Politics in
ENGLAND

We live under a system of tacit understandings.
But the understandings are not always understood.
Sidney Low, *The Governance of England*

*The Little, Brown Series
in Comparative Politics*

Under the Editorship of

GABRIEL A. ALMOND

JAMES S. COLEMAN

LUCIAN W. PYE

A COUNTRY STUDY

Politics in
ENGLAND

**PERSISTENCE
AND CHANGE**

Fourth Edition

Richard Rose

Centre for the Study of Public Policy
University of Strathclyde
Glasgow

LITTLE, BROWN AND COMPANY
Boston   Toronto

Library of Congress Cataloging in Publication Data

Rose, Richard, 1933–
  Politics in England.

  (Little, Brown series in comparative politics.
Country study)
  Includes bibliographical references and index.
  1. Great Britain—Politics and government. I. Title.
II. Series
JN231.R67 1985b   320.941   85-5784
ISBN 0-316-75647-4

ISBN 0-316-75647-4

9 8 7 6 5 4 3 2

ALP

Published simultaneously in Canada
by Little, Brown & Company (Canada) Limited

Printed in the United States of America

TO MY FATHER

Acknowledgments

This book sums up the experience over three decades of studying politics while moving back and forth between America and Britain. To an American with an English wife and binational children, the experience has been personally congenial as well as professionally stimulating. It also provides a perspective in which no system of government appears better or worse just because it is different.

In this fourth edition of *Politics in England,* every chapter has been thought about afresh and revised in the light of contemporary conditions. A very substantial amount of fresh material is contained in the tables and citations as well as in the newly written prose. Drawing on the experience of England under confident Conservative and Labour governments and under governments that have lost both self-confidence and national confidence guards against ephemeral generalizations. There is little point in facing the 1990s with a stock of knowledge based solely on current anxieties, the optimism of a quarter-century ago, or the communal courage of wartime.

The enormous expansion of political studies in the past two decades confronts an author with a plethora of materials. I myself have published more than a million words about politics in England since the first edition of this book. The result is a need to synthesize information and ideas rather than simply record or summarize studies; hence, the footnotes offer a guide to books and articles that expand points made herein. At times the train of thought leads to ideas not yet confirmed by research. Understanding can be advanced by raising questions as well as by answering them.

The terminology of politics in England is more complicated than most English people realize. While there is no doubt about the identity of England or of the Queen of England, in law the government is the government of the United Kingdom of Great Britain and Northern Ireland. The Parliament at Westminster represents and is responsible for governing Scotland, Wales, and Northern Ireland as well as England. Yet the United Kingdom government is described by the adjective British, not "UKish." The term *Britain* has no consistent meaning. To most English people it is interchangeable with the use of the word England. But to most Scots, Welsh, and Ulster people, the word connotes a loyalty to the United Kingdom as a whole. The resulting complexity of identities and institutions is too much to be dealt with properly in a book concerned principally with the Westminster government. It is examined in six books on the non-English parts of the United Kingdom that I have authored or edited.

Politics in England is the title of this book because England is in so many ways dominant in the United Kingdom. Its people constitute five-sixths of its population; the remainder is divided among three noncontiguous nations. The largest, Scotland, though more populous than such European Community countries as Denmark and Ireland, has only 9 percent of the population of the United Kingdom. Where differences cause friction, non-English people are expected to adapt to English ways. What is important to England will never be overlooked by any United Kingdom government. Politicians who wish to prosper in Parliament must accept English norms if they wish to advance. It is thus appropriate to write about British government and English society.

Since this book was first written, politics in England and the study of politics have changed substantially. Yet two assumptions continue to be important in the analysis presented here. The first is that the actions and attitudes of the mass of the population, as they are expressed in elections and opinion surveys, cannot be ignored in the study of representative government. With V. O. Key I share the assumption: "Voters are not fools." Secondly, in democratic politics, consent is more important than effectiveness. The economic difficulties of England are evidence of a loss of effectiveness, not consent. The maintenance of political consent for generations makes England different from major countries with undoubted economic superiority, such as France, Germany, and Japan. It also contrasts with Westminster's record in Northern Ireland, described in two of my books, *Governing without Consensus* and *Northern Ireland: A Time of Choice.*

In addition to information drawn from published books and articles, unpublished survey data has been courteously made available by the Gallup Poll, Marplan, MORI (Market and Opinion Research International), by National Opinion Polls (NOP), and by the Economic and Social Research Council Archive at Colchester. The facilities of the University of Strathclyde Social Statistics Laboratory have been helpful in processing machine-readable data, and assistance has also come from colleagues in the Centre for the Study of Public Policy. The discussion of public policies in Chapter XI draws upon a CSPP program of research on the growth of government in the United Kingdom since 1945, supported by grant HR7849/1 from the British Economic and Social Research Council.

Many debts have been accumulated in writing a book as wide-ranging as this. The suggestion that started it all came from Gabriel Almond. In preparing the original study and in much else, I have benefited specially from comments and talks with J. A. T. Douglas and W. J. M. Mackenzie. The following have kindly made useful comments upon all or part of the manuscript of this edition: Phillip Davies, Wynford Grant, Brian Harrison, Dennis Kavanagh, Eugene Lee, and J. M. Ross. Mrs. J. M. Roberts has promptly and accurately transcribed a rough manuscript into a neat typescript.

None of the individuals or organizations mentioned by name necessarily endorses any particular point in this study; they share responsibility for merits, not demerits.

Richard Rose

Contents

Tables and Figures

Only connect . . .

E. M. Forster, *Howards End*

The United Kingdom
(Standard Regions)

ATLANTIC

OCEAN

SCOTLAND

Aberdeen

Glasgow Edinburgh

North Sea

NORTHERN
IRELAND
Belfast

Newcastle
Tyne R.

NORTH

REPUBLIC

OF

IRELAND

Dublin

Irish Sea

YORKSHIRE
Leeds
AND

Liverpool Manchester
Mersey
Sheffield
HUMBERSIDE
NORTH
WEST

EAST MIDLANDS

WEST
Birmingham
MIDLANDS

EAST ANGLIA

WALES

Severn R.

SOUTH

Cardiff
Bristol

Greater
London
Thames R.

EAST

SOUTH WEST

English Channel

FRANCE

0   100
Scale of Miles

Persistence and Change

> *There is a great difficulty in the way of a writer who attempts to sketch a living Constitution, a Constitution that is in actual work and power. The difficulty is that the object is in constant change.*[1]

ENGLAND SUFFERS TODAY from the aftereffects of early success. In the late ninteenth century, England led the world both politically and economically. Since then, it has had nowhere to go but down. The difficulties are most evident in the economy. Two centuries after giving birth to the Industrial Revolution, England labors with an economy less modern than those of more recently industrialized countries such as Germany and Japan. Whereas some Americans express anxieties about living in a postindustrial society, more English people worry about the consequences of deindustrialization. Yet the rhetoric of dissatisfaction or despair is contradicted by the substantial and continuing postwar rise in the material living standard of the great majority of the population.

The political record mixes persistence and change. More than a century ago, the Victorian governors of England successfully adapted centuries-old traditional institutions to the imperatives of governing an urban industrial society. The result is a durable system of representative government. Critics charge that the very persistence of established institutions is a fault. Continuity and stability are interpreted as evidence of political stagnation. Change is said to be stifled by practices reflecting past rather than future needs. Today, there are dangers that past political

1

achievements are taken for granted, as well as contemporary difficulties being dismissed out of hand. The more contradictions a country's politics displays, the more important it is to try to understand what is happening.

For more than two decades parties and politicians have promised to "remodernize" England. In 1964 Harold Wilson claimed that his new Labour government would mark a turning point in the country's history. But change did not come. In 1979 Margaret Thatcher launched a Conservative government pledged to reverse the country's economic decline. The economy continued to deteriorate. In 1983 an Alliance of Liberal and Social Democratic politicians promised to "break the mould" of the old party system. But the system they campaigned against broke their electoral hopes.

In a contemporary mixed-economy welfare state, the problems of government are not confined to politicians. The actions of government affect everybody, for public policies influence the economy, the cost of living, and employment, and education, health, and pensions programs affect the well-being of tens of millions of people.

The problems facing England in the 1980s are neither transitory nor imported. They reflect the cumulation of problems that governments have sidestepped or grappled with unsuccessfully for generations. In Victorian times, the governors of England successfully faced the challenge of modernization. Today, their heirs face the challenge of remodernizing many of the country's institutions.

ENGLAND IN COMPARATIVE PERSPECTIVE

A distinctive feature of this book is that England is viewed in an international perspective. We can better appreciate the continuity of political institutions and political liberties in England if we compare its record with those of other countries such as Germany or Italy. Comparisons also emphasize England's relatively slow economic growth. To study England in comparative perspective is justified by history, for England has long been a major influence upon other nations.

A Prototype System. Understanding England is important, because for generations it has been the prototype of a country enjoying both stable and representative government. Its political institutions have served as a model on every continent. As the author of *The Origins of American Politics* emphasizes, "The pattern of political activity in the colonies was part of a more comprehensive British pattern, and cannot be understood in isolation from that larger system."[2] Parliaments can be found in India, Kenya, and Canada, as well as in London.

For a quarter-century the alleged ills of England have been subject to persistent diagnosis. Books and articles have appeared with such titles as *Is Britain Governable? The Breakup of Britain, Is Britain Dying?* and, with apparent conclusiveness, *The Suicide of a Nation.* So numerous and recurrent have been the jeremiads of the doom-mongers that they have generated a counterliterature. An American journalist, Bernard Nossiter, wrote a book entitled *Britain: A Future that Works.* Another group concluded that Britain exemplifies *both* progress *and* decline.[3]

Because self-criticism erupted dramatically in the early 1960s and has persisted steadily since, England has gained international notoriety as a negative reference group. Politicians in other lands often refer to England as a country *not* to imitate. President Gerald Ford cautioned his fellow Americans, "It would be tragic for this country if we went down the same path and ended up with the same problems that Great Britain has."[4] The editor of a state-of-England symposium, *The Future That Doesn't Work,* proclaimed: "The United Kingdom has become the latest version of the Sick Man of Europe and, as the United States has been on a similar diet, one might well ask if this nation is fated to go the way of the United Kingdom, and what, if anything, can be done to duck such a fate."[5] Such remarks prompted a former Labour Cabinet minister, Barbara Castle, to remark, "It is a curious form of special relationship that casts the United States as mourner-in-chief over Britain's corpse."[6]

But distance can distort perceptions. Foreign critics of England sometimes show that it is easier to see the mote that faults another country than the beam that conspicuously disfigures their own appearance. So well known a scholar of British affairs as Samuel Beer of Harvard can attack British government today for exemplifying "a fragmentation of political life" that is alleged to have culminated in incoherence, immobilism, and pluralistic stagnation.[7] Yet these are just the faults that his Harvard colleagues (and many other Americans as well) attribute to government in Washington today.[8] A perceptive American journalist, Anthony Lewis, has noted that compared with "America's problems of war and poverty and social division, in Britain, after all, the problem is only money."[9]

A historian, Paul Kennedy, argues that it is evidence of success that England was able to maintain a world position for a century of decline from its Victorian peak. Making provocative use of understatement, Kennedy suggests that England's ability to maintain political consensus in the face of other nations becoming economically and militarily stronger contains a moral for leaders of both the United States and the Soviet Union:

> In the longer-term perspective—on the fundamental issue of how to preserve a worldwide Empire for as long as possible once the economic and strategic tides had turned — was not this flexible, reasonable, compromise-seeking policy preferable to the assertive "no surrender" one? It was not a bad performance, on the whole, not a bad diplomatic juggling-act.[10]

Comparison need not imply global judgments about the superiority of one society to another. The author has lived too long on each side of the Atlantic to believe that such a comparison is practicable. As any traveler can verify, the grass *is* greener on the moister, cooler, and English side of the Atlantic. But the machinery for gardening is more advanced in America, and the sun shines more on American soil. Comparison must always involve careful specification of the topic: different (or better) compared to what?

Evaluation by Multiple Criteria. Analyzing economics and politics separately does not mean that the two can be separated in practice. There is a tendency to want to combine England's political stability, German or Japanese economic dynamism,

French food, and Spanish sunshine. However, the circumstances of each nation — for better *and* for worse — must be taken altogether. This is particularly true when a cause of success in one domain — e.g., military defeat as a precondition for economic reconstruction, or political stability as a cause of relative economic decline — may also be a cause of dissatisfaction in another.

Evaluating the state of England is difficult, for there is no consensus about how the performance of governments should be evaluated. Judged against the political experience of European neighbors, across the centuries the government of England has a record of* great achievement. England, unlike Germany or Italy, has no modern experience of fascist dictatorship; unlike Czechoslovakia, no experience of a communist coup d'etat; unlike Spain, no experience of military dictatorship arising from civil war; and unlike France, no modern experience of military occupation, the collapse of a regime, and the creation of a constitution around a charismatic leader.

The first things to examine are the essentials of government. No government that failed to defend its national boundaries, to maintain domestic peace, civil liberties and free elections could be considered successful as success is judged by conventional Western values. When politics in England is compared with the experience of America, France and Germany, and Japan, the record is outstanding, emphasizing the continuity of representative institutions in England, and security from foreign invasion or excepting Ireland domestic upheaval (Table Intro. 1). France, Germany, and Japan have seen representative government suspended by force one or more times in the twentieth century. Moreover, England enjoys a high standard of civil liberties as well as internal order.

Political achievements stand out when citizens are asked to say how proud they are of their country. The proportion expressing pride in being British is 86 percent, second highest among a range of major nations. Moreover, the very high level of national pride is achieved without the aggressive promotion of patriotism in schools and in the media, as occurs in the United States. National pride is higher than in France, Germany, and Japan, countries in which the Second World War

TABLE INTRO. 1   *England Compared to Other Major Countries*

	England	America	France	Germany	Japan
1. Last foreign invasion	1066	1812	1940	1944	1945
2. Last internal revolution, coup	1688	1861	1958	1933	1940
3. Current constitution dates from	17th cent.	1789	1958	1949	1946
4. Mass suffrage continuous since:	1885	1828[b]	1945	1949	1946
5. Deaths in military battle 1816–1980 (000)	1,295	664	1,965	5,353	1,371
6. Deaths from internal political violence 1948–1977	0[a]	434	164	61	60

[a]Excluding Northern Ireland, where about 1,500 deaths from political violence occurred in the period through 1977, and more than 2,400 through 1984.

[b]Not allowing for de facto disfranchisement of blacks in the American South until the 1960s.

Sources: Lines 1–4 calculated by the author. Line 5 calculated from Melvin Small and J. David Singer, *Resort to Arms* (Beverly Hills: Sage Publications, 1982), table 10. Line 6 from Charles L. Taylor and David A. Jodice, *World Handbook of Political and Social Indicators* Vol. 2 (New Haven: Yale University Press, 1983), Table 2.7.

and its aftermath have left many citizens with less cause for pride (Table Intro. 2). The maintenance of free representative government in peace and in war is in England a continuing source of national pride.[11]

Political values are not the only values by which a government can be judged. Harsh judgments about British government usually concentrate attention upon the country's economic performance, and particularly its recent economic performance.[12] When economic growth is the criterion, then England's record is poor. The economy has grown at less than half the rate of Japan or France, and one-third slower than

TABLE INTRO. 2 *National Pride: A Comparative Analysis*

National Pride	Britain %	America %	France %	Germany %	Japan %
Very proud	55	80	33	21	30
Quite proud	31	16	43	38	32
All proud	86	96	76	59	62
Not very proud	8	2	8	18	28
Not at all proud	3	1	9	11	3
All not proud	11	3	17	29	32
Don't know	3	2	7	12	7

Source: European Value Systems Study Group surveys, in Gordon Heald, "A Comparison Between American, European and Japanese Values," (Hunt Valley, Md.: WAPOR, annual meeting, 1982), Table 2.

Germany or America since 1960. Its annual average growth rate of 2.3 percent is the lowest among twenty-four industrially advanced nations that constitute the OECD (the Organisation for Economic Co-operation and Development). The country's inflation rate has been consistently higher than those of other major nations, and so too have been its long-term interest rates. Until the 1980s England had a level of unemployment below the OECD average, and lower especially than the United States. Since then its unemployment rate has risen sharply, both absolutely and relatively. The underlying economic problem of Britain has been slow economic growth.

The political direction that a government gives to the economy is conventionally measured by taking public expenditure as a percentage of the national product. By this measure, Britain has a medium-size government, not a big government. Government expenditure is higher than in the United States and Japan, but lower than in France and Germany (Table Intro. 3).

If reconciling conflict is the chief criterion of success, then British government can claim a record of success that none of its major continental neighbors — France, Germany, or Italy — can match. Twentieth-century England has been better at governing with consensus than in mobilizing economic resources.

TABLE INTRO. 3   *British Economic Performance in Comparative Perspective, 1960–1980*

	Britain	America	France	Germany	Japan
			(Annual %)		
Growth, Gross Domestic Product	2.3	3.5	4.6	3.7	7.7
Unemployment	2.8	5.5	2.8	1.7	1.5
Increase, price index	8.8	5.3	6.8	3.9	7.4
Interest rates (1974–1980 average)	13.1	7.9	11.1	7.8	8.2
Govt. outlay as % GDP (1980)	39.7	31.3	40.0	39.9	24.4

Source: Organisation for Economic Co-operation and Development, *Historical statistics, 1960–1980* (Paris: OECD), Tables 3.1, 2.14, 8.11, 10.8, and 6.4.

THE BOOK'S OBJECTIVES

The primary object of this book is deceptively simple: to analyze how politics in England works today. It starts by examining the historic and geographic setting of contemporary England. Chapter I considers the mixed inheritance of modern England, and the following chapter the constraints of place. Chapter III examines the institutions by which the Crown in Parliament rules, and Chapter IV the political culture that supports the legitimacy of authority. Three crucial functions of any political system — socializing individuals into the political culture, recruiting political participants, and communicating and withholding political information — are then scrutinized. The articulation and aggregation of interests by pressure groups and parties are the subject of Chapters VIII and IX. The three concluding chapters consider how the parts of the political system combine to make and implement policies in a changing world.

To analyze politics in its social context is to follow a tradition that goes back to Bagehot's late Victorian study of *The English Constitution* and yet is as modern as contemporary social science. The boundaries between parts of society are not so clear as those separating academic disciplines. Whereas professors can easily be divided into political scientists, economists, and sociologists, an ordinary English person cannot be viewed solely as a citizen, consumer, or friend: each person combines all these roles in his or her everyday life.

The methods of social science have been used to produce a large number of tables, using data about England, and about other countries with which England can be instructively compared.[13] If facts could be left to speak for themselves, then any kind of tables, whether of the census, public expenditure, or election results, would suffice as a guide to politics. But statistical facts require just as much interpretation as do the self-interested statements that politicians offer as facts in their diaries and memoirs. It is as important to take care in interpreting the meaning of numbers as it is to reflect about whether literary statements are (or can be) supported by quantitative evidence.

Secondly, this book is intended to show the impact that society has upon government, and the impact of government upon society. The exchange of influence is a two-way street: a Cabinet minister's decisions may influence programs affecting the lives of many citizens, and the electoral choices of citizens affect the fate of Cabinet ministers. No one who reaches the top in politics arrives there by his or her efforts alone. Every politician is subject to a host of social and economic influences in the process of a political career.

To examine the impact of government upon society we must look at what government does as well as what it is. The institutions of government can be used for many different political purposes. Each general election sees politicians announcing that they have the capacity to redirect their country. Yet the record of a party in office is often different from what a politician promises in a campaign. In politics, intentions should not be confused with achievements. As the late Aneurin Bevan, an outspoken Labour politician, once remarked: "Why use a crystal ball when you can read the bloody book?."[14]

Finally, this book seeks to examine how politics in England has been changing and is likely to evolve in the future. To do this we must understand what present trends imply for the future, and how the past influences the present. The fourth edition of a book first published twenty years ago is particularly suited to underlining both persistence and change. A newly elected British government does not start with a blank sheet on which to write a record; it takes over a set of commitments that fill many volumes of law books, and it inherits spending commitments of tens of billions of pounds. The commitments of contemporary big government were not created in a day. In England they reflect the accumulation of influences through decades, generations, and even centuries.

Fifty years ago the distinguished French writer Andre Siegfried diagnosed England's position thus: "To turn the corner from the nineteenth into the twentieth century, there, in a word, is the whole British problem."[15] Since then, England has achieved great changes. In the turbulent world of today, it faces a new challenge: the need to prepare for entry into the twenty-first century.

NOTES

1. The epigraphs in this book are taken from Walter Bagehot's classic, *The English Constitution,* first published in 1867.

2. Bernard Bailyn, *The Origins of American Politics* (New York: Vintage, 1970), p. ix.

3. William B. Gwyn and Richard Rose, eds., *Britain — Progress and Decline* (London: Macmillan, 1980). See particularly Gwyn's chapter, "Jeremiahs and Pragmatists: Perceptions of British Decline," for a review of critical writings.

4. Quoted in "Ford Fear of Carter Promises," *Daily Telegraph* (London), 4 January 1977.

5. Cf. R. Emmett Tyrrell, Jr., in his editor's introduction to *The Future that Doesn't Work: Social Democracy's Failures in Britain* (Garden City, N.Y.: Doubleday, 1977), p. 2.

6. "Americans Told Britain Still Lives," *The Times* (London), 17 April 1978.

7. Samuel H. Beer, *Britain Against Itself* (London: Faber & Faber, 1982), pp. 1f.

8. See e.g., Hugh Heclo, "Issue Networks and the Executive Establishment," in A. S. King, ed., *The New American Political System* (Washington, D.C.: American Enterprise Institute, 1978), pp. 87–124; and Samuel P. Huntington, "Postindustrial Politics: How Benign Will It Be?" *Comparative Politics,* 6:2 (1974), pp. 163–191.

9. "QE2 and other Sore Points," *Sunday Times* (London), 12 January 1969.

10. Paul Kennedy, *Strategy and Diplomacy, 1870–1945* (London: Allen & Unwin, 1983), pp. 217–218.

11. See Richard Rose, "Proud to be British," *New Society* (London), 7 June 1984, and "National Pride in Cross-National Perspective," *International Social Science Journal,* 36:1 (1985).

12. For reviews of the British economy, see e.g., J. Dow, *Management of the British Economy, 1945–1960,* (London: National Institute of Economic and Social Research, 1970); F. T. Blackaby, ed., *British Economic Policy, 1960–74* (Cambridge: Cambridge University Press, 1978); Wilfred Beckerman, ed., *Slow Growth in Britain* (Oxford: Clarendon Press, 1979).

13. Government statistics are inconsistent in territorial scope, sometimes referring to England, and sometimes to England and Wales, or Great Britain, or the United Kingdom as a whole. Official inconsistencies do little to affect substantive conclusions, given that England constitutes five-sixths of the population of the United Kingdom. For statistics on the non-English parts of the United Kingdom, see Richard Rose and Ian McAllister, *United Kingdom Facts* (London: Macmillan, 1982).

14. On the intentions of politicians, see Richard Rose, *Do Parties Make a Difference?* expanded 2nd ed. (Chatham, N.J.: Chatham House, 1984). On what governments do, see Richard Rose, "The Programme Approach to the Growth of Government," *British Journal of Political Science,* 15,1 (1985), pp. 1–28.

15. *England's Crisis* (London: Jonathan Cape, 1931), p. 11.

CHAPTER I

The Constraints of History

Each generation describes what it sees, but it uses words transmitted from the past. When a great entity like the British Constitution has continued in connected outward sameness, but hidden inner change for many ages, every generation inherits a series of inapt words — of maxims once true, but of which the truth is ceasing or has ceased.

EVERY COUNTRY IS CONSTRAINED by its history, for past actions limit the choices open to present governors. For example, the 1921 Anglo-Irish treaty gave de facto independence to two-thirds of the population of Ireland, but it left a virulent challenge to political authority in that part of Ulster remaining within the United Kingdom. Past events can also be important when they leave no heritage. In the eighteenth century, slave traders exported slaves to the New World but not to England, thus avoiding the legacy of racial problems that have tormented America.

To understand politics in England, we must understand the evolution of institutions as well as their current rationale. A deductive approach, inferring an explanation of institutions from their contemporary consequences, cannot properly explain politics in England, because it has developed a system of government within the constraints of a feudal and monarchical tradition. English people have never had to sit down under pressure of military defeat to deduce a constitution from first principles. This has been the fate of all the major powers in

Europe as of 1900: France, Germany, Italy, Russia, and successor states of the Habsburg and Ottoman empires.

In England, government has evolved very gradually. Old institutions have been adapted to new tasks, and new institutions have been grafted onto old. Like a well-established garden, the major features of the British Constitution today reflect the work of far more hands than those who presently tend it. For example, that central institution of democracy — elections — involves procedures dating back to the seventeenth century. In apportioning electors into parliamentary constituencies, the Boundary Commissioners are not expected to apply mechanically the formula "one person, one vote, one value." They are also expected to make allowance for the representation of "communities that are integral, human entities which have both a history and a very lively sense of corporate feeling."[1] Notwithstanding centuries of history, the boundaries of every constituency are reviewed each decade to remove anomalies arising from the continuous movement of population.

Symbols of continuity often mask great changes in English life. Much of what we think of as typical of old England — the ceremony of the monarchy, the urbane detachment of a non-party civil service, and the social exclusiveness of public boarding schools — reflects nineteenth-century reforms, or the conscious invention of tradition.[2] The contrast between traditional symbols and practice is particularly great in what Bagehot described as the "undergrowth of irrelevant ideas" enveloping the Constitution.

History is more than a record of past events; the residues of history constitute the period we familiarly name the present. Nowhere is this more true than in the politics of England. The heir to an ancient crown pilots jet airplanes and a medievally styled Chancellor of the Exchequer tries to steer the pound through the deep waters of the international economy. Clement Attlee summarized the interpenetrating periods of the past in a tribute to Winston Churchill:

> There was a layer of seventeenth century, a layer of eighteenth century, a layer of nineteenth century and possibly even a layer

of twentieth century. You were never sure which layer would be uppermost.[3]

The history of England has normally been taught in schools as a success story. But today many attack what they view as the dead hand of the past, or the comforting but mistaken assumption that past success guarantees future success. In the caustic words of the radical historian E. P. Thompson, "We lie upon our heritage like a dunlopillo mattress and hope, in our slumbers, that those good, dead men of history will move us forward."[4] The first part of this chapter shows how the country's resolution of past problems can contribute to present difficulties; the second contrasts the political and economic implications of this mixed inheritance. A long and continuous political history is neither good nor bad of itself: failures as well as successes can endure.

THE MAKING OF MODERN ENGLAND

England was fortunate in resolving many fundamental problems of governance before industrialization. The Crown was established as the central political authority in late medieval times, and the supremacy of secular power over spiritual power was settled in the sixteenth century, when Henry VIII broke with the Roman Catholic Church to establish a national Church of England. Characteristically, the conflict between Crown and Parliament in the civil war of the 1640s was followed by a Restoration. The monarchy continued, but with less power. The Constitution prevailing in England at the time of the Industrial Revolution in the late eighteenth century was a mixed Constitution, with authority divided between the Crown and Parliament. The result was limited but effective government.

Industrialization, not political revolution, was the great discontinuity in English history. By the middle of the nineteenth century, England was the world's first modern industrial society. The repeal of the Corn Laws in 1846, removing the import duty on a basic food, symbolizes the shift from a self-reliant agrarian society to an industrial economy trading its manufactured goods for food imported from other countries. At that point in time, England could claim to lead the world both economically and politically.

The Long Transition. Social scientists have no agreed means for dating the point at which England gained a modern system of government.[5] A political historian might date the change at 1485, when a civil war about royal succession was ended with the start of the Tudor monarchy under Henry VII, and major developments in the administration of royal authority. A parliamentary historian might date modern times from the seventeenth century, when Parliament asserted its authority against the King, first in arms and then peacefully. A specialist in party politics might date modern times from the grant of the right to vote to the majority of men in 1884, or to all men and women in 1918. A frustrated radical might proclaim that by his or her values, England hasn't become modern yet.

The Constitution of England at the time of the industrial revolution was designed for a rural society, and justified by tradition. Until 1834 the Treasury kept the nation's accounts in Roman numerals and Latin prose. Reformers declared that this Gothic constitution could not deal with problems of modern (i.e., early nineteenth-century) English society. The governors of Old England adapted slowly but realistically to political change. The prime minister, Earl Grey, endorsed the 1832 Reform Act with the argument, "Unless the privileged sections of the community were prepared to adapt and to improve, waves of dangerous and uncontrollable innovation would completely drown the existing social order."[6]

The simplest way to date modern government is to say that it came about in Victorian times, for Queen Victoria had a lengthy reign from 1837 to 1901. During this era, the principal features of the Old Constitution were altered so that government could cope with the problems of a society that was increasingly urban, literate, and critical of unchanged traditions.

A great transformation of society and economy occurred in the nineteenth century. From 1800 to 1900 the population of the United Kingdom increased from 16 million to 41 million people. The gross national product increased more than eleven times. Thanks to the increase in national wealth, public expenditure per person could increase almost three times, yet fall as a proportion of the national product. In 1800, at the height of England's successful war against Napoleon's France, public expenditure accounted for 22 percent of the national product. By 1850 it had decreased its share to 11 percent, but because the national product was so much larger, total spending rose by one-quarter in real terms. By 1900, at the time of the Boer War in South Africa, public expenditure accounted for 14 percent of the national product. Increased public expenditure in the nineteenth century was financed by the fiscal dividend of economic growth. Government grew greatly, but the economy grew even more.[7]

The 1832 Reform Act was a landmark, establishing the principle that constitutional traditions are subject to alteration by Parliament. It commenced the rationalization of the franchise; the majority of English males gained the vote in 1884. As the electorate expanded, party organizations began to develop along recognizable modern lines. Innovations promoted by followers of Jeremy Bentham's rationalistic philosophy led to a large, bureaucratic, and effective civil service. England's constitutional bureaucracy was capable of organizing everything from the economic saving of candle ends to prototype laws of the modern welfare state.[8]

By the middle of the nineteenth century, government had evolved from being a few central institutions around the monarch, supported by a landed gentry and nobility, to an incipient bureaucratic organization capable of delivering major public services nationwide.[9] In 1837, the Post Office was given a modern form of organization. The first minister responsible for health was appointed in 1854, for education in 1857, and for local government in 1871. Government was beginning to demonstrate that it could not only protect the country against foreign invasion and ensure domestic order, but also deliver welfare services.

Three Challenges. The creation of a modern system of government did not make the problems of governing disappear. What it did do was to create institutions of representative government that could respond to challenges confronting England in the twentieth century. The first of these challenges has been national defense in a war-ravaged world. In the First World War, Britain and France held Germany at bay in a trench war of bloody attrition, finally winning in 1918 with American support. In the Second World War, Britain stood alone against Nazi Germany in 1940 and 1941, until the war broadened to include Russia, America, and Japan. In 1945 Britain once again was on the winning side.

The second great challenge, the incorporation of the working class into the full rights of citizenship, was accomplished gradually. Most of the populist political demands made by the Chartists in 1837 were met by 1918. The supremacy of the elected House of Commons over the aristocratic and hereditary House of Lords was established by legislation in 1911. The right to vote was granted all adults in 1918. The Labour Party, founded in 1900 to secure representation in Parliament for manual workers, first formed a minority government briefly in 1924. The nonviolent General Strike of 1926 demonstrated the commitment of trade union leaders to constitutional action. When union leaders saw the revolutionary implication of a general strike, it was disowned, and the strike collapsed.[10]

Third, government began distributing the fruits of economic growth through welfare policies benefiting the mass of citizens. The Liberal government of 1906–1914 laid foundations for the contemporary welfare state by guaranteeing pensions in old age, and programs expanded slowly. Notwithstanding interwar unemployment rates fluctuating between 11 and 23 percent, the country's national product more than doubled between 1913 and 1938, a rate of economic growth faster than that of France, Germany, or Sweden. Public spending on social services increased from 2.6 percent of the national product in 1900 to 11.3 percent of a much larger national product in 1938.[11]

The Second World War and its aftermath brought about great changes within England. The wartime all-party coalition government of Winston Churchill in mobilizing the population for all-out war, sought to provide fair shares for everyone. From the wartime coalition came the Beveridge Report on Social Welfare, Keynes's Full Employment White Paper of 1944, and the Butler Education Act of 1944. These three measures — the first two named after Liberals and the third after a Conservative — remain major landmarks of the contemporary mixed-economy welfare state.

The wartime fair-shares policy was continued by the Labour government of Clement Attlee elected in 1945. It maintained rationing and controls, resulting in austerity while the economy was being rebuilt. The National Health Service was established, providing medical care for all. Coal mines, gas, electricity, the railways, road transport, and the steel industry were nationalized as part of Labour's program of increasing government's influence in the economy. By 1951 the Labour government had accomplished the measures on which there was agreement within the party; its economic policies had yet to produce prosperity. A much reformed Conservative party under Winston Churchill was returned to power by the electorate.

For more than three decades, Conservative and Labour governments have sought to promote economic prosperity, provide generous welfare services, and increase the take-home pay of ordinary citizens. The 1950s saw a rise in living standards after years of wartime scarcity and postwar austerity. Consumer goods once thought the privilege of a relative few, such as automobiles and refrigerators, became widespread. The Conservatives won general elections with unprecedentedly increased parliamentary majorities in 1955 and 1959. The Prime Minister, Harold Macmillan, summarized the economic record of the 1950s by saying, "Most of our people have never had it so good." But Macmillan was cautious about the future. When praising prosperity in 1957, he warned:

> What is beginning to worry some of us is, "Is it too good to be true?" or perhaps I should say, "Is it too good to last?" Amidst all this prosperity, there is one problem that has troubled us — in one way or another — ever since the war. It's the problem of rising prices.

Doubts Arise. The 1960s cast doubt upon the government's ability to guarantee continued affluence, for the British economy grew more slowly than the government wished, and more slowly than foreign competitors. The Macmillan government turned to economic planning in hopes of stimulating steady growth, and in 1961 unsuccessfully applied to join the European Common Market. In opposition, Labour leaders argued that socialism provided a technically superior means to develop the economy. But the promises of the 1964–1970 Labour government under Harold Wilson were shattered by a classic economic dilemma: how to stimulate a domestic economic boom without simultaneously risking inflation and the devaluation of the pound because of foreign creditors' reactions. The Wilson government tried to prevent devaluation, but failed. By the time Labour left office in 1970 the nation's economy was growing more slowly than at any time since 1945.

The 1960s were also important as the beginning of public disillusionment with British government. Continuities with the past were attacked as evidence of the dead hand of tradition. In 1963 the fourteenth Earl of Home, then a member of the House of Lords, was chosen as Prime Minister by a small clique of Conservative notables. This was attacked as a retrograde step. (Sir Alec Douglas-Home replied to the attack by remarking, "I suppose Harold Wilson must be the fourteenth Mr. Wilson.") A new wave of satire on television, on the stage, and in periodicals such as *Private Eye* mocked that which was formerly held in esteem. A series of Royal Commissions and inquiries proposed reforms of the civil service, local government, Parliament, the mass media, industrial relations, and the Constitution. New titles were given Whitehall offices to signify the desire for change for its own sake. Behind the entrance, the same people went through the same administrative routines as before.[12]

The 1970s intensified anxieties about the government (or even, some argued, the governability) of England.[13] Taken together, the experience of the Conservative government under Edward Heath from 1970 to 1974 and of the 1974–1979 Labour government under Harold Wilson and James Callaghan have demonstrated that difficulties are not unique to any particular individual or party. The Heath government promised major changes in policies as well as in institutions of government. But the biggest changes of the decade were neither intended nor desired by the Prime Ministers who presided over them.

Trying to limit unprecedented inflation in 1974, Edward Heath risked the authority of his office by confrontation with the National Union of Mineworkers, which defied the government's pay policy by striking to secure a wage increase. The impasse was broken by the general election of 28 February 1974, called by the Prime Minister to ascertain: Who governs? The electorate returned a vote of no confidence in both major parties. The Conservative share of the vote dropped by 8 percent, and the Labour vote by 6 percent, producing the lowest level of popular support in a generation for either party.

A minority Labour government was formed under Harold Wilson. In October, 1974 Labour won a bare parliamentary majority with 39 percent of the vote. This was the lowest share of the vote won by any majority government in British history, and little more than the vote won by Barry Goldwater or George McGovern in their landslide defeats in American presidential elections. By 1977, because of by-election defeats and defections by sitting MPs, the Labour government had lost its parliamentary majority. A pact with the Liberals was required to guarantee the government a majority in the House of Commons.

The major achievement of the 1974–1979 Labour government was to maintain political consensus in the face of economic difficulties. Instead of confrontation with the unions, the Labour government sought a social contract. Initially, this was intended to provide higher welfare benefits and avoid any government restrictions upon wage increases. In July 1975 the first of a series of pay policies was adopted limiting wage increases, and real take-home pay fell. In 1976, the problems of the political economy were such that the government was forced to seek a loan from the International Monetary Fund, and impose severe cash limits upon public-sector spending. By the spring of 1979, unemployment stood at the highest since the 1930s, 1.5 million; prices had doubled since 1974; and the economy had actually contracted instead of growing in two of the preceding four years.

The British general election of 3 May 1979 saw the two major parties reverse their traditional roles. The Labour government under James Callaghan argued against the risk of change.

The nominally Conservative party led by Margaret Thatcher called for a radical change in the country's economic policy. The Conservatives won an absolute majority in Parliament, and 44 percent of the popular vote. Labour's share of the popular vote fell below 37 percent, its lowest since 1931. The Liberals won 14 percent of the vote, but very few seats in the House of Commons. On 4 May 1979, Margaret Thatcher became the first woman Prime Minister of a major European country.

The Thatcher Response. Margaret Thatcher entered office in 1979 determined to make a break with the past, in terms of both style and substance.[14] The economic failures of past governments were diagnosed as arising from too much continuity in the management of the mixed economy, and too many political compromises. In place of consensus, she offered conviction, telling a 1979 election rally: "The Old Testament prophets did not say 'Brothers, I want a consensus. They said: This is my faith. This is what I passionately believe. If you believe it too, then come with me.' " Substantively, her conviction was that market-oriented monetary policies would right the country's economic difficulties. While a break with the postwar consensus, Mrs. Thatcher's views are consistent with an older tradition. Professor Milton Friedman, a Nobel Prize-winning economist whose views she endorsed, noted:

> Mrs. Thatcher represents a different tradition. She represents a tradition of the nineteenth century Liberal, of Manchester Liberalism, of free market free trade.[15]

In its first term of office, Mrs. Thatcher's government was frustrated in its hopes; reality was not what rhetoric promised. Unemployment doubled to 3 million, more than 12 percent of the labor force. Instead of growing faster, the economy slowed down, and in some years contracted. Between spring 1979 and spring 1983, the gross national product actually fell by 2 percent. One success was in reducing the rate of inflation. Whereas the cost of living rose 115 percent from 1974 to 1979, its rise was reduced to 55 percent from 1979 to 1983.

The Labour Party found coping with opposition even more difficult than coping with government. Left-wing critics of the

Wilson and Callaghan governments succeeded in gaining control of the party's annual conference, and forcing through a series of rules changes that shifted power from the party in Parliament to the extraparliamentary party. When 68-year-old James Callaghan resigned in 1980, he was succeeded by 67-year-old Michael Foot, who was acceptable to the party's left. In protest against the shift left within the party, four Cabinet ministers in the 1974–1979 Labour government resigned to form a new Social Democratic party in spring 1981. The SDP then concluded an Alliance with the Liberals; by autumn 1981, the Alliance was winning by-elections and leading in opinion poll support; the lead was short-lived.

In the 9 June 1983 general election, the Conservatives won a landslide majority in the House of Commons. The Conservatives owed some of their success to the fortuitous outbreak of a war between Britain and Argentina over the Falkland Islands in spring 1982. Mrs. Thatcher stood firm on the principle that Britain should regain the islands from Argentine invaders, and her conviction was rewarded with success. The war was short, virtually bloodless, and very popular in domestic politics; it also achieved the immediate military objective of regaining control of the South Atlantic islands from Argentine invaders. But the Conservatives owed their electoral success to divisions among their opponents. Together, the Labour and Alliance parties won 53 percent of the popular vote, as against 42 percent for the Conservatives. But because that vote was almost equally divided between the opposition parties, the Conservatives elected 387 MPs, as against 209 Labour MPs and 23 Alliance MPs.[16]

The Conservative government elected in 1983 is not the same as the group of politicians who entered office in 1979. In her second term of office Mrs. Thatcher faces evidence that conviction is not necessarily sufficient to achieve her political goals. The economy has grown much less than the government desired. Whereas the 1979 Conservative manifesto called for reversing the process of growth in government, by 1984 Mrs. Thatcher could tell a television interviewer, "I must be candid; I don't believe it is possible to cut public expenditure below the levels we have indicated." After experiencing the frustrations of office, Mrs. Thatcher avoids optimism about the ease of change: ''You cannot doubt that I shall strain to go on in the direction I have indicated, but I must be realistic about the speed at which I can go.''[17]

A MIXED INHERITANCE

One great premise of English politics is that the past is assimilated by adapting rather than by abolishing aging political institutions. The adaptation of Parliament since its thirteenth-century beginning is an outstanding example of continuity. The spirit is summed up in the motto of Lord Hugh Cecil's study of the philosophy of conservatism: ''Even when I changed, it should be to preserve.''[18] In Cecil's sense, conservatism is not bounded by party, for the Labour left can be fervently conservative in the face of demands to alter Socialist principles, and Labour ministers can be fervent in assimilation to established institutions.[19]

The founding leader of the Social Democratic party, Roy Jenkins, similarly sees the SDP as upholding continuity with the middle-of-the-road consensus rejected by both Mrs. Thatcher and the Labour left. Even though he has spent more than thirty years in Parliament, Jenkins argues, ''We must escape from the tyranny of the belief that one government can make or break us.'' According to Jenkins, political change is possible, but it is slow.

> A governing party must have the self-confidence to want power and to believe that its exercise of it can tilt the country in the right direction. But it should also have the humility to recognise that, on any likely projection of the past, its power will come to an end in about six years. The test of its statesmanship will not therefore be how many trees it pulls up by the roots, but how it fits into a continuous process of adaptation.[20]

The sentiments are not those of a missionary for the market economy or a builder of a Socialist New Jerusalem. They could be characterized by the slightly right-of-center label Whiggish, or the slightly left-of-center label Fabian, because they emphasize both continuity and change.

The Force of Inertia. The inertia of past choices constrains what any government can immediately do. For example, whatever the housing policy of the govenment of the day, it must accept that in the course of a five-year Parliament the number of new houses that can be built will be a relatively small addition to the total housing stock of the country. Nine-tenths of the people will continue to live in houses that were not built by the government of the day. The most a government can do in the course of a single Parliament is to take initiatives that will alter the pattern of housing in future.

The consequences of past choices cannot always be foreseen, because they continue far beyond the lifetime of the government that makes them, or of the politicians who vote for them. For example, the first pensions act introduced in 1908 was strictly limited in its expenditure commitments. Pensions were to be paid to persons from age 70, whereas the life expectancy of the average Briton was only 52. The pension of five shillings a week was a small fraction of the average worker's wage. But by a process of raising benefit levels and extending coverage, by the 1980s more than one-eighth of the population is receiving a pension.

Even when the long-term consequences of an immediate policy choice are evident, a politician may opt for the short-term advantage, thus leaving a legacy of problems for the future. For example, if instead of raising taxes, government borrows more money to meet the rising cost of public expenditure, this will cumulatively increase the amount of money it must pay as interest on past debts. The total paid in debt interest may be further increased if the rise in government borrowing also leads to higher interest rates. In the 1970s both Conservative and Labour governments resorted to borrowing rather than raising taxes to finance much of the increase in public expenditure. In consequence, the current money cost of interest payments rose sixfold between 1970 and 1980, a faster increase than spending on any welfare state program.[21]

Whereas Prime Ministers and parliamentary majorities are transient, government is continuing. Today's commitments of British government are not what any one party or politician has chosen. They are the consequence of past choices. A newly elected government is responsible for administering the laws inherited from its predecessors. Public institutions, public employees, and popular expectations all assume that pensioners, hospital patients, pupils in school, and holders of government debt will be treated much the same from year to year. In England today, government is not so much about making fresh choices; it is principally directed by the inertia force of past choices.

The current force of past commitments is most evident in the mixed-economy welfare state. In the postwar era successive Labour and Conservative governments have made commitments to increase public spending on the assumption that this would be paid for by the additional tax revenue generated by economic growth. The ideal was treble affluence: a bigger national product, which in turn would produce more money for public programs, and higher take-home pay as well. This was the consensus view of a generation of politicians raised on Keynesian doctrines, such as Prime Ministers Harold Macmillan and Harold Wilson, and influential party thinkers such as Labour's Anthony Crosland and R. A. Butler of the Conservatives.

In the 1950s Britain's achievement of treble affluence meant that the economy grew steadily, albeit slowly, and so did public expenditure. In consequence, take-home pay could grow as well. Thanks to economic growth at an average annual rate of 3.1 percent, public spending rose by 1.5 percent annually and take-home pay by 36 percent in the period. From 1961 to 1972 the economy continued to grow at the same annual rate as before; public expenditure grew faster, 2.5 percent. Take-home pay grew, but by a lesser extent, 14 percent in the period.[22]

The outbreak of worldwide economic difficulties in 1973 brought about a fundamental transformation in the relationship between growth in the national product, in public expenditure, and in take-home pay (Table I.1). The national product has continued to increase, albeit more slowly; the average annual growth rate from 1973 to 1983 was only 1.1 percent. The inertial spending commitments of government have continued to grow. The average increase of 1.6 percent is less than in the 1960s, but public spending now grows faster than

TABLE I.1   *The Consequences for Take-Home Pay of Low Economic Growth and Rising Public Expenditure*

	National Product	Public Expenditure	Take-Home Pay
	(1973 = 100)		
1973	100.0	100.0	100.0
1974	98.9	101.5	99.4
1975	98.2	107.1	94.3
1976	102.1	108.5	93.2
1977	103.1	106.7	92.3
1978	106.8	109.1	99.4
1979	109.1	111.3	103.3
1980	106.8	113.0	101.7
1981	105.5	113.0	97.8
1982	107.6	113.9	97.8
1983	111.1	116.9	100.6

Sources: Gross national product at market prices in real terms, and general government expenditure in real terms from *United Kingdom National Accounts 1984* (London: HMSO, 1984) Table 1.5. Take-home pay is the real net income of the average industrial worker, as calculated by the Inland Revenue.

the economy as a whole. Increased taxes and inflation have together resulted in the average industrial worker's wage falling rather than rising. Treasury figures show that the real post-tax wage of the average industrial worker fell in all but three of the past ten years. In the decade from 1973 to 1983, the overall net rise in earnings was less than 1 percent. Successive Labour and Conservative governments have not entered office with the intention of cutting the real wage of workers. That has nonetheless been the result, because of the present consequence of past commitments.

Past success cannot be extended indefinitely into the future. The House of Commons today has only a handful of members who were there when Clement Attlee's 1945–1951 Labour government was giving full momentum to the mixed-economy welfare state, or when Winston Churchill was in his last appearance on the world stage as Prime Minister from 1951 to 1955. More than two-thirds of Members of Parliament today first entered the House of Commons in 1970 or later. We are closer to the year 2000 than to a time in which politicians were confident about the state of the British economy. We no longer have good reason to refer to contemporary England as living in the post-

war era. Future historians will not characterize our time by
what went before, but by what it is a prelude to.

NOTES

1. Home Secretary Chuter Ede, quoted in Vincent Starzinger, "The British Pattern of Apportionment," *Virginia Quarterly Review,* 41:3 (1965), p. 328.

2. See Eric Hobsbawm and Terence Ranger, eds., *The Invention of Tradition* (Cambridge: Cambridge University Press, 1983).

3. *The Guardian* (London), 21 April 1963.

4. E. P. Thompson, "An Open Letter to Leszek Kolakowski," in Ralph Miliband and John Saville, eds., *The Socialist Register, 1973* (London: Merlin Press, 1974), p. 24. Cf. Brian Harrison, *Peaceable Kingdom: Stability and Change in Modern Britain* (Oxford: Clarendon Press, 1982).

5. For a much fuller development of points discussed herein, see Richard Rose, "England: a Traditionally Modern Political Culture," in Lucian W. Pye and Sidney Verba, eds., *Political Culture and Political Development* (Princeton, N.J.: Princeton University Press, 1965).

6. Cf. G. Kitson Clark, *The Making of Victorian England* (London: Methuen, 1962).

7. See Jindrich Veverka, "The Growth of Government Expenditure in the United Kingdom since 1790," *Scottish Journal of Political Economy,* 10:2 (1963). Cf. B. R. Mitchell, *European Historical Statistics, 1750–1970* (London: Macmillan, 1975), table K1.

8. See Henry Parris, *Constitutional Bureaucracy* (London: Allen & Unwin, 1969); and Sir Norman Chester, *The English Administrative System 1780–1870* (Oxford: Clarendon Press, 1981).

9. Richard Rose, "From Government at the Centre to Nationwide Government," in Y. Meny and Vincent Wright, eds., *Centre-Periphery Relations in Western Europe* (London: Allen & Unwin, forthcoming).

10. Cf. Krishan Kumar, "Can the Workers Be Revolutionary?" *European Journal of Political Research,* 6:4 (1978).

11. See Alan T. Peacock and Jack Wiseman, *The Growth of Public Expenditure in the United Kingdom* (Princeton, N.J.: Princeton University Press, 1961), p. 190.

12. A. H. Birch, "Westminster and Whitehall," in Gwyn and Rose, eds., *Britain — Progress and Decline,* pp. 57–72.

13. For distinctly British discussions of ungovernability, see Anthony S. King, "Overload: Problems of Governing in the 1970s," *Political Studies,* 23: 2–3 (1975), pp. 284–296; and J. A. T. Douglas, "The Overloaded Crown," *British Journal of Political Science,* 6:4 (1976), pp. 483–505. For more general discussions, see Samuel Brittan, "The Economic Contradictions of Democracy," *British Journal of Political Science,* 5:2 (1975), pp. 129–159; Richard Rose, "Ungovernability: Is there Fire behind the Smoke?" *Political Studies,* 27:3 (1979), pp. 351–370; and A. H. Birch, "Overload, Ungovernability and Delegitimation," *British Journal of Political Science,* 14:2 (1984), pp. 135–160.

14. For differing views of this controversial figure, see e.g., Patrick Riddell, *The Thatcher Government* (Oxford: Martin Robertson, 1983); Nicholas Wapshott and George Brock, *Thatcher* (London: Futura, 1983); and Stuart Hall and Martin Jacques, eds., *The Politics of Thatcherism* (London: Lawrence

& Wishart in association with *Marxism Today*, 1983). For the author's interpretation, see Rose, *Do Parties Make a Difference?* (expanded 2nd ed.).

15. Quoted in "Thatcher praised by her guru," *The Guardian* (London), 12 March 1983.

16. On the allocation of seats and votes, see Ian McAllister and Richard Rose, *The Nationwide Competition for Votes: The 1983 British Election* (London: Frances Pinter, 1984).

17. "Tax cuts depend on growth, says Thatcher," *Daily Telegraph,* 16 January 1984.

18. Lord Hugh Cecil, *Conservatism* (London: Williams & Norgate, no date, c. 1912), p. 243.

19. For a conventional leftwing attack upon Labour leaders for class collaboration, see Ralph Miliband, *Parliamentary Socialism* (London: Allen & Unwin, 1961). For sympathetic analyses that yet emphasize the limits of Labour's achievements, see Wilfred Beckerman, ed., *The Labour Government's Economic Record, 1964–1970* (London: Duckworth, 1972); and Nick Bosanquet and Peter Townsend, eds., *Labour and Equality: A Fabian Study of Labour in Power, 1974–79* (London: Heinemann, 1980).

20. Roy Jenkins, "Home Thoughts from Abroad," *The Listener* (London), 29 November 1979.

21. Her Majesty's Treasury. *The Next Ten Years: Public Expenditure and Taxation into the 1990s* (London: Her Majesty's Stationery Office, henceforth abbreviated to HMSO, Cmnd. 9189) pp. 30f.

22. For data and a general statement of the model invoked here, see Richard Rose and Terence Karran, "Inertia or Incrementalism? A Long-Term View of the Growth of Government," in A. J. Groth and L. L. Wade, eds., *Comparative Resource Allocation* (Beverly Hills and London: Sage Publications, 1984).

CHAPTER II

The Constraints of Place

Are they [the English] not above all nations divided from the rest of the world, insular both in situation and in mind, both for good and for evil?

THE ISLAND POSITION of Great Britain is its most significant geographic feature; insularity is one of its most striking cultural characteristics. London is physically closer to France than to the geographic center of England, but for centuries the English Channel has symbolized the psychological gulf between England and the continent of Europe. Although there is no other continent to which the island could conceivably be assigned, English people do not think of themselves as Europeans. A French writer has said, "We might liken England to a ship which, though anchored in European waters, is always ready to sail away."[1]

When Europe was the center of world affairs, England held aloof from commitment there, intervening only when necessary to maintain a balance of power, and entry to the European Community in 1973 occurred in spite of perceived differences between the English and Europeans. The country's military dependence upon America is as meaningful politically as is its geographical nearness to France, Belgium, and the Netherlands. Historic links with Commonwealth countries in other continents further reduce the significance of physical geography. Politically, England may claim to be equally close to or

29

distant from Europe, America, and the nations of a global Commonwealth.

When the Gallup Poll asks which countries England should work closely with, there is a desire to keep a foot in three worlds: 85 percent say it is important to have close relations with Europe, 81 percent think close relations with Commonwealth countries are important, and 78 percent believe close relations with the United States are important. No one thinks that Russia is a good friend of Britain. These views have been stable since the 1960s. When asked which relationship is most important, people divide into three principal groups: 39 percent today put Europe first, 26 percent put America first, and 25 percent put the Commonwealth first; the rest are don't knows.[2]

In an interdependent world, England is more dependent than most major nations. Instead of England leading the world as in Victorian times, international political and economic constraints today severely limit the government's scope for action. An empire turned into a multiracial Commonwealth now poses problems too. The arrival of more than a million new Commonwealth immigrants faces England with the problem of adapting a formerly all-white society to multiracial life. Within the United Kingdom, expressions of nationalism in different ways in Northern Ireland, Scotland, and Wales have forced Her Majesty's Government to think about the means by which a single Parliament at Westminster can govern a multinational political system. In turn this chapter reviews England's place in the world, the place of nonwhite Britons in a society that is overwhelmingly English, and the place of England within the United Kingdom.

INSULARITY AND INVOLVEMENT

For centuries England's insular position was a great asset, saving it from military invasions that have cost European countries so much in the twentieth century. The last successful foreign invasion of England — excluding border wars with Scots — was the Norman conquest in 1066; in France, it was the German invasion of 1940. In both world wars of this century, England did not suffer occupation, while the continent of Europe was a battlefield. Unlike France, Germany, Italy, and Japan, contemporary England has not had to build new political institutions after the havoc of war.

Insularity is not to be confused with isolation. As an island with a seafaring tradition, it has been, as Sir Eyre Crowe wrote, long ago, "a neighbour of every country accessible by sea." By acts of policy and by the adventurous initiatives of public officials and private traders, an empire was built up that at one time included nearly one-fifth of the population and land area of the world. The Empire drew together territories as scattered and various as India, Nigeria, and Palestine, as well as the old Dominions of Canada, Australia, New Zealand, and South Africa. At the end of the Second World War the past achievements of empire builders left the country with political commitments on every continent.

Imperial Decline. The end of empire began with the granting of independence to India and Pakistan in 1947. In the decades since, government has accepted that from a distance of thousands of miles it could no longer enforce its authority against colonial peoples demanding independence. More than three dozen colonies with a population of 800 million were part of the Empire in 1945; today they are independent states.

The Empire has been replaced by a free association of forty-seven sovereign states, the Commonwealth. The independent status of its chief members is shown by the removal of the word British from the title of the Commonwealth. A number of Afro-Asian nations have also exchanged loyalty to the Crown for the status of a republic, and the old Dominions of Canada and Australia have symbolically abandoned "God Save the Queen" as their national anthem. Only a miscellany of island colonies and small trading enclaves such as Gibraltar remain from days of the Empire. Meetings of Commonwealth countries today emphasize many political and social conflicts among its very heterogeneous membership.[3]

Foreign policy since 1945 is a story of gradually contracting commitments. Initially, Britain (as the United Kingdom of Great Britain and Northern Ireland is often referred to) was an important partner of America in organizing alliances. In 1947 the Labour government took the lead in organizing a European response to the United States offer of economic aid in the Marshall Plan. In 1949 Britain was important in founding The North Atlantic Treaty Organization (NATO), and after the Korean War broke out in 1950, it took the lead in European rearmament.

The country's inability to pursue an independent foreign policy was made evident in 1956. In collaboration with France, Britain organized an abortive military invasion of Egypt to seize the Suez Canal, regarded by Prime Minister Sir Anthony Eden as vital to England's trade routes. The military force was withdrawn in the face of American and Russian opposition; its objective was not achieved.

Contraction of diplomatic commitments has been matched by decline in military strength. Initially, the United Kingdom sought to develop an independent nuclear weapon. Since 1962 it has been reduced to dependence upon the United States for the sophisticated research and development technology required for modern weapons delivery systems. In 1965 the Labour government showed itself unable (or unwilling) to use force against 200,000 white settlers in Southern Rhodesia who unilaterally declared independence, defying until 1979 London's preference for a multiracial government. In the 1970s England found its military force so limited that at times it withdrew troops from its principal NATO bases in Europe in an attempt to contain violence in Northern Ireland.

As part of its heritage from the past, the United Kingdom remains one of five permanent members in the Security Council of the United Nations. Like France, it has influence of a different and lesser order than the three Council superpowers America, Russia, and China. It is a member of 126 international organizations. But some government officials now question whether the country today needs — or can afford — diplomatic commitments that it took for granted half a century ago. Official reports recommend closing down embassies in lands where the benefits are not perceived as equal to the cost.[4]

In April 1982, Britain showed that it could independently use military force, in response to the Argentine invasion of the Falkland Islands, a British colony in the South Atlantic with a population of 1,800 people. The United Nations Security

Council condemned the Argentine invasion and called for a diplomatic resolution of disputed claims to the territory by Britain and Argentina. After negotiations produced no settlement, a British task force landed in the islands; Argentina surrendered on 14 June 1982. The military victory gave evidence of the Conservative government's readiness to meet force with force in defense of British territory.[5]

The Falklands War is atypical of the conduct of British foreign policy. It involved no other major power. Argentina was led by an unpopular dictatorship without any effective allies, and its military forces were badly organized and equipped. The war was very short; it cost 255 British lives, fewer than have died in a bad year of fighting in Northern Ireland. Nor has the Falklands been a precursor of military intervention elsewhere. In 1983 the British government conspicuously held aloof from the troubles of the West Indian island of Grenada, notwithstanding concern expressed by its Commonwealth Caribbean neighbours about Soviet influences there. The United States then sent troops to Grenada without consulting the British government.

The Falklands War did not increase British commitment to international affairs. Less than a year after the Falklands invasion, 67 percent told a Gallup Poll that the government should have done more to prevent a war, and 53 percent said they thought it was not worth the money being spent to keep the Falklands in British hands.[6] Whereas before the 1959 general election, 42 percent thought that foreign affairs and defense issues were the most important problems facing the country as against 39 percent naming economic issues, before the 1983 general election only 1 percent thought this; 88 percent put economic issues first.[7]

Economic Difficulties. Force is used only occasionally, whereas economic transactions are continuous. The economy is unusually subject to influence by world conditions. Its exports flow to more countries than those of any other modern land. International trade is almost three times more important in relation to the gross national product than is the case for America. In order to pay for the food and raw materials that the country imports, exports to other countries must also be high. Imports equal almost one-quarter of the country's national product, more than double the level of imports of the United States. In addition to exporting manufactured goods, England also exports such invisible services as banking and insurance. The City of London is one of the world's great financial centers. The development of North Sea oil fields between Scotland and Norway has made Britain one of the few European nations to benefit from oil price rises. But it also underlines the relative weakness of exports of nonoil products.[8]

In the world economy England has increasingly become a decision-taker rather than a decisionmaker. While politicians have sought to increase the influence of the government over the nation's economy, the influence of international forces upon the national economy has grown even more. The most visible evidence is the decline of the value of the pound in relation to other major currencies in the world (Table II.1). In 1948, the pound was worth $4.20, and the German Deutsche Mark was of no value in the chaotic state of that country. In an era of fixed exchange rates, the pound was twice devalued, once in 1949 to $2.80 and again in 1967 to $2.40. The pound fell against the Deutsche Mark as well.

Along with other major trading nations, in 1972 Britain decided to abandon efforts to maintain a fixed exchange rate between the pound sterling and other currencies. Since then the

TABLE II.1 *The Changing Foreign Exchange Value of the Pound*

	US $	German Deutsche Mark
	(£1 equals)	
1940–1948	4.03	(not applicable)
1949–1967	2.80	11.12–11.74[a]
1967–1972	2.40	7.68–9.61
1976	1.64–2.03	3.91–4.62
1980	2.20–2.42	3.76–3.96
1984	1.16–1.46	3.64–3.96

[a]1953–1967

Source: Central Statistical Office *Annual Abstract* (London: HMSO, annually); Central Statistical Office *Financial Statistics* (London: HMSO, monthly).

pound has floated; that is, its value fluctuates daily in relation to other currencies, according to pressures in money markets from London to Hong Kong. Floating the pound has resulted in very substantial short-term fluctuations. For example, in 1980 the pound fluctuated in value between $2.20 and $2.42; in 1984 it fluctuated between $1.16 and $1.46.

The value of the pound has tended to float downwards. This helps Britain's exports by making goods more competitively priced, but it also makes dearer the goods that it imports. Since the floating of currencies in 1972, the pound has fallen against the dollar by as much as 52 percent and by as much as 53 percent against the German Deutsche Mark. Thus, at the request of a German plaintiff, an English High Court judge rendered judgment against a British company in Deutsche Marks because, he said, "Sterling floats in the wind; it changes like a weathercock with every gust that blows."[9]

To meet the balance of payments problems resulting from the decline in the pound, British governments have had to go to the International Monetary Fund to secure loans in 1967 and again in 1976. In negotiating these loans, the government promised to undertake economic measures that it had been unwilling to take before its hand was forced by external events.[10] The measures taken, such as raising interest rates and reducing public expenditure, were unpopular with Labour party supporters. But the Labour governments negotiating the loans have taken them in the belief that the alternatives would have been worse. In justification, James Callaghan, Labour Chancellor of the Exchequer at the time of the first IMF loan and Prime Minister at the time of the second loan, declared:

> No one owes Britain a living, and may I say to you quite bluntly that despite the measures of the last twelve months we are still not earning the standard of living we are enjoying. We are keeping up our standards by borrowing, and this cannot go on indefinitely.[11]

Into Europe. As England's position in the world has declined relative to other countries, government has looked to Europe. Joining with the increasingly prosperous countries of the European Community (or Common Market as it is often called in England, to stress its economic rather than political significance) was said to offer the best hope to secure continued economic growth and diplomatic influence.

The United Kingdom did not join the Community when it was established in 1957, considering its position superior to that of continental neighbors ravaged by war. In 1961, the Conservative government of Harold Macmillan first unsuccessfully sought entry, an application reactivated by Harold Wilson's Labour government in 1967, and pressed successfully by the 1970–1974 Conservative government under Edward Heath.

Concurrently, many changes in European societies have drawn the island nation much closer to its continental neighbors. The changes have ranged from joint participation in televised Eurovision song contests and European Football Cup matches to integrating operations of American multinational corporations such as the Ford Motor Company on both sides of the English Channel. Jet aircraft have made the English Channel less a barrier to travel than city traffic is. A businessman traveling from London to Paris, Brussels, or Frankfurt spends twice as long getting to and from the airport as in flight.

The United Kingdom joined the European Community on 1 January 1973, but a question mark hung over its membership, for ordinary voters and politicians disagreed about whether the decision was the right one. Parliament approved entry by 356 to 244 votes; differences about membership cut across party lines. A majority of Conservative and a minority of Labour Members of Parliament voted for entry, and were opposed by a majority of Labour and a minority of Conservative MPs.[12]

In 1975 the Labour government took the unprecedented step of calling a national referendum to determine whether or not Britain should remain a member of the European Community. The referendum showed a majority of 67 percent in favor. But the one-third who voted against have not abandoned their opposition; support for the Community has fluctuated since. In the first popular election of Members of the European Parliament in 1979, only 33 percent of the electorate turned out to vote, less than half the number voting at the general election a month before. In the 1984 European Parliament election, turnout was 32.4 percent, compared to a turnout of 72.7 percent in the 1983 general election.[13] In both European elections, voter apathy was higher in the United Kingdom than in any other European nation.

Economic arguments were the chief reasons given for entering the Common Market. The economy was pictured as likely to benefit from the stimulus of wider markets and competition. If Britain remained outside the Community, exclusion from continental markets was depicted as a risk that the country could not afford to run. But prosperity did not follow. Instead, in October 1973 the oil crisis triggered a world recession, and the Common Market has been blamed by its critics for economic difficulties that have since befallen Britain. In the 1980s, England is one of the less prosperous members of the European Community; its national product per head approaches that of Italy rather than Germany or France.

Politically, membership in the European Community has drawn politicians and civil servants into bargaining relations with their opposite numbers in continental countries. Diplomats may still feel more attracted to Washington, because it is central for international security. But other ministers can now look to meetings in Brussels for decisions about such bread-and-butter issues as agricultural and industrial policy. Today, almost every government department must at some time take European Community politics into account, and politicians and civil servants are increasingly involved in the bargaining that produces vast numbers of small-scale Community regulations that become binding laws in Britain. After a decade of membership, however, there is no agreement about how much influence the Community has upon Britain, or Britain upon the Community.[14]

The more England has become open to international influences, the more insular public opinion has become. Notwithstanding the patriotic fervor whipped up by the Falklands War, most English people have no desire to see their country again be a world power. A 1983 Gallup Poll found that 53 percent said that they would like to see the country be more like Sweden and Switzerland, as against 33 percent wanting it to try to be a leading world power. Moreover, the proportion favoring England's being on the sidelines of world affairs is increasing; in 1971 the proportion favoring a role like that of the Swedes or Swiss was 10 percent less.[15]

England's future place in the world will not be determined by popular wishes alone. The constraints of history and of place limit the extent to which the government can insulate the country from world events, particularly economic trends. Today, the effective choice of government is not whether England should be a small, rich country, resembling Sweden or Switzerland, but whether it should remain a big, rich country or gradually become a big and relatively (though not absolutely) poor country. By refusing to face this choice, England's governors demonstrate that the judgment of the American diplomat, Dean Acheson, remains apt: "Great Britain has lost an empire and has not yet found a role."[16]

NONWHITE BRITONS

As citizens of a world power, Britons have long moved around the world without constraint. For centuries, England has also received a small but noteworthy number of immigrants from other lands, principally Europe. The present Royal Family is the most notable of immigrants to England. The Queen is immediately descended from the heirs of Princess Sophia of Hanover. George I came from this German princely state to assume the English throne in 1714, succeeding the Scottish-bred Stuarts. German connections were maintained by Queen Victoria's marriage to Albert, Prince of Saxe-Coburg and Gotha, and by their offspring. Until the outbreak of anti-German sentiment in World War I, the surname of the Royal Family was Saxe-Coburg-Gotha. By royal proclamation, George V changed his name to Windsor in 1917.

Through the centuries, less eminent immigrants have also come to London; as a great port and trading center it has been accessible to all Europe. The chief influx of immigration in the first half of the twentieth century consisted of Jews from Eastern Europe, refugees from Nazi Germany in the 1930s, and then Poles and Hungarians. However, by the standards of America, Canada, or Australia, immigration has been slight.[17]

The English use of the word race not only to refer to differences
of skin color (e.g., West Indians) but also religion (e.g., Jews)
or nationality (e.g., Irish) emphasizes the varied ways by which
cultural differences are defined.[18]

New Commonwealth Immigration. In the late 1950s a few British
subjects from populous parts of the new Commonwealth, especially the West Indies, Pakistan, and India, began migrating
to England to benefit personally from their land's colonial past.
The great majority of the immigrants have been attracted to
England by the prospect of a job, whether as a doctor, factory
worker, or hospital orderly.[19] Those who dislike England and
return home have been fewer than those who like it and have
sent for their relatives and friends to join them.

Decades of immigration followed by decades in which immigrants have settled, married, and had children have cumulatively increased the nonwhite proportion of the population of
Britain from 74,000 (0.2 percent) in 1951 to an estimated
2,250,000 to 2,500,000 (about 4.5 percent) by 1981. Of this
total, about 670,000 have come from India and another 180,000
are Asians who have fled from East African countries; 550,000
have emigrated from Pakistan; 550,000 from the West Indies;
about 150,000 from Africa; and the remainder from Cyprus,
Malta, Hong Kong, Singapore, and other territories historically part of the British Empire.[20]

Immigrants have had little in common upon arrival. British
West Indians came as native English-speakers, albeit some
spoke with a calypso accent. The bulk of the early immigrants
from the Indian subcontinent — whether from India or
Pakistan — came from alien cultures: the majority were uned-
ucated and unskilled workers. Muslims and Sikhs follow religious practices that have made them especially distinctive. In
several cities Sikhs have had to fight political campaigns to become bus conductors, because the municipally owned bus companies said they would not employ Sikhs unless they wore caps
rather than their ritual turbans. The small number of African
immigrants have been divided among themselves by tribe and
citizenship. Differences among immigrants have made it difficult to establish an American-style political movement, for

the immigrants do not share a common black (that is, African) heritage; they share a negative characteristic (that is, they are all nonwhite).

As the result of its imperial past, the United Kingdom has never had a clear-cut definition of who is and who is not a British citizen. When immigration started in the 1950s, almost all of upwards of 1 billion residents of the Commonwealth from India to Newfoundland were British subjects, even though most had never come within a thousand miles of Dover. A series of Acts of Parliament progressively reduced the proportion of British subjects living in other parts of the Commonwealth who could enter the country as a right. There are now three principal categories of people with some claim to being British — those who are born and live in Britain; those who are born elsewhere in the Commonwealth and have no right of free entry to Britain; and citizens of the Republic of Ireland, who are counted as neither British nor foreign, and have an unqualified right to enter Britain, vote in British elections, and sit in the House of Commons.[21]

The entry into England of a relatively small number of nonwhite immigrants has had a significance far out of proportion to their number. From the first, public opinion has opposed such immigration. In 1958, two-thirds endorsed stricter controls upon immigration, and by 1968, 95 percent wanted stricter controls on immigration. MPs were shocked out of a complacent belief that their fellow countrymen were free of racial animosity in the 1964 election, when a racialist candidate, running on the Conservative label, won an upset victory at Smethwick. By 1970, Enoch Powell had become prominent as the proponent of a white England.[22] Successive Conservative and Labour governments have responded in 1962, 1968, and 1971 by passing laws intended to limit the number of nonwhite Commonwealth immigrants entering the United Kingdom.

From Immigration to Integration? Today racial issues are less about immigration and more about the place of immigrants in English society. Even more important is the place of children, born and educated in England, but of alien parentage. A melting-pot theroy emphasizes that racial differences will gradually disappear through a process of assimilation. Another theory posits that racial conflicts will increase unless positive policies are adopted to assist youths who are British in every conventional respect except their skin color.

The proportion of British-born people who are not white is increasing. As of 1982, an estimated 42 percent of the nonwhite population was British born, and the population is rising because of higher birth rates in the immigrant community.[23] This challenges the white majority to abandon its traditional assumption that England is an all-white society, and accept that it is now multiracial. Americans, by contrast, have never doubted that America is multiracial: the challenge that the United States faced in the 1960s was to alter relations between blacks and whites.

Politicians who have prided themselves on England's tolerance do not like to admit that racial discrimination occurs in England. Insofar as discrimination is known to occur, politicians may interpret this as an argument *against* passing laws to benefit a small percentage of blacks for fear of alienating a larger number of white voters. Laws intended to improve race relations were passed in 1965, 1968, and 1976. By comparison with American legislation, their scope is narrow, and provisions for judicial enforcement of rights are very much weaker than in the United States.[24] A government-sponsored Commission for Racial Equality established to oppose discrimination, relies primarily on investigation and conciliation rather than the courts.

The leaders of the major parties differ in degree, not principle, about race relations. The two crucial issues are defined as: (1) How few nonwhite immigrants should be admitted to Britain in the coming years? and (2) How much (or how little) should government do to promote good race relations within Britain?

Although nearly every conceivable white minority is found in the House of Commons, no political party has a nonwhite MP. Only the nonelected House of Lords has nonwhite members. In a limited number of constituencies, efforts are made to court the immigrant vote; immigrants who do vote tend to favor Labour.[25] When immigrants have stood independent of party, their vote has been minimal.

From time to time, white racist groups attract public attention by protest marches and counterdemonstrations. But their electoral appeal has been very slight. In the October 1974 general election, 90 National Front candidates polled 0.4 percent of the vote; in 1979, 303 National Front candidates won 0.6 percent of the vote; and in 1983, 60 National Front candidates secured 0.1 percent of the vote.

In the summer of 1981 riots in inner-city areas of London and Liverpool spotlighted the problem of young people of immigrant parentage. The riots did not, however, produce agreement about their causes or consequences. Diagnosis of the cause of the riots ranged from racial discrimination or police misbehavior through youth unemployment to hooliganism.

An imperial past has made Britain a multiracial society in fact, but it is not yet multiracial in political values. Politicians act on the assumption that the transition is so difficult that the slower the pace, the less the friction. The question for the 1990s is whether this characteristically gradualist approach will lead to the acceptance of nonwhite Britons, or whether a small, politically alienated, and active group will identify themselves as blacks rather than Britons.

ONE CROWN AND MANY NATIONS

The English Crown is the oldest and best known in the world. Identifying those subject to its authority is no problem, because English people for centuries have had a secure national identity. This identity is so taken for granted that the government does not think it necessary to put the name of the country on its postage stamps; the head of the Queen is regarded as sufficient. Yet there is no such thing as an English state.[26]

In international law as in the title of the Queen, the state is the United Kingdom of Great Britain and Northern Ireland. The island of Great Britain, the major part of the United Kingdom, is divided into three parts: England, Scotland, and Wales. England, smaller than Alabama or Wisconsin, constitutes 55 percent of the land area of Great Britain. The other part of the United Kingdom, Northern Ireland, consists of six counties of

Ulster that have remained under the Crown rather than join an independent Irish Republic ruled from Dublin. Insofar as territorial contiguity is politically significant, a state might occupy an island to itself or a pair of neighboring islands (see map, facing p. 1). Irish nationalists have always argued that geography implies the existence of two island states, Ireland and Britain. Unionists have argued for a United Kingdom of the two islands. The international boundary of the United Kingdom today cuts across the northeast of Ireland, the one arrangement that is not implicit in insular geography.

The boundaries of the United Kingdom, as of other European countries, were drawn by centuries of diplomatic negotiations, battles won and lost, and accidents of dynastic succession. Wales was joined to England by dynastic inheritance, formalized by legislation in 1536. Scotland was similarly joined in two stages in 1603 and 1707. England has been sending troops to Ireland intermittently from 1169 to the present, in efforts to maintain sovereignty in at least part of the island. Although the ancestry of the Crown may be traced back to Alfred the Great in the ninth century, the current boundaries of the United Kingdom date only from 1921.

The United Kingdom is a multinational state.[27] Most Welsh people think of themselves as Welsh, and Scottish people think of themselves as Scots. In Northern Ireland there is no agreement about national identity; most Protestants see themselves as British and most Catholics see themselves as Irish (Table II.2). Just as a Texan or a Californian also thinks of himself or herself as an American, so a Scot or a Welsh person is also ready to identify with being British. When asked whether they are proud to be British, 86 percent of Welsh people and of Scots give the same answer as 86 percent of English respondents: they are proud of being British.

Scotland. In Scotland the established church is Presbyterian, whereas the Church of England is Episcopal; the Queen, by a political compromise that long antedated the ecumencial movement, worships as a Presbyterian in Scotland and as an Episcopalian in England. Scotland maintains a separate legal system, influenced by the Roman law tradition. Its educational

TABLE II.2 *National Identity within the United Kingdom*

	England	Scotland	Wales	Northern Ireland	
				Protestant	Roman Catholic
% Thinks of self as:					
British	38	35	33	67	15
English	57	2	8	—	—
Scottish	2	52	—	—	—
Welsh	1	—	57	—	—
Ulster	—	—	—	20	6
Irish	1	1	—	8	69
Other, don't know	1	10	2	5	10
Total	100	100	100	100	100

Source: Richard Rose, *Understanding the United Kingdom: the Territorial Dimension in Government* (London: Longman, 1982), p. 14.

system also differs from England's in such matters as the provision of separately organized Roman Catholic schools, and a broader, less specialized secondary education. The universities of Scotland were the model for American liberal arts colleges.

The industrialized Scottish Lowlands concentrate most of Scotland's population around Glasgow and Edinburgh. The area is distinct from England in many ways from architecture to drinking habits. The Scottish Highlands lie outside industrial civilization, except for the occasional incursion of North Sea oil activities. The Highlands have most of Scotland's scenery but less than 5 percent of its population.

A separate legal system has meant that Scotland has always had some political institutions distinct from those of England. Since 1885 there has been a government minister as the head of the Scottish Office, and since 1939 the administrative headquarters of the Scottish Office has been in Edinburgh. The Scottish Office gradually acquired many responsibilities for health, education, housing, economic development, agriculture, and local government. Today, the functional responsibilities of the Scottish Office substitute for or overlap with eleven Whitehall departments.[28]

Wales. The most distinctive feature of Welsh society is language. The proportion of people speaking Welsh has declined from 53 percent in 1891 to 19 percent in 1981. Many with Welsh ties, like Charles, the royal Prince of Wales, show a little knowledge of Welsh in tribute to the very different cultural values implied by the gulf between the English and Welsh languages. In religion, Welsh people are Protestant but often not Episcopal. Welshmen campaigned for generations against the established Episcopal Church of Wales; it was finally disestablished in 1920. Within Wales there are marked contrasts between the English-speaking, industrial, and more populous South and the Welsh-speaking, rural North West.[29]

Since the sixteenth century, when Wales was amalgamated with England, it has almost invariably been governed by the same laws as England. In 1746 Parliament declared that the word "England" in an Act of Parliament was deemed to include Wales, a provision not repealed until 1967. The introduction of compulsory education in the nineteenth century promoted Anglicization in Wales, for Welsh-speaking children were required by law to attend English-language schools. In 1907 the first step was taken to treat Wales distinctively for administrative purposes, with the appointment of a Welsh Secretary of Education. In 1964 a separate Welsh Office was established, with its head a Cabinet minister. The laws that the Welsh Office administers are normally Acts of Parliament that apply equally to England and Wales.[30]

Northern Ireland. The most un-English part of the United Kingdom, by the common agreement of both English and Irish people, is Northern Ireland.[31] Formally, Northern Ireland is a secular state, but in practice differences between Protestants and Catholics dominate its politics. Protestant loyalty to the Crown rests upon the English monarch's historic status, proclaimed in the Bill of Rights of 1688, as "the glorious instrument of delivering this kingdom from Popery and arbitrary power." Protestants constitute two-thirds of the population. Following secession of Southern Ireland from the United Kingdom, Protestants held power locally from the etablishment of a Northern Ireland Parliament at Stormont in Belfast in 1921, until the Stormont Parliament was suspended in 1972. Most Catholics have refused to support the regime, holding that national identity justifies Ulster's merger in a thirty-two county Republic of Ireland, with its capital in Dublin. Such a merger would result in a society in which Catholics outnumbered Protestants approximately three to one. Protestants reject belonging to a United Ireland.

Since 1968 Northern Ireland has been in turmoil. In that year Ulster Catholics began demanding what they regarded as the civil rights of Englishmen. In default of laws allowing pursuit of these claims through the courts and lacking electoral influence because of minority status, Catholics turned to internationally publicized street demonstrations. Successive British Labour and Conservative governments forced the Stormont government to make token concessions, which created a backlash among Protestants fearful of being forced into a United Ireland. Demonstrations turned to street violence in August 1969, and the British Army intervened. The Irish Republican Army (IRA) was revived, and in 1971 began a military campaign to withdraw Northern Ireland from the United Kingdom. In retaliation, Protestants too organized illegal armed groups.

Since August 1969, more than 2,400 people have been killed in political violence in Northern Ireland, the equivalent in population terms of more than 80,000 killed in Britain, or more than 360,000 killed in political violence in America. The dead include hundreds of civilian bystanders, as well as hundreds of British soldiers, Ulster policemen, and Irish Republicans and Protestant Loyalists killed in active service with illegal military units.

British policy has been erratic and unsuccessful. In 1969 British troops provided full support for the Unionist (and Protestant) Northern Ireland government at Stormont. In 1971 the army helped to intern hundreds of Catholics without trial in an unsuccessful attempt to break the IRA; the IRA flourished. In 1972 the British government abolished the Stormont Parliament, and took direct responsibility for affairs there, creating a Northern Ireland Office under a British Cabinet minister. In reaction, Protestant violence flourished.

In 1974 the British government temporarily succeeded in creating a Northern Ireland Executive, sharing power between one faction of the Unionists and the pro-Irish unity Social Democratic and Labour Party. The Executive collapsed in the face of the Ulster Workers' Council general strike organized by Protestants. The government refused to grant the strikers' demand for a general election to test whether or not there was majority support for the biconfessional power-sharing government. In 1975 the government authorized the election of a Constitutional Convention. When the Unionist majority in the Convention recommended adopting an Ulster constitution modeled on British parliamentary practice, the government rejected it as unsuitable for the least united part of the United Kingdom.[32]

Whereas the government has always upheld the supremacy of Parliament in dealing with nationalists in Scotland and Wales, in Northern Ireland it has consistently been prepared to say that it has the right to secede from the United Kingdom, if and when a majority of its population might wish to do so. But this has not happened. There is an impasse between the pro-British and pro-Irish groups within Northern Ireland; the former is in the majority.

The chief institution of government in the Province, the Northern Ireland Office, exercises statutory authority that must be annually renewed. Northern Ireland is thus governed by "temporary" direct rule. In 1982 the Northern Ireland Office sought to encourage political bargaining by authorizing the election of a Northern Ireland Assembly. The result underlined the extent of polarization. In a proportional representation ballot pro-Union parties won three-quarters of the seats. The two Irish unity parties, the nonviolent Social Democratic and Labour Party, and Sinn Fein, which supports the IRA's use of violence, both abstained from participation in the Assembly. The government of the Republic of Ireland responded by lobbying the British government to come to an agreement with it about the future of Ulster. But consensus between the two governments of the British Isles would still mean governing without consensus within Northern Ireland.[33]

An Upsurge of Nationalism. For generations differences between nations within the United Kingdom were confined to differing levels of support for the Conservative and Labour parties. With the invariable exception of Northern Ireland, nationalist parties were always weak. This was the steady-state United Kingdom (see Table II.3). In the 1970s the party system was temporarily destabilized by the challenge of nationalist parties. The Ulster Unionists broke their link with the British Conservative party, the Northern Ireland Labour party disappeared, and a new Democratic Unionist party led by Dr. Ian Paisley came forward on the Protestant side. The net effect is that no British party now seeks votes in Northern Ireland; all votes cast there are for parties not fighting anywhere else in the United Kingdom.

In Scotland the Scottish National party vote rose to a peak of 30 percent in October, 1974, only 6 percent less than that of the front-running Labour party. In Wales, Plaid Cymru has polled upwards of one-tenth of the vote; in October 1974, it was able to win three seats in Parliament as well.[34]

In response to the rise in Nationalist votes, the 1974 Labour government pledged to devolve some government responsibilities to popularly elected Assemblies in Scotland and Wales. The attempt to implement these pledges provoked strong reactions in Parliament. Members of Parliament jealously sought reassurance that the devolution of power to Assemblies in Edinburgh and Cardiff would not detract from Parliament's authority. Moreover, many MPs believed the Labour government was overreacting to Nationalists, pointing out that 89 percent of Welsh voters did *not* vote Nationalist in October 1974, and the same was true of 70 percent of Scottish voters.

Parliamentary opposition forced referendums asking Welsh and Scottish voters whether they wished the Devolution Acts approved in Parliament in 1978 to go into effect. A novel feature of the referendums was the requirement that if 40 percent of persons deemed eligible to vote did not approve devolution,

TABLE II.3   *Divisions of the Vote within the United Kingdom, 1964–1983*

	Conservative	Labour	Liberal/ Alliance	Nationalists
		(% vote within nation)		
England				
1964	44.1	43.5	12.1	n.a.
Oct 1974	38.9	40.1	20.2	n.a.
1983	46.0	36.9	26.4	n.a.
Wales				
1964	29.4	57.8	7.3	4.8
Oct 1974	23.9	49.5	15.5	10.8
1983	31.1	37.5	23.2	7.8
Scotland				
1964	40.6	48.7	7.6	2.4
Oct 1974	24.7	36.3	8.3	30.4
1983	28.4	35.1	24.5	11.8
Northern Ireland				
1964	63.0[a]	16.1	4.7	18.2
Oct 1974	0	1.6	0	62.1 Un'st 29.8 Irish
1983	0	0	0	57.1 Un'st 33.2 Irish
United Kingdom total				
1964	43.4	44.1	11.2	0.9
Oct 1974	35.8	39.2	15.3	5.5
1983	42.4	27.6	25.4	2.5

[a]Vote for the Ulster Unionist Party, which broke its links with the British Conservative Party in 1972.

Source: Calculated from Richard Rose and Ian McAllister, *United Kingdom Facts* (London: Macmillan, 1982), Chapter 4.

the government would be compelled to give Parliament a chance to repeal the Acts. In the referendums of 1 March 1979, Welsh voters unequivocally rejected devolution; 80 percent voted against, and 20 percent in favor. In Scotland a narrow majority of Scots who voted gave approval to devolution; 51.6 percent voted yes, and 48.4 percent voted no. But the proportion of eligible voters endorsing devolution was only 32.8 percent of the Scottish electorate. In consequence, Parliament repealed the Devolution Acts for both Scotland and Wales.

Two general elections since have confirmed the Unionist (that is, pro-United Kingdom) sentiment in all parts of the United Kingdom. In 1979 the Scottish Nationalist vote dropped by nearly half, and the party lost nine of its eleven MPs; it fell again in 1983. The decline in the Plaid Cymru vote has brought it down to its lowest level since 1966. In Northern Ireland the vote for United Ireland candidates has grown, but pro-United Kingdom parties continue to poll up to two-thirds of the popular vote there.

Regionalism. Like every modern state, the United Kingdom is divided along geographical lines for purposes of administration as well as elections. Divisions occur within each of its national territories, as well as among them.[35] This is very evident within England itself. The North of England is much more industrial than the South of England and, because of a different social structure, more inclined to elect Labour MPs.

Within England, London is preeminent. With 7 million people, Greater London is seven times larger than Birmingham, the second largest city in the United Kingdom. Whereas New York City is as large as London, it does not similarly dominate American society. London contains one-sixth of the population of England; New York contains less than one-thirtieth of the population of the United States. Unlike Washington and Bonn, London is simultaneously the center of government, finance, the mass media, and the arts. More than two-thirds of people receiving a biography in *Who's Who* live within a 75-mile radius of the capital. Most of society's leaders are thus geographically segregated from the bulk of English people, who do not live within commuting distance of the capital. They live in places symbolically called the provinces.

The provinces of England have no political identity, unlike the regions and departments into which France and Italy are divided. Government has no standard definition of region; England is divided by dozens of different regional boundaries. The particular set of boundaries in use varies from program to program even within a government department.[36] There are

no elected regional assemblies, or regional headquarters that
are centers of political power. Within Scotland, within Wales,
and within Northern Ireland, regional differences are great,
dividing the Scottish Highlands and Lowlands, Welsh-speaking
North Wales and English-speaking South Wales, and industrial
Belfast from rural border areas.

Paradoxically, the pervasiveness of political divisions within
every town, region, village, and parliamentary constituency of
the United Kingdom contributes to unity Britainwide.[37] Insofar as votes for Conservative and Labour candidates reflect
the class structure of a constituency, then working-class constituencies will tend to elect Labour MPs, whether they are in
London, Cardiff, or Glasgow, and middle-class constituencies
will elect Conservative MPs, whether in Bristol, Cardiff, or
Perthshire. Systematic analysis of the 1983 general election emphasizes that apparent differences in votes between and within
England, Scotland, and Wales are not so much the result of
cultural differences between nations and regions, but principally reflect differences in social structure having much the
same impact throughout Britain. The importance of nationalism and religion in Northern Ireland is shown by people elsewhere in the United Kingdom regarding it as un-British.[38]

The government of Britain today is constrained by both history and geography. Political relationships are not defined in
a logically structured constitution. The government is the
product of a series of settlements occurring in different centuries in different places. The triumph of particular customs
over general principles is demonstrated by the lack of consistency in the territorial scope of a typical government department. The typical ministry will exercise some of its powers for
the United Kingdom as a whole, others throughout Great Britain (that is, for England, Scotland, and Wales), some for England and Wales, and some for England alone. Territorial
inconsistencies within the government of the United Kingdom
must inevitably be reflected in this text.[39]

The most important characteristic of United Kingdom government is that it is a Union. The Union reflects the disparate
origins of its parts, which accounts for the lack of uniformity
in some of its institutions today. Even more, the Union stands

for the common features of the whole. One unintended consequence of the surge in nationalist voting in the 1970s was the demonstration that most Scots, Welsh, and Ulster voters support parties determined to maintain the Union. The Union is expressed in Cabinet by the fact that the ministers in charge of the Scottish Office, Welsh Office, and Northern Ireland Office sit there by virtue of the seats their party holds in the United Kingdom Parliament. In government there is only one source of authority, namely the institutions that exercise the prerogatives of the Crown in Parliament.

NOTES

1. Andre Siegfried, *England's Crisis* (London: Jonathan Cape, 1931), p. 303.

2. *Gallup Political Index* (London), No. 279 (November 1983), p. 14. Less than 1 percent regard Russia as a good friend of Britain; *ibid.*, No. 284 (April 1984), p. 13.

3. See Sir Nicholas Mansergh, *The Commonwealth Experience* (London: Weidenfeld & Nicolson, 1969).

4. Cf. the *Report of the Review Committee on Overseas Representation, Chairman: Sir Val Duncan* (London: HMSO, Cmnd. 4107, 1969); the Central Policy Review Staff, *Review of Overseas Representation* (London: HMSO, 1977).

5. For an official review, see the *Report* of the Falkland Islands Review Committee chaired by Lord Franks (London: HMSO, Cmnd. 8787, 1983), and press comment after it was published on 18 January 1983. For an unofficial review see *Sunday Times* Insight Team, *The Falklands War* (London: Sphere, 1982). Cf. Walter Little, "The Falklands Affair: a Review of the Literature," *Political Studies*, 32:2 (1984), pp. 296–310.

6. *Gallup Political Index*, No. 270 (February 1983), p. 15.

7. *Gallup Political Index*, No. 274 (June 1983) p. 15; and Gallup Poll Election Release, No. 108 (London: Social Surveys, 1959).

8. C. L. Taylor and David A. Jodice, *World Handbook of Political and Social Indicators* 3rd ed. (New Haven: Yale University Press, 1983), Vol. I, table 6.9. Cf. Andrew Gamble, *Britain in Decline* (London: Macmillan, 1981); and Stephen Blank, "The Politics of Foreign Economic Policy," *International Organization*, 31:4 (1977), pp. 673–722. On the earlier period, see Andrew Shonfield, *British Economic Policy since the War* (Harmondsworth: Penguin, 1958).

9. See the statement by Lord Denning in *Shorsch Meier* v. *Hennin*, 1974, cited in Richard Vaughan, ed., *Post-War Integration in Europe* (London: Edward Arnold, 1976) p. 191.

10. On Britain's dealings with the IMF in 1976, see the series of articles by Stephen Fay and Hugo Young "The Day the £ Nearly Died," *Sunday Times* (London), 14, 21, 28 May 1978.

11. Prime Ministerial broadcast, 5 April 1976.

12. For details, see Uwe Kitzinger, *Diplomacy and Persuasion* (London: Thames & Hudson, 1973).

13. See David Butler and Uwe Kitzinger, *The 1975 Referendum* (London: Macmillan, 1976); Anthony King, *Britain Says Yes* (Washington, D. C.: Amer-

ican Enterprise Institute, 1977); and David Butler and David Marquand, *European Elections and British Politics* (London: Longman, 1981).

14. See e.g., Helen Wallace, William Wallace, and Carole Webb, eds., *Policy-Making in the European Communities* (London: John Wiley, 1977); and William Wallace, ed., *Britain in Europe* (London: Heinemann, 1980).

15. *Gallup Political Index*, No. 276 (August 1983) p. 16, and No. 172 (November 1974) p. 15

16. "Britain's Independent Role About Played Out," *The Times* (London), 6 December 1962.

17. See C. Holmes, ed., *Immigrants and Minorities in British Society* (London: Allen & Unwin, 1978); and E. Krausz, *Ethnic Minorities in Britain* (London: Paladin, 1972).

18. See R. M. White, "What's in a Name? Problems in Official and Legal Usages of Race," *New Community*, 7:3 (1979) 333–349. See also L. P. Curtis, Jr., *Anglo-Saxons and Celts* (Bridgeport, Conn.: Published for the Conference on British Studies by Bridgeport University, 1968).

19. On the first wave of immigration, cf. E. J. B. Rose and associates, *Colour and Citizenship* (London: Oxford University Press, 1969); and Michael Banton, *Promoting Racial Harmony* (Cambridge: Cambridge University Press, 1984). On continuing developments, see articles in the journal *New Community*.

20. For this estimate see Roger Ballard, "Race and the Census: What an 'Ethnic Question' Would Show," *New Society*, 12 May 1983, p. 212.

21. See Richard Rose, *Understanding the United Kingdom: The Territorial Dimension in Government* (London: Longman, 1982), pp. 35f.

22. Cf. Douglas E. Schoen, *Enoch Powell and the Powellites* (London: Macmillan, 1977); William L. Miller, "What Is the Profit in Following the Crowd?" *British Journal of Political Science*, 10:4 (1980), pp. 15–38; and Z. Layton-Henry, "Race, Electoral Strategy and the Major Parties," *Parliamentary Affairs*, 31:3 (1978).

23. See Central Statistical Office, *Social Trends*, No. 14 (London: HMSO, 1983), table 1.12 and *General Household Survey*, 1982 (London: HMSO, 1984), table 3.23.

24. See Donley T. Studlar, "Political Culture and Racial Policy in Britain", in R. Rose, ed., *Studies in British Politics* 3rd ed. (London: Macmillan, 1976), pp. 105–14; Ken Young and Naomi Connelly, *Policy and Practice in the Multi-Racial City* (London: Policy Studies Institute, 1981); and Z. Layton-Henry, *The Politics of Race in Britain* (London: Allen & Unwin, 1984).

25. See, e.g., Donley T. Studlar, "The Ethnic Vote, 1983: Problems of Analysis and Interpretation," *New Community*, 11:1–2 (1983), pp. 92–100. See also Ivor Crewe, "Representation and Ethnic Minorities in Britain," in Nathan Glazer and Ken Young, eds., *Ethnic Pluralism and Public Policy* (London: Heinemann, 1983), pp. 258–284.

26. On the absence of thinking about the state in England and America, by contrast with Continental Europe, see J. P. Nettl, "The State as a Conceptual Variable," *World Politics*, 22 (1968), pp. 559–581. For an illustration of this, see Richard Rose, "Is the United Kingdom a State? Northern Ireland as a Test Case," in P. Madgwick and R. Rose, eds., *The Territorial Dimension in United Kingdom Politics* (London: Macmillan, 1982), pp. 100–136.

27. See Richard Rose, *Understanding the United Kingdom*, chapter 1.

28. For studies of Scotland stressing its distinctiveness, see James G. Kellas, *The Scottish Political System* 3rd ed. (Cambridge: Cambridge University Press, 1984), J. A. Brand, *The National Movement in Scotland* (London: Rout-

ledge & Kegan Paul, 1978).

29. For studies sympathetic to Welsh distinctiveness, see K. O. Morgan, *Rebirth of a Nation: Wales 1880–1980* (Oxford: Clarendon Press, 1981); and Alan Butt Philip, *The Welsh Question: Nationalism in Welsh Politics, 1945–70* (Cardiff: University of Wales Press, 1981). Cf. Denis Balsom, Peter Madgwick and Denis Van Mechelen, *The Political Consequences of Welsh Identity* (Glasgow: U. of Strathclyde Studies in Public Policy No. 97).

30. See Ian Thomas, *The Creation of the Welsh Office: Conflicting Purposes in Institutional Change* (Glasgow: U. of Strathclyde Studies in Public Policy No. 91, 1981).

31. See Richard Rose, *Governing Without Consensus: An Irish Perspective* (London: Faber & Faber, 1971). For a guide to institutions and individuals, see W. D. Flackes, *Northern Ireland: a Political Directory* (London: BBC, 1983).

32. See Richard Rose, *Northern Ireland: A Time of Choice* (London: Macmillan, 1977); and Robert Fisk, *The Point of No Return* (London: Andre Deutsch, 1975).

33. For a review of alternative forms of government and the objections thereto, see David Watt, ed., *The Constitution of Northern Ireland* (London: Heinemann, 1981).

34. For analyses of voting in this period, see Ian McAllister, "United Kingdom Nationalist Parties: One Nationalism or Three?" pp. 202–223; and William L. Miller, "Variations in Electoral Behaviour in the United Kingdom," pp. 224–50, both in Madgwick and Rose, eds., *The Territorial Dimension in United Kingdom Politics*.

35. See McAllister and Rose, *The Nationwide Competition for Votes;* Richard Rose and Ian McAllister, *United Kingdom Facts* (London: Macmillan 1982); and Rose, McAllister, and Richard Parry, *United Kingdom Rankings* (Glasgow: U. of Strathclyde Studies in Public Policy No. 44, 1979).

36. See Brian W. Hogwood and Michael Keating, eds., *Regional Government in England* (Oxford: Clarendon Press, 1982).

37. For a cluster analysis grouping constituencies on social rather than geographical lines, see McAllister and Rose, *The Nationwide Competition for Votes,* chapter 10.

38. See Richard Rose, Ian McAllister, and Peter Mair, *Is There a Concurring Majority about Northern Ireland?* (Glasgow: U. of Strathclyde Studies in Public Policy No. 22, 1978).

39. On the confusion of England and Britain as labels, see Rose, *Understanding the United Kingdom,* pp. 28–31; on institutional complexity, *ibid.,* chapter 5.

CHAPTER III

The Institutions of the Crown

*"On all great subjects," says Mr. Mill, "much remains to be said,"
and of none is this more true than of the English Constitution. The
literature which has accumulated upon it is huge. But an observer
who looks at the living reality will wonder at the contrast to the paper
description. He will see in the life much which is not in the book;
and he will not find in the rough practice many refinements of the
literary theory.*

BEFORE STUDYING WHAT GOVERNMENT DOES, we must understand what government is. The conventional way to describe
a government is by referring to its constitution. We cannot do
so here, for England has no written constitution. At no time
in the past was there a break with tradition, as in the American
Revolution, forcing politicians to think about the basis of authority, and write down how the country should be governed
henceforth. The English Constitution has persisted for centuries without ever having been written down or subject to formal
approval. Its authority derives from its traditional origins.

The English Constitution is normally described as a mixture
of Acts of Parliament, judicial pronouncements, customs, and
conventions about the rules of the game.[1] Some of these elements are at least three centuries old, including the methods
by which Parliament can limit the Crown's right to tax and
spend public monies. Others, like the powers granted the European Community in 1973 to make laws binding in England,
are only a decade old, and their full meaning has yet to be

55

tested. Other elements are impossible to date, as when the Constitution is identified with something as general as the English way of life. Because of the jumble of unwritten and written elements in the Constitution, an introduction to a collection of written documents relevant to constitutional issues remarks: "It would be foolish to suppose that this mode of systematizing the material gives a complete picture of the British Constitution."[2]

The absence of a written constitution is often said to be a great advantage, because it allows greater flexibility to the government of the day. It can adapt institutions and actions to changing circumstances without the difficulties of amending a written document. The doctrine of parliamentary sovereignty means that the government can alter any institutions or procedures, as long as it can secure endorsement by a majority vote in Parliament. Laws of constitutional status are not entrenched; they are no more difficult to alter than any ordinary statute. The doctrine of parliamentary sovereignty means that the power of the government is not subject to any judicially enforceable constraints.

The flexibility of the Constitution results in vagueness about the conventions that politicians are bound to accept. Disputes about conventions and about the introduction or repeal of laws of constitutional status are resolved by political power. The party with a majority in Parliament carries the day. As the immediate cause of controversy recedes into the past, all sides usually come to accept yesterday's disputed actions as part of today's constitutional practice.

Whether an unwritten and sometimes vague set of ideas evolved in much earlier and different historical periods entirely suits contemporary England is today a subject of dispute. Critics allege that there is a "constitutional wasteland" because there is no charter clearly setting out the powers and limits of government. Nor is there any charter of citizens' rights enforceable in the courts. While admitting that "the idea sounds strange," Lord Scarman, a leading judge, has called for action to remedy "the helplessness of the law in face of the legislative sovereignty of Parliament . . . to accommodate the concept of fundamental and inviolable human rights."[3]

In a political system with a well-defined central authority

and a weak sense of constitutional constraints, the Mace is the appropriate symbol of political authority. The Mace is an ornate staff shaped like a club; it represented the power of the King in medieval times. As well as symbolizing the Crown, it also refers to the representative nature of government, for only when the Mace is in position in Parliament is the House of Commons deemed to be in session. With appropriate mystical overtones, the Mace symbolizes the unity of the Crown in Parliament.[4]

In everyday conversation, English people do not talk about the Constitution or the Mace but about government. The word can be used in many senses, as shown by the variety of adjectives that are used to modify it. One may speak of the Queen's government, to emphasize its enduring and nonpartisan features. Referring to a Labour or Conservative government emphasizes partisanship. The term government officials indicates civil servants rather than elected politicians. Adding the name of a Prime Minister (e.g., the Thatcher government), stresses personal and transitory features.

When a national survey asks people to say what first comes to mind when the word government is mentioned, three-fifths reply in terms of representative institutions, namely Parliament and parties (Table III.1). Only one-fifth mentions Cabinet ministers and civil servants as the principal symbol of government, and less than that think first of individual MPs and councillors. The institutional image of government contradicts the belief that television is personalizing politics. The impersonal view of government is confirmed when people are asked which part of government is most important: ministers and Whitehall officials move up, ranking equal with parties and Parliament.

Collectively, government departments are often referred to as *Whitehall*, after the London street in which many ministries are located. *Downing Street*, the home of the Prime Minister, is a small lane off Whitehall, and the *Palace of Westminster*, home of both the House of Commons and the House of Lords, is at the bottom of Whitehall. The historic clustering of government offices in the *Westminster* area symbolizes the centralization of government, just as the increasing dispersion of government

TABLE III.1   *The Public Image of the term Government*

	First comes to mind %	Most important %
Parliament	37	28
Parties	22	9
Total, Parliament & parties	(60)	(37)
Government ministers	18	30
Civil servants	2	7
Total, ministers & civil servants	(20)	(37)
MPs	15	14
Local councillors	4	9
Total, MPs & councillors	(19)	(23)
Don't know, None	(2)	(3)

Source: Louis Moss, *People and Government in 1978: A Survey of Opinion in England and Wales* (London: duplicated Birkbeck College, U. of London, 1982), p. 68.

offices throughout London symbolizes the growing complexity of government.[5]

Government is a set of impersonal institutions. Queen Elizabeth II is a figurehead, not an individual wielding authority as a person. Unlike in the United States, with its separation of powers, the authority of the Crown is meant to be unitary. But the chief institutions of the Crown are plural. This chapter concentrates first upon Whitehall, with the offices of the Prime Minister, the Cabinet, and civil servants, which are central in the exercise of authority. Parliament is necessary to give support and consent to government, but it is secondary in an era in which party discipline joins the fate of Members of Parliament with government. These institutions constitute a community of interests as well as a collective authority.

WHITEHALL

When a leading constitutional authority writes, "The Crown represents the sum total of governmental powers,"[6] this does not mean that Queen Elizabeth II personally determines the major activities of Her Majesty's Government. The Crown is a symbol of the institutions of government. Government property is held in the name of the Crown, not in the name of someone as transitory as a Prime Minister, or something as abstract as the state or as diffuse as the people of England. In the law courts, criminal actions are entered as the case of *Regina* (that is, Queen Elizabeth II) vs. the person accused of offending the Queen's peace.

The question thus arises: What constitutes the Crown? No simple answer can be given. The Crown is an idea to which people are asked to give loyalty. Like postage stamps bearing the face and emblem of the reigning monarch, the Crown has no name. It is also a concept of indefinite territorial domain; it refers to no particular primordial community of people. Today, as in Bagehot's time, the idea of the Crown confuses the dignified parts of the Constitution, which sanctify authority by tradition and myth, with the efficient parts which carry out the work of government.

The Queen. The reigning monarch deals almost exclusively with the dignified aspects of government.[7] The duties of Queen Elizabeth II are few in relation to what is formally called Her Majesty's Government. The Queen must give formal assent to laws passed by Parliament, but she may not state publicly her own opinion about legislation. The Queen is also responsible for naming the Prime Minister and dissolving Parliament before a general election. These actions are expected to be consistent with the will of Parliament, as communicated to the Queen by the leader of the majority party there.

The Queen receives major government papers, including reports of Cabinet meetings. She usually receives the Prime Minister once a week to discuss current affairs. The Queen has the opportunity to encourage the Prime Minister or to warn privately about the points that Cabinet deliberations have overlooked. No Prime Minister in modern times has suggested that a policy was followed because of the monarch's wishes. The responsibility for government rests with elected politicians.

If no party had a majority in the House of Commons, the Queen could be faced with conflicting advice about calling an election from the Prime Minister and a majority of MPs. In the uncertain circumstances of minority government, 1974–1979, the Queen was not confronted with conflicting advice; the Labour Prime Minister negotiated parliamentary support for major measures and, when this was lost, called a general election. A monarch forced to make a real political choice could lose his or her position as an institution above the party-political battle.[8]

The ceremonial role of the Queen as head of state consumes a substantial portion of royal time. The Queen and other members of the Royal Family appear at a great range of public functions, from horseraces and air shows to laying cornerstones for new local government buildings. The Royal Family is also in demand for goodwill tours abroad. Because these time-consuming dignified tasks are performed by the Royal Family, leading elective politicians have more time for the efficient work of government. In America, by contrast, the president is not only the ceremonial head of government and symbol of national unity, but also the head of a political party that divides the electorate by competing for votes.

The Royal Family is aware of the limits of its anachronistic office. In the words of Prince Charles, the heir to the throne: "Something as curious as the monarchy won't survive unless you take account of people's attitudes. I think it can be a kind of elective institution; after all, if people don't want it, they won't have it." The Gallup Poll finds that 81 percent of English people prefer a Queen, as against 10 percent favoring a president.[9]

The formal responsibilities of the Queen are necessary but unimportant. Her principal political significance is negative: by providing a head of state outside Parliament the monarchy denies this office to those who might exploit it for partisan ends.

The Cabinet. If British government is to be characterized in a phrase (a practice that may be questioned), it is best described as Cabinet government, for the powers and prerogatives nominally vested in the Crown in Parliament are effectively vested in the Cabinet. The Cabinet was described by Walter Bagehot as the efficient secret of the English Constitution, securing "the close union, the nearly complete fusion of the executive and legislative powers.'' Fusion is possible because Cabinet ministers come from the majority party in the House of Commons; this ensures control of legislation. Concurrently, they are the heads of the major departments of central government.

The Cabinet mobilizes the collective authority of government as well as representing the division of Whitehall into subgovernments, that is, separate ministries.[10] At the head of each ministry is a politician drawn from the ranks of the majority party in Parliament — one with a personal interest in advancing his views and his department as well as depending upon the Cabinet to back whatever is done there.

The day-to-day work of Cabinet ministers is focused within their department, but such are the interdependencies of policies that ministers can take few major steps without securing the support of other departments in Whitehall.[11] Spending measures require Treasury consent. The successful implementation of many measures requires the cooperation of other ministries responsible for activities which could help or hinder the achievement of a particular department goal. For example, measures affecting Industry may also affect Employment, and Foreign Office policies are often relevant to Defense. Inevitably, discussions between departmental ministers articulate differing views and interests, notwithstanding the fact that all are of the same party.

The Cabinet is the court of last resort for the resolution of differences between ministers.[12] But the Cabinet actually makes relatively few decisions. One reason is the pressure of time: the Cabinet usually meets no more than twice a week, and its agenda is extremely crowded by routine business, such as reports on pending legislation and on foreign affairs, and by the need to deal with emergencies. A second reason is practical: most Cabinet ministers will not be informed about most of the work of other departments, and have little interest in discussing activities for which they are not personally responsible. A third reason is organizational: it is possible to devote far more time and attention to matters by having them discussed in formal or informal Cabinet committees.

Within the framework of a Cabinet system, decisions can be

taken in many different settings. Actions that give little prospect of political controversy and do not require coordination with other departments can be taken within a ministry. Measures low in controversy may be settled by bilateral discussions between two ministries. When decisions affect a number of departments or are political hot potatoes, they are likely to be the subject of a formal Cabinet committee. The committee may be chaired by the Prime Minister if the issue is deemed very important; by a senior departmental minister if one ministry is deemed to have the principal responsibility; by a minister without departmental ties if a disinterested chairperson is wanted; or, on matters classified as technical, by a very senior civil servant. Unofficial networks are also important. For example, private discussions between the Prime Minister and the Chancellor of the Exchequer and the Foreign Secretary are frequent; other ministers are seen for select matters deemed of concern by the Prime Minister.

At any given moment, the Cabinet has dozens of committees covering economic and industrial affairs, intelligence and security, overseas affairs and defense, home affairs, and legislation.[13] In many important fields, committees exist at two levels, an official committee of ministers and a parallel committee of their civil servants. The latter is meant to clarify matters of fact and matters deemed technical; the ministerial committee is meant to concentrate on major political points. The distinction between minor matters suitable for civil servants to agree on and major political matters affecting ministers is easier to talk about than to apply. Sometimes ministers feel that their scope for choice and maneuver is restricted by agreement that their officials make with other departments.

In the process of negotiation that culminates in formal Cabinet decisions ministers will often clash with each other. Moreover, they will seek allies among ministers who are not parties to a dispute, among back-bench MPs, and among interest groups. Leaks to the press may be used as well to affect the climate of opinion. One minister's loyalty to advancing his cause may look like disloyalty to a colleague.

The end product of negotiation is meant to be a decision that all ministers directly affected can present to Cabinet as an agreed recommendation. The Cabinet more often ratifies than makes decisions. Ministers who have not been involved in negotiations prefer to let most recommendations go by without questioning, in expectation that their bargains will be similarly approved when they appear on the Cabinet agenda.

Endorsement by the Cabinet is the strongest sanction that a policy can have. Once the Cabinet has approved a policy, endorsement by the House of Commons can normally be taken for granted, because the Cabinet consists of leaders of the majority party. Even in the atypical Parliament of 1974–1979, when the Labour government lacked a working majority, it was nonetheless able to secure Liberal endorsement of nearly all its proposals, because it was the Labour leaders who had the resources of Whitehall behind them. Their Liberal partners were confined to Parliament, where they were ill-informed about how Whitehall works.[14]

After a Cabinet decision has been taken, ministers are expected to accept it. Even more important, the civil servants who provide the principal momentum for the work of departments will be bound by the decision. The doctrine of collective responsibility requires that all ministers must refrain from making public criticism of Cabinet decisions once taken. If a minister does not wish to go along with colleagues, he is expected to resign. Such is the political pain of giving up office that few ministers will make the giant step from questioning a Cabinet decision to resigning from Cabinet. Since 1945 fewer than a dozen Cabinet members have resigned because of political disagreements with their colleagues.[15]

The doctrine of collective responsibility has been suspended only twice in the past half-century, both times in the face of divisions within the 1974–1979 Labour government about the European Community. It is now less rigid than a generation ago, and ministers try to advance their individual interests by more or less veiled expressions of disagreement with colleagues in nonattributable leaks to the press. While this can cause political embarrassment, it rarely alters the direction of Whitehall.

Within a Cabinet there is no equality of political influence. While all ministers are formally equal, some are more equal than others. One way in which Cabinet ministers exercise influence is by chairing Cabinet committees. Of twenty-seven committees chaired by ministers, the Prime Minister herself chairs ten; the Chancellor of the Exchequer or his deputy, the Chief Secretary, chairs six; the Lord President of the Council, a nondepartmental neutral minister, chairs seven; the Foreign Secretary, the Home Secretary, the Leader of the House of Commons, and the Secretary of State for Trade and Industry each chair one. Thirteen of the twenty-one Cabinet ministers are not recorded as chairing any Cabinet committee.[16]

The Departments. While the Cabinet is the keystone in the arch of central government, the departments are the building blocks.[17] Departments, singly or in collaboration, administer the Cabinet's collective responsibilities. An individual minister's standing in Cabinet depends on his ability to show other ministers that he can convincingly present what his department is doing and cooperate as necessary with colleagues in other departments.

From time to time, politicians or professors suggest that the involvement of Cabinet ministers in departmental affairs prevents the Cabinet from being a proper planning body. Critics usually advocate a small Cabinet of half a dozen to act as overseers of Whitehall. No Prime Minister has accepted this view, except in wartime. The majority have agreed with Herbert Morrison that "a Cabinet without departmental ministers would be deficient in that day-to-day administrative experience which makes a real contribution to collective decisions."[18]

The composition of the British Cabinet, unlike that of the American Cabinet, is not fixed by law. The Prime Minister determines how the government's work is divided among departments, and can make alterations easily. There is no agreement about how British government ought to be organized into departments. The last major review of the departmental structure of government, Lord Haldane's Report of 1918, enunciated two contrasting principles: division into client groups such as pensioners, employees, and Welshmen; or, organization according to the services to be performed, for example, dividing responsibility for children among Education, Health, and custodial sections of the Home Office.[19]

Every Cabinet has some departments organized primarily by clients, and other departments organized by services. Whereas the functions of Whitehall persist, the names of departments are changeable. When Mrs. Thatcher formed her second-term Cabinet in June 1983, the departments were:

Economic Affairs. The Treasury; Trade and Industry; Employment; Energy; Agriculture; Transport.

External Affairs. Foreign and Commonwealth Office; Defense.

Social Services. Health and Social Security; Education and Science.

Territorial. Environment (including English Local Government and Housing); the Scottish Office; the Welsh Office; the Northern Ireland Office.

Law. Lord Chancellor's Department; Home Office; the Attorney-General and the Solicitor-General for England and Wales; the Lord Advocate and the Solicitor-General for Scotland.

Managerial and Nondepartmental. Leader of the House of Commons (job doubled with the nondepartmental portfolio of Lord Privy Seal); Lord President of the Council (and Leader of the House of Lords); Paymaster General; Chancellor of the Duchy of Lancaster; Parliamentary Secretary of the Treasury (Chief Whip in the House of Commons).

The compound labels and phrases in parentheses indicate the complexity of departmental structures. This tangle is accentuated by the readiness of Prime Ministers to put new labels on old or rearranged government functions, or to abolish old titles by merging responsibilities in superdepartments such as Environment.

One reason why departmental titles and duties can easily be altered is that government departments are usually not single-purpose institutions, but agglomerations of more or less related administrative units brought together by a process of expansion, fusion, and fission. Since 1952 successive Prime Ministers have merged nineteen old departments into five mammoth superdepartments.[20] A Ministry of Technology was created by the Labour Government in 1964 simply by placing a new Cabinet minister atop a collection of government bureaus previously the responsibility of a variety of ministers. Reciprocally, the abolition of the Ministry of Technology by the Conservatives in 1970 did not mean the wholesale dismissal of civil servants, but reassignment of the parts of the ministry to other departments, especially the new Department of Trade and Industry. In 1974 a newly installed Labour government divided this superdepartment into separate departments of Trade, Industry, and Prices and Consumer Protection, the last abolished by the Conservatives in 1979.

The limiting consideration in creating a government department is the political controversy that its work is likely to generate.[21] A department cannot be any larger than one minister can answer for in Cabinet and in the House of Commons. The Post Office, a department dealing routinely with a heavy volume of work, required so little ministerial attention that its work was hived off to a separate Post Office Corporation outside Whitehall. By contrast, as troubles in Northern Ireland grew following civil rights demonstrations in 1968, responsibility for monitoring events shifted from a Home Office civil servant to a junior minister, and then to the Home Secretary. By 1972 the troubles were so great that a separate Northern Ireland Office was created.

The ability of a minister to answer for a department also depends upon the coherence of its subject matter. The Department of Education and Science covers a number of interrelated functions, whereas the Home Office is responsible for a very disparate range of policies. The smaller and more homogeneous the groups being served by a department, the more focused its work becomes. The agricultural pressure groups are so thoroughly centralized that the Ministry of Agriculture, Fisheries and Food is much more easily administered than the Foreign and Commonwealth Office, which is concerned with many countries on many continents. Having a well-organized client group can be dangerous, for if it is politically powerful the minister may become its captive. If several groups exist, making conflicting demands upon a minister, it is easier to play one off against another.

The Treasury and the Home Office illustrate the differences between Whitehall departments. The Home Office has a staff of approximately 25,000 and the Treasury, 1,000. The Home Office has many tasks that can be kept administratively separate: police, fire, prison, drugs, the prevention of cruelty to animals, control of obscene publications, and race relations. By contrast, the Treasury has a few interrelated tasks: management of the economy, protecting the balance of payments, and control of public expenditure. Because of the importance of its tasks, the Treasury has more senior civil servants than the Home Office. The Home Office has more staff at lower levels, because of its much greater volume of routine work. The job of Home Secretary is burdensome. The Home Secretary is always vulnerable to adverse publicity, if a convicted murderer escapes from prison or a newspaper stirs up concern about drugs. Responsibility for the economy is much more diffuse, and the Chancellor of the Exchequer has a ministerial colleague, the Chief Secretary, to carry the burden of managing public expenditure.

The two departments vary greatly in procedure and style.[22] The Home Office has a tradition of advice moving slowly up through the civil service hierarchy; recommendations reflect a desire for consistency in handling the details of administration. When abolition of capital punishment was being debated, one senior Home Office official opposed it on the ground that it would be manifestly unfair to those who had already been hanged. In the Treasury, the Chancellor is likely to receive a variety of opinions from civil servants, who can be as varied and changeable in their outlooks as academic economists. Not least significant is the difference in power. A Home Secretary can expect that his decisions will usually be enforced, because they involve administering the laws of the land. By contrast, a Chancellor of the Exchequer has to accept that whatever he decides can easily be upset by international economic trends over which British government has no control, and little influence.

Every minister has a multiplicity of roles, but ministers dif-

fer in the emphasis they give to each.[23] First, a minister deals
with policies. He may initiate policies; select between alternative policies brought forward within the department; or seek
to avoid difficulties by minimizing any policy decisions. Taking
policy initiatives sounds appealing, but in practice much time,
energy, and political capital are risked in efforts to advance
from a ringing declaration of good intentions to an Act of Parliament. Many ministers prefer to have civil servants identify
policies regarded as administratively practicable, and then select a few to sponsor. To influence policies, a minister must
have a point of view clear enough so that civil servants can
correctly infer what the minister would wish done with dozens
of matters that cannot be referred to him for lack of time. In
default of a clearly defined ministerial viewpoint, civil servants
fall back upon a departmental point of view, or do nothing.

Second, a Cabinet minister is the executive head of a large
bureaucracy, formally answerable to Parliament for all that is
done in his name by thousands of civil servants. A minister is
less a manager than an overseer of departmental activities,
scrutinizing files and memoranda to ensure that nothing is said
or done in his name that will prove politically embarrassing to
explain to Parliament. A minister may also meet with officials
in the field as well as in Whitehall, in order to see that they
understand his point of view, and to understand their problems
better. Answerability for actions is not tantamount to control.
Often, when a department makes an administrative blunder
the minister has no prior knowledge of the mistake, and is thus
not regarded as personally culpable.[24]

A minister's third role is that of departmental ambassador
to the world at large. This determines the influence a department will have in a world where many compete for influence.
A minister is the department's ambassador to the Cabinet,
seeking Cabinet endorsement for the department's handling of
controversial issues, for legislation it wishes to promote, and
for the department's claims for money. A minister is the department's spokesman in the House of Commons, defending
its actions from criticism as well as promoting legislation there.
The minister is a department's chief spokesman in consultations with pressure groups, determining which demands are

rejected or accepted, and seeking group support for departmental initiatives. Last and not least, the minister represents the department in the press and on television, promoting its policies and defending it from critics when things appear to go wrong.

A minister is often an ambitious politician, looking upon a particular job as a stepping stone in a career. A minister considered good in heading a lesser department hopes for promotion to a major post, such as the Treasury, the Home Office, or the Foreign Office, and senior ministers will usually nurture an ambition to become Prime Minister. In career terms, a minister can rise within Whitehall by gaining a reputation for being good at understanding the department's work, and by winning battles in the Cabinet. In Parliament, a minister can rise in esteem by skill in debating, dominating critics by the adroitness and quickness of his replies. Developing a good reputation within the party requires careful attention to endless committee meetings, and the ability to demonstrate that whatever a department is doing, it is consistent with party principles. Skill in garnering favorable newspaper and television reports enhances a politician's visibility outside Parliament.

The Prime Minister. Within the Cabinet the Prime Minister occupies a unique position, sometimes referred to as *primus inter pares* (first among equals). But as Winston Churchill once wrote, "There can be no comparison between the positions of number one, and numbers two, three or four."[25] Yet the preeminence of the Prime Minister is ambiguous. The politician at the apex of government can be very remote from what is happening on the ground. The more responsibilities attributed to the Prime Minister, the less time there is to devote to any one task. Because of the collective nature of Cabinet government, the Prime Minister has a narrower range of personal responsibilities than an American president, and must work with politicians who are colleagues rather than subordinates. Matters of domestic policy that would be pushed up to the White House in Washington are usually kept in the hands of departmental ministers in Whitehall.

Every Prime Minister must live with the knowledge that the number of the things he or she can do is limited by the hours in the week (see pp. 313–16). What is done by a Prime Minister's government is principally done within departments. The Prime Minister is confronted with major tasks that cannot be delegated because they are important to the Prime Minister's political standing.[26] Each illustrates both the resources and limitations of Downing Street.

1. *Party management* is the first and foremost task. A Prime Minister may be self-interested, but he or she is not self-employed. Before becoming Prime Minister, a politician has normally spent a quarter-century working in the party in Parliament, culminating in election as the party's leader. To remain Prime Minister, a politician must retain the confidence of those who have elected her or him, and whose withdrawal of confidence could lead to the collapse of the government. In managing the party in Parliament, the Prime Minister has many resources.

Patronage is the most tangible resource that a Prime Minister can use to ensure loyalty. A Prime Minister has the sole power to determine which of several hundred MPs in the governing party will receive an appointment as one of twenty or so Cabinet ministers, fifty junior ministers outside Cabinet, or several dozen unpaid parliamentary private secretaries. As the work of government has grown, the number of patronage appointments has grown too.[27] In 1900 Conservative government ministerial jobs were given to one-tenth of the MPs. In 1975 Harold Wilson gave one-third of Labour MPs a job as minister, junior minister, or parliamentary private secretary. In 1983 Mrs. Thatcher gave patronage appointments to one-quarter of Conservative MPs. The number of ministerial appointees is augmented by those back benchers who want to receive an appointment, and work for this by energetically showing their support for the Prime Minister. The patronage power of the Prime Minister of the day is sufficient to give jobs to most of the MPs whose votes would be needed to ensure a majority, if her or his leadership were challenged in the parliamentary party.

In making appointments, a Prime Minister combines four different criteria: personal loyalty (rewarding friends); cooptation (bribing enemies, or stopping their attacks by enfolding them within the cloak of collective ministerial responsibility); representativeness (for example, appointing a woman); and competence in giving direction to a government department. Of these criteria, three are meant to maintain the support of the governing party for the Prime Minister; only one refers to skills relevant to running government. Every Prime Minister wishes to appoint MPs who are administratively competent *and* give personal support. But a Prime Minister cannot err by having insufficient personal support, for the resulting government, no matter how competent, may no longer be hers or his.

2. *Parliamentary performance* is the second means by which a Prime Minister can stamp her or his authority upon the party. In the corridors of Westminster, a Prime Minister can have a quiet word with colleagues, flattering their egos, reassuring their doubts, or calling their attention to some hard facts of political life. A Prime Minister can also address party meetings, seeking to encourage belief in the wisdom and success of government policies.

Twice a week the Prime Minister appears in the House of Commons to answer parliamentary questions, testing debating skills against hundreds of opposition MPs. Unprotected by a speechwriter's script or television's opportunities for recording statements, the Prime Minister must show that she or he is a good advocate of the government's actions, or face the demoralization of parliamentary party supporters.

Prime Minister's question time is not usually an attempt to ascertain information about specific government policies. More than one-third of questions are debating points, seeking to test the Prime Minister's mettle in the cut-and-thrust of parliamentary repartee; one-quarter of the questions concern foreign affairs, and one-quarter economic matters.[28] The departmental policies of more than two-thirds of the Cabinet, including the departments spending the most public money, such as Health and Social Security and Education, are rarely the subject of questions to the Prime Minister. The only full dress parliamentary debates in which the Prime Minister normally speaks are those which focus upon major foreign affairs or economic issues, or questions of confidence in the government.

3. *Media performance* is a third way in which a Prime Minister can strengthen her or his hold upon the party. A Prime Minister does not have to seek publicity; attention is thrust upon the incumbent of Downing Street. But a Prime Minister does have to work hard to receive *favorable* publicity. Unlike the Queen, she is the object of partisan controversy, and opposition politicians are always trying to put the Prime Minister in a bad light.

The media do not create the Prime Minister's image; their role is to amplify it. Journalists are on intimate terms with politicians in Westminster, and the Prime Minister will be on intimate terms with a few journalists whose goodwill and favorable words are valued. Because journalists look to Westminster opinion for their assessment of the Prime Minister, a Prime Minister successful in securing the good opinion of the House of Commons will usually be reported positively in the mass media as well.

Today, television is often the favored medium of a Prime Minister who believes in appealing to the ordinary viewer and voter. Television enables a politician to cut out the middle man, the newspaper reporter or editor, and speak directly through the camera to the viewer. But television success depends heavily upon personal qualities. A politician may learn to repress mannerisms that annoy viewers and exploit personal characteristics that are appealing, but there are limits to which television advisors can change the personality or the message of a 50- or 60-year-old politician whose profession is the conduct of government, not conducting a TV chat show.

4. *Winning elections* is important in party management. The only election a Prime Minister must win is election as party leader.[29] Of the nine persons who have held the office since 1945, five — Winston Churchill, Anthony Eden, Harold Macmillan, Sir Alec Douglas-Home, and James Callaghan — first entered Downing Street during the middle of a Parliament. Clement Attlee, Harold Wilson, Edward Heath, and Margaret Thatcher first became Prime Minister by leading their party

to victory in a general election. To retain the leadership of the nation, a Prime Minister must also win the next general election.

Within the lifetime of a Parliament, the Prime Minister's standing waxes and wanes with MPs' evaluation of their leader as an electoral asset. The publicity that goes with the office is usually a wasting asset for a Prime Minister. Every Prime Minister has seen popularity, as measured by the Gallup Poll, fluctuate during his or her term of office, and most have seen their popularity decline.[30] MPs have a vested interest in this, for an unsuccessful government can cause dozens to be defeated at the next general election. Unlike an American Congressman's, an MP's fight for reelection is largely determined by nationwide trends.

The party's electoral strength is tested during the life of a Parliament by frequent opinion polls and at by-elections. A Prime Minister whose party is behind in the opinion polls can be considered an electoral liability rather than an asset. Most of the time the Opposition rather than the governing party is ahead in opinion polls. Most by-elections show a swing of votes against the government. When this leads the governing party to lose a seat in the Commons, it is a pointed reminder of political mortality to MPs of the governing party.[31] In the twelve elections since 1945, the Prime Minister has six times led the governing party to victory, and six times to defeat.

Managing a political party is as complicated as it is important. Nor can the Prime Minister ignore completely tasks that are delegated, such as managing the party outside Parliament. A party leader must inspire extraparliamentary followers with confidence that the party is being led successfully, and in the direction that party activists will want to follow.

5. *Leading the government is a political, not a managerial task.* A Prime Minister cannot expect to be successful in Parliament or with the electorate, if the government of the day's record is a record of failures. The Prime Minister's chief responsibility is not to make every decision of government: this responsibility is dispersed among more than twenty Cabinet ministers. The Prime Minister's responsibility is to choose the people who make most of the day-to-day decisions of government; to or-

chestrate the overall pattern of government by imposing a more or less clear sense of direction and purpose; and, upon select occasions, to work closely with a few ministers in determining policies deemed of particular political importance.

As the spokesperson of British government, the Prime Minister's political leeway is greatest when away from a Cabinet meeting. A Prime Minister can make public speeches that mobilize support for particular policies that may or may not appeal to every Cabinet colleague. A Prime Minister can pointedly ignore topics or ministers, thus downgrading their influence with their colleagues. But a Prime Minister cannot normally commit the government to a course of action without checking first with the minister or ministers responsible. A more or less public controversy with a colleague, noncooperation, or even the threat of resignation could arise, if no advance consultation occurs with the minister meant to carry out a Prime Ministerial pledge. Not to consult colleagues before making a commitment means that a Prime Minister risks making a promise that the government cannot (or will not even try to) deliver.

A Prime Minister is ex officio involved in the substance of international affairs and economic issues.[32] In international affairs, the Prime Minister represents the British government in negotiations with leaders of other countries. The Prime Minister must also balance Foreign Office diplomacy and Ministry of Defence military concerns. The sensitivity of some topics, including intelligence, espionage, and counterespionage, requires Prime Ministerial attention. The House of Commons will want the Prime Minister to explain every intelligence mistake that occurs. In international affairs, the Prime Minister is in effect the leader of a team, which includes the Foreign Secretary and the Defence Secretary. While the Prime Minister speaks as the ultimate authority for government, nearly all the work is done by the Foreign Office or the Ministry of Defence. The Prime Minister must often rely upon the judgment of colleagues there, in view of the volume of information and the amount of foreign travel required to deal with international affairs.

Because the management of the economy is today the chief

political priority of government, a Prime Minister cannot be indifferent about the subject. But no Prime Minister can devote the time to the subject given by the half a dozen Cabinet departments affecting the economy. Nor does Downing Street have a staff that can produce economic policies in competition with the large and sophisticated Treasury staff. As the politician most concerned with the broad aims of government policy, the Prime Minister is uniquely placed to see the interconnections between economic issues and other political objectives. Moreover, the Prime Minister must defend unpopular consequences of policies. Therefore, the Prime Minister engages in a continuing dialogue with the Chancellor of the Exechequer, asking questions and giving advice. When disputes arise between the Chancellor and spending departments, the Prime Minister can act as the ultimate arbiter.

When the Cabinet faces a difficult or controversial decision, the Prime Minister is in the chair. A Prime Minister can encourage a discussion in which colleagues identify the political elements of greatest importance, and indicate their support for conflicting views. If a subject generates great controversy within Cabinet, a Prime Minister may postpone a decision. After an issue has been ventilated in Cabinet, no vote is taken. The discussion ends with a summing up by the Prime Minister. Clement Attlee described the task thus:

> The job of the Prime Minister is to get the general feeling, collect the voices. And then, when everything reasonable has been said, to get on with the job and say, "Well, I think the decision of the Cabinet is this, that or the other. Any objections?" Usually there aren't.[33]

A Prime Minister who commits herself or himself to a particular course of action before opinions are collected around the Cabinet table — and Mrs. Thatcher has been known to do this — can sometimes impose a policy upon the Cabinet. But sometimes this tactic leads to a Prime Minister being rebuffed, or made to change her mind by colleagues; this too happens to Mrs. Thatcher.

In the office of Prime Minister, individual personalities can make some, albeit a limited, difference (Figure III.1). Biogra-

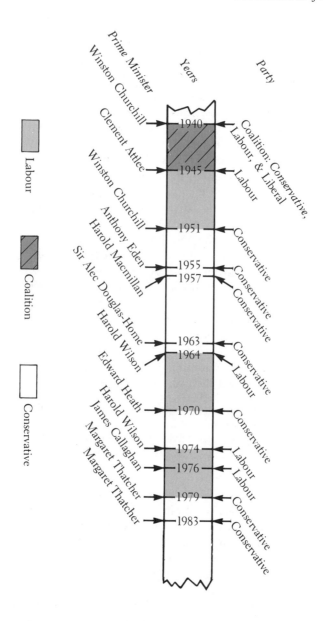

FIGURE III.1   *British Prime Ministers and Governments since 1940*

phies and autobiographical memoirs inevitably emphasize the personal element in the job. But the office exists before the individual. Histories — including those written by past Prime Ministers such as Harold Macmillan and Harold Wilson — tend to emphasize the continuity of the office.

Individual politicians vary substantially in the way in which they have approached the office of Prime Minister. Winston Churchill saw himself in the darkest hours of the Second World War as above party politics, a military strategist and a leader rousing patriotic fervor. Clement Attlee very much saw himself as the servant of the Labour Party, expressing the lowest common denominator of opinion within it. By contrast, Margaret Thatcher sees herself as a conviction politician who wishes to give a lead, even if all her own supporters, let alone opponents, are not ready to follow.

The time that a party leader has to prepare for office is variable. Sir Anthony Eden was heir apparent to Churchill for a decade before entering 10 Downing Street, and Edward Heath spent five years of intense preparation of policies in opposition before becoming Prime Minister in 1970. By contrast, in 1963, following the resignation of Harold Macmillan because of illness, Sir Alec Douglas-Home became Prime Minister unexpectedly, with virtually no time to think about what he might like to accomplish in office.

Circumstances are at least as important as personality in determining what a Prime Minister can do. This is made evident by the actions of persons who have been Prime Minister more than once. When Winston Churchill entered office in 1940 as the leader of a coalition facing grave threats to national existence, his immediate task was to give direction to a nation united to fight. When Churchill returned to office at age 77 in 1951, he had less energy, and the country was divided about economic matters, which interested him less. When Harold Wilson entered office in 1964 he was new to the job and prepared to devote six years to managing the Labour party and Cabinet. By the time he returned to office in 1974, he had had eleven years as party leader; Wilson stayed in office only two years before retiring voluntarily at age 60. Margaret Thatcher entered office in 1979 full of convictions about what she would like to do in government. In 1983 she entered Downing Street for a second term after fighting an election in defense of what British government had actually done.

The very high degree of institutionalization of British government is made evident by the fact that a party leader can move into Downing Street on a few hours' notice after the election results are announced. The Whitehall administrative machine is ready to tell the new incumbent what is expected, and the new incumbent will usually have had years of experience of watching other Prime Ministers do the job.

As an individual officeholder, a British Prime Minister has less formal authority than an American president. The most authoritative phrase in Washington is: the president wants this. The equivalent phrase in Whitehall is: the Cabinet has decided that. Insofar as British government is more subject to central direction, the Prime Minister is more powerful than an American president. Armed with the authority of the Cabinet and support from the majority party in the House of Commons, the Prime Minister can be certain that nearly all legislation introduced during the year will be enacted into law. By contrast, a president must suffer the slings and arrows of Congressional opposition that nullifies much of his legislative program. The Prime Minister is on top of a unitary government, influencing local as well as central government, and without judicial limitations on its powers. By contrast, the president is without authority over state and local government and the judiciary.

The Civil Service. Government could continue for months without ministers introducing new legislation, but it would collapse overnight if hundreds of thousands of civil servants stopped administering prosaic laws about taxes, pensions, health, and other responsibilities of the welfare state. Because British government is a big government, even a middle-ranking civil servant may be responsible for a staff of several thousand people or for spending tens of millions of pounds. Only if these duties are executed routinely—that is, quietly and effectively —will ministers have the time and opportunity to debate new policies.

Substantial legal and theoretical problems make it hard to

define the boundaries of the civil service. The author of a legal textbook concludes that in order to determine whether an official is or is not a civil servant, "The facts of each appointment must be considered."[34] Whatever the task, civil service jobs normally have in common: recruitment by examination, long-service employment guaranteed by public funds, and an inflation-proof pension upon retirement. Many of the bureaucratic characteristics attributed to civil servants, such as preoccupation with paper work, obedience to rules, and promotion by seniority, are increasingly found outside as well as inside government. Large organizations — both public and private — are usually bureaucratic in structure, albeit private sector organizations are far less ridden by rules and procedures, as they are not answerable to Parliament.[35]

The 630,000 civil servants constitute fewer than one-tenth of all those working for government (cf. Table XI.3), but are of central importance because they serve as the staff of Whitehall ministries. The civil service is divided into categories unequal in size and political significance. At the base of the pyramid are some 120,000 *industrial* civil servants, principally in defense-related work, and 185,000 *clerical* staff, whose work is the routine of bureaucracy: typing letters, filing forms, and other tasks allowing little discretion. Responsible posts are of three different types: *specialist and technical* (240,000); *executive* (80,000); and *administrative* (6000). Specialist officials are recruited because of particular knowledge, for example, of public health, highway construction, or museums. Their contribution to Whitehall is expertise or skills relevant to particular programs, such as social security or tax collection. Executive officers are meant to carry out policies laid down by others, for example, supervising regional offices implementing policy guidelines laid down in Whitehall.

The administration group is at the apex of the Whitehall pyramid. Within the administration group of 6,500 all of whom have high educational qualifications and well-above-average salaries, there is a fundamental division between those who work in specialist roles and the few thousand *senior civil servants* who advise ministers and oversee the work of other civil servants.[36] Prior to reorganization in the late 1960s, this group was known as the administrative class; the word class was an apt description of officials who are separately recruited for assignment to work that is primarily political rather than bureaucratic, scientific, or technical. The motto of the senior civil service (the term to be used henceforth for politically relevant officials within the administration group) is: The expert should be on tap, but not on top. Ordinary members of the public are more likely to meet clerical staff or technicians. Ministers in Whitehall deal with senior civil servants.

Senior civil servants usually deny publicly that they are political; the handbook for recruits goes so far as to declare: "Administrative trainees and those in equivalent grades are precluded from engaging in political activities."[37] What this means is that senior civil servants cannot engage in party politics or in public controversy about issues. But insofar as politics concerns making choices about the policies of government and reconciling different views about what government ought to do, then civil servants are very much politicians. They advise ministers about issues confronting them and anticipate and deal with the consequences of ministerial statements.

The immediate responsibility of senior civil servants is to look after the needs of their departmental minister. They are the principal staff to whom a minister can turn for help, and the relationship is intimate. As Headey notes, "In an average week a Cabinet Minister is likely to see at least two civil servants — his Permanent Secretary and his Private Secretary — far more frequently than he sees the Prime Minister or any of his party colleagues."[38]

The first thing a minister wants from civil servants is assistance in reviewing the activities and policies of the department for which he is responsible. A minister may enter office with an idea of what he would like to do or what his party would like to do, but without a clear idea of how this aim might be achieved, or even whether it is do-able. Senior civil servants are expected to respond to ministerial initiatives sympathetically but not uncritically, pointing out difficulties that the minister may not be aware of, as well as suggesting ways toward the political goals identified. If it turns out that a minister simply wants to get publicity, civil servants are expected to suggest means for him to achieve this goal.

Second, a minister looks to senior civil servants to defend him from mistakes. Civil servants spend much time scrutinizing the continuous flow of information that moves through a ministry, trying to spot problems before they can blow up in the minister's face. If the department is the object of criticism in Parliament and the press, civil servants are expected to construct the arguments that a minister can use to defend actions for which he is formally responsible.

Third, a minister needs the help of civil servants to market policies. Marketing begins within Whitehall; the department's position needs advocacy against criticisms from other departments represented on Whitehall committees. Increasingly, senior civil servants are expected to play a discrete role in affecting the climate of opinion within which the department's policies are put forward, appearing before parliamentary committees, briefing journalists, and talking with pressure groups. Advocacy occurs in support of the government rather than the governing party, a fine distinction not always easy to draw. Senior civil servants leave to lower-ranking officials the management of departmental programs.

Although senior civil servants work for a minister, they are also servants of the Crown. From this derives an important additional responsibility: to see that the Queen's government is carried on. Others may take for granted that the institutions and conventions developed over generations will persist; senior civil servants see as one of their primary tasks ensuring that changes in party control of government or in the wishes or whims of individual ministers do not disrupt the institutions of Whitehall.

As permanent employees of permanent institutions of government, civil servants have a much greater incentive to consider the long-term interests of government than do transient ministers representing the government of the day. Because career prospects of civil servants are largely determined by the evaluation of their colleagues within the civil service, they have an interest in maintaining their reputation for adhering to standards of good government, as that term is defined by colleagues.

Many roles undertaken by civil servants elsewhere in Europe or America are not performed by senior British civil servants.

They are rarely responsible for the hands-on management of major government programs. Nor do British civil servants engage in overt political activity; the good (or ill) they do is done anonymously; engaging in public controversies is left to ministers. Traditionally, senior civil servants have regarded their job as a lifetime career. It is not seen as a stepping-stone to a well-paid job, as can happen in Washington, or to election to Parliament on a party ticket, as may happen in continental Europe.

Ministers and civil servants need each other. A minister looks to senior civil servants as his principal source of help in a Whitehall in which a minister competes with party colleagues for influence in Cabinet and must defend departmental actions in Parliament, the press, and in face-to-face meetings with pressure groups. Ministers expect their civil servants to be partial to the government of the day. The idea is found in many other professions. For example, a lawyer is expected to advocate his client's case whether or not he believes it, just as a civil servant is meant to have a portable commitment carried from a Conservative to a Labour government and back. The central political question is whether officials are willing to serve a government loyally even when its views are very different from their own.

Civil servants want their minister to give clear and prompt decisions about memoranda that they present, and to stick to a decision when it attracts criticism as well as praise. Given a clear lead by their minister, civil servants are willing and able to exercise authority in his name. Civil servants also like a minister to be successful as the department's ambassador, winning battles in Cabinet, defending the department from criticism in Parliament and the press, and securing public recognition and praise for its achievements. A minister who is indecisive when action is imperative makes life difficult for civil servants. A minister who is unsuccessful as an ambassador makes the department a loser in the Cabinet competition for scarce public funds and legislative time, and thus lowers departmental morale.

Jointly, ministers and senior civil servants are responsible for *political administration*. At the apex of Whitehall, civil servants are expected to give advice about policies, the very stuff of what government does. Any issue worth calling to the attention of a minister is by definition political, that is, subject to differences of opinion. In reviewing alternative policies, a civil servant is making political as well as administrative judgments. Whitehall administrators accept this fact; a survey found that 76 percent believe political concerns more important than technical considerations, and 89 percent do not resent politicians being involved with administrative issues.[39]

Ministers and civil servants usually work well together, because each contributes different skills; their joint efforts are more than either could achieve singly. After acknowledging that differences between the two groups can make for tensions, Sir Patrick Nairne, a senior civil servant, declares: "The real question is not 'Are the civil servants outwitting the politicians, or the politicians outwitting the civil servants?' but rather 'Is this partnership adequately fruitful?' "[40]

Within the world of political administration the predisposition of civil servants is to deemphasize conflict; consensus-mongering is a major activity. In the words of Sir William Armstrong, one of the most formidable of postwar civil servants, "There is indeed a great deal of common ground — what I have called ongoing reality — which is properly, necessarily and desirably the concern of a permanent civil service."[41] The room allowed politicians for maneuvre within the dictates of "ongoing reality" is seen as limited.

The bias of the senior civil servant is not so much toward the view of any one party — they are paid to be bipartisan rather than apolitical — but rather toward the status quo. By definition, the status quo is do-able, because it is already being done. When advising about new policies, civil servants may be more interested in maintaining continuity than in securing radical change. This can lead civil servants to challenge Conservative proposals to reduce the size of government, as well as Labour proposals to expand it. Because senior civil servants are prepared to accept the status quo and because in postwar Britain control of government has alternated between the Conservative and Labour parties, civil servants are alternately attacked for being right-wing or left-wing.

Whatever may be the status quo, it is always subject to change, and this is as true of the role of senior civil servants as it is of government policies. Pressures have arisen first of all within government. The growth of Whitehall's responsibilities has led to an enlargement of the senior civil service, and made the highest-ranking civil servants more remote from the point at which low-ranking officials deal with specific cases and difficulties. The growth of government's responsibilities outside Whitehall has fragmented the community of policymakers; local authorities, nationalized industries, and the health service have their own staffs and responsibilities independent of Whitehall.

Accepting responsibilities to manage the economy and to improve social conditions faces civil servants with opposition from organizations completely outside the Westminster network. No longer can success be defined simply as a neatly drafted departmental minute or a private word of advice to the minister. The more public the activities of government, the more informed and potentially critical is popular judgment of successes and failures.

The difficulties of British government in the past two decades have made the senior civil service a target for criticism. Demands for reform have stressed both apolitical management objectives and a desire for more political inputs. Major management reforms were recommended in 1968 by the Fulton Committee on the civil service, including changes in recruitment, training, and promotion of civil servants. Nine years later a House of Commons committee endorsed many of these reforms, and called for more. The call for reform continues because the changes made are relatively few; they are determined principally by the senior civil service itself. Gradual alteration, not rapid change, is the essence of a civil service.[42]

Committed partisans wanting to change the policies of government at a faster rate or in a different direction than successive British governments have been moving see the senior civil service as a major obstacle to change in Whitehall. Anthony Benn, a left-wing Labour Cabinet minister for a decade, alleges that cooperation between ministers and civil servants is on the terms of "always trying to steer incoming governments back to the policy of the outgoing government, minus the mistakes that the civil service thought the outgoing government made.'' Sir John Hoskyns, advisor to Margaret Thatcher, has also attacked the civil service for its caution:

> The first thing to realize about civil servants is that few, if any, believe that the country can be saved. . . . They have seen politicians trying to do the wrong thing and succeeding, or the right thing and failing. As each government retires exhausted the service has somehow to continue with the next, persuading itself that the problem was insoluble in order to conserve its self-respect.[43]

One reform endorsed by critics is the introduction of a number of partisan political advisors into Whitehall departments and into the Prime Minister's residence in 10 Downing Street. These advisors are seen as capable of providing a partisan influence to set against the bipartisan outlook of civil servants. Because civil servants have been cloistered politicians in Whitehall, they are less likely to be sensitive to the nuances of party politics outside Whitehall. Since 1964 more and more ministers have had at least one partisan appointee in their office, but continue to have far more civil servants close to them.[44]

Political advisors have been of two types. One category consists of senior policy advisors, individuals who have considerable knowledge of the substance of a department's work from previous experience in a pressure group or business, or from research in its field. The primary focus of the senior policy advisor is upon the programs of the department. Party links are useful too, but secondary to expertise.

The other type is a partisan advisor, a personal assistant who knows the party in power well, and is often personally committed to a minister, moving with him from department to department. Partisan advisors are expected to maintain contact with groups outside Whitehall, such as the governing party's back-bench MPs, pressure groups, and the press. Both types of political advisors are expected to offer their minister companionship, for a politician may feel lonely when surrounded by a vastness of civil servants.

Political advisors have fitted into Whitehall because most of their work complements rather than conflicts with that of the civil service. One or two advisors in a department with a staff of ten or twenty thousand does not threaten the established civil service. A partisan advisor can even assist a department by advocating his minister's (and the department's) case in party circles from which civil servants are barred. A policy advisor who is well informed about the department's subject may create difficulties, if advising the minister to follow ways that most civil servants are disinclined to go. But policy advisors, like partisan advisors, must come to terms with the civil servants around them, if they are to get essential information about what is going on in the department.

The Thatcher government in 1979 brought forward a new phenomenon in Whitehall: a Prime Minister predisposed to dislike and distrust the civil service. The distrust was first of all derived from Mrs. Thatcher's ideological belief in the superiority of the market to government, and by implication of business firms to Whitehall ministries. To encourage greater efficiency in Whitehall, she established an efficiency unit under Derek (now Lord) Rayner to recommend savings in the housekeeping activities of government. The number of civil servants has been reduced by 14 percent under her leadership, in part by transferring the burden of work elsewhere, and in part by increasing the burden on those remaining in place. The Civil Service Department was abolished, and its work divided between the Treasury, strengthening financial control, and the Cabinet Office, bringing it closer to the Prime Minister. Civil service pay has not been allowed to rise in line with the private sector. The result has been demoralization in the civil service, including its higher ranks.

The political animus in Mrs. Thatcher's attack on the civil service has arisen from her belief that the views she espouses in favor of radical change are not welcomed by many senior civil servants. (This view has also been voiced from the left by such ex-Labour ministers as Anthony Benn.) That charge was not so much denied, as cited as an argument against her convictions by the secretary of the First Division Association of senior civil servants: ''The civil service provides an important and unique stabilising role. . . . It is absolute rubbish to pretend, as some politicians do, that electorates vote for governments to implement their policies in full."[45]

In order to strengthen the direction of departments, Mrs. Thatcher has taken an unusual degree of interest in the promotion of senior civil servants to the very top post as Permanent Secretary to a minister. Winning reelection in 1983 has meant that most of the several hundred top policymaking officials in Whitehall have been promoted during her period in office. F. F. Ridley, a professor of public administration, concludes: "The radicalization of British politics as expressed in Thatcherite Conservatism and Bennite Socialism makes the idea of a neutral civil service harder to sustain than in past decades of broad agreement between successive governments on fundamental issues."[46]

Criticisms of civil servants, whatever their source, are often equally applicable to ministers. Both are generalists; neither is expected to have professional skills or expertise relevant to the substantive problems of the department, whether it is the Treasury, Education, or Social Security. Neither MPs nor civil servants have experience of managing large organizations, except what they learn on the job in Whitehall. Ministers are shuffled from department to department in response to the political exigencies of the moment, and civil servants are sent from one post to another without regard to whether there is time for them to master a post's technical features. Civil servants are experts if their job is defined as political administration. But by comparison with many specialists outside government, they often lack knowledge of the substance of the problems confronting them.

Because Whitehall is run by a combination of ministers and civil servants, anything that affects either group affects the system as a whole. If the caliber of the civil service deteriorates, this affects what the Cabinet can achieve. If a Prime Minister or Cabinet is uncertain or unrealistic in setting policy objectives, this limits what civil servants can achieve. When one falters, the whole falters. Insofar as the combined skills of civil servants and ministers are not adequate to today's problems, the aggregate capability of government is diminished.

Since the Prime Minister, Cabinet, and senior civil servants collectively constitute the directive force in British government, the capabilities of each are best seen as complementary. In the view of a leading civil servant, Sir Patrick Nairne:

> If reality — immovable facts, unanswerable argument, uncontrollable pressures—is to be the touchstone, or continuity of policies, and the need to reap what a previous administration has sown, or not to change what the public has come to accept or expect is to be regarded as paramount, then no one is better at fostering and defending the policies to be followed than the average civil servant.

But the acceptance of the status quo and the maintenance of continuity is only one side of government. As Sir Patrick goes on to add:

> The promotion of policy change is the principal challenge of politics. Only when ministers are determined to pursue new, and perhaps radical policies — challenging the arguments of reality and continuity in the process — will the politicians exercise real power and be effectively on top.[47]

THE ROLE OF PARLIAMENT

In its dignified aspect, Parliament is very impressive. The Palace of Westminster, the home of the House of Commons and House of Lords, is a building familiar as a symbol throughout the world. Parts of the building date back to the eleventh century; the bulk is of Victorian Gothic design, as massive as it is nonutilitarian. Officers of the House emphasize its dignity by wearing elaborate formal dress, including wigs. The late Aneurin Bevan, a left-wing Labour MP, described his first impression of Parliament as a church dedicated to "the most conservative of all religions—ancestor worship."[48]

In efficient power, Parliament is not so impressive, because its role in making policy is strictly limited. The Cabinet controls most of its proceedings; by convention, the Leader of the Opposition is also allowed to fix topics for a number of major debates. The Prime Minister can be sure that any proposal the government puts forward will be promptly voted on in the form desired by the government. It not only drafts legislation but also controls amendments. Furthermore, the power of the purse rests with the Treasury; parliamentary debate about the budget rarely alters its content.

The limited influence of Parliament is made clear by comparison with the United States Congress. In America each house of Congress controls its own proceedings, independent of the other and of the White House. When one party controls the presidency and the other Congress, party loyalties reinforce congressional independence. An American president can ask Congress to enact a bill, but he cannot even compel it to vote on the measure he recommends. A bill may receive many amendments that reduce its attractiveness to the White House. Congress can increase or decrease presidential requests for appropriations; the president's budget is not a final document, but an attempt to get Congress to vote money as he wishes. Parliament lacks each of these powerful congressional checks upon the executive.

Enacting Legislation. The general principles of bills are decided by ministers. Bills are prepared by specialist parliamentary draftsmen acting on instructions given by civil servants seeking to express ministerial wishes. Details are discussed at length with affected and interested parties *before* a bill is introduced in the Commons. Such influence as the Commons exerts upon legislation is felt at the drafting stage, when Whitehall seeks to anticipate what MPs will criticize when a bill comes forward for debate. Consultations required for preparing a bill usually take a year or more, whereas the time required for a bill to become law after it is introduced in Parliament is seven weeks on average. Laws are described as Acts of Parliament, but it would be more accurate if they were stamped: Made in Whitehall.

The enactment of legislation is complex. A bill is introduced in the House of Commons by a minister at first reading, and published without debate. In the second reading debate, the general principles of the bill are discussed. Major bills are then usually referred to the Committee of the Whole House (MPs meeting with special rules of procedure). Lesser legislation is considered by standing committees containing a fraction of the

House. Party discipline is effective in both places. A report stage follows, giving all MPs a chance to discuss the bill once again.

After a third reading, a bill proceeds to the House of Lords. If it is passed in the same form as in the Commons, it receives the royal assent, a formality, and becomes the law of the land. If the Lords amend or vote against a bill, it returns to the Commons for further consideration. A money bill is exceptional; it automatically becomes law within a month after approval by the Commons. The Commons may accept the amendments of the Lords. If the Commons rejects them, the Lords may bow to the wishes of the Commons, or again endorse their amendments. If the Lords do so, the Commons version of the bill becomes law, if it is approved by the Commons twice in a period of more than one year. The Lords has the power to delay a bill, but not the power to filibuster it to death. The less strict attention to party lines makes the Lords different from the Commons; the lack of elected members makes it weaker.

In a year's parliamentary business, the government can secure passage of 100 percent of the bills that it introduces; it has done so eight times since 1945. Since 1945 a government has secured on average nearly 97 percent of the legislation that it introduces during a Parliament (see Table III.2). The government's ability to get its way is not influenced by party colors: Labour governments get their proposals endorsed as easily as the Conservatives. Even in the 1974–1979 Parliament, when Labour had no overall majority, it nonetheless enacted more than 90 percent of the bills that it introduced.

While the bills that government promotes are often amended in the House of Commons, the government almost invariably determines whether or not proposed amendments will succeed. In a three-year period the government moved 1,772 amendments at committee and report stages of legislation; 1,770 were approved by Parliament. Opposition MPs and back-bench MPs in the government party moved 4,198 amendments; of these, only 210 were accepted by the government and approved by Parliament. The government introduces and enacts 89 percent of amendments to laws, as well as securing the passage of nearly all substantive legislation. Certainty results in a state of mind expressed by a Labour Cabinet minister thus: "It's carrying

TABLE III.2   *The Proportion of Government Bills Approved by Parliament*

Parliament (Government)	Bills introduced	Approved	Percentage approved
1945–1950 (Labour)	310	307	99.0%
1950–1951 (Labour)	99	97	98.0
1951–1954[a] (Conservative)	167	158	94.6
1955–1959 (Conservative)	229	223	97.4
1959–1964 (Conservative)	251	244	97.2
1964–1965[a] (Labour)	66	65	98.5
1966–1969[a] (Labour)	215	210	97.7
1970–1973 (Conservative)	192	189	98.4
1974–1979[a] (Labour)	260	236	90.8
Totals	1,688	1,638	96.6

[a]Omits final session of Parliament, interrupted by government calling a general election, voiding all pending bills.

Sources: 1945–1969: Calculated from Valentine Herman, ''What Governments Say and What Governments Do: An Analysis of Post-War Queen's Speeches,'' *Parliamentary Affairs,* 28:1 (1974), table 1; 1970–1979: Calculated from Gavin Drewry, ''Legislation,'' in S. A. Walkland and Michael Ryle, eds., *The Commons Today* (London: Fontana, 1981) pp. 96, 113.

democracy too far if you don't know the result of the vote before the meeting.''[49]

Party loyalty explains why the government consistently wins votes in the House of Commons. The government represents the majority party in the Commons, and MPs in the majority party are expected to support Cabinet measures (and vote against motions by the Opposition) in order to keep their party in control of government. The principal division in central government does not run between Parliament and Whitehall, but within the House of Commons, separating the majority party, which controls both Commons and Cabinet, and the opposition.

When a major vote occurs in the House of Commons, it is normally treated as a vote of confidence in the government. The party line is officially stated in a weekly memorandum issued by the party's Chief Whip. The MPs of the governing party accept the whip, because they recognize that only by voting as a bloc can their party continue to control government.

To defy the whip by abstaining or by voting for the other side is acceptable only if it does not lead to the downfall of the government. Cabinet ministers benefit most from party discipline, for their proposals are supported by the feet of back-bench colleagues tramping through the division lobbies. MPs vote as their leaders direct, even when they do not accept a measure fully with their hearts and minds.

Back benchers of the governing party go along with the Cabinet because of trust in leaders, a belief that frequent rebellion may cost them chances of promotion to a ministerial post and, above all, because they accept the overriding claims of party loyalty. Although party discipline is often criticized by independent commentators, most MPs consider it necessary and desirable.

Within the governing party there are opportunities for backbench MPs to influence government, individually and collectively. The whip's office is expected to listen to complaints from back benchers and convey their concerns to ministers. In the corridors and club rooms as well as in the committee rooms of the Commons, back benchers can tell ministers what they think is wrong with the party's policies. Disagreement can be carried to the floor of the Commons as well. An individual MP may abstain or even vote against the government whip in an effort to make ministers think again about a government policy. Individual rebels, however, have an inconsequential effect upon the outcome of the vote.[50]

An MP who makes a habit of rebellion or threatens to rebel to the party's collective damage faces the risk of expulsion from the party and almost certain electoral defeat, because MPs are elected primarily because of their party label, and not because of personal qualities. Knowing this, Harold Wilson, as Prime Minister, could threaten Labour MPs thus:

All I say is "watch it." Every dog is allowed one bite, but a different view is taken of a dog that goes on biting all the time. If there are doubts that the dog is biting not because of the dictates of conscience but because he is considered vicious, then things happen to that dog. He may not get his licence renewed when it falls due.[51]

The opposition in the House of Commons cannot expect to alter major government decisions; by definition it lacks the votes in the House of Commons. The opposition accepts defeat on nearly every one of its motions for up to five years, the maximum statutory life of a Parliament, because it hopes for victory in the next election. As long as the major parties alternate in winning control of a parliamentary majority, each can expect to enjoy all the powers of British government part of the time.[52]

The experience of the minority Labour government in the 1974–1979 Parliament emphasizes the importance of party discipline. Labour was the largest party in the Commons, but it was without an absolute majority of votes for most of the period. In March 1977, the Prime Minister emphasized how important it was to have a secure parliamentary majority, concluding a pact with the Liberals in the House of Commons. The pact promised the Liberals consultation about legislation in return for a Liberal promise to refrain from defeating the government on a vote of confidence. Interparty agreement thus temporarily replaced intraparty solidarity as the means by which government dominated Parliament.

Ironically, the one role that an MP will rarely undertake is that of legislator. Each year the government sets aside a small amount of time for MPs whose names are drawn by lot to introduce private members' bills. Because government support is not ensured, less than a dozen such bills pass in a session. A number are noncontroversial measures, covering such things as litter in the street. A few are issues so controversial that neither party will officially take responsibility. Private member bills secured reform of the law on abortion and on homosexuality. However, a controversial private member's bill may never be adopted, because without whips to enforce disciplined voting, a small group of MPs opposed to a measure can obstruct its passage.

Collective Functions. The daily routine of the House of Commons is that of a talking shop; its procedures allow discussion in many ways. A typical day begins with a number of MPs at morning committee meetings, some attending to correspondence or gossip in the Palace of Westminster, and a few, especially lawyers, pursuing normal jobs. At 2:30 P.M. the House assembles for prayers, followed by an hour of parliamentary questioning of ministers. At 3:30 P.M. ministers, opposition leaders, or back benchers may briefly raise exceptional or urgent items, such as an international or economic crisis. By 3:45 P.M. the House is usually dealing with pending legislation or debating issues, with ministers and front-bench opposition spokesmen speaking first. By the time the ordinary back bencher rises to speak, many MPs will have left the chamber to have their evening meal, or to attend meetings in the Palace of Westminster with other MPs or visitors. The chamber is likely to fill up again for major speeches (and perhaps a vote) at the end of the major debate of the day at 10 P.M. The final half hour of each day is reserved for an adjournment debate, in which an individual back bencher can raise an issue and receive a reply from a junior minister.

The House of Commons, sitting for about 190 days annually, spends far more days each year talking than do the Parliaments of other major Western nations. It spends one-third more time in full session than does the United States Senate, three times more than the French Assembly, and nearly five times more than the West German Bundestag.[53] It also spends more time talking because each day's session usually lasts at least eight hours. MPs have limited time to spend in their constituencies, or to see people outside London or abroad.

During the year the House of Commons spends more time talking about nonlegislative than legislative matters. In a typical year 38 percent of Commons' time is devoted to discussing government bills, 5 percent to statutory instruments promulgated by government departments subordinate to Acts of Parliament, and 3 percent to private members' bills brought forward by back-bench MPs. The bulk is devoted to discussing actions of government taken under authority of already enacted laws, or actions that the government is urged to take within existing statutory authority.

Among all the functions of Parliament, the first and foremost is weighing men, not measures. MPs continuously assess their colleagues as ministers and potential ministers. A minister may win a formal vote of confidence but lose standing among colleagues if his arguments are demolished in debate, or if he shows little understanding of the case that his civil servants have briefed him to argue. The clublike atmosphere of the Commons permits MPs to judge the personal character of their colleagues; through the years it separates those who merit personal confidence from those who do not. By the continuing assessment of persons, MPs make uncoerced judgments about the Cabinet and opposition leadership. Although not recorded in division lists, party leaders notice carefully which of their colleagues have the confidence of back benchers, and journalists write reputations up and down according to fluctuations in the judgments that Parliament makes of its individual members.

Scrutinizing the activities of government is the second major function of Parliament. Debates on the floor of the House provide a major means of ventilating opinions about how government does (and ought to) manage the economy, conduct foreign policy, reduce unemployment, improve health, education, and social welfare, and a host of other things for which ministers in Whitehall are more or less responsible. Before the government of the day has made a commitment, the views of back benchers and opponents give ministers an idea of the relative support for alternative courses of action. After the government makes a commitment, the Commons can tell the government what it thinks of the government's choice.

Because a small group of MPs can give more time to detailed consideration of an issue, much of the formal discussion of the Commons is done by committees. There are standing committees to review legislation: the Scottish Grand Committee, the Welsh Grand Committee, the Northern Ireland Committee, ad hoc Statutory Instruments committees to review particular regulations, and ad hoc committees denominated A, B, C, etc. (to *avoid* being considered subject-matter committees) for detailed discussion of legislation that does not require consideration by the Committee of the Whole House. By asking responsible ministers to explain details of legislation, MPs can test whether Whitehall has considered a bill to their satisfaction and to that of pressure groups briefing MPs on points of detail. But because party lines normally prevail in committee voting and are invariably enforced on committee reports back to the House, they lack the power of American congressional committees to rewrite or block legislation.

The House of Commons also maintains a series of select committees to scrutinize specific aspects of government administration. The Public Accounts Committee, always chaired by a leading opposition MP, reviews government expenditure after the event, publicizing instances of waste and financial mismanagement. Its existence as a watchdog is a caution to administrators of public money. The Statutory Instruments Committee scrutinizes rulings laid down by the executive under powers delegated by Act of Parliament. It can call the attention of the House to statutory instruments that it believes inconsistent with parliamentary practice and legislation. A Committee on European Legislation acts as a political filter for hundreds of Community documents issued each year.[55] It can call the attention of the Commons to those few Community proposals that it may wish to debate because of their potential impact on Britain. A Commons debate cannot veto Community actions, although the British government can. It gives the minister responsible for arguing Britain's case a sense of domestic attitudes about issues subject to multinational bargaining in the European Community.

In response to lobbying by back-bench MPs and academic specialists in the unofficial Study of Parliament group, the House of Commons established fourteen select committees to monitor the policies and activities of Whitehall departments following the 1979 general election. At their most optimistic, reformers hoped that the new select committees would provide a means for back benchers to influence government policy across a range of subjects from agriculture to Welsh affairs. Notwithstanding some initial scepticism, the select committees have succeeded in engaging the activities of many back benchers, holding hundreds of meetings in each annual session; interviewing ministers, civil servants, and outside experts; and filling thousands of pages with their reports.[56] Equally important, the select committees survived in the Parliament elected in 1983.

The capacity of the new select committees can be no more than that of the House of Commons. A select committee can devote time to a particular issue and, because ministers and civil servants are subject to continuing questioning there, spotlight areas of departmental activity or inactivity. The select committees also offer extraparliamentary groups an opportunity to press their case on Whitehall departments. Committee reports can direct more publicity to a particular point of view than can speeches of individual MPs. But none of these activities compels the government to change any policy. Committees exhort rather than require departments to act. Insofar as a committee examines issues relevant to partisan controversies, the chances are that the committee will split along party lines and become another forum for the discussion of differences which Whitehall has already considered and discounted.

The third function of the Commons is expressive: to give voice to the collective concerns of 650 politicians elected to represent diverse geographical and functional constituencies within the United Kingdom. By virtue of membership in the Commons, an individual MP has many opportunities to make his voice heard in the Palace of Westminster, Whitehall, and in the press and on television. The distinctive feature of speaking as an MP is that an individual's voice then becomes part of the collective embodiment of an intangible but not unimportant sense of the House. Since the careers of Cabinet ministers are affected by their ability to sense and deal with the mood of the House, an MP giving expression to opinions there, like the member of a jury, voices an opinion of disproportionate importance.

The attention given to Parliament in Westminster guarantees that ministers and civil servants are not entirely introverted, thinking only of the concerns of their department or of Whitehall. They are continuously concerned with presenting to the House of Commons the case for what they are doing. But concentrating upon the presentational aspects of policies has disadvantages too. A department or a minister may become more interested in what is said about its activities in the Commons than what gets done in the country. A former head of the civil service relates this experience:

> I happened to be visiting the Welsh Office in Cardiff on the day when there had been an oil slick in the Bristol Channel. So

naturally there was a great deal of activity going on, and when I arrived at the office the man in charge there was beginning to get people in to start assessing the situation.

The first question dealt with was: What was to be said in the House? It was not: How much mess was there on the beaches and what damage had been done, and how progress could be made in clearing it up? That came next.[57]

Individual MPs. A newly elected MP, contemplating his or her role as one among 650 individuals in the House of Commons, immediately notices the advantages that election brings. Remarks that went unnoticed when the MP was a private citizen now appear in print. An MP is able to direct inquiries to any branch of British government and expect prompt, very detailed answers. As an MP a person will have the opportunity to meet people in many walks of life, and travel at government expense or at the expense of an interest group. Entering Parliament opens opportunities to do freelance journalism or to be paid for part-time consulting. The Palace of Westminster also provides the facilities of a good London club, and has some of the cloistered in-group aspects of a boarding school in the countryside. The disadvantages of membership slowly dawn upon members — irregular hours, frequent travel separation from family, and a salary ceiling and career uncertainties — but few MPs find the disadvantages so great that they wish to retire from the House.

Whereas an individual MP's vote is virtually predetermined by party commitment, an MP's behavior outside the division lobbies is completely open. There are many roles open to a newly elected MP, regardless of party. These can be grouped under two broad headings: inner-circle roles oriented toward the actions of government, and outer-circle roles where there is greater scope for individual expression but less scope for influencing by Whitehall.[58]

Among *inner-circle* roles, the most important is that of a ministerialist. At any given time, about one-sixth of the Commons holds ministerial appointments, and fifty or more opposition MPs are shadow ministers, expecting office if there is a change of government. Their ranks are further augmented by those who aspire to office. Ministerialists dominate most of the work of the House because they are sure to speak in debates, whether for or against government bills. While personal ambition often drives an individual to want to be a minister, to succeed in that ambition an MP needs to demonstrate that he or she is good at whatever Cabinet ministers are expected to be good at, such as understanding the problems of departments, the procedures of Whitehall, and the tactics of the House of Commons.

Advocates of causes and interests are prominent too, because MPs have privileged access to the ear of Whitehall, and Whitehall is concerned with programs. Often a newly elected MP will be identified as an advocate of a particular cause or interest, whether partisan (e.g., the nationalization of industries, or increasing the size of the Royal Navy) or nonpartisan (promoting fishing interests, or nursery schools). To advocate a cause or interest, an MP will need to do more than make speeches: he will also need to influence other MPs to share his cause, working as a group to influence Whitehall.

Managing party and parliamentary business is a third important role. The whip's office is not only responsible for informing MPs what the party line is but also for informing party leaders what objections there are to actions under consideration by party leaders. Organization breeds counterorganization: the opposition is organized to use parliamentary procedures to exploit government weakness. Both government and opposition can have more or less formally organized factions, seeking to promote particular positions that are strongly held by some but not all within a party. A small number of MPs contribute to the Commons in nonparty ways, helping conduct its business by chairing debates, or advising on the management of Parliament and its business.

The least conspicuous but perhaps the most important role of MPs is that of party loyalist. Nearly all MPs are party loyalists when the whips are on. Loyalists usually say little and attract no attention to themselves. They see their role as maintaining party unity. As a former Conservative Prime Minister noted long ago, ''An MP may further party ends by his eloquence; he may do so even more effectively perhaps by his silences.''[59]

An MP who turns his or her back on government can face in many different directions. Among *outer-circle* roles the most common is that of expressive enthusiast. The difference between an enthusiast and an advocate of causes is that the latter tries to influence the government, whereas an enthusiast expresses feelings about an issue, whether or not anyone is listening. An enthusiast believes it important to make speeches in the Commons and attract publicity, whereas an advocate of a cause would rather listen to a minister announce a change in policy, knowing that it was his efforts that helped produce the change.

Publicity-seeking roles are always on offer in the Commons; a pointed question to the Prime Minister may enable an MP to grab a headline or be interviewed on television. Concentrating on issues that are of popular interest, even if of little substantive importance to government, such as the Royal Family or a prison escape, can gain an MP publicity but does not gain influence in Whitehall.

A half-century ago many MPs were extraparliamentary careerists; an elder son of a peer could serve as an MP from a sense of *noblesse oblige,* spending most of his time fox-hunting or managing family estates. A lawyer could use a seat in the Commons as a means of advancing a career at the bar, or gaining a judgeship. Today, the demands upon an MP's time are such that it is difficult to combine two careers. For example, teachers, a very numerous occupational group in the Commons, must choose between classroom teaching or a seat in the Commons.

Ironically, the role of constituency representative, a role taken with increasing seriousness by many MPs, is of little importance to government. MPs can devote time to looking after the concerns of individual constituents, such as securing a disability pension, or a government grant for small business, or rehousing. This relationship can flatter an MP who is a small fish in the big pond of Westminster. It is also prudent, for even if many votes are not won, there may come a day when a small number of votes makes the difference between winning or losing reelection.[60] In the Labour party today, it is also necessary to cultivate good relations with the local party to avoid losing renomination to fight the seat. But an MP cannot gain government favors for his constituency by trading his vote in return for local benefits; the whip, not constituency interest, determines an MP's vote.

The roles of MPs are multiple, and an individual MP can undertake several, for example being both a party loyalist and a good constituency representative, or a ministerialist and advocate of a cause. At any given time, the work of the Commons requires that MPs collectively be distributed among a wide variety of roles. A Commons that had nothing but ministerialists would be as difficult as a Commons in which everyone was nothing but a publicity-seeker. The size and variety of the Commons provides MPs with a repertoire of opportunities to advance their career and to advance political objectives within a single institution.

The House of Lords. The House of Lords is unique among the upper chambers of Western parliaments because its membership of more than 1,200 is primarily hereditary. In addition to hereditary peers, whose recent or remote ancestors have been ennobled for their activities, the Lords include up to eleven judges sitting as Lords of Appeal in Ordinary, twenty-six bishops of the Church of England, peers who have had hereditary titles conferred for their public services, and since 1958, distinguished men and women appointed to life peerages.[61] Members of the Royal Family do not sit in the Lords, although they hold titles. Hereditary peers constitute three-quarters of the membership of the Lords, but more than one-third of the hereditary peers do not attend the Lords even once a year. Only one-sixth of the Lords attend at least half its sessions. Life peers, numbering more than three hundred, can speak from extraparliamentary experience in varied walks of life: industry, finance, trade unions, education, and the mass media. Many active peers are retired members of the House of Commons who find the three-afternoons-a-week pace of the Lords suited to their advancing years. Nearly half the peers attending a majority of debates are life peers.

Like the House of Commons, the Lords weighs people fit or unfit for ministerial office. Because of the peers' high average

age, few expect office. Only in the Conservative ranks are there younger peers seeking to establish themselves politically. Since 1963 the most politically ambitious can disclaim a hereditary peerage and stand for the House of Commons. Because convention requires that every minister be in Parliament, a seat in the Lords can be given a minister brought in from outside Westminster to contribute expertise to government. Once in office, the minister will have to prove his worth in debate in the Lords, a less difficult audience than the Commons. The absence of responsibility for a constituency gives a peer an advantage in a ministry requiring much traveling, such as the Foreign Office, and freedom from constituency pressures can be useful in dealing with such issues as race relations.

The Lords' power to reject bills passed by the House of Commons was formidable until the Parliament Act of 1911 abolished its unlimited right of veto, substituting the power to delay enactment of legislation. Since the Parliament Act of 1949, this delay is limited to little more than one year. Occasionally, the Lords have used their powers to delay passage of a major Labour government bill, to oppose a nonparty measure, such as abolition of capital punishment, or to harass a Conservative government with a large majority in the Commons. The use of delaying powers is exceptional; the threat of their use occasionally worries a government.

The Lords normally avoid rejecting measures from the Commons, for to do so would raise questions about their status. The Lords cannot claim to represent the nation, because they are neither popularly elected, nor are they drawn from anything like a cross-section of the population. Moreover, the Lords have always had a Conservative majority. Before passage of the Life Peerages Act, Conservatives outnumbered Labour peers by about eight to one; since then, the Conservative advantage over Labour has dropped greatly. As Liberals, Social Democrats, and nonparty members are more numerous in the Lords than in the Commons, the Conservative majority over all other parties is reduced.

The Lords can initiate or amend legislation. The government often introduces legislation in the Lords dealing with technical matters or with nonparty matters such as animal welfare. The government can use the Lords as a revising chamber to incorporate amendments suggested in debate in the Commons. Members of the upper house can also introduce private peers' bills, but these are rarely of political consequence.

Like the Commons, the Lords can discuss public issues without reference to legislation. The government or opposition may initiate a debate on foreign affairs, or individual back benchers may raise such topics as pornography or the future of hill farming. Peers may scrutinize administration by questioning ministers. Media coverage is slight. A peer who wishes to influence public opinion is more likely to get publicity by making his remarks on a public platform outside the Palace of Westminster than by stating views in the little-read House of Lords *Hansard*. Members of the Commons are unenthusiastic about the Lords. Five-sixths of Labour MPs and half of Conservative MPs say they pay little or no attention to its debates.[62]

Dissatisfaction without Reform. The limited influence of both Houses of Parliament perennially stimulates demands for reform by back bench MPs, active peers, and political commentators. While many demand reform of the House of Lords, there is fundamental disagreement about the direction of change.[63] Labour critics talk about abolishing the House of Lords, regarding its functions as a hindrance rather than a help to the elected House of Commons. Conservatives have promoted the idea of removing or reducing the hereditary element of the Lords in order to improve its political status. As long as its composition is an anachronism, the House of Lords cannot compete successfully against the House of Commons for influence.

Criticisms of the House of Commons are multiple. It is said to do a bad job of reviewing and revising legislation, scrutinizing administration, representing and educating public opinion, or preparing younger MPs for the job of a minister. The remedies prescribed are equally varied. Since 1964 many minor reforms have been introduced into the work of the Commons, affecting the procedures of the House and the facilities of individual MPs. But an academic survey of these reforms concludes with "pronounced pessimism" that the changes have been "puny . . . in the extent to which they have failed to grip the essential problem": the need to diminish the power of the government, if Parliament is to become more influential upon government.[64]

One reason why reform proposals have languished is that proponents disagree about the part that the Commons ought to play in government. Some reformers believe that it should have power to prevent Whitehall from acting, whereas others simply wish greater powers to scrutinize and criticize what it does. The former wish to transfer power from Whitehall to the House of Commons; the latter, to improve the work of Whitehall by strengthening the Commons' capacity for oversight. Reformers also disagree about the role of an individual MP. Some assume that being an MP is a full-time job and that facilities should be appropriate. Others argue that day-and-night immurement in the Palace of Westminster threatens to make MPs remote from those they claim to represent.

The most important obstacle to reform reflects the principal grievance of back-bench proponents of change: powers of decision effectively rest with the leaders of the governing party in the Cabinet, and not with the House of Commons as a whole. Whatever MPs say from the back benches or in opposition, once in Cabinet they argue that the present powers of Parliament are all that can be granted it. In 1978 the Labour Prime Minister rejected a Commons committee recommendation to expand the work of select committees with the argument that this would "involve a fundamental change in our parliamentary system and in the relationship between the Executive and Parliament." Back-bench MPs of both parties are rightly skeptical of Cabinet ministers' readiness to give them greater influence. Only one-sixth think that ministers even wish to see MPs well informed about the work of Whitehall.[65] The result is that Whitehall rather than Parliament is the prime lawmaking institution in England.

Although Whitehall is more powerful than the Palace of Westminster, it is not all-powerful. It can govern only through Parliament; the government must win parliamentary votes of confidence to stay in office, and Parliament must approve each Whitehall proposal before it can become a law. The procedures of the House of Commons limit the amount of legislation that a government can enact in a year. Some three hundred proposals are put to the Cabinet annually by ministers; only a sixth succeed in gaining a place in the year's crowded parliamentary timetable. Introducing a major bill is a lengthy and tiring process that can take up to three years from the time a Cabinet decides in principle to promote legislation to a bill receiving the Royal Assent. Members waiting unsuccessfully for time to speak in a debate have as their counterparts Cabinet ministers waiting to get authorization from the Cabinet to put a major bill forward in Parliament.

Members of Parliament, especially in the governing party, collectively influence government by voicing demands that it do something about an issue that they believe to be important. If the clamor is widespread and persistent, the government may amend a bill, or even withdraw it for further consideration. But it is up to the government to decide whether or not Commons' talk will change its policy. A majority of MPs will rarely vote to veto a government action.

The experience of the minority Labour government from 1974 to 1979 emphasizes the limits of Parliament. Votes in the House of Commons were important then only because no party had a majority. The Commons gained influence because of an accident of the electoral system, not because of actions of MPs. The 1979 general election returned things to normal: one party won 100 percent control of government by winning 53 percent of the seats in the Commons. In 1983, the Conservative government won 100 percent control of government by electing 397 MPs with 44 percent of the popular vote.

Parliament is a necessary part of British government because it must concur in what government does. But its ability to scrutinize and criticize the ministers and measures of government should not be confused with the ability to exercise the powers of the Crown. That power rests with government departments in Whitehall.

A COMMUNITY OF INTERESTS

The public is the intended beneficiary of government policies, but the public is distant from the world of Westminster.

Immediately, MPs, civil servants, and ministers respond to the demands of office and to the demands that each makes upon others in the process of carrying on the Queen's government.

Government is a community of people. Group values tend to determine what individuals in office wish to do, and what they can do. Whereas the federal government in Washington may be described as a government of strangers, because so many people in it are unfamiliar with one another, Whitehall is like a village, where most people feel that they belong to a single community. Like any group of villagers, people are much more interested in maintaining the standards of their community than in worrying about what happens in places as distant as Bournemouth or Barnsley.[66]

Whitehall is in many respects a small community.[67] Although few ministers or civil servants now live in or near Whitehall, the people who work there spend most of their waking hours together, developing an intimacy like that found within an English boarding school or a small American liberal arts college. The top of Whitehall is not a vast sprawling institution like the University of London or the University of California. Within this village, everyone knows or knows about everyone else's strengths, weaknesses, and ambitions.

Ministers may find the life trying, as they compete against each other for scarce resources: money, parliamentary time, press headlines, and Prime Ministerial favor. Civil servants can take a different view; while ministers (and governments) come and go, they remain forever. The ethos of Whitehall is set by civil servants who are more numerous as well as more durable than ministers. The dozen or two ministers who carry political influence must work in tandem with several hundred very influential civil servants. The hundreds of thousands of civil servants meant to carry out the decisions of these several hundred top people are kept at arm's length by conventions of the bureaucracy.

In the village of Whitehall, civil servants are not anonymous. Each has a reputation to maintain with peers and superiors who determine promotion. What is it that gives a civil servant good repute? First and foremost, trustworthiness. One must be scrupulously honest in money matters and in keeping knowledge of public affairs private. One must not try to pull a fast one on colleagues in other departments by withholding information from colleagues in other departments. A senior civil servant should also be reliable; predictability of actions is important when time is pressing. Coordination occurs best when officials know what their colleagues in other departments expect them to do.

Soundness is another cardinal virtue. A civil servant who repeatedly voices clever but controversial ideas will become a bore as more experienced hands explain, for the hundredth time, why a bright idea is simply not practical politics. Intelligence is demonstrated by showing awareness of a problem's complexities, by finding one more snag than anyone else has found, or one more awkward objection to a proposal for change. Whitehall, like much English university education, prizes critical rather than constructive intelligence.

Within the Whitehall community, ministers' reputations are determined by different criteria than in Parliament. A minister who is known to be good at presenting or defending a department in parliamentary debate is always welcome, as is a minister who can secure favorable press publicity or counter unfavorable publicity. But civil servants also care about what a minister is like in private. A minister who values a good repute among civil servants will be willing to listen to and able to understand complex briefings about administrative matters, intervening selectively on political or policy points, but not overturning the work of months spent in committee drafting documents. Ministers also value colleagues who are easy to work with on interdepartmental matters affecting the daily activities of government. Once a decision is made, a minister who wishes a good reputation will not second guess the decision or heap blame on others if things go wrong.

The knowing, impassive figure of the mandarin is the symbol of the English civil service, just as the Washington counterpart is symbolized by the aggressive athlete, the man with clout. "Why are your officials so passionate?" a British Treasury official asked presidential adviser Richard Neustadt. Neustadt turned the question around, asking why British civil servants are so dispassionate about the outcome of their activ-

108 *The Institutions of the Crown*

ities.[68] He concluded that American civil servants care about policies because their careers are wrapped up with their success in getting things done for their department. To win a political battle advances an American official personally, as well as advancing a government policy.

In England, civil servants know that their minister will get the credit or the blame for the results of their work. They are personally detached, because they have little career stake in the outcome of what they are doing. A reputation for upholding the Whitehall code is more important than winning a battle about a particular issue. The style of governing is that of the amateur cricketer, not the professional hardball player. British civil servants do not play to win; the important thing is how one plays the game.

Whitehall civil servants are perennially skeptical of politicians' claims to reform the world within the lifetime of a Parliament. Their daydream of paradise is not of megalomaniac power, but of a world in which there are few decisions to make because ministers, MPs, and subjects have left them undisturbed in the orderly administration of routine affairs of state. Sir William Armstrong, former permanent head of the civil service, argued that the chief danger in government is not "that obstructive bureaucrats will drag their feet" but that "optimism will carry ministers into schemes and policies which will subsequently be seen to fail — failure which attention to the experience and information available from the service might have avoided." An experienced minister, Roy Jenkins, half agrees. Looking back upon decisions in which his personal preferences differed from civil service advisers, he regretted some decisions "made with advice, and some made against it."[69]

The Constitution of the Crown is not so much a mechanism for resolving problems as it is a device for coping with or adapting to them. Whitehall officials talk about the machinery of government, but the last thing that they believe is that government is a machine capable of manufacturing solutions to pressing problems, or being improved by advances in technology, whether mechanical or electronic. The language of

Whitehall mandarins often obscures rather than sharpens analysis.

"Running the economy is more like gardening than operating a computer," remarked Denis Healey about his experience of a decade in government.[70] Within the year there is a familiar cycle of planting, cultivating, and reaping the results of a year's work: Acts of Parliament, white papers, and the prevention of measures that could have spread like weeds through Whitehall. A gardener does not expect to control the environment, but to respond to it, planting seeds that might grow, watering plants when rain is short, pulling weeds when and where they sprout, pruning back plants that grow too fast, and fertilizing those which fail to grow as desired.

The work of a well-planted garden is continuous: things are always blooming or growing. But the yield is also uncertain. Civil servants cannot be sure of the product of their work until after it is accomplished, just as gardeners may either see their efforts rewarded by a good summer or ruined by too much or too little rain. As in gardening, the great bulk of Whitehall's work consists of daily and recurring routines: preparing briefs for committee meetings or answers to parliamentary questions, repairing damage done by past mistakes, or planting ideas or proposals that may blossom a year or two hence. Just as there are thousands of gardeners for every plant geneticist trying to improve the breed, so there are hundreds of civil servants trying to preserve the garden of Whitehall for every person consciously trying to improve it.

Both ministers and civil servants see themselves as persons with great responsibilities. Ministers are ultimately responsible to the electorate; immediately they are responsible to their colleagues in the Cabinet and to their patron in Downing Street. The longer they remain in office, the more they are also likely to develop a sense of responsibility to the department that gives them their status in government. Civil servants are ultimately responsible to the Crown; immediately they are responsible to their minister and to the head of the civil service. Civil servants have little personal contact with party politics and even less with the electoral hurly-burly of representative government. A comparative European-American study found that senior British civil servants ranked sixth and last in frequency of contact with MPs, political party leaders, or ordinary citizens.[71]

The closeness of the Whitehall community has its dangers. Generalizing from a study of financial control by the Treasury, Heclo and Wildavsky argue:

> Political administration in Great Britain is profoundly narcissistic, because each participant must and does care greatly about what his fellows are doing and thinking. To be more precise, it is not so much the individuals who are self-absorbed as the governmental apparatus of which they are a part and to which they must necessarily respond. To say that British political administrators care more about themselves than about the country would be wrong; to say that more of their time and attention is devoted to themselves than to outsiders would be closer to the truth.[72]

The strength of the Whitehall community is the ease with which it can despatch business. Its method of policymaking emphasizes the process of government more than the substance of policies. The community is thus vulnerable to events outside Whitehall, particularly when they threaten changes that are unpleasant or cannot readily be accommodated within standard Whitehall operating procedures. A good policy can be defined as one that both ministers and civil servants of different departments find acceptable. But none of the economic policies enthusiastically agreed by ministers and civil servants has yet to have the desired impact upon the world outside Whitehall. The fact that Whitehall's leaders have their hands on the tiller of the ship of state is not evidence that they can steer it in any direction that they wish; the aim may simply be to keep afloat.

The denizens of Westminster have ample evidence of their inability to control major events, both domestic and international. Like all villagers, they are vulnerable to decisions made in cities elsewhere, such as Washington or Zurich or Tokyo. At times of economic crisis, the community threatens to become a community of despair. The crucial question today is whether this community can adapt to the pressures of the world outside Whitehall, or whether Whitehall will respond only when a problem threatens to become, in a phrase that is a masterpiece of English understatement, "too disastrous."

NOTES

1. See Geoffrey Marshall, *Constitutional Theory* (Oxford: Clarendon Press, 1971), and *Constitutional Conventions* (Oxford: Clarendon Press, 1984). For a lawyer's approach, see, e.g., S. A. de Smith, *Constitutional and Administrative Law* 4th ed. (Harmondsworth: Penguin, 1981, revised by H. Smith and R. Brazier).

2. Leslie Wolf-Phillips, *Constitutions of Modern States* (London: Pall Mall, 1968), p. 182. For another attempt to put down on paper the terms of the Constitution, see S. E. Finer, *Five Constitutions* (Harmondsworth: Penguin, 1979, pp. 33–87.

3. Nevil Johnson, *In Search of the Constitution* (Oxford: Pergamon, 1977), p. 35; Sir Leslie Scarman, *English Law — the New Dimensions* (London: Stevens, 1974), p. 15. For a review of criticisms, see Philip Norton, *The Constitution in Flux* (Oxford: Martin Robertson, 1982), pp. 1–36.

4. See Richard Rose, *Understanding the United Kingdom,* pp. 86ff.

5. In this book the term Whitehall describes what in America is called the executive branch of government, that is, ministers, civil servants, and Cabinet. Parliament usually means the House of Commons, and the term MP always refers to a member of the Commons. Westminster refers to all who cluster in and around Whitehall and the Houses of Parliament.

6. E. C. S. Wade and G. G. Phillips, *Constitutional and Administrative Law* (London: Longman, 1970), p. 171.

7. For the best-informed description, see Dermot Morrah, Arundel Herald Extraordinary, *The Work of the Queen* (London: William Kimber, 1958). For an empirical social science analysis, see Richard Rose and Dennis Kavanagh, "The Monarchy in Contemporary Political Culture," *Comparative Politics,* 8:3 (1976), pp. 548–576.

8. For the problems confronting a monarch in the event of the House of Commons lacking a dominant party to give advice, see David Butler, *Governing Without a Majority* (London: Collins, 1983), pp. 80 ff.

9. *Gallup Political Index,* No. 190 (May 1976), p. 12. Cf. Prince Charles's interview in Anthony Sampson, *The Changing Anatomy of Britain* (London: Coronet, 1983), p. 14.

10. For a comparison of the British, American, and other systems, see Richard Rose, "Government against Sub-Government: A European Perspective on Washington," in R. Rose and E. Suleiman, eds., *Presidents and Prime Ministers* (Washington, D.C.: American Enterprise Institute, 1980), pp. 284–347; and Richard Rose, *The Capacity of the President: A Comparative Analysis* (Glasgow: U. of Strathclyde Studies in Public Policy No. 130, 1984), especially pp. 40–62. See also Colin Campbell, *Governments under Stress* (Toronto: U. of Toronto Press, 1983).

11. For studies of the Cabinet see, Valentine Herman and James E. Alt, eds., *Cabinet Studies: A Reader* (London: Macmillan, 1975).

12. For views of the same Cabinet by different members, see accounts of the 1964–1970 Labour Cabinet by e.g., Patrick Gordon Walker, *The Cabinet* (London: Jonathan Cape, 1970); Richard Crossman, *Inside View* (London:

Jonathan Cape, 1972), and *The Diaries of a Cabinet Minister* (London: Hamish Hamilton and Jonathan Cape, vol. 1 (1975), vol. 2 (1976), and vol. 3 (1977). Sir Richard Marsh, *Off the Rails* (London: Weidenfeld & Nicolson, 1978); George Brown, *In My Way* (London: Victor Gollancz, 1971); and Harold Wilson, *The Governance of Britain* (London: Sphere Books, 1977).

13. See Peter Hennessy, "Whitehall's Real Power House," *The Times,* (London) 30 April 1984; T. T. Mackie and Brian W. Hogwood, *Cabinet Committees in Executive Decision-Making* (Glasgow: U. of Strathclyde Studies in Public Policy No. 111, 1983).

14. See Alistair Michie and Simon Hoggart, *The Pact* (London: Quartet Books, 1978); David Steel, *A House Divided* (London: Weidenfield & Nicolson, 1980).

15. For a discussion of departures from the complete and continuing public unanimity of Cabinet, see Philip Norton, *The Constitution in Flux,* pp. 61-71, and sources cited therein.

16. Calculated from Peter Hennessy, "Whitehall's Real Power House."

17. The term department is not used consistently in British government. See Christopher Hood and Andrew Dunsire, *Bureaumetrics* (Farnborough: Gower, 1981), chapter 3.

18. Lord Morrison of Lambeth (Herbert Morrison), *Government and Parliament,* 3rd ed. (London: Oxford University Press, 1964), p. 48.

19. For classification schemes, see W. J. M. Mackenzie, "The Structure of Central Administration" in Sir Gilbert Campion et al., *British Government since 1918* (London: Allen & Unwin, 1950).

20. Cf. Sir Richard Clarke, *New Trends in Government* (London: HMSO, 1971); F. M. G. Willson, "Coping with Administrative Growth," in D. Butler and A. H. Halsey, eds., *Policy and Politics: Essays in Honour of Norman Chester* (London: Macmillan, 1978), pp. 35–50; and C. Pollitt, *Manipulating the Machine: Changing the Pattern of Ministerial Departments, 1960–83* (London: Allen & Unwin, 1984).

21. See Hood and Dunsire, *Bureaumetrics,* chapter 5.

22. For an insider's view, see Roy Jenkins, "The Reality of Political Power," *Sunday Times* (London), 17 January 1972. More generally, see Hugo Young and Anne Sloman, *No, Minister: An Inquiry into the Civil Service* (London: BBC Publications, 1982), especially pp. 23ff.

23. The typology of ministerial roles is taken from the major study by Bruce Headey, *British Cabinet Ministers: The Roles of Politicians in Executive Office* (London: Allen & Unwin, 1974).

24. On ministerial responsibility, see S. E. Finer, "The Individual Responsibility of Ministers," *Public Administration,* 34 (Winter 1956); Maurice Wright, "Ministers and Civil Servants", *Parliamentary Affairs,* 30:3 (1977); and Marshall, *Constitutional Conventions,* pp. 61ff.

25. Winston S. Churchill, *Their Finest Hour* (London: Cassell, 1949), p. 14.

26. See Richard Rose, "British Government: the Job at the Top," in Rose and Suleiman, *Presidents and Prime Ministers,* pp. 1–49.

27. See David Butler and Anne Sloman, *British Political Facts, 1900–1979* 5th ed. (London: Macmillan, 1980), p. 78.

28. See Rose, "British Government: the Job at the Top," pp. 12ff.

29. Prior to 1965, the Conservative party did not elect its leader; a person was selected by a small, informal coterie of elder statesmen. See R. T.

McKenzie, *British Political Parties* (London: Heinemann, 2nd edition, 1963), chapter 2.

30. See Rose, *The Capacity of the President,* chapter 4.

31. Rose, "British Government: the Job at the Top," pp. 7–11.

32. *Ibid.,* pp. 32–43.

33. Quoted in Francis Williams, *A Prime Minister Remembers* (London: Heinemann, 1961), p. 81.

34. See Wade and Phillips. *Constitutional Law,* 8th ed., p. 218. Cf. W. J. M. Mackenzie, "The Civil Service, the State and the Establishment," in Bernard Crick, ed., *Essays on Reform* (London: Oxford University Press, 1967).

35. See David Howells, "Marks and Spencer and the Civil Service: a Comparison of Culture and Methods," *Public Administration,* 59 (1981), pp. 337–352.

36. For a fuller discussion of this group, with copious citations to relevant sources, see Richard Rose, "The Political Status of Higher Civil Servants in Britain," in Ezra Suleiman, ed., *Bureacrats and Policy Making* (New York: Holmes and Meier, 1984).

37. Civil Service Commission, *Appointments in Administration, 1981* (London: HMSO, 1980), p. 23. For accounts of work by civil servants, see e.g., Neil Summerston, "A Mandarin's Duty," pp. 400–421, and David Lewis, "The Qualities of Future Civil Servants," pp. 422–433, in *Parliamentary Affairs,* 33:4 (1980).

38. Bruce W. Headey, *British Cabinet Ministers* p. 153.

39. For this and many other data on the attitudes of British higher civil servants vis à vis Continental and American counterparts, see Joel D. Aberbach, Robert D. Putnam, and Bert A. Rockman, *Bureaucrats and Politicians in Western Democracies* (Cambridge, Mass: Harvard University Press, 1981).

40. Quoted in Young and Sloman, *No, Minister.*

41. Sir William Armstrong, *The Role and Character of the Civil Service* (London: Oxford University Press, 1970), pp. 14–15.

42. See the Fulton Committee, *Report: The Civil Service,* vol. 1 (London: HMSO, Cmnd. 3638, 1968), and the *Report* of the House of Commons Committee chaired by Michael English MP (London: HMSO, HC 535-I, 1976–1977). Cf. Peter Kellner and Lord Crowther-Hunt, *The Civil Servants* (London: Macdonald, 1980).

43. Cf. Sir John Hoskyns, "Whitehall and Westminster: An Outsider's View," *Parliamentary Affairs,* 36:2 (1983), p. 142; for Benn, see Young and Sloman, *No, Minister,* p. 20, and more generally, Anthony Benn, "The Case for a Constitutional Premiership," *Parliamentary Affairs,* 33:1 (1980).

44. See Rudolf Klein and Janet Lewis, "Advice and Dissent in British Government: the Case of the Special Advisers," *Policy and Politics,* 5:1 (1977). Cf. Rob Shepherd, "Ministers and Special Advisers," *Public Money,* 3:3 (1983), pp. 33–35.

45. Quoted in F. F. Ridley, "The British Civil Service and Politics: Principles in Question and Traditions in Flux," *Parliamentary Affairs,* 36:1 (1983), p. 44. See also G. K. Fry, *The Changing Civil Service* (London: Allen & Unwin, 1984).

46. Ridley, "The British Civil Service and Politics," p. 47.

47. Quoted in Young and Sloman, *No, Minister,* p. 110.

48. Aneurin Bevan, *In Place of Fear* (London: Heinemann, 1952), p. 6.

49. Eric Varley, quoted in Alistair Michie and Simon Hoggart, *The Pact,*

p. 13. For statistics, see J. A. G. Griffith, *Parliamentary Scrutiny of Government Bills* (London: Allen & Unwin 1974).

50. See Richard Rose, "Still the Era of Party Government," *Parliamentary Affairs*, 36:3 (1983), pp. 282–299. For a different interpretation of the same evidence, see Philip Norton, *Conservative Dissidents* (London: Temple Smith, 1978) and related writings.

51. Quoted in *The Times* (London), 5 March 1967.

52. On the position of the opposition, see R. M. Punnett, *Front-Bench Opposition* (London: Heinemann, 1973). For the consequences of a Parliament without a majority party, and thus a government lacking a majority to control Parliament, see Butler, *Governing Without a Majority.*

53. For comparative data about Parliaments, see Valentine Herman with Francoise Mendel, *Parliaments of the World* (London: Macmillan, 1976), especially table 24.

54. See R. L. Borthwick, "The Floor of the House," in S. A. Walkland and Michael Ryle, eds., *The Commons Today* (London; Fontana, 1981), p. 66.

55. David Coombes, "Parliament and the European Community," in Walkland and Ryle, *The Commons Today,* p. 243.

56. See *Report from the Liaison Committee: The Select Committee System* (London: HMSO House of Commons paper 92, Session 1982–1983).

57. Quoted in *The State of the Nation* (London, Granada Television, 1973), p. 30.

58. For a more detailed discussion of roles of MPs, see Richard Rose, "British MPs: More Bark than Bite," in Ezra Suleiman, ed., *Parliaments and Parliamentarians in Democratic Politics* (New York: Holmes & Meier, forthcoming).

59. Earl Balfour, *Chapters of an Autobiography* (London: Cassell, 1930), p. 134. For much information about the individual behavior of MPs, see also Anthony Barker and Michael Rush, *The Member of Parliament and His Information* (London: Allen & Unwin, 1970).

60. Cf. Bruce E. Cain, John A. Ferejohn, and Morris P. Fiorina, "The Constituency Service Basis of the Personal Vote for US Representatives and British Members of Parliament," *American Political Science Review,* 78:1 (1984), pp. 110–125, and Ivor Crewe, "British MPs and their Constituents: How Strong are the Links?" (Colchester: University of Essex unpublished manuscript).

61. For basic data on the Lords, see Butler and Sloman, *British Political Facts, 1900–1979,* pp. 196–203.

62. See Barker and Rush, *The Member of Parliament and His Information,* pp. 144–147.

63. See e.g., Donald R. Shell, "The House of Lords," in David Judge, ed., *The Politics of Parliamentary Reform* (London: Heinemann, 1983), pp. 96–113 and Janet Morgan, *The House of Lords and the Labour Government, 1964–1970* (Oxford: Clarendon Press, 1975).

64. S. A. Walkland, "Whither the Commons?" in Walkland and Ryle, eds., *The Commons Today,* pp. 280, 284. Philip Norton, *The Commons in Perspective* (Oxford: Martin Robertson, 1981) especially chapters 9, 10.

65. Barker and Rush, *The Member of Parliament and His Information,* p. 363.

66. Cf. Hugh Heclo, *A Government of Strangers* (Washington, D.C.: Brookings Institution, 1977); and Hugh Heclo and Aaron Wildavsky, *The Private Government of Public Money* (London: Macmillan, 1974).

67. See F. M. G. Willson, "Policy-Making and the Policy-Makers," in

Rose, ed., *Policy-Making in Britain* (London: Macmillan, 1969).

68. Richard E. Neustadt, "White House and Whitehall," in Rose, ed., *Policy-Making in Britain,* p. 292. For views emphasizing differences between civil servants, see Hugo Young and Anne Sloman, *But Chancellor: An Inquiry into the Treasury* (London: BBC, 1984), pp. 21 ff.

69. Cf. Sir William Armstrong, *The Role and Character of the Civil Service,* and Roy Jenkins, "The Reality of Political Power."

70. Quoted in Paul Mosley, *The Making of Economic Policy* (Brighton: Wheatsheaf, 1984).

71. See Aberbach, Putnam, and Rockman, *Bureaucrats and Politicians in Western Democracies,* p. 231.

72. Heclo and Wildavsky, *The Private Government of Public Money,* p. 9.

CHAPTER IV

Political Authority and Political Culture

It is the dull traditional habit of mankind that guides most men's actions and it is the steady frame in which each new artist must set the picture that he paints.

THE POLITICAL AUTHORITY of a regime is defined by two characteristics: popular compliance with the basic political laws considered necessary for its survival, and popular support for the character of the regime. Whereas compliance is about the behavior of individual subjects, support is about intangible attitudes. If citizens both support the regime and also comply with its basic political laws, then authority is fully legitimate; that has normally been the case in England. If people comply with basic political laws but refuse to support the regime, then it is coercive; this is today the case in such East European countries as Poland. A system of government that loses both the support and compliance of many citizens, such as the Stormont Parliament that governed Northern Ireland up to 1971, is headed toward overthrow.[1]

The political culture (and the subcultures into which it can be divided) is important, whether there is conflict between the culture and the regime, or whether there is consensus. The political culture concerns intangible but important values, beliefs, and emotions that influence support for authority and compliance with its basic political laws.

Political values are ideas about what justifies and ought to guide political choices. A political culture is a more or less harmonious mixture of the values, beliefs, and emotions dominant in society. Political values cannot be isolated from political beliefs and emotional symbols. For example, freedom of speech may be regarded as a value in itself; it may be thought to lead to the best choice of public policy; and it may also be cherished as a symbol of good government.

Beliefs about what is expected to happen have both an empirical and normative dimension. For example, the government is expected to call a general election even if the governing party is likely to lose, because elections are institutionalized in the process. People also believe that it is morally right that a government ought to be periodically subject to electoral judgment. Even when beliefs are clear they are not always determinant. Twice in this century, in the exceptional circumstances of wartime the government has postponed a general election after first obtaining the consent of all parties in Parliament.

Emotional symbols significant in the political culture concern fundamentals of government, such as the national identity of the community being governed. Tradition has given the English an extraordinarily strong sense of national identity. Its strength is shown by the absence of intensely nationalistic symbols, often the sign of a frustrated sense of nationhood. In two world wars of this century, patriotism has been strong enough to sustain the sacrifice of hundreds of thousands of lives in battles for national survival.

As Bagehot emphasizes, the political culture reflects "the dull traditional habit of mankind." While the cultural outlooks of Englishmen are not inherited biologically, they are transmitted from generation to generation. Through political socialization English people learn about events and ideas from a time long before they were born (see Chapter V). In a lifetime every citizen learns new ideas from personal and national experience. Elderly English people may combine many strata of beliefs, ranging from those prevalent in Victorian times through wars and depression to the present. The outlook of young voters will be greatly influenced by events since 1980; to young voters the era of Sir Winston Churchill and Clement Attlee will seem a part of prehistory.

Collectively, the values, beliefs, and emotional symbol that constitute the political culture of England are "a system of tacit understandings."[2] They are tacit because they are taken for granted. Ordinary citizens do not speak the language of political theorists or political sociologists, nor do they readily articulate their thoughts about government. The chapter draws upon a mixture of sources to depict the political culture of England today. It gives particular attention to the views of the politically active minority; this group is not only articulate but also disproportionately influential in government.

Bagehot told only half the story when he wrote that cultural norms guide most actions. Immediately, this is true: each person is constrained by his or her values, beliefs, and emotions. But cultural outlooks are not fixed, nor are they enforceable in a court of law. They are derived from past experience of political authority. English people are unconcerned with the risk of a coup d'etat because it has never happened. By contrast, many politicians in Latin American and Third World lands expect coups to recur because they have experienced illegal seizures of power. The political culture, reflecting what has been done by rulers in the past, is as much a consequence as a cause of political action.

THE MAINTENANCE OF AUTHORITY

Compliance with Basic Political Laws. While all Acts of Parliament have the same formal authority, they are not all equal in political significance. The very existence of law-enforcement agencies emphasizes that government expects some people to break some laws. The crucial point for political authority is whether basic political laws or conventional regulations are broken.[3] Basic political laws are those few laws that governors deem important for the maintenance of the regime. For example, inciting a group to refuse military service in time of war would be considered subversive of political authority, whereas encouraging a group of motorists to have one more drink before leaving a pub could be an antisocial act causing an accident by a drunken driver, but not a challenge to political authority.

Breaking a basic political law is a political crime. The IRA, the most experienced revolutionary group within the United Kingdom, is well aware of this. It claims that when it shoots a policeman it is not committing a murder but a political act. When Republican demonstrators peacefully assemble in defiance of a court order, the act is equally a political crime, because it is intended to subvert the authority of the Crown. The fact that a demonstration may be less violent than a group of football fans coming back from a match does not alter its significance. Any violation of a basic political law has serious political implications, whereas football hooliganism is a social problem.

National politicians are particularly committed to upholding Westminster's authority — even when it is used in pursuit of objectives that they reject. The readiness to comply with basic political laws was made explicit during the Suez War of 1956 by the then leader of the opposition, Hugh Gaitskell, who told the House of Commons that the Labour party would be:

> bound by every constitutional means at our disposal to oppose it. I emphasize the word ''constitutional.'' We shall, of course, make no attempt to dissuade anybody from carrying out the orders of the government, but we shall seek, through the influence of public opinion, to bring every pressure to bear upon the government to withdraw from the impossible situation into which they have put us.[4]

The alternation of Conservative and Labour parties in office gives an incentive to party leaders to uphold the authority of Westminster, for a party in opposition expects to benefit from future compliance with laws it enacts. Left-wing unions today press Labour party leaders to support the defiance of industrial relations acts, but the party wishes to avoid supporting defiance of the law. Instead, the repeal of acts unpopular in the Labour movement is pledged—once the legitimate authority of government is put in Labour's hands.

At election after election, voters have refused to give support to antisystem parties. This has been demonstrated most strikingly in Scotland and Wales, where Scottish Nationalist and Welsh Nationalist parties regularly run candidates demanding independence from Westminster. From 70 to 90 percent of the electorate within these parts of the United Kingdom *reject* the party that claims to represent their nation. The great majority of Scots and Welsh identify with and vote for parties that define national interest in British term. (Cf. Tables II. 2–3). Moreover, nationalist parties do not reject the idea of parliamentary government; it is authority being placed in London rather than Edinburgh or Cardiff that is the root of their objection.

Popular support for authority is also evidenced by rejection of extreme left- and right-wing political movements. The Communist Party of Great Britain has always polled a derisory vote. Its best (*sic*) election was in 1945, when Communists won 0.4 percent of the vote; in October 1974, at a time of high industrial tension and militancy Communist candidates polled less than 0.1 percent of the vote. In 1983, Communist candidates polled less than 0.05 percent of the vote. The British Communist party has even been described as "overwhelmed by the British political culture and forced to accommodate to the country's political tradition."[5]

In reaction against the assimilation of the Communist party to consensus norms, a variety of self-styled revolutionary groups have formed, split, and reformed, such as the Militant Tendency, the Socialist Workers' party and the Socialist League. They avoid testing their popular support at elections. The most significant group is *Militant,* a Trotskyite organization that greatly multiplies its influence by the role that some of its members play within the Labour party.[6]

From time to time self-styled fascist movements appear and nominate candidates for parliamentary elections; their popular support is also miniscule. In the 1930s the British Union of Fascists, led by a former Labour MP, Sir Oswald Mosley, failed to gain any support at a time of high unemployment and the approach of world war. In the 1970s the National Front sought to stimulate support for a radical reaction against established parties and institutions. When anti-immigrant marches have been organized in areas with many black immigrants, violence has resulted. Electorally the National Front has been a failure. In 1983, it contested one-tenth of Britain's constituencies and won 0.1 percent of the vote.[7]

The efforts of the extreme left and the extreme right to defy the law in the name of a self-proclaimed superior political morality is not accepted in England. Whereas in Eastern European countries the government accuses people of subversive crimes against the state, in England the very idea of a political crime is unknown. When asked whether or not there are some circumstances in which political terrorism can be justified, 84 percent say that it must *always* be condemned, as against 12 percent believing that somewhere in the world there may be a justification for violence against an established regime.[8]

When people are asked whether they consider organizations such as the IRA terrorists or freedom fighters, 91 percent tell the Gallup Poll that they consider the IRA as terrorists, and only 3 percent see the IRA as freedom fighters. By contrast, in Northern Ireland, where political legitimacy *is* contested, the IRA, which is in armed insurrection against the Crown, and the armed Protestant Ulster Volunteer Force are integral to politics.

Even though conventional crime has been increasing through the years, in England as elsewhere in the Western world the police continue to work on the assumption of maintaining order with the consent of nearly everyone within the community. The sense of trust is demonstrated by the fact that the police patrol unarmed, and criminals are usually unarmed too. When people are asked how much confidence they have in a variety of major institutions in society, 83 percent express a great deal or quite a lot of confidence in the police, placing it second in popular confidence ahead of Parliament, the civil service, and the courts.[9]

England has no paramilitary security force to compel obedience to the law, nor has it anything like the American national guard for use in the event of domestic political disorder. The internal security forces of England are, in proportion to population, one-third smaller than those in America, France, or Italy. The navy is England's premier military service; by its nature the navy cannot be deployed within the country, and the army is hardly ever used to enforce public order within England.

The importance of cultural attitudes in maintaining law and order is best demonstrated by the contrast between England and the most disorderly part of the United Kingdom, Northern Ireland. The Westminster Parliament has never been successful in efforts to export English police, courts, or military organization to any part of Ireland, because these institutions can operate only with the consent of the population. Irish Republicans have always refused such consent. Ulster Protestants, determined to maintain their own political position, have only given consent with reservations.

Westminster's first reaction to civil rights disorders in Ulster in 1968 was to encourage the Northern Ireland government to imitate English ways; a year later, troops were also introduced. A decade and one-half of governing without consensus has failed to produce what one Home Secretary has called "an acceptable level of violence."[10] It is painfully clear that England's rule of law is not for export to all parts of the United Kingdom.

Trust between police and the policed is today subject to erosion on three fronts. First of all, the revelation that some policemen abuse their authority or commit illegal acts reflects against the police as a whole. Second, the politics of confrontation pursued by some unions in defiance of Acts of Parliament has led to the mobilization of police at strike scenes, as in the 1984 coal strike. In turn, this has led some Labour party and trade union leaders to call for workers to "fight, oppose and break unjust and anti-democratic class laws." During the miners' strike, their union leader, Arthur Scargill, declared: "We have no intention of abiding by laws either civil or criminal which restrict our ability as a trade union to fight for the rights of our members."[11] Third, in immigrant areas there is ambivalence because of a desire of many immigrants to enjoy protection by the law against crime and against racial discrimination, yet concern that law-enforcement officials may themselves discriminate against immigrants.

The importance of trust is emphasized by the Lord Chancellor, Lord Hailsham: "Law is a confidence trick. Law depends upon *asabia,* that is, a sense of solidarity between people who regarded themselves as the members of a society accepting certain values.''[12] Particular protest incidents show that there are at least a few English people today prepared to attack political authority. But a Marxist critic of established authority concludes, ''It is an assault that has taken place without very evident mass support.''[13]

Ironically, the rise of unorthodox methods of political activity in the late 1960s — protest marches, rent strikes, sit-ins at public buildings, and occasional violence to property — has reaffirmed the commitment of the great majority of English people to compliance with basic political laws. A nationwide survey concentrating upon unorthodox political protest found little support for political action outside the law (see Table IV.1). A majority approved signing petitions and lawful demonstrations, but disapproved of eight other forms of political protest ranging from boycotts and rent strikes to violence. Approval is low (16 percent) for unconventional but legal protest measures such as unofficial strikes, as well as for measures that are illegal but well publicized, such as the occupation of buildings.

The commitment of English people to lawful political action reflects values about how people ought to act, and not simply calculations about what will work. Consistently, the minority

TABLE IV.1 *The Limits of Support for Unorthodox Political Behavior*

	Approve %	*Believe effective* %	*Have done* %
Sign petitions	86	73	23
Lawful demonstrations	69	60	6
Boycotts	37	48	6
Rent strikes	24	27	2
Unofficial strikes	16	42	5
Occupying buildings	15	29	1
Blocking traffic	15	31	1
Painting slogans on walls	1	6	—
Damaging property	2	10	1
Personal violence	1	11	—

Source: Reprinted from Alan Marsh, *Protest and Political Consciousness,* Sage Library of Social Research, Vol. 49, Table 2.1, by permission of the Publisher, Sage Publications, Inc. Copyright © 1977 by Sage Publications, Inc.

who believe unorthodox measures are effective is larger than that approving unlawful measures. For example, 11 percent believe violence is effective but only 1 percent approve of using violence (Table IV.1). Because most people disapprove of unorthodox political behavior and do not believe it effective, very few engage in such protest; only 6 percent report involvement in boycotts and 5 percent in unofficial strikes.

The commitment of English people to established political authority is also shown by popular readiness to support the government in taking strong measures to defend itself, if its authority is challenged by violation of basic political laws. Surveys show that 80 percent approve courts giving severe sentences to protesters who disregard the police, and 73 percent approve police using force against demonstrators. Similarly, a large majority believe that a tough line on law and order will also be effective.[14]

Most English people reject unorthodox or illegal political activities, but they also reject the government bending the law to repress lawful disagreement with public policies. A majority would not endorse the government using troops to break strikes, and only one-quarter would infringe freedom of speech and assembly by making political protest demonstrations illegal. The median person takes a middle-of-the-road position, wanting public officials as well as antigovernment protesters to support the institutions of government and comply with basic laws.[15]

Readiness to comply with basic political laws deemed central to the maintenance of authority does not mean the unthinking endorsement of each and every law, nor does it mean opposition to changes through alteration of the Constitution. People often support the regime while voicing specific criticisms favoring reform. But a desire to reform particular institutions should not be confused with the unconditional rejection of authority. Surveys of popular attitudes toward three alternatives — revolution, reform, and rigid defense of the status quo — show that two-thirds of English people consistently endorse a reformist approach to society (Table IV.2). Among the minority that does not, those favoring defense of the status quo substantially outnumber the handful who endorse revolutionary actions.

TABLE IV.2 *Popular Attitudes toward Social Change, 1976–1983*

	1976 %	1980 %	1983 %
Society must be radically changed by revolutionary action	7	6	5
Society must be gradually improved by reforms	60	56	62
Society must be defended against all subversive forces	25	32	27
Don't know	8	6	6

Source: *Euro-Barometre* No. 20 (Brussels: Commission of the European Communities, December 1983) p. A46.

Support for the Regime. Compliance with basic political laws goes hand in hand with support for the political regime. The idea of a revolution overthrowing representative parliamentary institutions is inconceivable to the great bulk of English people; only 7 percent say they think it likely that government might be overthrown in the next decade. When public opinion is asked to evaluate government by elected representatives, 94 percent support it as very good or fairly good; only 3 percent consider it a bad way to run the country. Politicians too almost unanimously support the established system of representative government; only 2 percent of MPs say there should be big changes in the way England is governed.[16]

The question then arises: why do people support the regime? The great books of political philosophy cannot provide a satisfactory explanation, for philosophers have disagreed fundamentally. In the seventeenth century Thomas Hobbes disagreed with John Locke; at the end of the eighteenth century Edmund Burke disagreed with Jeremy Bentham, and John Stuart Mill disagreed with his Victorian contemporary in London, Karl Marx. The great books of political philosophy can have only a limited effect upon popular opinion; even after a century of compulsory education these texts are read by only a very small minority of the electorate. Popular political outlooks are derived primarily from experience, not books.

Past traditions are sometimes cited as an explanation of the unreflective, even unconscious English acceptance of political authority. But the events of a thousand years of English history offer precedents to justify political revolt as well as political allegiance. Regicide is an older tradition than parliamentary government. High-status Englishmen have been committing treason against the Crown since the time of Thomas A. Becket in the twelfth century. Lowly Englishmen have been revolting against the Crown at least since Wat Tyler's peasant rising of 1381.

Traditional symbols transcending divisive issues are also cited as causes of popular allegiance to authority. The monarchy is the most prominent symbol of political authority. Public opinion overwhelmingly favours having a Queen or King as head of state; positive regard for the monarchy is common throughout society. But survey evidence rejects the theory that positive regard for the Queen creates or strengthens allegiance to political authority.[17] The Queen is viewed as a nonpolitical figure above the everyday activities of government; the positive emotions inspired by monarchy are not strong. The hurried abdication of King Edward VIII in 1936 in order to marry an American divorcee occurred without difficulty because popular regard was immediately transferred to his hitherto little-known brother, who then became King George VI.

The greatest difficulty in explaining political allegiance by invoking symbols is that we cannot separate cause and effect. The regard in which English people hold their Crown, their traditions, and their institutions is a consequence of centuries of legitimate government. Nothing is compelling about the symbols in themselves. Northern Ireland shows that symbols of British government can stimulate conflict between antimonarchical Irish Republicans and Protestants proclaiming loyalty to the Crown.[18]

Support for authority is not the result of carefully calculated policies pursued by politicians. Politicians try to avoid raising constitutional issues because they are so difficult to resolve, especially without a written Constitution. One political commentator, Hugo Young, writes:

> Preserving constitutional order could be called the highest task of politics. Yet the effort applied to it has been derisory. Half of Whitehall devotes itself to the economy, which it can but slightly

tinker with. Virtually none of Whitehall has been concerned with the Constitution. . . . To almost all concerned, constitutional issues exist in order to be denied, circumvented or reduced to an administrative inconvenience.[19]

Nor can ordinary citizens rely upon constitutional rights to justify support for the regime. An unwritten Constitution that does nothing to limit the authority of the Crown offers no protection to an English person seeking redress against government. The 1688 Bill of Rights, unlike the American version enacted a century later, contains no fundamental principles that a citizen can invoke against an Act of Parliament.

The government's statutory powers are broad enough to sanction it's doing almost anything. In a single day in 1940, Parliament approved an Emergency Powers (Defence) Act that allowed the government to compel persons "to place themselves, their services and their property at the disposal of His Majesty."[20] Even if the courts rule against the executive, the effect of a judgment can be cancelled by a subsequent Act of Parliament retroactively giving statutory justification for what the courts ruled should be done. In 1965 the Burmah Oil Company won a lawsuit claiming government compensation for property damaged in the Second World War. The government promptly passed a retrospective law abolishing the grounds for claiming compensation.

Today, as in the past, the chief constraints upon British government are cultural norms about what government should and should not do. Written formulas cannot by themselves restrain government. In England little attempt is made to employ formal constitutional constraints. As a High Court judge has noted:

> The safeguard of British liberty is in the good sense of the people and in the system of representative and responsible government which has been evolved.[21]

The trust that English people show is not derived from a belief in the effectiveness or competence of government. When people are asked whether they think the actions of government have helped to make their position better or worse than it might have been, the most frequent response, given by 47 percent, is to say that government has not had much effect; another 11 percent see its impact as better in some ways and worse in others. The proportion who see government as unambiguously making their lives worse is 18 percent; the proportion seeing government as unambiguously improving their lives is also limited, 24 percent.[22] Moreover, the great majority of respondents think the impact of government is much the same whichever party is in office. There are always lots of people who think that government is doing some things wrong, and could do many things better.

Insofar as people do trust government, they show confidence that the governors of the day will not go "too far" in the use of power. Avoiding the abuse of power, rather than effectiveness in its use, is the cornerstone of support for government in England. There is not an uncritical endorsement of every feature of the political system. There is socialization into a political system in which positive support for the regime is very much the norm, a norm reinforced by experience. Among those who have tried to get government to act upon a complaint and contacted a public official or politician, the proportion reporting satisfaction is usually twice as great as the proportion expressing dissatisfaction.[23]

Positive readiness to support the system as it is, including a capacity for gradual reform, is consistent with dissatisfaction about specific actions of government. Surveys that report very few people favoring revolutionary change in government also show that a substantial fraction of the British public is not satisfied with the way that democracy works. In 1983, 32 percent reported themselves dissatisfied with democracy but only 5 percent reported that they favored revolutionary change (cf. Table IV.2).[24]

When surveys ask English people to evaluate reasons for giving allegiance to authority, the reason most often endorsed is pragmatic: 77 percent believe "it's the best form of government we know." Such a judgment does not regard authority as perfect or even trouble-free. Government is regarded as good enough, or simply as the least of many possible evils. "It's the kind of government the people want" is also thought a good reason for supporting government by 66 percent. A majority

(65 percent) also recognizes the inevitability of government: "We've got to accept it whatever we think."[25]

The effectiveness of government in providing the right things for people is considered less important; 49 percent think it is a good reason for accepting authority. Contrary to the argument sometimes offered by economic determinists, popular allegiance is not bought by providing public benefits. A government that is ineffective in managing a mixed-economy welfare state can still enjoy authority if people consider it the best form of government that they know. After all, the legitimacy of government in England was secured long before it became a great provider of welfare benefits.

WHOSE AUTHORITY?

Governors are a small, select fraction of the population, whose authority is justified because they are believed to represent the country as a whole. But there is no agreement about how representation works, or whose authority governors exercise.[26] Three theories of representation are often mentioned.

Trusteeship. Traditionally politicians were said to have a duty to act as trustees of the nation, taking the initiative in determining what government does. Writing before the First World War, A. L. Lowell described England's governors as holding office "by the sufferance of the great mass of the people, and as trustees for its benefit." According to this doctrine, MPs and the Cabinet are not expected to ask what people want, but to use their independent judgment to determine what is in the best interests of society. L. S. Amery, a former Conservative Cabinet minister, wrote after the Second World War that England is governed "for the people, with, but not by the people."[27]

Before industrialization, aristocratic trustees justified their power on the grounds that most of the population was considered unfit — by birth, upbringing, and interest — to participate in government. Writing in 1867, Bagehot argued that anyone who doubted this had only to go into the kitchen to talk with the cook. Bagehot thought a democratic franchise would work well only if the mass of the electorate showed deference to their betters. Today, only an aging and very small (less than one-tenth) fraction of English people are prepared to defer to others on grounds of social status.[28]

Today, university education rather than aristocratic birth is the best way to become a political trustee. Superior education often characterizes radicals who challenge the authority of elected governments as well as established politicans. Radicals justify challenge on the assumption that they are the best trustees of the national interest. Marsh's survey of *Protest and Political Consciousness* found that radical criticism of existing trustees of government has "less to do with altruism and much more to do with their urge to hasten the day when the existing elites have been ousted by themselves."[29]

The trusteeship view of government is summed up in an epigram: The government's job is to govern. The outlook is popular with any party in office, because it justifies government's doing whatever it wishes. Civil servants find the doctrine congenial too, because they permanently serve the governing party, and can therefore see themselves as the continuing, albeit nonelected, trustees of the public interest.

Collectivism. A second doctrine of representation assumes that social groups are the constituent units of politics; individuals are considered politically important only insofar as they are represented collectively through groups. Collectivists argue that the aggregation of individual preferences by groups is inevitable in decision making in a country with more than 55 million citizens. It is usually assumed that the chief political interests in society are organized into economic groups. An alternative collectivist formulation is that each ministry or institution of government has its own policy-specific network of groups; groups concerned with environmental policy or abortion for example, differ from those concerned with industrial relations or foreign affairs.[30]

The Conservative version of group politics emphasizes harmony. The traditional Conservative view of society saw the different strata of society as organically linked, like the parts of the human body, with the head having a directing role and other parts responding naturally. Each group could make a contribution, and receive esteem and benefits. The outlook is summed up in the funeral monument to an eighteenth-century Oxford servant "who, by an exemplary life and behaviour, obtained the approbation and esteem of the whole society."

By contrast, the Labour version of group politics emphasizes political differences between employers and employees. This is an interest group more than a class analysis, for a large proportion of manual workers do not belong to a trade union, and a substantial fraction of middle-class employees do. The Labour Party sees itself as a party representing one organized interest, trade unions. The outlook is represented in the cry of Frank Cousins, formerly leader of the Transport and General Workers, the country's largest trade union: "We represent Britain, we represent the working class of Britain, and they are Britain."[31]

Classical Marxists see authority as a function of class: capitalists have power in society, making the forms of government more or less irrelevant. By definition, those without capital are powerless, whether or not they have the vote. British government is said to be an agent of the capitalist class, which is organized internationally. Neo-Marxists give greater emphasis to government's autonomous influence upon class relations. All Marxists stress irreconcilable political conflicts arising from class divisions within England.[32]

The collectivist concept of authority sees government principally as the resultant of group pressures. In Samuel Beer's perspective, the Labour and Conservative parties represent the principal groups in society. Thus, party government and group representation in government are merged.[33] The formulation, however, omits consideration of the Liberal Party's role; the Alliance claims to represent those who do not wish to be aligned with business or labor interests.

Corporatist models of policymaking identify three groups as of crucial importance: business, trade unions, and government. The process of policy making is seen as the outcome of discussions amongst leaders of these groups within tripartite institutions that are called corporatist, emphasizing the extent to which the three different groups have become incorporated in a single body. The purpose of corporatism is to reconcile group differences. If the leaders of these three groups spend more time accommodating each other than pressing their own sectional demands, they risk suffering repudiation by supporters. This has frequently happened with attempts to impose wage and price regulations upon business and labor in Britain.[34]

The collectivist model of politics gives greater emphasis to the authority of organized groups than to the authority of government. In its moderate form, corporatist theories admit that government is one among several participants in the policy-making process. Carried to their logical extreme, corporativist theories reduce government to an institution for squaring powerful group interests. In the words of W. J. M. Mackenzie: "The state is submerged by the interests; it continues, but only as a form of contest. The so-called government is like a medieval king amid the barons' wars; his body is a symbol and a prize that the factions strive to possess."[35]

Individualism. The liberal model of political authority takes democracy literally; it sees authority as derived from individuals. It differs from the trusteeship model in giving far greater weight to those who are represented than to their representatives. It differs from the collectivist approach in denying that pressure group leaders are legitimate makers of public policy. Liberal individualism sees government by popularly elected representatives, responsive and accountable to the electorate, as the primary justification for authority.

Political authority was established in England for centuries before the King's ministers became accountable to Parliament and the right to vote was widespread.[36] Thus, theories of government by public opinion must be imposed upon predemocratic institutions and attitudes. A proponent of collectivist doctrines such as Beer argues that popular political expression is a sign of political decay because it weakens groups.[37] The persisting strength of the elitist trusteeship doctrine reflects the contrast in origins between Westminster and the liberal-individualist Constitution of the United States.

The liberal doctrine is often conveniently invoked by the winning party after a general election; it claims that victory is proof that the policies in the party's manifesto must be what the people want.[38] Popular support, whether given because of or in spite of specific manifesto commitments, is considered a mandate for the governing party to act. But opponents of any particular government action can cite public opinion polls showing that few electors are familiar with the contents of party manifestos, and sometimes a majority of the public is ignorant of or does not approve of particular government measures.

Nineteenth-century liberal doctrines of individual choice favor individual participation, rather than collective representation through parties and interest groups. The decline of confidence in government management of the economy has brought about a revival of neoliberal economic doctrines.[39] Relatedly, the decline of confidence in Conservative and Labour party leadership has revived arguments for voting by proportional representation, perceived as a mean of giving each individual's voice equal weight in government.[40]

The government held a referendum in 1975 giving individuals the opportunity to express their views on the Common Market, and about Scottish and Welsh devolution in 1979. The occasional use of referendums does not signify the conversion of politicians to faith in popular decision making. Instead, it reflected the desire of the Labour government of the day to minimize the costs of intraparty divisions by asking the electorate to endorse what the Cabinet proposed but a minority of Labour politicians opposed. Many MPs reject the principle of the referendum, believing that it undermines their position as trustees of authority. The late Labour minister R. H. S. Crossman argued against the referendum on the ground that majority opinion is often opposed to many reforms that can secure parliamentary approval.

> Better the liberal elitism of the statute book than the reactionary populism of the marketplace. Referenda or plebiscites notoriously confirm right-wing acts: they do not voice left-wing opinions.[41]

The evidence shows Crossman wrong in his assumption that public opinion is right-of-center on all issues; his remarks are nonetheless a revealing indication of the elitism of self-styled political trustees.

The Mix of Authority. The unitary authority of the Crown is consistent with a multiplicity of institutions making use of that authority. Political authority is not concentrated in one institution or justified by only one theory; it involves a mixture of values and beliefs.

When asked directly, almost all MPs say that individual citizens ought to influence government; and 91 percent say that people ought to be allowed to vote even if they cannot do so intelligently. However, most MPs also see their primary role as being that of a group representative or trustee for the nation. Only one in five thinks that a political leader should primarily respond to the views of followers. A Labour MP says:

> The essential thing in a democracy is a general election in which a government is elected with power to do any damned thing it likes and if the people don't like it, they have the right to chuck it out.

A Conservative MP with an aristocratic background endorses much the same view in a characteristically mock diffident manner:

> I personally consider myself capable of coming to decisions without having to fight an election once every four or five years, but on the other hand, the people must be allowed to feel that they can exercise some control, even if it's only the control of chucking somebody out that they don't like.[42]

Most individuals see two groups of elected trustees, the Prime Minister and Cabinet, and two collectivist institutions, big business and trade unions, having a lot of influence upon the country. Relatively few see more traditional institutions, such as the Royal Family, the House of Lords, the Army, or the Church, as having a lot of influence. Consistent with the historical evolution of authority from the top down, only 8 percent see people like themselves as having a lot of influence.[43]

Many groups can be seen as exercising some political influence because the institutions of government are composite rather than monolithic. Westminster institutions give preeminence to politicians acting as trustees on behalf of those they represent. Collectivist parties and pressure groups are important as constraints upon politicians acting as trustees. Individual judgments are intermittently but crucially significant in a general election.

The mixture of authoritative institutions in society generates popular confidence, and particularly popular confidence in major political institutions. A major international study of values shows that British people on average tend to have more confidence in their major institutions, including political institutions, than the French, Germans, or Italians (Table IV.3) and about as much confidence as do Americans.

British people tend to show a higher level of confidence in public than in such nongovernmental institutions as the press and trade unions. Confidence in the persisting institutions of the regime is demonstrated by the fact that far more English people endorse nonparty (sometimes mislabeled nonpolitical) institutions than vehicles of party politics. More than four-fifths express confidence in the police and armed forces, the most authoritative and the most coercive institutions of governance. The legal system, the education system, the civil service and also the Church (for most, the established Church of England) generate more confidence than does Parliament.[44] Diverse

TABLE IV.3 *Popular Confidence in Major Institutions*

	Britain	America	France	Germany	Italy
	(% expressing a great deal or quite a lot of confidence)				
	%	%	%	%	%
Police	86	76	64	71	68
Armed forces	81	81	53	54	58
Legal system	66	51	55	67	43
Education system	60	65	55	43	56
Civil service	48	55	50	35	28
Church	48	75	54	48	60
Major companies	48	50	42	34	33
Parliament/Congress	40	53	48	53	31
Press	29	49	31	33	46
Trade unions	26	33	36	36	28
Average	53	59	49	47	45

Source: Gordon Heald, ''A Comparison between American, European and Japanese Values'' (Hunt Valley, Md.: Annual WAPOR Conference, 21 May 1982), Table 4, a 1982 survey by the European Values Systems Study Group.

institutions of authority mobilize support in a multiplicity of ways; most support is given institutions central in the exercise of political authority.

CULTURAL INHIBITIONS
UPON AUTHORITY

In theory Parliament can enact any law that the government of the day recommends; in practice the actions of every government are limited by what people will stand for. The diffuse legitimacy that English people confer upon government is not a blanket endorsement for doing anything. From the time of Magna Carta in 1215 legal limits have been set to the actions of the Crown. Today, the norms of the political culture constitute the chief practical limitation upon the actions of politicians: they identify things that are not done and, even more, preclude measures inconceivable in an English context but perfectly normal in authoritarian regimes. In the words of Bernard Crick:

> The only restraints are political. Governments are restrained by what they think the country will stand for come the general election, and they adhere to things like general elections because they prefer (whether out of ethics, habit or prudence, or all three) to settle disputes politically rather than despotically and coercively.[45]

The Slight Relevance of the Courts. Courts have relatively little influence upon Westminster, because the role of law is narrowly defined. Whereas in past centuries judges proclaimed the doctrine of the rule of law in efforts to restrain royal absolutism, twentieth-century English judges do not consider themselves arbiters of what government may or may not do. Instead, they assert that it is up to Parliament, acting under the direction of the Cabinet, to decide this.

English courts claim no power to declare an Act of Parliament unconstitutional, nor will they accept a claim that an Act should be set aside because it conflicts with a previous Act of Parliament or with what claimants describe as natural rights.[46] If a statute delegates discretion to a public authority, the courts do not question the motives of the officials exercising discretion. While English judges believe that the unwritten Constitution must be constantly adapted, they want no part of the job. That is the responsibility of Parliament. The final court of appeal is political rather than judicial.

The principal activity of the courts is to resolve disputes about the application of the law to particular events, or to ascertain facts indicating whether or not a law has been violated. Government actions can be challenged on a factual basis or because a ministry is said to act outside its statutory powers. If the action of central government or a local authority is *ultra vires* (outside its powers), the courts can order it to desist. If the courts do rule an action of government *ultra vires*, government can retrospectively legitimate what it has done by an *ex post facto* act, or it can free itself from future judicial constraint by an Act of Parliament explicitly conferring powers that the courts had said were previously lacking.[47]

The courts are not so much the source as the beneficiary of authority. Whereas in the United States the Supreme Court determines what the Constitution says and others must obey, in England a judicial decision is meant to be a clarification of what Parliament has already decided. If the governing party disagrees strongly with a judicial decision, it can use its majority in Parliament to overturn the court's ruling. Judges normally seek to avoid party political controversy. When appointed by the government of the day to undertake an extrajudicial role, such as chairing a government committee dealing with controversial issues, there is a risk that "a little of the long-standing esteem in which judges are held and some of their authority is undermined."[48]

When an individual citizen does have a grievance against government, it is much more likely to involve a specific administrative action, such as a claim for a welfare benefit or planning permission for a house, rather than a major constitutional issue. A variety of administrative institutions and special tribunals exist that individuals can, if they wish, use in seeking redress for their grievances. By contrast with those in the United States, the courts are not normally used to resolve political disputes, and by contrast with those in France, there is no separate system of administrative law. Usually, an aggrieved citizen will make informal representations to administrators to reappraise the case, and if still dissatisfied, seek help from a local councillor; write an MP; or use media publicity to secure what is believed to be his or her due, but what is not a legal right.[49]

In England the liberties of the subject are principally guaranteed by cultural norms. Both governors and governed expect that everyone, whether or not he or she agrees with the government of the day, will be free to speak his or her mind. The laws of libel restrict what can be said about individuals but do not restrict political freedom of speech. Any group that wishes to nominate candidates can contest a general election; there is no test that political parties must meet, nor are candidates asked to swear a loyalty oath. In the extreme case of Northern Ireland, the Republican Sinn Fein party is pledged to *dis*loyalty to the Crown. It nominates candidates who express their rejection of the Crown's authority by refusing to take a seat in Parliament if elected.[50]

In matters of personal morality, British practice has been to use the law sparingly to enforce social norms. While the United States was experimenting with the legal prohibition of the sale of alcohol to curb drunkenness, England adopted the simpler tactic of requiring public houses to close at specified hours each day. In the 1960s a series of legislative measures expanded further the scope of what was legally permissible, repealing laws against homosexual relations and the censorship of books, films, and plays, and legalizing abortion. What individuals do in private is not considered a subject suitable for public regulation today.

The Scope of the Mixed Economy Welfare State. Commitments to provide health, education, pensions, and unemployment benefits, to maintain major nationalized industries, and to promote individual savings and private enterprise are today accepted by the government of the day. The frequent rotation of Conservative and Labour governments in office since 1945 demonstrates that whatever the rhetoric neither party repeals the bulk of measures enacted by its predecessor. Changes in the scope of the mixed-economy welfare state do not alter core commitments; they occur at the margin.[51]

Although English people agree about many things that government ought to do (e.g., provide schools and police services) and many things it ought not to do (regulate tastes in food and reading matter), at any point in time there is political controversy about the boundaries of state intervention. Today, the greatest controversy about the limits of government action concerns the direction of the economy. Since politicians are not inhibited by the logic of formal economic models, they are free to articulate views that may be collectively incoherent or contradictory.

Trade unions argue that they should be free from regulation by statute and free from government intervention in wages bargaining. Union claims of freedom from regulation by industrial relations laws is unique in Western nations. Unions do not want a Labour government to give them statutory benefits, preferring to secure these through industrial bargaining, and they certainly do not want a Conservative government to impose statutory restrictions on unions. The unions view courts and Acts of Parliament as constraints upon their activities; the unions want to be free to pursue their own interests in the marketplace. In the words of the former general secretary of the Trades Union Congress, Len Murray:

> If it's a free-for-all then we are part of the all. We will do our thing like other people will do their thing. If we take the view that the way in which the government is operating through its impact on employment or prices or the social wage or whatever is against the interests of our members, then we shall get up and say so, and if necesary we'll go and walk up and down the streets to say so.[52]

Debate about the economy is often stated in moral terms rather than technical language or economists' equations. Inflation and unemployment are considered bad and economic growth, good. When asked to say what the symbols of capitalism and socialism represent, people respond positively to the symbol of socialism (39 percent), most frequently characterizing it as about equal rights or about a fair standard of living. Among the 27 percent who respond negatively, socialism is usually seen as about government controls. As for capitalism, the 47 percent making negative responses do so because it is associated with inequalities of power as well as money; by contrast 37 percent endorsing capitalism see it as representing private business, and freedom from government interference.[53]

When asked directly about how the British economy does and ought to work, the majority perceive it as a mixed economy, based on private enterprise with some government controls, and this is regarded as generally desirable (Table IV.4). Questions about wages and profits show that the majority accept the basic market concepts of profit, investment, and wages being related to the market performance of their employer. Concurrently, the majority also believe that the average citizen needs government as a protection against business abusing its influence.

At any given point in time political controversy focuses upon disagreements about what government ought to do. In England, debate is not about whether the economy should be run free of any government intervention, nor is it about taking all major firms into public ownership. Public opinion rejects such extreme alternatives. Nor is debate about whether inflation and unemployment are desirable or undesirable. Controversy is about the best means of promoting economic growth, inflation, reducing unemployment, and dealing with a host of related problems that face the Cabinet weekly. Successive government attempts to fix wages and prices have collapsed because of a

TABLE IV.4 *Descriptions of and Aspirations for the British Economy*

	Believes best describes %	Preferred system %
Private enterprise with enough government controls to curb business abuses	44	39
Private enterprise with only a minimum of government regulation	25	38
The government involving itself with the day-to-day planning of companies	16	13
All industry owned and controlled by the government	6	5
None of these	8	6

Source: Nationwide survey by Marplan, London (April 1981). Reprinted by permission.

lack of normative agreement about what is a fair wage or price. Such is the normative dissensus about fair (*sic*) wages that a government seeking to define and enforce wage standards in the absence of consensus "would carry the very real threat of extending economic into political instability."[54]

Inhibitions upon government are both normative and practical. Businessmen can refuse to invest in England or can invest abroad in search of profits for their own firm rather than respond to an elected government's definition of the national interest. As a part-time director of the government-owned Bank of England said to a private client during a sterling crisis with reference to speculation against the pound: "This is anti-British and derogatory to sterling but on balance, if one is free to do so, it makes sense to me."[55]

As well as accepting the market role in determining the size of the national product, the majority of English people believe that government should provide a high standard of welfare services. From three-fifths to four-fifths consistently endorse present or higher levels of spending on welfare state programs, even when it is made clear that this requires present or higher levels of taxation (Table IV.5). The proportion favoring a reduction in welfare state expenditure in order to reduce taxes has fallen from 34 percent when Margaret Thatcher was first elected in 1979 to 14 percent in 1984. Mrs. Thatcher's rhetoric in favor of reducing the activities of government appears to have stimulated a countermobilization in support of a broad range of programs involving big benefits and big costs for nearly every family in England.

Although government is responsible for the economy, it is not all-powerful. For more than a generation both Conservative and Labour governments have endorsed the same goal: the growth of the economy. Moreover, they have exhorted citizens to assist in promoting faster growth in the economy. Successive governments have failed.

CONSENSUS AND CONTROVERSY

The dichotomy between consensus and controversy is false. In every political system, there must be consensus about at least a few fundamental features of government. But because the

TABLE IV.5 *Popular Attitudes toward Taxes and Welfare Benefits*

	May 1979	Mar 1981	Mar 1983	Mar 1984
	(% for each preferred option)			
Taxes should be cut, even if it means some reduction in government services, such as health, education, and welfare.	34	20	23	14
Things should be left as they are.	25	23	22	25
Government services such as health, education, and welfare should be extended, even if it means some increase in taxes.	34	49	49	54
Don't know	7	8	6	7

Source: *Gallup Political Index* for the month indicated.

system is political, by definition it involves controversy, for politics is about articulating conflicting values and beliefs as well as about their reconciliation.

Consensus here refers to the readiness of nearly all English people to comply with basic political laws, and to support the parliamentary system of government. It is this that a former Prime Minister, the Earl of Balfour, had in mind in writing a year after the General Strike of 1926, "Our whole political machinery presupposes a people so fundamentally at one that they can safely afford to bicker: and so sure of their own moderation that they are not dangerously disturbed by the never-ending din of political conflict."[56]

Controversy is the stuff of parliamentary democracy: the adversary arrangements of Westminster actively encourage the opposition to attack whatever measures are put forward by the government of the day. Cultural norms are consensual because they do not become implicated in party political debate. To a party politician, it is the differences between parties that are important. By definition, any political issue will reveal a variety of conflicting opinions about the form, the direction, and the tempo of government action. Disagreement about government policies can be conducted more easily when politicians agree about the rules of the game for resolving their disagreements.

It is tempting to describe differing outlooks toward government as subcultures. We can speak of a subculture of the left or right, or of a materialist or postmaterialist subculture. However, the important qualifying term *sub*culture is often omitted. The result is that points of difference within an overarching fundamental consensus are made to appear as if they were irreconcilable conflicts. Error is compounded if the subcultures thus created are assumed to be uniform within a class, region, or nation of the United Kingdom. There is no agreement among social scientists about the constituent elements of subcultures, or the methodology for distinguishing them from each other. Dennis Kavanagh's wide-ranging review identifies nine different models of English political culture and subcultures.[57]

Differences between political subcultures rarely set Englishman against Englishman, because individuals are themselves often divided in their own mind. Surveys of public opinion repeatedly show that people can endorse policies of all three parties, differing with each in turn according to the issue.[58] *The Civic Culture,* a cross-national survey of basic political outlooks by Gabriel Almond and Sidney Verba, attempted to classify English respondents according to three ideal-type categories: the participant citizen, the loyal undemanding subject, and the parochial person remote from government. But more than two-thirds of the respondents could not be fitted into any of these categories; in their own minds they mixed values, beliefs, and emotions from each.[59]

The political controversies that exist in Britain cannot be neatly packaged without doing an injustice to differences within political groups.[60] This is most evident in attempts to identify a distinctive ideology of the Conservatives or the right, or of Labour or Socialism. The literature of Conservative politics is replete with disagreements about the meaning of the term, and this is expressed in Parliament too. The division in the Thatcher government between so-called "wets" and "dries" (that is, more right-wing monetarists and more middle-of-the-road Keynesians) is only the latest in a long history of disagreements among Conservatives.

On the left, fundamental disputes within the Labour party have erupted recurrently and in 1981 led to the more centrist Social Democrats leaving to form their own party. This reduced the range of opinions within the Labour party without ending disagreement within Labour's ranks. Is socialism a set of doctrines that can be identified independently of Westminster politics? Or, as a leading parliamentarian, Herbert Morrison argued, "Socialism is what the Labour government does."[61]

The Alliance of the Liberal party and Social Democrats provides two parties to represent centrist positions.[62] The Liberals express views drawn from across the political spectrum. When the leader of the Social Democrats, Dr. David Owen, endorses support for market principles in managing the economy and welfare principles in social policy, the result is a different mixture of policies from that of the Conservative and Labour parties. The positions are not novel per se.

The politicians most steeped in day-to-day controversy and most dependent upon the maintenance of consensus about the system, Members of Parliament, have differences about policies, but are prepared to work within the existing political system. Robert Putnam's in-depth study of *The Beliefs of Politicians* found that the great majority concentrate on the political and administrative practicality of programs. Whatever they say in public most MPs do not privately see party differences as threatening the Westminster system. The confrontational rhetoric of a Margaret Thatcher or an Anthony Benn is less representative of the way that politicians think about each other than a backbench MP's calm characterization of partisan opponents thus:

> Well, they're different men with different policies, and some of them I quite like. They seem decent chaps, but I don't know . . . I don't agree with their policies.[63]

The everyday language of politics concentrates attention upon political differences because, by definition, politics is about the articulation of conflicting opinions. But political parties in England have been noteworthy for their readiness to assimilate ideas from their opponents. When an election transfers control of government from one party to another, the winning party does not use its newly gained power to reverse all the actions of its predecessors. To a surprisingly large extent it carries on as before. At the level of actions, not words, continuities are more substantial than differences.[64]

NOTES

1. For a fuller discussion of legitimacy, see Rose, *Governing Without Consensus,* chapter 1. Cf. the very English study of Brian Harrison, *Peaceable Kingdom: Stability and Change in Modern Britain* with the attempt by Keith Middlemass to describe England as if it could be fitted to German traditions, *Politics in Industrial Society: Experience of the British System since 1911* (London: Andre Deutsch, 1979). For cross-cultural contrasts, see the shrewd assessment by the Anglo-German sociologist, Ralf Dahrendorf, "The Politics of Economic Decline," *Political Studies,* 29:2 (1981), pp. 284–291.

2. Sidney Low, *The Governance of England,* rev. ed. (London: Ernest Benn, 1914), p. 12. For a discussion of links between tacit understandings and political values, see Richard Rose, "England: a Traditionally Modern Political Culture," in L. W. Pye and Sidney Verba, eds., *Political Culture and Political Development* (Princeton: Princeton University Press, 1965), pp. 83–129.

3. See Richard Rose, "Dynamic Tendencies in the Authority of Regimes," *World Politics,* 21:4 (1969), p. 605ff.

4. House of Commons, *Debates,* 5th series, vol. 558, col. 1462 (31 October 1956).

5. Robert Kilroy-Silk, in a book review in *Political Studies,* 18:4 (1970). See also D. T. Denver and J. M. Bochel, "The Political Socialization of Activists in the British Communist Party," *British Journal of Political Science,* 3:1 (1973); and Kenneth Newton, *The Sociology of British Communism* (London: Allen Lane, 1969).

6. For informed but unsympathetic accounts, see Blake Baker, *The Far Left* (London: Weidenfeld and Nicolson, 1981); and David Kogan and Maurice Kogan, *The Battle for the Labour Party* (London: Fontana, 1982). For a discussion of trends from within the left cf. e.g., the periodical *Marxism Today* and Austin Mitchell, *Four Years in Death of the Labour Party* (London: Methuen, 1983).

7. Cf. Stanley Taylor, *The National Front in English Politics* (London: Macmillan, 1982); and Christopher Husbands, *Racial Exclusionism and the City: The Urban Support of the National Front* (London: Allen & Unwin, 1984).

8. *Gallup Political Index,* No. 269 (January 1983), p. 13.

9. *Gallup Political Index,* No. 273 (May 1983) p. 11. See also Table IV.3. On policing generally see reflective accounts by policemen, e.g., Sir Robert Mark, *Policing a Perplexed Society* (London: Allen & Unwin, 1977); and D. W. Pope and N. L. Weiner, eds., *Modern Policing* (London: Croom Helm, 1981); and compare the views of outsiders, e.g., Ben Whitaker, *The Police in Society* (London: Eyre Methuen, 1979); R. Baldwin and R. Kinsey, *Police and Politics* (London: Quartet Books, 1982); and Stuart Morris, "British Chief Constables: the Americanization of a Role," *Political Studies,* 29:3 (1981), pp. 352–364.

10. Cf. Richard Rose, "On the Priorities of Citizenship in the Deep South and Northern Ireland," *Journal of Politics,* 38:2 (1976), pp. 247–291.

11. Scargill, quoted in "'MPs' motion attacks 'Above Law' Scargill," *Daily Telegraph,* 22 June 1984; Eric Heffer, quoted in "Traditional to Break Bad

Laws," *ibid.*, 7 April 1984. Cf. "NGA Votes to Obey Judges," *ibid.*, 19 January 1984.

12. Lord Hailsham, quoted in Terry Coleman, "His Lordship in the City of Destruction," *The Guardian*, 25 May 1984.

13. Martin Kettle, "The Police," in H. Drucker et al., *Developments in British Politics* (London: Macmillan, 1983), p. 28.

14. See Alan C. Marsh, *Protest and Political Consciousness* (London: Sage Publications, 1977), table 2.1.

15. *Ibid.* Middle-of-the-road attitudes toward changes in the system of government are also reported by Louis Moss, *People and Government in 1978* (London: Birkbeck College, U. of London, 1982) pp. 124 ff.

16. See R. Jowell and C. Airey, eds., *British Social Attitudes: the 1984 Report* (Aldershot: Gower, 1984), p. 31. See Mary Horton, *The Local Government Elector* (London: HMSO, 1967), pp. 60 ff.; and Robert D. Putnam, *The Beliefs of Politicians* (New Haven: Yale University Press, 1973).

17. See Richard Rose and Dennis Kavanagh, "The Monarchy in Contemporary Political Culture," *Comparative Politics*, 8:4 (1976), pp. 560 ff.

18. See Richard Rose, *Governing Without Consensus*, p. 244.

19. "Into the Golden Future," *Sunday Times* (London), 7 August 1977.

20. Quoted in G. H. L. LeMay, *British Government, 1914–1953: Select Documents* (London: Methuen, 1955).

21. Lord Wright, in *Liversidge* v. *Sir John Anderson*, quoted in G. LeMay, *British Government 1914–1953* (London: Methuen, 1955), p. 332. For a discussion of the problem of maintaining civil liberties in such a constitutional setting, see Harry Street, *Freedom, The Individual and the Law*, 5th ed. (Harmondsworth: Penguin, 1981).

22. Louis Moss, *People and Government 1978*, p. 23.

23. *Ibid.*, pp. 36 ff. More generally, see Dennis Kavanagh, "Political Culture in Great Britain: the Decline of the Civil Culture," in Gabriel Almond and Sidney Verba, eds., *The Civic Culture Revisited* (Boston: Little, Brown, 1980), pp. 124–176, and conceptually, Bernard Barber, *The Logic and Limits of Trust* (New Brunswick, N.J.: Transaction Books, 1983).

24. *Euro-Barometre*, No. 20 (December 1983), p. A36.

25. Richard Rose and Harve Mossawir, "Voting and Elections: a functional Analysis," *Political Studies*, 15:2 (1967), pp. 173–201.

26. For a wide-ranging review of these theories, see A. H. Birch, *Representative and Responsible Government* (London: Allen & Unwin, 1964).

27. L. S. Amery, *Thoughts on the Constitution*, 2nd ed. (London: Oxford University Press, 1953), p. 21; and A. L. Lowell, *The Government of England*, Vol. 2 (London: Macmillan, 1908), p. 508.

28. Cf. Bagehot, *The English Constitution*, and evidence cited in Dennis Kavanagh, "The Deferential English: a Comparative Critique," *Government and Opposition*, 6:3 (1971).

29. Marsh, *Protest and Political Consciousness*, p. 197.

30. Cf. Christopher J. Hewitt, "Policymaking in Postwar Britain," *British Journal of Political Science*, 4:2 (1974).

31. *Labour Party Conference Report* (1962), p. 182.

32. See e.g., Ralph Miliband, *Capitalist Democracy in Britain* (London: Oxford University Press, 1982); and Barry Hindess, *Parliamentary Democracy and Socialist Politics* (London: Routledge & Kegan Paul, 1982).

33. For a detailed historical examination of the collectivist outlook, see Samuel H. Beer, *Parties and Pressure Groups in the Collectivist Age: Modern British*

Politics, 3rd ed. (London: Faber & Faber, 1982). For a very different perspective, see R. Currie, *Industrial Politics* (Oxford: Clarendon Press, 1979).

34. For discussions of corporatism in a British context see e.g., W.P. Grant and D. Marsh, "Tripartism: Reality or Myth?" *Government and Opposition,* 12 (1977).

35. W. J. M. Mackenzie, "Models of English Politics," in R. Rose, ed., *Studies in British Politics,* 3rd ed. (London: Macmillan, 1976), p. 59.

36. C. S. Emden, *The People and the Constitution* (Oxford: Clarendon Press, 1933), especially Appendix A.

37. Cf. Beer, *Britain Against Itself.*

38. Cf. Dennis Kavanagh, "The Politics of Manifestos" *Parliamentary Affairs,* 34, 1 (1981) pp. 7–27.

39. Nick Bosanquet, *After the New Right* (London: Heinemann, 1983).

40. Vernon Bogdanor, *The People and the Party System* (Cambridge: Cambridge University Press, 1981).

41. *New Statesman,* 7 August 1970. Cf. David Butler and Austin Ranney, eds., *Referendums* (Washington, D.C.: American Enterprise Institute, 1978).

42. Quoted from Putnam, *Beliefs of Politicians,* part III.

43. See *Gallup Political Index,* No. 268 (December 1982) p. 11.

44. The expression of confidence is also persisting. See *Gallup Political Index,* No. 273 (May 1983).

45. Bernard Crick, *The Reform of Parliament,* rev. 2nd ed. (London: Weidenfeld & Nicolson), p. 16.

46. Cf. Louis L. Jaffe, *English and American Judges as Lawmakers* (Oxford: Clarendon Press, 1969), p. 4. See also Lawrence Baum, "Research on the English Judicial Process," *British Journal of Political Science,* 7:4 (1977).

47. See Gavin Drewry, *Law, Justice and Politics* (London: Longman, 1975).

48. *Solicitors' Journal.* Quoted in Gavin Drewry, "Judges and Political Inquiries: Harnessing a Myth," *Political Studies,* 23:1 (1975), p. 60.

49. For a thorough and comparative overview of this subject, see F. F. Ridley, "British Approaches to the Redress of Grievances," *Parliamentary Affairs,* 37:1 (1984), p. 32. See also Geoffrey Marshall, "Parliament and the Redress of Grievances: the Role of the Parliamentary Commissioner," in Walkland and Ryle, eds., *The Commons Today,* pp. 260–278.

50. Cf. Cornelius O'Leary, "The Wedgwood Benn Case and the Doctrine of Wilful Perversity," *Political Studies,* 13 (1965), pp. 65–78.

51. See Rose, *Do Parties Make a Difference?*

52. Brian Connell, "Len Murray: A Life in the Movement," *The Times,* 22 August 1977.

53. For supporting evidence for this and following paragraphs, see Richard Rose, "Two and One-Half Cheers for the Market in Britain," *Public Opinion* (Washington, D.C.), 6:3 (1983), pp. 10–15.

54. J. H. Goldthorpe, "Social Inequality and Social Integration in Modern Britain," in Rose, ed., *Studies in British Politics,* 3rd ed.

55. Quoted in Mackenzie, "Models of English Politics," p. 60.

56. "Introductions" to Walter Bagehot, *The English Constitution,* p. xxiv.

57. See Kavanagh, "Political Culture in Great Britain," pp. 164–165.

58. See the discussion in Chapter IX, and especially Tables IX.3–5.

59. The proportions with a mixed outlook varied from 63 to 87 percent; see Rose and Mossawir, "Voting and Elections," pp. 191 ff.

60. For a brief overview, see Rodney Barker, *Political Ideas in Modern Britain* (London: Methuen, 1978). Cf. Norton, *The Constitution in Flux,* 261 ff.

61. Quoted in Peter Jenkins, *The Battle of Downing Street* (London: Charles Knight, 1970). p. 101.

62. Cf. Hans Daalder, "In Search of the Centre of European Party Systems," *American Political Science Review,* 78:1 (1984), pp. 92–109.

63. Putnam, *The Beliefs of Politicians,* part II.

64. Rose, *Do Parties Make a Difference?*

CHAPTER V

Political Socialization

People who learn slowly learn only what they must. The best security for a people doing their duty is that they should not know anything else to do.

THE VALUES, BELIEFS, AND EMOTIONS of the political culture are transmitted from generation to generation through a series of socializing experiences in the family, at school, and at work. Political outlooks today reflect attitudes learned early in life as well as responses to contemporary events. Socialization experiences influence the antisystem views of the youthful radical as well as the positive allegiance of the ordinary adult. Because of the continuity of English institutions, many values transmitted through political socialization antedate the birth of an individual.

Most socializing agents are not political in their primary intent. Parents teach their children about many things besides politics, and very few couples in England would have children for the good of the party. Schools are established to teach children reading, writing, arithmetic, and other skills valued in nonpolitical contexts. Neighbors may influence political outlooks, but a house is rarely chosen for political reasons. Parties are the only social institution primarily concerned with political socialization, for parties have an interest in recruiting as many long-term supporters as possible.

Political socialization is a continuing process. When an English person begins to learn about politics in childhood, he or she first may respond emotionally to the monarch, or to symbols of Parliament. By the time a person reaches 18, the minimum age for voting, many political predispositions have been developed. But adult political behavior is not simply determined by these predispositions.

Adult life offers many opportunities to learn about politics from experience as a citizen. Political events too may force an individual to alter views. A person predisposed to vote for the Liberal party will have to adopt another party if the Liberals fail to contest the constituency, and a person with Scottish identity can translate this into a vote for the Scottish National Party only if living in a Scottish constituency. Individuals are always potentially open to learning new ideas or altering old ones. Because political socialization is continuous, new experiences can alter or reinforce what was learned previously.

Content is more important than process. What an English person learns about politics has greater significance than how an outlook is acquired. In England a history of legitimate government emphasizes support for authority and compliance with basic political laws; as Bagehot said, people hardly "know anything else to do." Allegiance to authority is a cause not a consequence of the pattern of political socialization. In Northern Ireland youths are socialized into conflict.[1]

Socialization influences the political division of labour. Children learn early that people differ from each other; these differences gradually become relevant politically. A young person not only learns about differences between political parties but also about the political role that he or she is expected to take. Socialization tends to differentiate partisan supporters; it also tends to divide electors into a small minority actively involved in politics, and a large group that is marginally active.

This chapter begins by examining socialization in the family, and then considers how sex roles influence political participation. Education provides a bridge between the family and the adult world, and the complexities of class joins many influences. The conclusion summarizes the cumulative effect of a multiplicity of socializing influences.

THE INFLUENCE OF FAMILY AND GENERATION

Examining the political outlooks within the family is not to assume that political harmony is important within the family. A MORI survey during the 1983 general election found that among married couples little more than half (55 percent) said that their spouse voted for the same party, 34 percent did not know how their spouse voted, and 10 percent reported that their spouse voted for a competing party. In many families politics is of no importance.

The family's influence comes first in chronological order; political attitudes learned within the family become intertwined with primary family loyalties. A child may learn little of what the Labour or Conservative party stands for except that it is the party of Mum and Dad. Family circumstances also determine the class milieu in which a child grows up.

Parental Influence. Politics does not need to have deep emotional overtones for children to follow the partisan cues offered by their parents. But to maintain continuity between generations, parents must make clear to their children what the family's party is. Often they do not (Table V.1). The party preference of both parents is remembered by less than half the electorate. Adults whose parents were both Conservatives usually are Conservative, and those with both parents Labour tend to be Labour. But the relationship is not invariable.[2]

A simple theory of intergenerational determinism fails, because 61 percent of the electorate does not acquire a lasting party identification from their parents. Most voters acquire a party identification without parental direction or in opposition to it. Even when young adults vote as their parents, they may think for themselves. Because less than half the support for the Conservative and Labour parties is, as it were, delivered by the obstetrician, each party has an incentive to seek recruits who are not life-long supporters.

Parental influence is evident when a person born into a politically active family enters politics. Entering politics is then the equivalent of going into a family business. The eldest son

TABLE V.1 *Party Identification within the Family*

	Respondent				
	Conservative %	Labour %	Liberal %	None %	Total %
Both parents:					42
Conservative	67	15	6	12	
Labour	10	71	6	14	
Liberal	39	33	18	10	
One parent unknown, other:					29
Conservative	55	30	7	8	
Labour	19	61	9	12	
Liberal	43	28	18	11	
Parents disagree	40	37	13	9	6
Neither parent's choice known	33	42	11	14	24

Source: British Election Survey (Colchester: ESRC Survey Archive, October 1964). By permission.

of a hereditary peer knows that he is guaranteed a seat in the House of Lords if his father predeceases him. Sir Anthony Wagner, Garter King of Arms, argues that a hereditary House of Lords is desirable because a peer may be groomed from childhood for political leadership. This view is rejected by the 55 percent of the nation who favor abolition of hereditary titles.[3]

The number of politicians from political families is disproportionately high in every Cabinet. In Harold Wilson's first list of appointments in 1964, ten of the forty-three named to ministerial posts had parents sufficiently involved in public life to merit notice in their offspring's biography. In 1979, eight of the twenty-two Conservative Cabinet ministers had family ties with politics. Prime Ministers, too, are disproportionately drawn from political families. Winston Churchill's ancestors had been in the Commons or the Lords since early in the eighteenth century. His son and grandson (as well two sons-in-law) also sat in the Commons. Harold Wilson's parents and grandparents, though never in Parliament, were also keenly interested in politics; he claims, "I was born with politics in me."[4] Margaret Thatcher's father was active in local politics as a Liberal.

Religion. A religious identification is likely to be acquired in childhood from parents, and insofar as religious differences affect party loyalties, this will influence political behavior. In the nineteenth century, laws and customs reserved many civic and social benefits to members of the established Church of England. Conservatives tended to be Anglicans, and nonconformist Protestants to favor the Liberals. In the twentieth century, the political importance of religion has gradually eroded, and church attendance has waned. Whereas 49 percent say they were very religious as children, and 33 percent somewhat religious, only 13 percent say that they are now very religious, and 18 percent that they are to some extent religious.[5]

Notwithstanding the decline in attachment to religion, it retains some influence on party loyalties. Systematic studies of electoral behavior have found even after allowing for the effect of class, Conservatives have polled disproportionately well in areas with a relatively strong Anglican tradition, and Labour has done badly. The Liberals are no longer so dependent upon nonconformist votes. Although religion is a much less important influence than class upon contemporary English politics, it is a secondary influence.[6]

Age and Generations. Every citizen goes through a series of stages in the life-cycle from childhood through adulthood to old age. Youth is the phase of the life-cycle with the greatest openness to change, since young people cannot base their political attitudes upon decades of experience, as do older adults.

The greater openness (or inexperience) of young people makes them readier to support new parties, such as the Liberal-Social Democratic Party Alliance and nationalist parties in Scotland and Wales.[7] Younger people are also more predisposed to engage in unconventional or unorthodox forms of political protest.[8] As adults move through the life-cycle, they are likely to become more consistent in their party loyalties, and less ready to vote for new parties or favor new ideas.

Whereas life-cycle influences are temporary, generational differences arising from the impact of distinctive historical events are life-long. Elderly voters can remember the interwar depression clearly, and some will have been unemployed or raised in the homes of long-term unemployed.[9] Some middle-aged people will recall the Second World War and the postwar austerity of the 1940s. By contrast, voters in their twenties are likely to have had their political ideas first formed in a period of peace and prosperity. Voters in their twenties will have their views formed in a period of economic recession and uncertainty.

Differences in generations influence party support. Twenty years ago voting studies found that older people tended to be Conservative, partly because they had formed party attachments before Labour was one of the two major parties. Labour was disproportionately strong among middle-age voters who had cast their first vote in 1945, a landslide Labour election victory. However, electors old enough to have voted in 1918 are now nearly all dead, and young voters who identified with Labour in 1945 are now becoming pensioners. By the next British general election, the median voter will have first gone out to work when the Beatles and Harold Wilson first became popular in the early 1960s, and more than one-third of the electorate will not have cast their first vote until after the world recession of the 1970s had hit Britain hard.

The continuity arising from political socialization is substantially offset by the discontinuities arising from political change. A century ago, Gilbert and Sullivan wrote in *Iolanthe*:

> Nature always does contrive
> That every boy and every gal
> That's born into the world alive
> Is either a little Liberal
> Or else a little Conservative!

By 1918 the Liberal party had collapsed, and the Labour party replaced it, disrupting more than the song's rhyme. In default of candidates, millions of voters from Liberal homes could no longer vote Liberal. In the 1980s, the Alliance is seeking to create another major disruption in the party system. In 1983 it won one-quarter of the vote from people who could not have been socialized into Alliance support, for the Alliance did not exist four years previously.

Extrapolating the political future from generational differences is very risky. Age-related differences are matters of degree, not kind, and are often small. Parties and pressure groups normally draw support from some people of every age. Groups specific to one age bracket, such as the National Union of Students, represent minorities. Moreover, students are a rapidly changing category in society. As students enter adult jobs, they may change their outlooks. Because the student generation of 18- to 21-year-olds changes every three years, its political character can also change rapidly. Consistently, party loyalties, not age, are the more important influence on political outlooks (see Table XII.3).

SEX SIMILARITIES AND DIFFERENCES

In law the rights of men and women to participate in politics were made equal by the grant of the vote to most women in 1918, and on the same age qualifications as men in 1928. Nearly the whole of today's female electorate has always had the right to vote, and most women voters today have grown up in a family where the mother as well as the father had the right to vote. Politicians too have spent all their lives appealing for the support of an electorate that contains about 2 percent more women than men, because women live longer.

All political parties pursue a strategy of seeking the votes of both women and men. The parties make their primary appeal to the electorate without regard to sex; specifically feminist issues are rare. Economic issues are stressed without regard to any differential between men and women. The emphasis is upon family income rather than the distribution of income or opportunities to each within the family.

At each general election, women divide in their votes between parties in proportions very similar to men. Since 1950 women have normally been slightly more inclined than men to favor the Conservatives, but the difference is usually only a few percent. In 1983 the Gallup Poll found women slightly more likely to vote Alliance and less likely to favor the Conservatives; but MORI found women 4 percent more likely than men to vote Conservative.[10] Hence, a general tendency for slight sex differences to appear in voting should not be interpreted as an invariant law.

Even the slight Conservative bias among women is not necessarily a reflection of sex differences, for it also reflects the
fact that women are disproportionately the elderly and church-
attenders, two pro-Conservative groups. Among women over
age 55 in 1983, the Conservatives received a 5 percent higher
share of the vote than among women under 25 according to
MORI surveys. The effect of age on the partisanship of women
is thus greater than the effect of sex differences.

When the political attitudes of men and women are compared, similarity is again the rule. Not only do women and men
each divide in their views, but also they divide in much the
same proportions (Table V.2). On a range of twenty questions,
covering a variety of subjects from inflation and unemployment to nuclear weapons and abortion, there is an average
difference of only 4 percent between men and women; three-
quarters of the differences are statistically insignificant, and the
others limited in degree.

Common political priorities characterize men and women on
such issues as abortion, which might be considered a feminist
issue. Outlooks are virtually identical on so-called tough proposals for bringing back the death penalty and nuclear arms as
well as so-called tender proposals such as giving more aid to
poor countries. The greatest difference of opinion — about the
amount of sex and nudity in the media — is a limited difference, 19 percent. There is thus no mass base in political attitudes for a feminist political party. There are feminist pressure
groups, but their activities should not be mistaken for actions
by government.[11] When attention is turned to participation in
party politics and government, women are usually a minority,
and often a small minority.

In 1975 the Sex Discrimination Act created an Equal Opportunities Commission to promote the elimination of discrimination and equality between the sexes. The legislation started
from the premise that neither unions nor employers would want
an activist monitoring of employment, as is done in the United
States. The Commission, like comparable official groups concerned with race relations, has excited little controversy because it has not sought to promote its mandate aggressively.

The one field of public life where women predominate is in

TABLE V.2 *The Similar Views of Men and Women about Issues*

	Men	Women	Difference (Women–Men)
		(% endorsing)	
Tenants have right to buy council house	81	81	0
Spending more to combat pollution	78	78	0
Bringing back death penalty	64	65	+1
Make abortion widely available on health service	46	47	+1
Take Britain out of Common Market	35	34	−1
Spend whatever needed to defend Falklands	37	39	+2
Sending colored immigrants home	28	30	+2
Increase public spending to reduce unemployment	75	78	+3
Cut public spending to reduce inflation	52	55	+3
Unilateral nuclear disarmament	20	23	+3
Redistribute wealth to poorer people	62	59	−3
Introduce stricter laws to regulate unions	55	59	+4
Spending more money on health service	88	93	+5
Do more to promote equal opportunities for women	74	79	+5
Re-establishing selective grammar schools	45	50	+5
Shift power from London to regions, local government	54	49	−5
Giving more aid to poor Afro-Asian countries	40	46	+6
Government influencing wages and prices	74	82	+8
Withdraw troops from Northern Ireland now	43	58	+15
Reduce sex and nudity on TV, films, magazines	<u>41</u>	<u>60</u>	+19
Average difference			4

Source: Unpublished analysis by the author of Gallup Poll survey, 19:24 (October 1983), for *Daily Telegraph*.

158 Political Socialization

public employment. Whereas women constitute 42 percent of
the total workforce, they are 47 percent of public employees.
Women are 89 percent of employees in social services, 78 percent in the National Health Service, and 72 percent in education. Only in the armed services and in nationalized industries are women underrepresented. Women are, however,
much less likely to be employed at managerial levels in the
health service, in local government, or in Whitehall.[12]

In local government, the fact that a councillor's job is unpaid
and meetings are often held in daytime might be expected to
give a competitive advantage to housewives, who would not
suffer a loss of income by becoming councillors. Women are
about one-sixth of the membership of local councils, and are
most likely to be elected to rural county councils, where the
Conservative Party is particularly strong. Women are less likely
to be appointed to important committee chairmanships than
men.[13]

In national politics women are about 10 percent of parliamentary candidates. When a woman seeks a party's nomination for Parliament, she is likely to face prejudice in the selection
of candidates, for there is a belief among some party officials
concerned with nominations that women are less good as vote-
getters. Once nominated, however, women candidates appear
to differ little from men in their electoral appeal. Women parliamentary candidates are less likely to be elected than men
because their party often nominates them to fight a hopeless
constituency. The proportion of women in the House of Commons is low. In 1979, Labour had eleven women MPs and the
Conservatives eight; in 1983 there were thirteen Conservative
and ten Labour women. The twenty-four women MPs is three
less than the number in October 1974, notwithstanding the activities of the 300 Group, which seeks to secure the election of
300 women MPs.[14]

At Cabinet level, the Prime Minister is expected to appoint
at least one woman, a figure in proportion to the number of
women in the Commons. From 1964 to 1979, four women
served in Cabinet — Margaret Thatcher, Barbara Castle, Ju-
dith Hart, and Shirley Williams. Each is a politician whose
stature is not derived from her sex or from the expression of

feminist views. The offices each held were determined by competitive abilities; none was confined to a department considered somehow appropriate for women. Margaret Thatcher's election as leader of the Conservative party in 1975 showed the readiness of MPs to judge women on political not sexist grounds. Both her supporters and critics react more strongly to Margaret Thatcher's political views than to her sex.

Differential levels of political participation cannot be ascribed to women's lacking an interest in politics. The proportion of women who are interested in politics is almost similar to the proportion of men: 54 percent of women describe themselves as having a great deal or some interest in politics, as do 68 percent of men, according to the 1979 British Election Survey. Studies by Dowse and Hughes have found that there is virtually no difference in political interest or attitudes among boys and girls in secondary schools.[15] Moreover, schools are today usually coeducational.

When women are asked their views about work, the majority state that a career is less important than the home. An NOP survey found that 89 percent of women of working age considered a woman's first duty should be to children, as against 10 percent saying it should be equally to a job and to children. Similarly, 61 percent said a woman's first duty should be to marriage, as against 36 percent saying it should be equally to marriage and a job. In each case, only 1 percent thought that women should put their career first. Moreover, 69 percent thought that a married woman should give her husband's career the priority, as against 19 percent saying it would depend upon who had the better job, and 9 percent flatly saying no. While attitudes are changing with the generations, the change is gradual. Not only are 80 percent of women over 45 ready to put their husband's career first, but also 55 percent of women under 25 would do the same.[16]

The relatively low proportion of women in national politics (including the senior civil service) is the result of a combination of influences.[17] Marriage and childrearing occupy many women in the years when young men build foundations for a political career. Within the Labour party, men are at an advantage, because they are more likely to enter occupations that are unionized, and to be elected to office in a union, a stepping-stone to a Labour parliamentary career. A woman who wants a career in national politics can succeed, but the effort required is great. By becoming Prime Minister, Margaret Thatcher has demonstrated that a woman can rise to the top in politics. But as the only woman in her Cabinet, she also makes it clear that a high position is the exception for a woman.

SCHOOLING

Although there is no formal educational requirement to vote or hold public office, education is potentially a major influence on political outlooks, for young people are in school from early childhood until they go out to work, and hundreds of thousands of voters are still students. Because schools are the product of society, education is best considered an intervening rather than an independent influence on political outlooks.

Aims of Education. English schools teach "life adjustment" as well as academic subjects. Implicitly as well as explicitly, schools prepare the young for adulthood by emphasizing behavior and attitudes appropriate to adult roles, as well as by teaching basic skills such as reading, writing, and arithmetic. Since English people take their national identity for granted, there is no emphasis on civic education in the schools.[18]

In England education has always assumed inequality.[19] Historically, most of the population has been considered fit for only a minimum of education. Until after the Second World War, the normal school-leaving age was 14. Today, the law requires youths to remain at school until age 16. The highly educated minority, a small fraction of the population, are expected to take a leading part in politics. Speaking as the Conservative minister of education, Lord Hailsham argued:

> Equality of opportunity in education or life does not mean either equality of performance or ability or uniformity of character. The object of education is to bring out differences just as much as to impose standards, and the democracy of the future will not be a drab mass of second-rate people in which distinction of intellect or character is described as eggheadness. It will be a society governed by its graduates — science and arts and social sciences —

and largely run by people who put public service in front of enjoyment, profit or leisure.[20]

By contrast, Socialists have viewed schools as institutions for changing society by reducing social differences. Ending segregation by academic ability in secondary schools is seen as a means to promoting social equality.

When secondary education was made compulsory by the 1944 Education Act, an examination at age 11-plus streamed pupils into separate schools according to academic ability, with about one-quarter attending academic grammar schools, where they were trained to pass external examinations qualifying for university entrance. The remainder were said to have failed, attending secondary modern schools giving an education for manual work or a routine white-collar job.

In 1965 a Labour government circular requested that all local authorities reorganize secondary education, abolishing the selective 11-plus examination. Although the circular met opposition from Conservative-controlled local education authorities, it has gradually become effective throughout the country. By 1982, only 3 percent of secondary pupils were in selective state grammar schools. The comprehensive school is now the norm for this generation of youths. But any effects of this change can work through society only slowly, for most voters will be products of the old selective system until about the year 2000.

Status in Education. Secondary schools discriminate by social status as well as intelligence. Today, about 6 percent of young people are in public schools, that is, private, fee-paying schools independent of the state. Most of these schools are chosen by parents in the belief that the schools offer a better formal academic education than neighboring state schools.[21] Whereas Americans may seek better education for their children by moving to a superior suburban school district, the limited variation within the state system causes English parents to seek a better education by paying private tuition. If only because they do not have to take students of all abilities, private schools usually have more students who do well in examinations.

Within the category of private schools are a small number

of extremely prestigious male public boarding schools, such as Eton, Harrow, and Winchester. The public schools developed to provide youths from well-to-do homes an education considered appropriate to a gentleman, emphasizing character, good manners, and sports as much as or more than intellectual achievement. Today, public schools continue to attract some pupils whose parents value their social status as much as educational achievements. One school, Eton, has become well known for producing a very disproportionate number of Conservative MPs, Cabinet ministers, and Prime Ministers. But most former public school students seek careers in industry or commerce, which offer a far greater number of job opportunities.[22]

Higher education further differentiates young people, for only one in four youths leaving secondary school goes on to further study, and only 8 percent of all young people follow a degree course at a university or polytechnic.[23] By comparison with America, England has few universities. As recently as 1956, half of English university students were attending one of three institutions: Oxford, Cambridge, or the University of London. A university degree was not required for entering business, for a commission in the army, or to become a lawyer. In the 1960s, rising birthrates and demand for higher education resulted in the creation of many new institutions: sixteen of the thirty-four English universities were founded between 1961 and 1967. New institutions cannot claim the social prestige of ancient institutions but they can compete academically.

State-financed scholarships, scaled according to the financial needs of students, have meant that graduates are today far more numerous than before. To be a graduate is no longer synonymous with being well born or a gentleman. Moreover, young people who have not attended a university face new barriers to career advancement, for professions formerly open to them today usually recruit only graduates. One writer describes the new class of state-financed graduates as a meritocracy.[24]

Home Influence Stronger than Schools. The stratification of English education has encouraged many social scientists to study the political attitudes of students, expecting to find that differences in schooling have a strong influence upon youthful political attitudes. The research demonstrates the opposite. Schools have a limited influence on youthful political outlooks compared to the family and class backgrounds of students.[25] The concept of citizenship, based on equality independent of educational achievement, dominates political learning. A young person learns more about common rights and duties of citizens than about differences in political roles.

The most striking evidence that home counts more than school was found in a survey conducted by Ted Tapper among students in a variety of English secondary schools from the most prestigious to the least. Young persons did differ in their partisanship, but parental influence explained 41 percent of the variance, whereas differences between schools accounted for only 2 percent of the variance. In determining youthful political interest, parental interest in politics is more important, explaining 13 percent of the variance.[26] Belief in the possibility of a political career was found among pupils in all types of schools. Parents and school together could explain only 8 percent of the variance. Equality of political opportunity is thus an ideal widely diffused among schools unequal in their educational character.[27]

Students at universities are volatile in their political outlooks. In the 1960s, surveys found more students ready to support Labour than would be expected of a largely middle-class group. Differences between students in different faculties were also significant, with social scientists tending more toward Labour, and engineers to the Conservatives. In 1976 a nationwide student survey by MORI found that undergraduates were very much less pro-Labour than young people not at universities.[28] University teachers have tended to be pro-Labour, whereas primary school teachers are strongly Conservative.[29]

Once students leave the university, attitudes change. In the 1964 Labour Cabinet many members had been contemporaries of Prime Minister Harold Wilson at Oxford in the 1930s. But in their student days these Labour ministers had belonged to the Labour, Conservative, Liberal, and Communist parties. Harold Wilson was himself a Liberal.

Differences in schooling imply differences in adult life. These most obviously affect choice of occupation. A doctor or a teacher requires formal educational qualifications, whereas a businessman, a bookmaker, or a lorry driver does not. The literature of political socialization predicts that the more educational advantages one has, the more a person is expected to: (1) favor the party historically identified with the educationally advantaged, the Conservatives; and (2) participate in politics. Because education affects occupation, which in turn affects position in the class structure, it can be important indirectly as well as directly.

The cumulative effect of greater postwar educational opportunity has been to eliminate any consistent influence of education upon party preference. In 1970 within each social class, those with more education were more likely to favor the Conservatives, and those with less, the Labour party. But further education for the offspring of Labour-voting working-class parents has created a significant fraction of middle-class people with non-Conservative loyalties. In 1983 there was a tendency within the middle class for persons with further education to favor the Alliance, and for Conservative support to be highest among middle-class persons with only a minimum of education. But in the working class, voters with a minimum of education favored Labour.[30]

Education does have a significant influence upon active participation in politics, even though there are some politicians without formal educational qualifications, and only a minority of the most educated go into politics. As one rises up the career ladder, an educational qualification becomes increasingly important. Persons with only a minimum of education constitute nearly three-quarters of the electorate but less than half of local government councillors, and less than one-tenth of MPs, ministers, and administrative civil servants.[31]

The 4 percent with a university degree constitute more than half the MPs, ministers, and high-ranking civil servants. The preeminence of university graduates among the ranks of senior civil servants is expected, because these officials are recruited by competitive examinations. But even though the House of Commons has no formal educational qualification, education also eases entry. The Labour party, claiming to represent working-class interests, draws more than half its MPs and ministers from the very small fraction of its supporters who are university graduates.

Because education in England often reflects social status as well as formal learning, the influence of the two must be separately assessed. Active politicians can be assigned to one of four groups, those whose education is prestigious and meritocratic (attended both public school and university), purely prestigious (public school only), purely meritocratic (grammar school and university), or lacking both prestige and high merit.

Table V.3 emphasizes the differences between Conservative and Labour politicians, as well as between politicians and those who elect them. Leading civil servants are university graduates; a majority also have a prestigious secondary education. The median Conservative MP and minister has "jam on one side and butter on the other," that is, a public school education and a university degree. It is a sign of social change that this proportion is substantially lower among Conservative MPs first elected in 1983, and the meritocratic Conservative MPs are becoming more numerous. Alliance MPs have a background more nearly resembling the Conservative than Labour MPs. Almost half of Labour MPs have no education to brag about,

TABLE V.3 *Prestige and Merit in the Education of Politicians*

Type of education	MPs			Ministers		Admin. civil servants
	Con. %	Labour %	Alliance %	Con. %	Labour %	%
Merit and prestige	53	14	39	67	22	56
Pure merit	18	36	26	24	65	44
Pure prestige	17	0	13	0	4	—[a]
Neither	12	49	22	9	8	—[a]
Number	397	209	23	21	23	—[a]

[a]In default of full details, all civil servants are classified as if graduates.
Sources: MPs derived from D. E. Butler and Dennis Kavanagh, *The British General Election of 1983* (London: Macmillan, 1984), p. 235; ministers calculated by the author from *Who's Who* data on Conservatives of Cabinet rank appointed in 1983 and Labour Cabinet ministers appointed in October 1974. Civil servants include persons promoted from lower ranks; based on *The Fulton Committee*, vol. III (1), pp. 64 ff.

whether in terms of prestige or merit. But most Labour Cabinet ministers have an education that is meritorious. James Callaghan has complained that his life was "less complete than it might be" because he had not gone to a university.[32] When Callaghan constituted his Cabinet as Prime Minister in 1976, more than three-quarters of his Labour appointees were graduates.

CLASS

To speak of class is to invoke an idea as diffuse as it is meant to be pervasive, for it is sometimes used to label the cumulative effect of all socialization experiences. Occupation is the most common indicator of class in England, and will be employed henceforth in this study. But to group people by one economic attribute does not mean that they are identical in every other respect. Whereas a coal miner usually lives in a mining village where his occupation is part of a network of social relations with family, friends, and neighbors, most social relationships of an electrician working in central London but living in a suburb are divorced from work.

Nearly every definition of occupational class places almost two-thirds of English people in the working class, and one-third in the middle class.[33] It is also important to distinguish differences among nonmanual workers. The handful of upper-class people living solely on inherited capital is politically less significant than the 5 percent of upper-middle-class people in leading positions in the professions, large organizations, and government. The middle middle class, which holds less important positions in business and industry, is numerically larger but politically less important. The lower middle class, holding routine white-collar jobs, is larger than the other two sections of the middle class. Studies of voting and political recruitment show differences between the upper middle class and lower middle class. Within the working class, sociologists often discriminate among skilled, semiskilled, and unskilled groups.

Does Class Equal Party? For most of the twentieth century political behavior and party competition in England have been interpreted in terms of class equals party. The Conservative party has been perceived as the party of middle-class interests supported by middle-class voters, and the Labour Party as the party of working-class interests supported by working-class voters. This viewpoint was summed up by Peter Pulzer thus: "Class is the basis of British party politics all else is embellishment and detail."[34]

Party politicians did not entirely accept the idea that class equals party, for Conservatives sought working-class votes and won a minority share, and Labour sought middle-class votes, and won a minority share. But at election after election, the broad picture remained the same: the majority of the middle class voted Conservative, and the majority of the working class voted Labour. The fit was not perfect; if it had been, Labour would have won every election, because the majority of the electorate consists of manual workers. Whereas Marxist interpretations emphasize the potential for conflict between classes, English politicians usually treat class differences as bargainable.

A generation of rigorous academic analysis of party competition has shown the class-equals-party model of voting to be limited in validity. Two alternative interpretations have emerged. A major study in the 1960s by Butler and Stokes emphasized the importance of parental influence upon party loyalties by their offspring. Insofar as adults' current occupational class tended to reflect parental class this was not a denial of the influence of occupational class. An alternative approach, propounded by Richard Rose, has emphasized the importance of such socioeconomic influences as trade union membership and housing choice. By contrast with the relatively deterministic Butler-Stokes emphasis upon influences from the past, the lifestyle approach emphasizes influences that can fluctuate with social change, and allows a significant scope for voluntary choice by individuals.[35]

The 1983 British general election provided a particularly strong test for the class-equals-party model and for theories of intergenerational determinism. The emergence of the Alliance party with an explicit appeal to "break the mould," offered voters a choice that did not fit the old two-class, two-party model. Futhermore, the Alliance challenge came after a twenty-five-year period in which the influence of occupational class had been steadily declining.[36]

A Model Rejected. The 1983 election departed from the pattern of electoral behavior since 1945, for it had no consistent correlation between class and party (Table V.4). The success of the Alliance in winning almost as big a popular vote as Labour demonstrated the limits of intergenerational influences. The middle class did tend to favor the Conservatives, but in no sense could the Conservatives be described as the exclusive choice of the middle-class voters, winning only four out of seven votes, and in the lower middle class hardly half the vote. The Alliance came second among the middle-class electorate.

The working-class was very divided in 1983. Among skilled manual workers, who enjoy many of the consumer benefits formerly associated with the middle class but continue to work with their hands, the Conservatives finished ahead of the Labour party, 40 to 31 percent. Among unskilled workers and those living on welfare state benefits, the Labour party finished ahead of the Conservatives, 42 to 31 percent. The inadequacy of the old class-equals-party model is emphasized by the fact that overall in the working-class votes divided 36 percent Conservative, 36 percent Labour, and 26 percent Alliance. No party could claim to represent a majority of manual workers.

The class-equals-party model could still apply if the competing parties each drew an overwhelming number of votes from one class only. But this is not the case. In 1983 the Conservative vote was drawn in almost equal numbers from the middle class and the working class, and the Alliance vote was

TABLE V.4 *The Relation of Class to Party Preferences, 1983*

Class	Conservative %	Labour %	Alliance %	As % of electorate
Solid middle class	62	12	24	15
Lower middle class	52	18	28	24
Skilled working class	40	31	27	31
Unskilled working class	31	42	24	30

Source: Calculated by the author from merged Gallup Poll surveys during the 1983 election.

drawn in equal proportions from the middle class and the working class (Table V.5). These patterns of support have persisted for many elections among Conservatives and Liberals. By contrast, nearly four-fifths of Labour's vote came from manual workers. But Labour could not claim to be the party of the working class, for it won little more than one-third of the votes of manual workers. Labour appears as a working class party only because it so failed to win middle-class support. In 1983, divisions within the working class were of far more political significance than divisions between classes.

The class-equals-party model was derived from a particular period of England's past, the process of industrialization described by Karl Marx, who wrote his magnum opus in nineteenth-century London. It was made the basis of electoral organization by the Labour party from the First World War, replacing earlier party divisions based on urban-rural and religious differences. Enormous changes, both social and political, have occurred since the publication of *Das Kapital* in 1867; since the first successful effort of unions to elect a working-class representative to Parliament in the 1880s, and since the emergence of the Labour party as the second party in Britain in 1922. It is hardly surprising that in the 1980s the model no longer fits England.

Today, the social difference most salient to party choice is housing.[37] People who own their homes (or are buying a home on a mortgage) are disproportionately Conservatives; homeowners now constitute three-fifths of the electorate. By contrast, people who live in council houses built and rented by local authorities, nearly 30 percent of the electorate, are disproportionately Labour. The importance of where you live is

TABLE V.5 *Party Support by Class, 1983*

	Conservative %	Labour %	Alliance %	Total electorate %
Middle Class	50	21	40	39
Working Class	50	79	60	61

Source: Calculated by the author from merged Gallup Poll surveys conducted during the 1983 election.

so great that it divides manual workers. Nearly half of all
working-class homeowners voted Conservative in 1983,
whereas a majority of working-class council tenants voted Labour. The influence of housing has been strong for nearly two
decades.

The electoral importance of housing derives from the distinctiveness of British housing. Council houses are concentrated in more or less self-contained neighborhoods. About five-
sixths of council tenants are working class. With the spread of
home ownership, council tenants increasingly represent a re-
sidual category of manual workers, those with insufficient income or inclination to buy their own home, thus differing from
the more affluent or upwardly aspiring manual workers. On a
council estate with very few middle-class people, Labour voting
is the norm; little support is voiced for the Conservatives. This
norm is reinforced by the fact that rents are set by elected local
councils. The Labour party is perceived as the party more sympathetic to building council houses, and keeping council house
rents low.

England today still has a class structure, but it is no more a
simple two-class structure than there is a simple two-party system. At least four different classes are politically salient: the
upper middle class, where Conservative support is normal; the
lower middle class, where Conservatives lead but do not dominate; and, within the *working class,* a group of Conservative-
voting *prosperous homeowners,* and a stratum of Labour-voting
lower-wage council house tenants. An occupational measure of class
is now too crude to catch the most salient political nuances of
social class, as defined by T. H. Marshall: "The essence of
social class is the way a man is treated by his fellows (and reciprocally, the way he treats them), not the qualities or the
possessions which cause that treatment."[38]

Overall, more than half of the electorate did *not* vote for
the party associated with their class; in 1983 middle-class
Conservative supporters and working-class Labour supporters
together accounted for only 47 percent of the vote. One explanation for this is that votes are principally determined by party
identification and attitudes toward issues.[39] But this begs the

question: To what extent does class influence attitudes toward issues and party identification?

Limits of the Influence of Class. The link between class models of politics and party preference is limited for at least three reasons. First of all, whereas 96 percent can readily identify their parents' class, awareness of class origins is not translated into an active consciousness of class today. When the same people are asked if they think of themselves as belonging to a particular class, only 32 percent say they think of themselves as working class, and 21 percent as middle class. Half do not think of themselves as belonging to a particular class.[40]

Secondly, class is no longer perceived as very important in social relations. When the 1979 British Election Study asked people whether or not they thought it would be difficult to have friends in other classes, 67 percent said it would make no difference, 22 percent a little difference, and only 6 percent saw it as making a lot of difficulties. Similarly, when the Gallup Poll has asked people to describe good things and bad things about each class, 55 percent can find no faults in the middle class and 50 percent no faults in the working class. When asked to describe good qualities, 62 percent can find nothing good to say about the middle class, and 47 percent nothing good to say about the working class. Most people today lack a clearly defined image of class.[41]

Thirdly, and most important, even when there is an awareness of class differences, these are not normally translated into a sense of class grievances leading to conflict. Only 6 percent told the 1979 British Election Study that they thought that everyone should have much the same wage, regardless of their skill or responsibility. More than five-sixths think that people who get ahead in life do so because of their ability. Only one in ten think that social background is of primary importance in getting ahead in Britain today. Butler and Stokes found that less than one-tenth of the electorate overall see politics in terms of opposing class interests.[42]

The influence of class is most apparent when one examines the family background of politicians. Educational data show that most Conservative MPs come from comfortably middle-class homes. Politics neither raises nor lowers their occupational status. The Labour party, by contrast, has always drawn a significant proportion of its MPs from working-class families. Educational changes since the Second World War have created a third type of Labour MP, a person born into a working-class home but with an ensured middle-class career thanks to a university education. The administrative civil service draws disproportionately from middle-class families, because it recruits primarily from the universities, whose students are disproportionately from middle-class homes.

The higher the political office, the greater the likelihood that it will be filled by someone who has always had a middle-class job. About one-sixth of the nation is employed in professional or managerial tasks, but more than three-quarters of all MPs come from higher social strata, being lawyers, teachers, journalists, or businessmen by occupation. Whereas more than three-fifths of the electorate is working-class, 11 percent of MPs started life as manual workers.

The Parliamentary Labour party's composition shows how even a party dedicated to advancing the interests of manual workers draws representatives from secure middle-class homes and from upwardly mobile homes. In terms of class background, Labour MPs divide into three groups: those from middle-class homes; those who rose by educational achievement into the middle-class through education; and those who started life as manual workers but rose through political activity in the Labour movement, and confirmed their middle-class status by becoming MPs. Today, more than half of Labour MPs sponsored by trade unions have been middle-class by occupation, rather than manual workers.[43]

Voters view their representatives in terms of party labels, not class characteristics. A National Opinion Polls survey found that a majority rejects the idea that class interests are defined by the social characteristics of their MP. Voters think it more important that an MP should live in his constituency than that the MP should be of the same class as most of the people who vote for him.

THE CUMULATIVE EFFECT

By comparison with many European countries, the most distinctive feature of political socialization in England is that there are few institutions dividing citizens into politically distinctive groups. In Belgium, Canada, and Switzerland, language creates a gulf in communication between communities. In the Netherlands, Northern Ireland, and until recently in France and Italy, religious differences have divided society into groups of believers and unbelievers or Protestants and Catholics. There is nothing in England comparable to the historic division between races in the United States.[44]

The degree of social homogeneity within England is also underscored by comparison with other nations of the United Kingdom. Language socializes Welsh people into two different groups. In Scotland, the division of youths into separate Catholic and non-Catholic schools emphasizes differences of religion. In Northern Ireland differences of religion are compounded by conflicts of national identity. By contrast, nearly everyone in England speaks English, is indifferent to religion, and lives in or near an urban area. Since England constitutes 83 percent of the population of the United Kingdom, divisions important in many countries are here sources of a common experience.

Class differences have been considered important because they are the only substantial division within English society. Like every other industrial society, England has a social structure divided into manual and nonmanual workers. But class differences have not translated into political differences to the degree implied by much social theory and political rhetoric. The largest group in the electorate — white urban manual workers of the dominant Protestant religion (that is, Church of England or nonconformist) — divide their support almost evenly between the Conservatives and Labour.[45]

In the course of a lifetime, socialization processes subject every person to a great variety of experiences, some emphasizing differences and others an identity of interests. Politically important influences can be grouped under two headings: *for-*

mative influences in the family, including parental class, parental party preference, and education; and *contemporary* influences, such as current occupational class, housing, union membership, and so forth. One academic tradition, rooted in social psychology, emphasizes the importance of formative influences. Another tradition, dominant in Britain, emphasizes current socioeconomic influences.

The relative importance of formative as against contemporary influences upon individual partisanship can be tested statistically by using AID (the Automatic Interaction Detector) to measure the amount of variation in current party preference explained by each. The impact of formative influences is calculated first; the additional impact of contemporary influences is then added.

Two-thirds of the explained variation in party preference can be accounted for by formative influences (Table V.6). Father's class and parent's party preference together account for more than half the variance explained. Neither generation nor sex explains as much as 1 percent of variation. Attendance at school beyond the required minimum has little additional effect upon party preference. Among contemporary influences, where one lives is more important than how one works; owner-occupiers are more often Conservative, and council tenants very heavily Labour.

Collectively, all these influences explain nearly one-third of voters' two-party preferences. But this also means that 68.3 percent must be explained by other factors independent of the socialization influences discussed here. One reason English people do not vote strictly along class lines is that a majority have no set of socialization experiences consistent with ideal-type definitions of class. Models of class determinism presuppose that working-class people have a minimum education, a trade union member in the family, and rent their homes. Middle-class people are expected to have had more than the minimum of education, not to belong to a trade union, and to own their homes.

In fact, only one English person in five conforms exactly to the ideal-type criteria of class.[46] Middle-class people are more likely to conform to their class stereotype than are manual

TABLE V.6 *The Cumulative Effect of Socialization Experiences*

	Division	Conservative % two-party vote	% Variation explained at each stage
Formative influences			
1. Generation	Born before 1935	48	0.4
	Born 1935 or after		
2. Sex	Male	43	0.2
	Female	48	
3. Father's class	Middle	69	9.2
	Working	36	
4. Father's party	Conservative	73	9.9
	Labour	25	
	Other or none	55	
5. Religion	Church of England	55	2.1
	Other	41	
6. Education	Academic	66	1.2
	Minimum	37	
			(23.0)
Contemporary influences			
7. Current class	Middle	62	2.4
	Working	29	
8a. Housing	Owners	61	5.5
	Tenants	29	
8b. Union membership	Yes	28	0.8
	No	60	
8c. Nation	England	48	0.0
	Non-England	31	
			(8.7)
Total variation explained			31.7

Source: October 1974 British Election Survey, analyzed by the author with AID III. The first seven items were entered in turn, to simulate their order of occurrence in the socialization process.

workers. As the number of reinforcing class characteristics increase, the likelihood of an individual's favoring the party of that class increases. In 1983, 69 percent of upper-middle-class voters with all the stereotypical characteristics of that class voted Conservative, as against 6 percent favoring Labour; in the lower middle class the ratio was 66 percent to 8 percent. Among working-class voters, 58 percent with all the stereotype manual worker characteristics favored Labour, more than twice the national average. But these groups are *atypical* of their own class:

only one-seventh of manual workers now conform to their class stereotype, and less than one-third of the middle class.

Youthful socialization is relatively important in recruiting a small proportion of persons for political offices. As one goes up the ladder of officeholders, the social distinctiveness of politicians increases. National politicians are better born, better educated, and have held jobs of higher status than the average voter. Yet the same evidence also shows that whatever their social origins, no one is barred from seeking office. Socialization experiences produce differences in degree, not in kind. Moreover, the majority of middle-class male university graduates, the group most predisposed to enter politics, do not seek public office.

Among active political participants, intensive socialization into the role of politician tends to override other influences. This is illustrated by what happens when an opposition party enters office. A newly elected Cabinet can alter policies of government, but accesssion to office also alters the politicians. Lord Balneil, heir to one of the oldest titles in Britain, has said that patterns of politics are preserved "not so much by the conscious efforts of the well established, but by the zeal of those who have just won entry, and by the hopes of those who still aspire."[47]

Political socialization influences the probabilities of political action: it does not produce certainties. Because socialization is continuous, individuals remain open to change in their political outlooks at any time in adult life. The likelihood of change depends upon an individual's involvement in politics. For most people pre-adult and parapolitical influences are likely to be important. They are carried forward by inertia in whatever political role they find themselves. They have enough interest and knowledge to vote, but not enough involvement to take up new political roles and ideas readily.

Political events can force a major change in individual behavior, whatever the formative influences. For example, the collapse of the Liberal party after the First World War forced many people raised in Liberal homes to find a party different from their parents in default of a Liberal candidate in their constituency. In international affairs, events in the 1930s and

1940s forced politicians to think of Germany as an enemy and Russia as an ally, and then to reverse these labels.

The decline in class-based support for parties shows that past socialization experiences predispose but do not predetermine political behavior. Loyalties to institutions formed in one era need not continue for a lifetime. Parties find that onetime supporters may deem them inappropriate in changing circumstances. The 1983 election showed how contemporary political influences can override long-term socialization. But the party identification of voters still shows long-term persistence. In 1983, the new Liberal-Social Deomocratic Party Alliance won nearly as many votes as the Labour party. However, the Labour party, with more than sixty years of active electioneering behind, had the party identification of twice as many voters as the Alliance party. The Alliance needs to convert short-term 1983 support into long-term party loyalty, and Labour needs to remove short-term liabilities in order to reclaim the votes of long-term identifiers.

NOTES

1. See Rose, *Governing Without Consensus,* chapter 11, and James L. Russell, *Socialization into Conflict* (Glasgow: University of Strathclyde Ph.D. thesis, 1974).

2. Cf. Hilde Himmelweit, Marianne Jaeger Biberian, and Janet Stockdale, "Memory for Past Vote: Implications of a Study of Bias in Recall," *British Journal of Political Science,* 8:3 (1978), pp. 365–375; and Richard S. Katz, Richard G. Niemi, and David Newman, "Reconstructing Past Partisanship in Britain," *British Journal of Political Science,* 10:4 (1980), pp. 505–515.

3. Cf. Sir Anthony Wagner, "Hereditary Peers Defended," *The Times* (London), 30 January 1969; and National Opinion Polls, *Monthly Bulletin* (June 1972), p. 27.

4. Quoted from "The Family Background of Harold Wilson," in Rose, ed., *Studies in British Politics,* 3rd ed., p. 192.

5. Calculated from data in the October 1974 British Election Survey, variables 4:49, 4:50.

6. For survey data on religion and voting, see Richard Rose, "Britain: Simple Abstractions and Complex Realities," in R. Rose, ed., *Electoral Behavior: A Comparative Handbook* (New York: Free Press, 1974), p. 518. For ecological analysis, see William L. Miller and Gillian Raab, "The Religious Alignment at English Elections between 1918 and 1970," *Political Studies,* 25:2 (1977). For historical background, see also Kenneth Wald, *Crosses on the Ballot* (Princeton: Princeton University Press, 1983).

7. See e.g., Richard Rose, "Britain: Simple Abstractions and Complex Realities," p. 521; Paul R. Abramson, "Generational Change and Continuity in British Partisan Choice," *British Journal of Political Science,* 6:3 (1976);

and Ivor Crewe, Bo Sarlvik, and James Alt, "Partisan Dealignment in Britian, 1964–1974," *British Journal of Political Science,* 7:2 (1977), pp. 161 ff.

8. See Marsh, *Protest and Political Consciousness,* especially chapters 3 and 8.

9. David Butler and Donald Stokes, *Political Change in Britain* (London: Macmillan, 1974 2nd ed.), chapter 3.

10. See the Gallup Poll, "Voting Behaviour in Britain, 1945–1974," in R. Rose, ed., *Studies in British Politics,* 3rd ed.; *Gallup Political Index* No. 275 (July 1983), p. 4; and MORI, *British Public Opinion: General Election 1983* (London: MORI, final report, 1983), pp. 21 ff.

11. See Elizabeth Vallance, "Writing Women Back In," *Political Studies,* 30:4 (1982), pp. 582–590, and the books cited therein.

12. See Howard Morrison, "Employment in the Public and Private Sectors, 1976–82," *Economic Trends,* No. 352 (February 1983).

13. See Stephen L. Bristow, articles in *County Councils Gazette* (November, December, 1978).

14. See Elizabeth Vallance, *Women in the House* (London: University of London Press, 1979), and "Women in the House of Commons," *Political Studies,* 29:3 (1981), pp. 407–414; Jill Hills, "Candidates, the Impact of Gender," *Parliamentary Affairs,* 34:2 (1981), pp. 221–228; and Vicky Randall, *Women and Politics* (London: Macmillan, 1982).

15. R. E. Dowse and J. A. Hughes, "Girls, Boys and Politics," *British Journal of Sociology,* 22:1 (1971).

16. NOP, *Review* (London: NOP Market Research No. 46, February, 1984), pp. 14 ff.

17. On women in the civil service, see the Fulton Committee, *The Civil Service,* vol. 3.2 (London: HMSO, 1968). More generally, see M. Fogarty et al., *Women in Top Jobs, 1968–1979* (London: Heinemann, 1981).

18. On civic education, see *Teaching Politics,* the journal of the Politics Association (a body of secondary school teachers) and its report, *Political Education and Political Literacy* (London: Longmans, 1978).

19. The discussion that follows explicitly excludes Wales, where education has historically been valued differently and language presents separate issues, and Scotland, where education is organized differently, both on academic grounds and by state-supported segregation by religion.

20. "A Society Governed by Graduates," *The Times* (London), 24 January 1962. For the viewpoint of ministers, see Maurice Kogan, *The Politics of Education* (Harmondsworth: Penquin, 1971). Cf. Paul E. Peterson, "British Interest Group Theory Re-examined," *Comparative Politics,* 3:3 (1971); and Raphaella Bilski, "Ideology and the Comprehensive Schools," *Political Quarterly,* 44: 2 (1973).

21. See Tessa Blackstone and Irene Fox, "Why People Choose Private Schools," *New Society,* 29 June 1978.

22. See S. G. Danks, "Destination of last year's school-leavers," *Careers Bulletin* (Camberley: a publication of ISCO, the Independent Schools Careers Organisation, no. 161, 1976), pp. 10–17; and, historically, T. J. H. Bishop with Rupert Wilkinson, *Winchester and the Public School: A Statistical Analysis* (London: Faber & Faber, 1967).

23. For statistics on educational achievement, see the annual HMSO publication *Social Trends,* from which data cited here are taken.

24. See Michael Young, *The Rise of the Meritocracy* (Harmondsworth: Penguin, 1961).

25. For a socialization study of young people that also interviewed parents, see Robert E. Dowse and John Hughes, "The Family, the School and the Political Socialization Process," in Rose, ed., *Studies in British Politics,* 3rd ed. The book includes a detailed bibliography of articles at pp. 514–521.

26. In addition, youthful commitment to further education, reflecting intelligence more than the school environment, explained a further 12.5 percent of the variance in political interest.

27. All findings from Tapper's work are based on this author's AID analysis of the original data, weighted to adjust numbers of respondents to proportions in different types of secondary schools at the time of fieldwork. For Tapper's account, see Ted Tapper, *Young People and Society* (London: Faber & Faber, 1971).

28. See "Unmilitant," *The Economist,* 23 October 1976.

29. See *Teachers in the British General Election of October 1974* (London: Times Newspapers, 1975), and National Opinion Polls, *Review,* No. 13 (February 1978), p. 24, and "Alliance Gains but Tories stay well in front," *Times Education Supplement,* 27 May 1983.

30. See Rose, "Britain: Simple Abstractions and Complex Realities," table 10, and author's analysis of 1983 Gallup Poll election surveys.

31. For further details, see Richard Rose, *Politics in England: An Interpretation for the 1980s* (London: Faber & Faber, 1980), table V.3.

32. "Farmer Jim from the JC Ranch," *The Guardian,* 6 June 1970; Cf. Martin Burch and Michael Moran, "Who Are the New Tories?" *New Society,* 11 October 1984.

33. The system of classification used here is that standard to market research in Britain: groups A, B, and C1 constituting the middle class, and C2, D, and E constituting manual workers. For distinctions by sociologists that are not necessarily relevant politically, see e.g. J. H. Goldthorpe, *Social Mobility and Class Structure in Modern Britian* (Oxford: Clarendon Press, 1980).

34. See Peter Pulzer, *Political Representation and Elections in Britain* (London: Allen & Unwin, 1967), p. 98. For a review of evidence showing how limited is the reality of this generalization, see Richard Rose, *Class Does Not Equal Party: The Decline of a Model of British Voting* (Glasgow: U. of Strathclyde Studies in Public Policy, No. 74, 1980).

35. Cf. Butler and Stokes, *Political Change in Britain,* 2nd ed.; Rose, "Britain: Simple Abstractions and Complex Realities," pp. 523–533; and Rose, *Class Does Not Equal Party,* pp. 45ff. Patrick Dunleavy has tried to refute these approaches, while tending to confirm the latter. Cf. Dunleavy, "The Urban Basis of Political Alignment," *British Journal of Political Science,* 9:4 (1979), pp. 409–444 and the analyses by Martin Harrop, "The Urban Basis of Political Alignment: A Comment," ibid., 10:3 (1980), pp. 388–398, and M. N. Franklin and E. C. Page, "A Critique of the Consumption Cleavage Approach in British Voting Studies," *Political Studies* 32,4 (1984), 521–536.

36. See Richard Rose, "From Simple Determinism to Interactive Models of Voting: Britain as an Example," *Comparative Political Studies,* 15:2 (1982), pp. 145–169.

37. See Rose, "From Simple Determinism to Interactive Models of Voting," table 4, and Jonathan Kelley, Ian McAllister, and Anthony Mughan, *The Decline of Class Revisited* (Glasgow: U. of Strathclyde Studies in Public Policy No. 135, 1984).

38. T. H. Marshall, *Citizenship and Social Class* (Cambridge: Cambridge University Press, 1950), p. 92.

39. See the emphasis in Bo Sarlvik and Ivor Crewe, *Decade of Dealignment* (Cambridge: Cambridge University Press, 1983).

40. Calculated from *British Electron Survey 1983,* Qs. 73, 78.

41. *Ibid.,* and *Gallup Political Index,* No. 261 (May 1982), pp. 11f; see also NOP, *Bulletin,* No. 109 (June 1972), pp. 17–18 for similar findings a decade earlier.

42. Martin Harrop, "Popular Conceptions of Mobility," *Sociology,* 14:1 (1980), pp. 88–98; Butler and Stokes, *Political Change in Britain,* 2nd ed., pp. 90 ff.

43. See Byron Criddle, "Candidates," in D. Butler and D. Kavanagh, *The British General Election of 1983* (London: Macmillan, 1984), p. 234.

44. Richard Rose and Derek Urwin, "Social Cohesion, Political Parties and Strains in Regimes," *Comparative Political Studies,* 2:1 (1969).

45. Rose, *Class Does Not Equal Party,* table 26.

46. Ibid., Table 14, and author's calculations from 1983 Gallup Poll election surveys. For a contextual analysis, see Elizabeth Bott, *Family and Social Network* (London: Tavistock, 1957).

47. Lord Balniel, "The Upper Classes," *The Twentieth Century,* No. 999 (1960), p. 432.

CHAPTER VI

Recruiting Participants

The principle of popular government is that the supreme power, the determining efficacy in matters political, resides in the people — not necessarily or commonly in the whole people, in the numerical majority, but in a chosen people, a picked and selected people. It is so in England.

POLITICAL PARTICIPATION REFLECTS individual aspirations and institutional opportunities. While every citizen is formally eligible to participate in politics, in a free society no one is compelled to participate. Furthermore, the institutions of representative government set very strict limits on the scope for individual participation. Everyone has the right to vote, but only 650 people can be MPs at any one time, and elective offices in local government are fewer than the proportion of persons with political aspirations.[1]

In the recruitment of politicians, the office comes before the individual. The institutions of British government define the jobs for which politicians can compete. An individual wanting to be somebody in politics in England must follow already laid down career lines: first to become active in party politics, then to become an MP, and finally to become a Cabinet minister. While political ambitions may be similar on both sides of the Atlantic, the offices that people seek and the methods used to win office are different, being shaped by national institutions.

An individual's political career depends first of all on his or her ability to do what is expected. These expectations are less the product of individual character than they are a reflection of political institutions. Even an individual with as strong a personality as Margaret Thatcher had no chance to impose her views on government until after more than thirty years in party politics.

Once active in politics, whether full time, intermittently, or as a volunteer, a person undergoes intensive socialization into a political role. This experience differentiates all politicians, whatever their social origins, from nonpoliticians. Political socialization in the family, in school, or at work influences predispositions. Role socialization within political institutions, such as parties, local government, or Parliament, is on-the-job learning.

Before asking who participates in politics we must ask: *How* can people participate in politics in England? The chief political offices open to aspiring politicians are of three different types. First there are elective offices in local government or as a Member of Parliament, which in turn can be a stepping stone to becoming a Cabinet minister. Secondly, there are offices in the senior civil service, where an individual has a permanent, albeit anonymous, position inside Whitehall. Thirdly, there is scope for people to be intermittent politicians, affecting public policy while in such jobs as a newspaper editor, trade union official, or banker, or temporarily taking a public post as a part-time member of a government commission or partisan advisor to the government of the day.

The process of political recruitment is inherently discriminatory: a large number of people end up in peripheral political roles, and a small number occupy leading offices. The first section of this chapter examines the roles of individuals for whom political participation is, at most, an occasional concern. Then, attention is focused upon the way in which a small number of people become involved in central political positions. The potential for converting high social or economic status into political office is the third topic of this chapter, which concludes by evaluating the political significance of a process that selects a few people into office, and leaves out the great majority.

THE PERIPHERAL PUBLIC

Everyone in English society has a multiplicity of roles, such as spouse and parent, worker and consumer, and taxpayer and beneficiary of public services. Most people do not view their lives in terms of what can be achieved in politics; therefore any analysis of political recruitment risks distorting the significance that individuals give to political activities. Instead of speaking of people as voters, it would make more sense to speak of the way ordinary individuals behave in electoral situations. The role of voter or citizen is not the chief role of people in England.

As Citizens. Consciously or not, nearly everyone in England participates in the political system. The great majority of English people are law-abiding subjects of the Crown. The readiness to follow the law of the land is crucial for the maintenance of political authority. When many people do so passively it is easy for government to exercise authority. Everyone who earns or spends money also contributes directly and indirectly to the cost of government by paying taxes on earnings and purchases.

Nearly every citizen participates in the contemporary welfare state as a beneficiary as well as a subject. Government provides a wide variety of benefits for individuals and families: health care from birth to old age, education in youth, a host of social services for families in trouble, often a council house, and a pension in old age. Government also provides many collective services, ranging from parks to military defense. So taken for granted are these familiar programs of the welfare state that they are often thought of as nonpolitical (*sic*). A person using a municipal swimming pool or an elderly person visiting a doctor does not think of himself or herself as participating in politics. Yet in both instances the services consumed are provided by government.

Representative institutions give every citizen at least three different ways of actively trying to influence government. First of all, a person can vote for candidates competing for public offices. Secondly, an individual can join a political party, and seek to influence the selection of candidates and the policies of the party, or join a pressure group that concentrates upon promoting a particular interest. Thirdly, an individual can approach an elected politician or a public official for assistance with a particular personal or neighborhood problem.

Local Politics. Local government offers unique opportunities for political participation to the peripheral public, because it is near at hand. To be involved in local government, a person does not need to give up a full-time job or travel to London. Furthermore, local government provides services that are immediately and visibly of concern, such as education, housing, roads, refuse collection, and social services. As many benefits of government are delivered by local government as by Whitehall ministries.[2]

Unlike the United States, England does not allow local electors to vote on a host of tax and bond issues or referendum questions, or for executive heads of local authority services. The only choice is the choice of a party to take responsibility for the local council.

Participation in local politics is very limited. Only about two in five voters bother to turn out to vote in local elections. In 1979, when district council elections were held the same day as a parliamentary election, the turnout was abnormally high, 77 percent; the following year, when there was no national election, turnout fell to 40 percent.[3] Thousands of councillors in small local authority areas are elected with little opposition. The proportion working for local authorities — about one in eight of the total labor force in Britain—is almost as numerous, and certainly more immediately influential, than those who regularly vote to elect the councils to which local employees are meant to be responsible.

A citizen is more likely to turn to paid officials of a local authority than to an elected councillor.[4] A survey estimates that one citizen in four contacts the local council office at least once a year. The problems that cause concern are such municipal services as housing, education, social services, and planning. In addition, some people are sporadic interventionists, becoming involved in local politics as and when an issue arises that concerns them directly, for example, a road problem on their housing estate, or an issue at the local primary school. They are stimulated to protest by a very local measure; when satisfied, they once again become politically inactive.[5]

About one person in twenty claims to have thought of becoming a candidate for local office, a figure roughly equal to the proportion who belong to a political party. But the number of people who are actually councillors at any one point in time is less than one-tenth of 1 percent. Activists do not stand in council elections for three major reasons: 36 percent say that they lack the time or the health to do the job, 32 percent lack the self-confidence and temperament, and 24 percent say they lack the knowledge or interest in local politics.[6]

A seat on the local council is the height of participation for an amateur politician. The job has no salary; councillors receive a daily attendance allowance, and many retain their everyday job. The average councillor spends more than twenty hours a week on political work, and leading councillors spend far more. Studies of local councillors find that most achieve great satisfaction from their work. Some see council work as a complement to other community activities; some see it as compensation for a dull job; others, such as retired persons and housewives, see council politics as a substitute for full-time employment. Because of the limited willingness of people to enter council politics, in most parts of the country a determined Conservative or Labour activist has a reasonable chance to become a councillor.

Increasing demands upon the time of councillors mean that many people cannot afford to hold local office. Conservatives are often well-to-do professional persons or own successful businesses. Labour councillors sometimes have been earning sufficiently little, being housewives, students or unemployed, so that the allowances paid councillors as expenses can provide an income to live on. Or a Labour councillor can have an employer, for example, a trade union or cooperative society, that will give staff time off to advance the Labour cause.[7]

Local pressure groups can be important on matters of limited local concern, but pressure groups are very much centralized to lobby in Whitehall.[8] This is true even of local authorities, which are banded into nationwide associations in efforts to influence Westminster politicians whose decisions affect all local government.

National Politics. Ironically, national politics is more likely to be the focus of individual political participation than is local politics. This is true even though the opportunity for one individual to exercise influence in an electorate of 42 million is much less than to exercise influence in a local electorate of 42,000. National politics is of primary concern to most people because institutions of government concentrate responsibility in Westminster. The media reinforce this, giving far more attention to Parliament and national political figures than to local events. In consequence, even local government elections now tend to reflect popular responses to nationwide trends in party politics more than specifically local conditions.[9]

A parliamentary election held about once every four years provides the chief (and for most, the only) occasion in which citizens actively participate in national politics. Almost every British citizen 18 years old or over is eligible to vote. Citizens of Commonwealth countries from Australia to Zambia and citizens of the Irish Republic are also entitled to vote while residing in Britain. The burden of registration is undertaken by local government officials; the register is revised annually. Election day is not a legal holiday, but widely dispersed polling stations, compact territory, and the individual citizen's sense of duty bring a high turnout of voters by American standards, although not by European standards.

In the eleven general elections since 1950, turnout has averaged 77.0 percent of the electoral register; adjusting for defects in this register, the average turnout is 80.8 percent. Many who do not vote in an election are prevented from doing so by temporary illness or holidays. There is no substantial group of people who persistently refuse to vote because of apathy or disaffection. Englishmen are well advised to vote when a parliamentary election is held. Casting a vote for one candidate for one seat in the House of Commons is the only chance there is to participate in a nationwide ballot.

In addition to being represented by a Member of Parliament, an individual can also be represented by belonging to organizations that seek to advance an interest by lobbying. Organizations are numbered in the tens of thousands, with a total membership in tens of millions, covering 61 percent of the electorate. But most organizations do not recruit members on political grounds, nor would they describe themselves as political organizations. Hence, the number belonging to organizations does not mean that more than half the population is actively trying to lobby Whitehall. The most common type of organization is a leisure, social, or sports club.

About one in five voters sees himself or herself as a member of an organization concerned with public issues, most often a trade union. Business groups are well organized, but their members are likely to be companies rather than individuals. Most issue groups are concerned with only a single cause. The smaller the interest group, the greater the scope for an individual to exercise influence within an organization. But small groups usually have less influence in Whitehall. One elector in seven reports holding an office or belonging to the local committee of an organization that has the potential to act as a political pressure group.[10]

Political parties provide another means by which individuals can participate in national politics. The Conservative and Labour parties have long maintained constituency associations throughout England, and the Liberals seek to do so. The parties have no restrictive entrance rules; they seek as many members as are willing to join. With a little effort, a person can become a ward secretary of a local party or a member of its general management committee. Political parties define membership by dues paid to constituency organizations.

The great majority of English people identify with a political party, but not so strongly that they become members. In the Labour party, 95 percent of the party's 6.5 million nominal members are affiliated by trade unions. Party dues are paid as part of union dues; trade unionists automatically become party members unless they take the trouble to contract out of their union's wholesale application to the Labour party. Many union members do not know that they belong to the Labour party, and some vote Conservative or Alliance. The Conservatives do not know how many members they have; estimates are that the party has about a million dues-payers. The Liberal Party's membership is the smallest of the three parties.[11] For most party members, paying annual dues is the extent of their participation in national politics.

The Social Democratic party, founded in 1981, has used modern technology to alter the idea of participation. The traditional English model of political participation is through an organization that has local branches affiliating to a headquarters. While local units are weak, they are meant to be centers of group activity. The SDP has been organized from the top down. Membership is solicited through national newspaper ads, and the party publicized principally through the press and television. Instead of soliciting members door-to-door locally, the SDP has solicited members through the mail. Instead of having constituency organizations, the SDP has a centralized computer register of all members in the country. Instead of a local affiliating to a London-based national organization, each member is directly linked by mail with London, and then assigned to an area group embracing several constituencies.

A variety of party and pressure-group organizations are kept alive by the efforts of a small number of political activists for whom politics is a principal avocation. A survey by Market and Opinion Research International (MORI) estimates that 7 percent of the electorate can be classified as political activists, taking part in at least five of ten common political activities such as voting, helping in fund-raising efforts, urging people to vote, holding office in an organization, and advising people to contact their MP, make public talks, and present their views to an MP. The activists are almost evenly divided among the parties. While not an exact social cross-section of the population, activists do include substantial numbers from all ages, classes, and educational backgrounds. MORI concludes that the activist is distinctive in what he or she *does* rather than for what he or she is.[12]

Ad hoc protest groups appear sporadically in local and national politics. Many reflect local interest in a single issue, such as a local council's failure to ensure pedestrian safety at a busy crossroads. The concentration of politics in London allows London-based protest groups to appear as nationwide organizations. In a metropolitan area of 16 million inhabitants, it is not difficult to attract hundreds of people to a protest meeting on almost any issue. One requires a cause, a speaker with a name or status, and money to hire a hall and advertise the meeting. Overall, only 6 percent of the electorate say they have taken part in a lawful street demonstration, and even fewer in illegal protests.[13]

The great majority of English people participate in national politics by voting, and a majority also belong to an organization (Table VI.1). The proportion regularly involved in politics is from 5 to 19 percent, depending upon the indicator selected. If holding elected office is the measure of being a politician, the proportion drops below 1 percent. By this standard, one could argue that the proportion of the adult population actively participating in politics in England today is scarcely higher than it was before democratic franchise reforms were enacted in the nineteenth century.

The line between politicians and those outside politics can be drawn in more than one place. If officers of organizations are considered to be at least intermittently politicians, because

TABLE VI.1 *Involvement in National Politics*

	Estimated number	*Estimated % adults*
Eligible electorate	42,000,000	98
Voters 1983	30,600,000	73
Organization members	24,000,000	61
Great deal of political interest	8,000,000	19
Official post in organization	5,500,000	14
Political activists	2,800,000	7
Protest demonstrations	2,500,000	6
Individual party members	2,000,000	5
MP, senior civil servant	4,000	0.01

Sources: Electorate and voters: Home Office. Organization members and officers, *The Local Government Elector* (London: Her Majesty's Stationery Office, 1967), pp. 113 ff. Political interest: SSRC *British Electoral Survey,* October 1974, Q. 44; Political activists: Robert M. Worcester, ''The Hidden Activists,'' *New Society,* June 8, 1972; Protest demonstrations: Alan C. Marsh, *Protest and Political Consciousness,* pp. 45 ff; Individual party members, MP, senior civil servant derived by author from official statistics and estimates.

190

Recruiting Participants

their representative status enables them to voice pressure-group demands, more than 5 million citizens are politicians. Even if one reduces the total to those who have run for election to local or national office, there remains the "as many as/but only" problem. Does one say: "as many as 2.8 million people are political activists"? or: "but only 2.8 million people are political activists"? Active participants in politics are a significant fraction of the Crown's subjects, but a limited fraction.

CENTRAL POLITICAL ROLES

Central political roles are held by three types of politicians: cabinet ministers, senior civil servants, and intermittent public persons. Members of Parliament are not central to government; they become so only by attaining ministerial office. Three characteristics are common in recruitment to central political roles.

Common Characteristics. First of all, experience is positively valued. Starting early in a political career is virtually a precondition for success. Civil servants normally enter Whitehall immediately after taking a university degree in their early twenties. Aspiring Cabinet ministers had better gain entry to the House of Commons in their late twenties or early thirties, because an MP must usually accumulate ten to twenty years seniority in the House of Commons before gaining a Cabinet post. Intermittent public persons also serve long apprenticeships before gaining political eminence. A trade union leader will usually enter his trade in adolescence and take thirty to forty years to reach the general secretaryship of a union. In making appointments to the chairmanship of government committees, Whitehall officials consider that sound judgment increases with age.

Second, persons who seek leading political roles are not expected to start at the bottom in local politics and work their way gradually to the top. Instead, early in a career an individual must gain "cadet" status (that is, a junior appointment high in the hierarchy), then gradually accumulate seniority and skill. The procedure might be described as working one's way sideways, inasmuch as seniority will carry a well-placed cadet politician a substantial distance forward. The method is most evident in the senior civil service, for no one is recruited from the ranks of local government. Similarly, Cabinet posts are not given to individuals because of their stature in local or regional politics, as might happen in a federal system such as America or Germany. Of MPs, 71 percent have not had any local government experience before election to Parliament, and it is even more rare for a Cabinet minister to have any firsthand experience of local government.[14] Whereas election to the local council is the high point of a peripheral citizen's career, becoming an MP is the starting point for a central political role.

A third influence upon recruitment is geographic. Members of Parliament, senior civil servants, and most intermittent public persons spend their working life in London. MPs are not required to have lived in the constituency that nominates them or to take up residence there. Among Conservative candidates selected for winnable constituencies, 22 percent had a direct constituency connection; in the Labour party the proportion is little more than one-quarter.[15] A defeated MP or candidate can move to another constituency to reenter the House and regain national political status. Nearly all politicians in central political roles think in terms of functional, not geographical representation. Insofar as they share a common sense of place, it is London, which is not typical of English cities.

Civil Servants. Whereas MPs come and go from ministerial office with great frequency — on average a minister lasts about two years in one job — civil servants have a job in Whitehall for almost forty years. Moreover, the recruitment process makes all civil servants very much aware of the views of their elders. For example, the present head of the civil service, Sir Robert Armstrong, entered government in 1950 as a principal in the Treasury, when its head was Sir Edward Bridges, who had entered the civil service in 1919, when it was under a head who had entered the service in 1882, shortly after the introduction of great Victorian reforms.

A distinctive feature of senior civil servants in Britain is that they are recruited without any specific academic qualification. In commenting upon the qualities required in a civil servant, the historian Lord Macaulay gave classic statement to the value of education:

> If, instead of learning Greek, we learned the Cherokee, the man who understood the Cherokee best, who made the most correct and melodious Cherokee verses, who comprehended most accurately the effect of the Cherokee particles, would generally be a superior man to him who was destitute of those accomplishments.[16]

Consistent with the tradition of liberal education, in the 1980s 70 percent of successful entrants to the administrative grade have arts degrees, as against 15 percent with a social science degree, and 14 percent with a degree in science and technology. The English practice of recruiting senior civil servants with a specialized education in Greek, Latin, or medieval or modern history is unparalleled in any other major Western nation.[17]

In reaction against this tradition, the Fulton Committee on the civil service recommended that administrative recruits should have "relevant" knowledge of the work of government, "minds disciplined by the social studies, the mathematical and physical sciences, the biological sciences or in the applied and engineering sciences." It did not however, explain why scientific or engineering subjects should be relevant to the work of Whitehall administrators. The Committee's uncertainties about what a civil servant should know were revealed when it failed to agree about a straightforward way to test for relevant knowledge.[18]

The Civil Service Commission has since remedied this deficiency. Candidates for entry to cadet status in the higher civil service are now examined for their ability to summarize lengthy prose papers, to resolve a problem by fitting specific facts to general regulations, to draw inferences from a simple table of social statistics, to follow logical diagrams, and to display verbal facility.

Because bright young persons enter the civil service with no specialized skill and spend decades before reaching senior posts, role socialization is especially important. Civil service recruits, whether their fathers were coal miners or members of the aristocracy, are expected to learn what to do by following those senior to them. Senior civil servants determine the promotion of their juniors. Cooptation ensures the transmission of established assumptions about *how* government should work; it need not imply agreement about what should be done. An individual gains promotion by knowing how Whitehall works rather than because of views about policies. A young civil servant is inoculated against deep involvement in subject matter by frequent moves from post to post; the median administrator is 2.8 years in a job.[19] Part of the training given cadet civil servants is intended to instruct them how "to write briefs on something you know nothing about."[20]

During their working lives, civil servants become specialists like members of other professions; they become specialists in the difficult task of managing Whitehall. Their knowledge of public administration extends far beyond what can be learned in textbooks. They know how to deal with the Treasury in annual negotiations about departmental estimates, how to remind a minister tactfully that his preferred policy may be a political disaster, how to produce a cover-up answer for an awkward parliamentary question, and how to arrive at a departmental policy when the mind of the minister is blank.

In a typical Whitehall career, a senior civil servant will tend to concentrate in a few departments; 48 percent have served in one or two departments, 27 percent in three, and 26 percent in four or more departments.[21] Within a department, an individual will frequently be posted from one job to another, for example, from a finance job to a personnel task, and then to negotiate with outside bodies concerned with the ministry. One effect of concentrating a career in a few departments is that a senior civil servant will know intimately the work habits of immediate colleagues; this greatly facilitates coordination within a ministry. But familiarity with a department does not lead to identification with a department's programs or interests. A senior civil servant is meant to identify with Whitehall first of all.

> About the worst thing that can happen to an ambitious Assistant Secretary, short of being caught accepting bribes, is to go native, to stay in the same division so long that he is thought to be lost to a particular specialism.[22]

Notwithstanding the high status and significance of the work, Whitehall has had difficulties in sustaining the recruitment of cadets for senior civil service posts. In the 1960s, a significant minority left the civil service within a decade of entry, evidence of low morale. In the 1970s, successive pay freezes eroded Whitehall's relative pay advantage, and since 1979 the Conservative government has been trying to reduce the number of civil servants, including the number of high posts to which cadets might aspire. Hence, the Civil Service Commission has noted the "disappointing quality of applicants" for some higher posts. Even in a period of high unemployment, the Commission has not been able to fill all the cadet posts, because of the substantial proportion of persons offered Whitehall jobs who turn them down in favor of working elsewhere.[23]

MPs. Election to the House of Commons is virtually a condition of becoming a Cabinet minister. Members are self-recruited, in the sense that those seeking a parliamentary nomination are expected to put themselves forward. Nomination for a winnable seat involves competition among aspirants for the favor of the selection committee in the dominant party of a constituency. A young person eager to take a central political role does not need to become an MP; entry to the senior civil service upon leaving the university provides a more secure post at the political center. MPs are personalities who prefer the promises and uncertainties of a public life in the Palace of Westminster to a cloistered life in Whitehall.

The motives leading people to seek election to Parliament are multiple, combining public and private interests.[24] Case studies, statistical analyses, and novels have been written about the trials to be surmounted after entering the House of Commons. An MP, his parliamentary agent, and his biographer might each emphasize different motives. One thing is certain: ambition for power is not the only motive; most candidates in each general election are defeated. In the Liberal party, defeat is so likely that the party's headquarters "discourages any potential candidate who indicates he is interested in standing because he hopes to get into Parliament." More than three-quarters of defeated candidates nonetheless consider their campaign enjoyable and satisfying.[25]

Once elected, most MPs can count on a career of fifteen years or longer in the Commons, because most parliamentary seats are safe against electoral tides. National influences determine the movement of the floating vote. It has been unusual for a sitting MP to lose the party's renomination, but changes in Labour party rules now make renomination, and thus retention of a safe seat, less certain (see Chapter IX).

Being an MP was historically not a full-time job but a part-time job for a wealthy person. Conservatives often argue that working outside the Commons keeps an MP in touch with the "real-world" problems of an ordinary citizen. Labour MPs argue that keeping in touch with the world of politics is a full-time job. Differences in occupational background help explain differences in party attitudes. More Conservatives can combine being an MP with their previous occupation as a professional or as a company director than can Labour MPs, who are more likely to be ex-school teachers. Half of Labour MPs can, however, supplement their parliamentary allowances by drawing upon trade union sponsorship.[26]

Ministers. Career MPs form the pool of individuals eligible for a ministerial post when their party has a parliamentary majority.[27] The discretion that a Prime Minister can exercise in recruiting ministers is limited. Many of the party's back-bench MPs are ruled out of consideration by parliamentary inexperience, old age, ideological extremism, personal unreliability, or even lack of interest in office. One analysis of Conservative and Labour MPs found that a chief requirement for securing office was survival in the Commons. A majority of MPs elected three times or more achieve a ministerial post. A Prime Minister is likely to spend as much time deciding what posts are to be offered individual MPs as in deciding which MPs are suited to office.

Experience in the Commons does not lead naturally to the work of a minister, as primary school leads to secondary school. The MP's chief business is dealing with people and talking about ideas. Doing these things well is useful in Whitehall, but a minister must have other skills too: knowing how to handle the paperwork required by a major administrative post; the ability to appraise the consequences of policy alternatives that will not be clear until long after he has left office; and the capacity to relate political generalities to the specifics of a technical problem. A minister may find the transition from the back benches to government greater than the shift from being a party activist to being a back-bench MP. A minister must learn what to do on the job.

An MP joining the government is usually appointed first to a junior ministerial post. Every Cabinet minister is assisted by several junior ministers assigned to the department by the Prime Minister. Junior ministers are sometimes delegated the job of overseeing substantial chunks of departmental work, such as prisons in the Home Office, or university affairs in Education. But a junior minister's power is limited to matters of lesser political significance. The doctrine of individual ministerial responsibility formally fixes the whole responsibility for the department upon its chief minister. A Cabinet minister will not readily trust a junior minister to make a decision when he will receive the blame if things go wrong.

When ministers are asked what they think their task is, nearly every minister makes some reference to policy making and to maintaining parliamentary support.[28] Half think it important to protect or advance their department against other departments in Cabinet deliberations and to maintain morale within their department. One-third stress the need for public-relations work with pressure groups and the general public. Different definitions of the job lead to differences about the skills considered most important in recruiting ministers. Half think that a good minister is a specialist in handling Parliament and a gifted amateur in the face of the problems of his department. But the other half think that specialist knowledge of a department's tasks is most important.

Recruiting Cabinet ministers from the ranks of MPs ensures that they have had ample experience to meet one important task, handling parliamentary business. But restricting appointments to established MPs prevents a nationwide canvass seeking persons with specialist skills for particular posts. Little more than one-tenth of ministers are appointed to departments where they can claim some specialized knowledge.[29]

The one way in which a minister can be sure of learning about a department's work is to learn on the job. Anthony Crosland, a minister with an unusually analytic mind, reckoned, "It takes you six months to get your head properly above water, a year to get the general drift of most of the field, and two years really to master the whole of a department."[30] The time from appraising a problem to implementing a policy can be as much as five years. The practice of Prime Ministerial patronage frequently brings about the reshuffling of ministers from department to department. The average minister stays about two years in one office; the turnover rate is one of the highest in Western nations. Nearly every move by a minister takes him to a job in a department where he has no experience, and on-the-job learning must start again.

The recruitment of ministers has come under criticism as part of a general cry for reform. Industrialists argue the need for more businesslike ministers; economists, the need for more economic expertise; and some academics praise the American system of in-and-outers, in which persons move between the federal executive and other organizations, such as state government, universities, or profit-making companies. In 1964, Harold Wilson named five individuals without previous parliamentary experience to ministerial posts, a practice that had previously been followed only in wartime emergencies. The most prominent appointee, Frank Cousins, resigned less than two years after his appointment. Mr. Heath did not emulate the tactic in 1970, nor has it been repeated since. Reviewing the recruitment of ministers, F. M. G. Willson concludes, "The pattern not only remains overwhelmingly similar to that established over the last hundred years, but if anything has moved slightly towards more orthodoxy in terms of parliamentary and administrative experience."[31]

The closed-shop conventions of Parliament virtually bar anyone from moving to a prominent ministerial post without an apprenticeship in the House of Commons. The civil service too has been opposed to recruiting staff from outside its ranks, especially at higher levels. It is argued that such a practice would make high-paying Whitehall jobs patronage plums to be awarded to partisan sympathizers inexperienced in Whitehall's ways. Civil servants expect that they will receive the top jobs in Whitehall after years of loyally accumulating seniority.

Temporary Whitehall appointments are given in small numbers to party workers, economists, and journalists in order to have political policy advisors within Whitehall. Samuel Brittan, an economic journalist turned Whitehall irregular, concluded from his experience that the contribution of any irregular is limited by the vice of his virtue.[32] The more novel the perspective brought to Whitehall, the more one must learn in order to operate effectively there. Yet the more an individual learns, the less likely he or she is to have a distinctive contribution to make. New recruits cannot by themselves make a "new" style of government. To change government they must learn the strengths as well as observe the weaknesses of the old ways.

Intermittent Politicians. Many individuals are involved in politics intermittently and may not even think of themselves as in a political role. If all those holding government appointments were defined as political, then such diverse persons as the Archbishop of Canterbury, the Director General of the British Broadcasting Corporation, the Regius Professor of Greek at Oxford, and the Astronomer Royal could be called politicians. If challenged, each would probably deny being a politician, yet also claim to be carrying out duties in the public interest.

Tens of thousands of people are recruited into part-time government service by being appointed to public bodies. Most part-time appointments are without salary. Civic-minded people are expected to give advice gladly on a committee, commission, or other advisory body, or to assist law enforcement as lay magistrates.

Many members of government advisory committees and commissions sit by virtue of their position in an organization affected by the committee's deliberations. Pressure-group officials are involved in politics informally as well as formally. Pressure-group appointees to a committee are often balanced by having as a chairman a lay gent, a person whose amateurism implies neutrality in government.[33] The Treasury keeps a list of "the great and the good" to act as lay representatives of the public on specialist committees. Politicians on the left sometimes criticize appointees to quangos (as quasi-nongovernmental agencies are sometimes called), on the ground that they overrepresent the professional middle class. Politicians on the right sometimes criticize the system on the ground that it provides influence and a useful part-time income for proteges of Labour politicians.

An official tabulation of public boards staffed by intermittent public persons found 310 variously denominated bodies with more than 10,000 full- and part-time members appointed by the Whitehall departments sponsoring the bodies.[34] Most individuals held only one appointment in their field of interest or expertise. Less than half the appointments carry a part-time salary or honorarium; appointees may be rewarded by an honor, ranging from the lowly rank of OBE (Order of the British Empire) up to a K (a knighthood), or occasionally a seat in the House of Lords.

Intermittent public persons come from greatly varied backgrounds. Analysis of a sample of members of ad hoc Royal Commissions shows that nearly half (46 percent) had social origins so ordinary that they did not list their father's status or occupation in standard biographical sources. Although 42 percent had an Oxford or Cambridge education, 30 percent had no education beyond secondary school. Among those on Royal Commissions, fewer than half were drawn from the old professions (law, civil service, Parliament, landowners, or the military).[35] The varied careers of recruits to intermittent public posts suggest that they bring to Westminster a greater range of viewpoints than are found in the ranks of full-time politicians.

The careers of intermittent political participants can best be seen in short biographies of a few prominent public persons.

Lord Goodman. Born 1913. Educated at secondary school in London, University of London, and Cambridge. Solicitor. Entered Royal Artillery as enlisted man, 1939; left as major, 1945. Solicitor to Harold Wilson for various personal matters. Chairman, Arts Council of Great Britain, 1965–1972. Member, Royal Commission on Working of Tribunals of Enquiry (Evidence) Act, 1966; Chairman, Committee of Inquiry on Charity Law, 1974. Member, British Council, 1967–; President, National Book League, 1972–; Chairman, Observer Newspaper Trust, 1967–1976; Newspaper Publisher's Association, 1970–1975. Member, Industrial Reorganization Corporation, 1969–1971. President, Institute of Jewish Affairs, 1975–; chairman, Housing Corporation; 1973–1977. Director, Royal Opera House, 1972–. Master, University College, Oxford since 1976. Created Life Peer, 1965.

Lady Warnock. Born 1926. Educated, St. Swithin's, Winchester; Lady Margaret Hall, Oxford. Fellow and tutor in Philosophy, St. Hugh's College, Oxford, 1946–66; Headmistress, Oxford High School, 1966–72; Member, Independent Broadcasting Authority, 1973–81; Member, Royal Commission on Environmental Pollution, 1979–; Social Science Research Council, 1981–; United Kingdom Commission for Unesco, 1981–. Chairman: Committee of Enquiry into Special Education, 1974; Advisory Committee on Animal Experiments, 1979–; Committee of Enquiry into Human Fertilization, 1982–84; Head, Girton College, Cambridge, since 1984. Created Life Peer, 1984.

Lord Rayner. Born 1926. Educated, City College, Norwich; Selwyn College, Cambridge. Retailer. Joined Marks & Spencers, 1953; director, 1967; chief executive since 1983. Fellow, Institute of Purchasing and Supply, 1970. Procurement Management Board, Ministry of Defence, 1972–; deputy chairman, Civil Service Pay Board, 1978–1980; Advisor to Prime Minister on improving efficiency and eliminating waste in government, 1979–1983. Member, Design Council, 1973–1975; Council, Royal College of Art, 1973–1976. Security Advisory Commission, 1977–1980. Created Life Peer, 1983.

Different as the careers of these three public persons are, all have two things in common. None has ever been a candidate for elective office, or held a post as an established civil servant.

Their abstention from conventional public offices does not mean that they are any less involved in central political roles.

POLITICIANS AND SOCIETY

Traditionally, political leaders were simultaneously leading social, political, and economic personages. Aristocrats could claim seats in Parliament by virtue of noble birth and inherited wealth. When the chief tasks of government were traditional tasks, social leaders could easily double in political roles. The twentieth century has accelerated the rise of the full-time professional politician, just as it has brought professionalization to many other social roles, from sports to scholarship.[36]

Politicians and students of politics may feel that political leaders are superior to economic leaders — but businessmen, economists, and trade unionists may believe the opposite. Those with inherited social status may feel superior to both, disdaining a career in politics or industry. The attractions of public office may be weighed against other jobs, and found wanting. Even more important, the attractions may not even be considered, because of the reputation of politics. Political, economic, and status leaders may each be amazed that the others regard their rewards as worth seeking.

In contemporary England it is necessary to ask how often those who have achieved high social status or leading economic positions are recruited into politics. The question is not about the social origins of politicians, but rather about the political inclinations of those with high nonpolitical status.

The qualities and achievements that confer social status today are multiple and diverse. No one seems to agree about what it is that puts top people on top.[37] Prestige can be accorded persons on grounds as different as traditional honor (the Queen), statesmanship (a former Prime Minister in old age), television personality (David Frost), or achievement in sports, whether as a jockey in the sport of kings or as a football hero in the sport of the working class. People with very different measures of prestige live without conflict as long as they do not meet. For example, the wife of an Army colonel welcomed a newcomer to a rural Oxfordshire village of five hundred with the statement that, except for three families, "nobody" lived in the village, that is, no one else significant by her criteria for status. In working-class communities, people with middle-class attributes may find themselves similarly isolated.[38]

Individuals with high social status cannot claim to govern by virtue of their celebrity. They may tell the government what to do in a public speech or a private conversation, but this right is also claimed by political activists, whatever their social status. Ministers will usually pay far more attention to someone who has earned a position in the party than to a person who has simply inherited a peerage. To be influential, social leaders must translate their diffuse status into specific public office in Westminster or Whitehall.

Interest in politics is a minority taste among those of high social status. Among members of the House of Lords, about one-third do not even bother to attend one sitting a year, and only one-sixth attend as many as half the sittings in a session. Moreover, hereditary peers are less likely than newly appointed life peers to attend and speak in the Lords.[39] The proportion of Oxbridge arts graduates seeking to enter the senior civil service is but a small fraction of each year's crop of graduates. Similarly, the proportion of Etonians in a Conservative Cabinet is an infinitesimal fraction of Old Etonians in society at any time, and a falling proportion. At one time nearly half the Cabinet of Harold Macmillan were Etonians. Mrs. Thatcher appointed six Etonians to her first Cabinet in 1979; in 1983 she appointed only one old Etonian.

In the eighteenth century holding public office could be considered a form of *noblesse oblige.* Now it means seeking favor from the democratic mass. Aristocrats and wealthy businessmen prefer to pursue less controversial and plebeian activities than local government. A study of local notables in Bristol found that 73 percent had never even thought of seeking election to the local council, and only 11 percent had become councillors. Local government was avoided because of a dislike of party politics, and many also held councillors in low esteem.[40] The Conservative Party in Parliament has changed too: "The pre-war influence of aristocrats and of very rich capitalists has given way both in the parliamentary party and in the constituencies to the dominance of the 'ordinary' upper middle classes.''[41]

The incentives for translating diffuse status into political position must be weighed against drawbacks. For a person of high social status, the title MP confirms but may not enhance prestige. A politically important post in the civil service may confer less social status than a politically unimportant post in the Royal Household. Political life is most rewarding to those who *lack* high inherited status. For most people to become an MP is to rise in status; even being a defeated parliamentary candidate can confer prestige. A senior civil service post has more social status than managing a factory, because the former work is for public good, not private profit.

Once an individual has been recruited into politics, prestige is measured far less by social origins than by political accomplishments. A local councillor will have more prestige than a ward secretary, Members of Parliament have more political prestige than local government councillors, and ministers sworn into the Privy Council take precedence over back-bench MPs. The civil service has many gradations in status and status symbols.

The most successful politicians and civil servants raise their social status by earning honors or titles for their political and public service. The honors list, issued twice a year by the monarch on the advice of the Prime Minister, provides incentives for intermittent public duties. When asked what he would do with his newly conferred middle-rank honor, one public person smiled and said, ''Work to improve it.'' Honors can also soften the blow of forced retirement. A Cabinet minister fired for inefficiency or old age can be consoled with a place in the House of Lords.

The financial rewards that politics offers are limited, and usually less than could be earned by the same effort in other occupations. An MP's salary of £16,904 a year is much less than that of a senior civil servant or a political journalist. A Cabinet minister's salary, £42,980, is low by comparison with salaries for persons with similar responsibilities outside government. The heads of nationalized industries are usually paid more than the Prime Minister, but their pay is less than could be earned in the private sector. Whereas in industry success usually brings valuable capital gains, a politician cannot realize money profits when the stock of the party rises. When it falls, he loses both office and official salary.

Politicians do have one thing in common with contemporary economic leaders: they must specialize to succeed. It is no longer easy for an individual to move back and forth between careers in different worlds. The proportion of businessmen with any political experience is limited, and has been falling. A study of company chairmen, the most political office in a large company, found that before the First World War a sizeable minority (three in ten) had been an MP at some stage in their career. But in contemporary England only one company chairman in twenty-five has been an MP, usually well before becoming a chairman. Another study of managers concludes, "All in all, top managers have not had marked experience outside industry, outside their own firm, or outside their own line of work."[42]

Trade union leaders, like businessmen, have dedicated a working life to their career. Unlike businessmen, their institutions are integrated in party politics through affiliation to the Labour party. Whereas a minority of businessmen are Alliance or Labour supporters, it is unheard of for a union leader to support the Conservative party. Union leaders who are not Labour party supporters prefer the Communist party or other Marxist groups. Although trade union leaders and Labour MPs share a common Conservative opponent, the lines of demarcation between the industrial and political wings of the labor movement are strict. Union leaders are very rarely MPs; of the thirty-eight members of the Trades Union Congress (TUC) General Council in 1984, not one was an MP. Similarly, union leaders cannot sit on the National Executive Committee (NEC) of the Labour party, because its monthly meetings occur at the same time as the General Council of the TUC. Union leaders send their deputies to NEC meetings. Unions sponsor more than one hundred Labour MPs, but few of these are national officers of their union. Once elected to Parliament, a union member exchanges a union career for parliamentary ambitions.

Industrial firms and city banks, like trade unions, are not

eager to see able young persons in their employment seek parliamentary careers. When one does, it is usually assumed that the aspiring politician will lose any chance of promotion in the firm. Just as the House of Commons jealously requires a minister to serve an apprenticeship on the back benches, so industry, commerce, and the trade unions expect a person to acquire experience on the job before being rewarded with a top position.

The careers of Cabinet ministers since 1945 emphasize the distance between political and economic leadership. No leader from the business world has been a senior minister since the end of the Second World War, and only two leading trade union officials have sat in Labour Cabinets (Ernest Bevin, 1945–1951, and Frank Cousins, 1964–1966). In Harold Wilson's 1964 Cabinet, no one could be described as a businessman by occupation; seven were trade unionists. When Wilson left office in 1976, his Cabinet had become a Cabinet of political professionals; it had but one trade unionist. In Margaret Thatcher's 1979 Cabinet, few ministers were businessmen, and no leader of the business world sat there. In her second term of office, the place of professional politicians in Cabinet increased.

The number of ministers with high social status has declined substantially since 1945. The 1945 Labour government had four peers, and in Sir Winston Churchill's 1951 Cabinet, six of sixteen Cabinet posts were held by members of the House of Lords. In the 1974 Labour Cabinet, the only members of the House of Lords were those required to sit there, the Lord Chancellor and the Leader of the House of Lords. In 1979 and 1983, Margaret Thatcher appointed three peers to her Cabinet, only one more than the minimum required.

Intensive apprenticeship is a prerequisite for success in most aspects of English life today. Just as a Cabinet minister must usually spend years as an MP, so a bishop must serve as vicar, a general as lieutenant, a professor as university lecturer, and a managing director of a firm must first work under others. Leadership positions in England today are far more differentiated than they were in 1832, when the local lord might also appoint the local clergy, lead the militia, sit as a magistrate, and send his son to the House of Commons, while himself attending debates in the House of Lords. After years of interviewing people in leading positions in many areas of English life, Anthony Sampson concluded:

> My own fear is not that the Establishment in Britain is too close, but that it is not close enough, that the circles are overlapping less and less and that one half of the ring has very little contact with the other half.[43]

SELECTIVE RECRUITMENT

The extent to which political recruitment is considered selective depends upon the definition of the political class. Nothing could be more selective than a parliamentary election that makes one person Prime Minister of a country with 55 million people. Yet nothing is considered more representative, because an election is the one occasion in which every adult can participate in politics. The greater the scope of activities defined as political, the greater the number of people who are participants. Government intervention in the economy has made company directors and trade union shop stewards at least intermittently politicians. Yet their economic position gives them freedom to act independently of government. Workers can vote with their feet by an unofficial strike. Businessmen can vote with their pocketbooks by investing money outside the United Kingdom.

The most analyzed features of political recruitment in England are the social origins of politicians. Whatever the criterion chosen—age, sex, education, or occupation—politicians differ in profile from those whom they represent. If the good fortune of Old Etonians in gaining a disproportionate number of nominations in safe Conservative seats is one form of "class nepotism,"[44] then trade union sponsorship of workers in safe Labour seats can also be seen as class nepotism, albeit favoring a different class.

The social origins of politicians do not, however, predict the outlooks of individual politicians.[45] Politicians gain promotion because of abilities relevant to Whitehall and Westminster rather than by conforming to the expectations of their former public school headmaster. If social origins were all-powerful, then Conservative MPs would hardly ever disagree, because they are virtually all middle class. Theories of social determinism deny the existence of politics (that is, disagreement about issues) within the Conservative party. Yet Conservatives are never all of one mind. In the late 1950s, Harold Macmillan suffered resignation by three Old Etonians from his government on political grounds. Their replacements were also Old Etonians. In the Labour party, disagreements are frequent, but they are not easily related to social characteristics. MPs from public schools and Oxford can be found on the left, and working-class Labour MPs can have conservative attitudes about many social issues.

Like success in polo, success in national politics is ultimately achieved by skill and experience. But the readiness and opportunity to develop the skill by playing the game are not determined solely by individual aptitudes. Opportunities depend upon personal and family circumstances as well as social background.

The contrast between the egalitarian basis of the electoral franchise and the selectiveness of political recruitment is undoubted: its political significance is arguable. Economic efficiency dictates that some people be selected to specialize in major political offices. The need for competent government justifies selection for civil service posts by criteria that favor university graduates. Yet the need for communication between representatives and the represented — by empathy as well as face-to-face dialogue — implies selecting some politicians because they are socially representative of the electorate.[46]

Debates about the recruitment of politicians cannot be resolved by stating that competence should be the criterion for selection. This begs the question: What is competence? In recruiting for the civil service, academic achievement is the customary sign of competence. Experience is highly valued for promotion; it is proof that an individual has undergone lengthy socialization into the norms of Whitehall. Members of Parliament gain preferment by demonstrating to the Prime Minister that they can conform to expectations specific to parliamentary party politics.

The lengthy role socialization of career politicians is the sin-

208

Recruiting Participants

gle most significant feature of political recruitment to central political roles in Britain. Civil servants spend most of their adult life being socialized into Whitehall norms *before* receiving senior posts. Members of Parliament undergo role socialization for a decade or two *before* becoming important ministers. Continuity makes the routine work of government, including party politics, move forward easily. Each politician knows what he can and cannot do within the confines of his current role, and what should be done to secure promotion. The resulting continuity is impressive, whether it is viewed as a means of preserving national traditions or as an obstacle to change when new political problems arise.

NOTES

1. For an overview of the literature of political participation, see Dennis Kavanagh, *Political Science and Political Behaviour* (London: Allen & Unwin, 1983), chapters 7, 9; for empirical analysis, see e.g., Colin Crouch, ed., *British Political Sociology Yearbook,* vol. 3 (London: Croom Helm, 1977); and George Moyser, "Modes of Mass Political Participation in Britain (Florence: ECPR Workshop on Political Participation, 1980).

2. See Richard Rose, *From Government at the Centre to Nationwide Government* (Glasgow: U. of Strathclyde Studies in Public Policy No. 132, 1974).

3. On participation in local elections, see F. W. S. Craig, *British Electoral Facts, 1832–1980* (Chichester: Parliamentary Research Services, 1981), pp. 129 ff.

4. See Mary Horton, *The Local Government Elector,* chapter 2; and Louis Moss and Stanley Parker, *The Local Government Councillor,* Vol. 2 (London: HMSO, 1967), p. 45.

5. See e.g., Robert E. Dowse and J. Hughes, "Sporadic Interventionists," *Political Studies,* 25:1 (1977); and Paul E. Peterson and Paul Kantor, "Political Parties and Citizen Participation in English City Politics," *Comparative Politics,* 9:2 (1977).

6. See Horton, *The Local Government Elector,* chapters 5, 6; cf. Moss and Parker, *The Local Government Councillor,* chapters 4, 9.

7. See John Gyford, "Our Changing Local Councillors," *New Society,* 3 May 1983, and sources cited therein.

8. Kenneth Newton, *Second City Politics* (London: Oxford University Press, 1976).

9. Butler and Stokes, *Political Change in Britain,* 2nd ed., pp 40ff.

10. For an exhaustive study of the subject, see Ivor Crewe, Tony Fox, and Jim Alt, "Non-Voting in British General Elections, 1966–October 1974," in Colin Crouch, ed., *British Political Sociology Yearbook,* vol. 3, pp. 38–109.

11. See the report of the Houghton Committee, *Financial Aid to Political Parties* (London: HMSO, Cmnd. 6601, 1976), 31 ff. See also *Gallup Political Index,* No. 200 (March 1977), pp. 12–15.

12. See Robert M. Worcester, "The Hidden Activists," in Rose, ed., *Studies in British Politics,* 3rd ed.

13. See Marsh, *Protest and Political Consciousness,* p. 45.

14. See Michael Rush, *The Selection of Parliamentary Candidates* (London: Thomas Nelson, 1969), pp. 60–181; and Peter G. Richards, *The Backbenchers* (London: Faber & Faber, 1972), p. 22. On the overlapping roles of local councillors and MPs in the scrutiny of constituents' problems, see Ronald Munroe, "Where Representatives Meet: Conflict or Co-operation?" *Public Administration Bulletin,* No. 27 (August 1978).

15. See Rush, *The Selection of Parliamentary Candidates,* pp. 74, 181.

16. *The Life and Letters of Lord Macaulay* (London: Longman, 1923 Volume II) pp. 585–586. See also Lord Bridges, *The Treasury* (London: Allen & Unwin, 1964), pp. 51–52, 101–102.

17. See Civil Service Commission, *Annual Report 1983* (Basingstoke: Civil Service Commission, 1984), p. 41. Cf. Aberbach, Putnam, and Rockman, *Bureaucrats and Politicians in Western Democracies,* p. 52.

18. See The Fulton Committee, *Report* vol. 1, pp. 27ff., and appendix E, especially p. 162. See also *Qualifications* (London: Management and Personnel Office, 1983).

19. See The Fulton Committee, *Report,* vol. 2, pp. 20ff. On the formal training of civil servants, see E. Grebenik, "The Civil Service College: the First Year," *Public Administration,* 50 (Summer 1972).

20. Comment by a teacher at the Civil Service College, quoted in Peter Kellner and Lord Crowther-Hunt, *The Civil Servants* (London: Macdonald, 1980) p. 145.

21. For career data on civil servants, see Rose, "The Political Status of Higher Civil Servants in Britain," and sources cited therein.

22. Kellner and Crowther-Hunt, *The Civil Servants,* p. 162.

23. Civil Service Commission, *Annual Report 1983,* p. 8. See R. G. S. Brown, "Fulton and Morale," *Public Administration,* 44 (Summer 1971), p. 193; R. A. Chapman, "Profile of a Profession," in The Fulton Committee Report, (1968) 3:2, pp. 1, 13, and Peta E. Sheriff, "Outsiders in a Closed Career," *Public Administration,* 50 (Winter 1972).

24. Note the catalogue of motives in Sir Lewis Namier, *The Structure of Politics at the Accession of George III,* 2nd ed. (London: Macmillan, 1957), ch. 1. Cf. Austin Mitchell, *Westminster Man* (London: Thames Methuen, 1982).

25. See Dennis Kavanagh, *Constituency Electioneering in Britain* (London: Longman, 1970), pp. 81ff; and Jorgen Rasmussen, *The Liberal Party: a Study of Retrenchment and Revival* (London: Constable, 1965), p. 212.

26. See the *Annual Register of Members Interests* (London: HMSO).

27. See Richard Rose, *The Problem of Party Government* (London: Macmillan, 1974), chapter 14, for a detailed development of points summarized here about the making of Cabinet ministers.

28. See Headey, *British Cabinet Ministers* 59ff.

29. *Ibid.,* pp. 90ff.

30. Quoted in Maurice Kogan, *The Politics of Education* (Harmondsworth: Penguin, 1971), pp. 155ff.

31. "Entry to the Cabinet, 1959–1968," *Political Studies,* 18:2 (1970), p. 238. See also by the same author, "The Routes of Entry of New Members of the British Cabinet, 1968–1958," *ibid.,* 7:3 (1959).

32. Samuel Brittan, "The Irregulars," in Richard Rose, ed., *Policy-Making in Britain* (London: Macmillan, 1969).

33. K. C. Wheare, *Government by Committee* (Oxford; Clarendon Press, 1955), pp. 15ff.

34. Civil Service Department, *A Director of Paid Public Appointments Made by Ministers* 2nd ed. (London: HMSO, 1978). Alan Doig, "Public Bodies and Ministerial Patronage," *Parliamentary Affairs,* 31:1 (1978).

35. Calculated from data in Charles J. Hanser, *Guide to Decision: the Royal Commission* (Totowa, N.J.: Bedminster Press, 1965), Appendix 3.

36. See J. M. Lee, *Social Leaders and Public Persons* (Oxford: Clarendon Press, 1963); and Anthony King, "The Rise of the Career Politician in Britain — and its Consequences," *British Journal of Political Science,* 11: 2 (1981), pp. 249–85.

37. See National Opinion Polls, *Monthly Bulletin,* No. 109 (June 1972).

38. Margaret Stacey, *Tradition and Change* (London: Oxford University Press, 1960), p. 145. See also Brian Jackson and Dennis Marsden, *Education and the Working Class* (London: Routledge and Kegan Paul, 1962), pp. 53ff.

39. See Bernard Crick, *The Reform of Parliament,* 2nd ed., p. 137 and *Social Trends,* Vol. 8 (1977), table 14.6

40. See R. V. Clements, *Local Notables and the City Council* (London: Macmillan, 1969), pp. 51, 156ff.

41. David Butler and Michael Pinto-Duschinsky, "The Conservative Elite, 1918–1978: Does Unrepresentativeness Matter?" in Z. Layton-Henry, ed., *Conservative Party Politics* (London: Macmillan, 1980), p. 198.

42. R. V. Clements, *Managers* (London: Allen & Unwin, 1958), p. 151; and Philip Stanworth and Anthony Giddens, "An Economic Elite: A Demographic Profile of Company Chairmen," in Stanworth and Giddens, eds., *Elites and Power in British Society* (London: Cambridge University Press, 1974), pp. 87, 90.

43. Anthony Sampson, *Anatomy of Britain,* p. 632 and endpapers. If Sampson had included leaders in local government or leaders in Scotland, Wales, and Northern Ireland, the lack of contact would have appeared even greater.

44. H. R. G. Greaves, *The British Constitution,* 2nd ed. (London: Allen & Unwin, 1948), p. 164.

45. Dennis Kavanagh, "From Gentlemen to Players," in W. B. Gwyn and R. Rose, eds., *Britain: Progress and Decline,* p. 75.

46. On these criteria for recruiting governors, see Robert A. Dahl, *After the Revolution?* (New Haven: Yale University Press, 1970).

CHAPTER VII

Communication
and Noncommunication

A parliamentary minister is a man trained by elaborate practice not to blurt out crude things.

COMMUNICATION IS THE HYPHEN that joins parts of the political system. Government wants citizens to know what it expects of them, and it needs information about what citizens are thinking and doing. Citizens want government to know what they would like, or at least what they will not stand for. Noncommunication is also important. A minister cannot act if he does not know that a problem exists, and a voter will ignore views confined to those in central political roles in Whitehall. Because politics is about differences of opinion, communication does not resolve conflicts. With perfect information, policymakers would still have to decide between competing opinions.

Political communication is simple in outline form: who says what to whom how?[1] A sender transmits messages to an audience through one or more media of communication. Channels of communication include public media, such as the press, television, and Parliament, and private media, such as conversations in the corridors of Whitehall. The influence of an audience varies inversely with its size: small, private meetings are often more important than televised political discussions. Only at election time does a mass audience determine political outcomes.

The roles of communicator and audience are often exchanged. Those who speak often, such as MPs, are also expected to listen to those who seek to influence them. Those who usually listen, the voters, speak decisively at elections. The dynamics of the policy process require politicians to propose a course of action, then listen for reactions from those affected. Once reactions are heard, this feedback can be used to revise ideas according to what has been learned.

Everyone, whether a politician or an ordinary citizen, is part of both horizontal and vertical communication networks. Horizontal communication involves people of similar political status, such as Cabinet ministers. Vertical communication links individuals differing in their political status. For example, the Employment minister must ensure that his views reach down to the local offices where unemployment benefits are paid. Reciprocally, an unemployed person wants his views to travel up to where economic decisions are made.

The fewer the channels of communication, the greater the opportunity for distortion. Insofar as messages move simultaneously through many channels, redundancy makes it less likely that a message will be lost; it also increases the burden of monitoring information. The greater a person's political involvement, the more complex his or her communications network will be. In theory, complexity offers more information. But it also makes it necessary to ignore or scan briefly much that is communicated.

Trying to keep political discussions quiet also creates difficulties. There is a risk that private negotiations will leak to the press, and that relevant ideas will be suppressed or excluded. For example, from 1964 to 1967 the Labour government did not wish to discuss the possibility of devaluing the pound, fearing that such news would lead to speculation against the pound. Devaluation was under consideration in the Treasury but, as one minister remarked, it was "a very difficult subject to discuss because it was absolutely essential that nobody should know that it was being discussed."[2]

In the liberal model of English politics, government is expected to communicate information freely because the public has the right to know. The greater the flow of information, the better informed the public can be. As the public is meant to be the ultimate arbiter of policy, a better informed public is also expected to make government better. In Washington, this doctrine of the public's right to know is given statutory expression in a Freedom of Information Act. By contrast, the White-hall model takes a very different view of supply-demand relationships. Information is assumed to be a scarce commodity and, "like all scarce commodities, it is not freely exchanged."[3] Publicity is considered costly, not only because of the time required to carry out an extensive public relations campaign, but also because public discussion might make private negotiations more difficult.

Whitehall laws and conventions assume that publicity is "not in the public interest."[4] David Butler, an academic and media commentator on politics, writes, "Conducting the whole business of advising and policy-forming in public just wouldn't work." A Foreign Office official says more bluntly: "It is no business of any official to allow the government to be embarrassed. That is who we are working for."[5]

The first analytic question concerns the mass public: How many individuals have political views that they wish to communicate to government? Second, we must examine the structure of the public media (broadcasting and the press), and how they communicate information about public affairs. The third topic, horizontal communication within government, depends upon what is not communicated as well as what is communicated. With this knowledge, the costs and benefits of the distinctive Whitehall approach to political communication can be assessed.

PUBLIC OPINION

Discussion of the role that public opinion ought to play usually starts from the assumption that members of the public have political opinions to communicate, and that there are no obstacles to their translation into government policies. Both these assumptions are rejected by the evidence.

The Limits of Opinion. Every survey of public opinion distinguishes between two groups of citizens: those who have an opinion about an issue and those who do not. The proportion of opinionated citizens is likely to be highest for issues immediately affecting them. When people are asked whether or not they are satisfied with their standard of living, 99 percent usually state a view. When voters are asked to choose between alternative government measures for handling an issue, the proportion of don't knows rises to a third or half on matters concerning Whitehall far more than the public.[6] If the same question is put to the same person at different times, a different answer may be given, for some political opinions are almost random responses to passing events. This is hardly the basis for a long-term commitment by government.

Insofar as political opinions ought to be based on knowledge, then many voters should withhold judgment on public policies. It was probably easier for the electorate in nineteenth-century England to understand issues than it is today. Fewer issues faced government, and often these required a simple decision of principle, such as whether or not to give everyone the right to vote. Today, the alternatives among which the government must choose are complex, and many choices must be based on disputed technical considerations about which most voters do not inform themselves. Voters concentrate more upon results, such as full employment, steady prices, and a rising standard of living than upon the means to these ends.

Knowledge of politics reflects interest in politics; the higher the interest, the more likely a person is to hold opinions about issues. Citizens have many reasons not to take an interest in politics. Talking about politics can lead to arguments threatening friendships, or reveal civic ignorance. Less than one-quarter of the electorate say that they often discuss politics. Low interest may also reflect reasoned calculation. Because the ordinary individual can exercise so little political influence, it is not economical to spend a lot of time and money to obtain political information. The best value-for-money strategy is to delegate responsibility for gathering information to trusted full-time politicians.[7] Citizens need only acquire sufficient information about competing parties to choose between them. This knowledge may be gained free, if friends and neighbors endorse one party as "the party for people like ourselves."

The public debate about the United Kingdom's entry to the European Community, a seemingly straightforward question, illustrates the difficulty of trying to relate public opinion to government. When the issue was first mooted in the early 1960s, the don't knows were sometimes the largest group, and often formed an absolute majority of the electorate when added to those with views but no knowledge. In the subsequent decade, as the Common Market became the object of much discussion in the media, the proportion of don't knows decreased, and opinion fluctuated greatly. The Gallup Poll proportion endorsing entry to the Common Market ranged from a high of 71 percent in July 1966 to a low of 16 percent in November 1970.

At the time of the 1970 general election, voters had no choice of pro- and antimarket parties, for all parties were then in favor of entry. The Labour and Conservative parties subsequently adopted contrasting positions, but within each party MPs disagreed among themselves about whether the terms negotiated were satisfactory. As the parties shifted, the views of voters altered. Voters with shifting, uncertain, or confused opinions could claim with justice that their views matched those of their party.

When the country entered the European Community, the median Englishman was literally a don't know; those with opinions were almost evenly divided, 39 percent for entry, and 45 percent against. Confusion was not confined to the ranks of the less informed. A survey of university economists found 40 percent favoring entry on economic grounds, 42 percent against, and the median economist undecided.[8] One person, the Prime Minister, Edward Heath, was without doubts. The Prime Minister knew what he wanted: entry to the Common Market. Britain joined.

The Limits of Voting. The public was able to pronounce its views — changing and partially informed as they were — in a 1975 referendum about continuing membership in the Common Market. This popular consultation was not undertaken because of politicians' deference to direct democracy or because politicians believed that ordinary people in the street knew better than they. The referendum was called because the Labour government was deeply split on the question, and the Prime Minister, Harold Wilson, reckoned that a referendum might resolve disputes between Cabinet ministers at minimal cost to the party and to his own personal position.[9]

The 1975 European Community referendum showed the electorate divided into three groups: 43 percent who voted for entry, 36 percent who did not vote, and 21 percent who voted against entry. The years since have shown Cabinet ministers divided about membership, alternatively complaining about Community actions and, when personally responsible for bargains with Community partners, claiming credit for benefits. When the country went to the polls for the second direct election to the European Parliament in 1984, the two-thirds who did not vote was as large as the proportion who had voted in favor of entry at the 1975 referendum. The Gallup Poll found the electorate as a whole divided into three almost equal groups in their views about the Community: 33 percent said it was a good thing, 32 percent a bad thing, and 35 percent said it was neither or were don't knows.[10]

A general election is the principal occasion on which the majority of the public speaks its mind. Elections, however, are blunt instruments infrequently used. Counting votes can decide who governs, but it does not tell governors what to do. Election results are only a rough judgment for or against parties. For propaganda purposes, the winning party speaks of receiving a mandate, as if every voter necessarily read and agreed with its pre-election proposals before casting a ballot. On some issues a majority of a party's voters have more confidence in the party they vote against than in the party they vote for.[11] The doctrine of an electoral mandate is a dignified symbol rather than an effective means of expressing popular opinion.

Between elections voters can communicate their views directly to their MP by letter or in person. But only one-tenth of the electorate says that in fact it has ever done so. More than nine-tenths of these communications are to ask the MP's assistance in dealing with administrative actions that directly affect the writer, such as a disability pension or allocation of a council house. In most cases these problems concern local government, not Westminster. When an individual voter turns to his or her MP, it is for help with personal problems involving government, and not to discuss political issues.[12]

Party headquarters commission public opinion surveys in efforts to learn what the silent majority of voters think, feel, and want. The Conservative party was the first to show an interest in market research techniques in the 1959 election. The Labour party attacked the Conservatives for allegedly trying to sell policies like soap, and then showed itself better able to use market research in the 1964 campaign. Since then both parties have made regular use of their own private opinion surveys to complement traditional party mechanisms for sounding opinion. Opinion researchers prepare profiles of the social characteristics of floating voters, and analyze the relative importance or unimportance of issues and the appeal of slogans and campaign themes.

Ironically, party use of public opinion surveys has demonstrated how ready British politicians are to ignore the views of those whose votes they seek.[13] MORI researcher Robert Worcester, who also works for the Labour party, has described a party leader as "a relatively unlistening client, who is much more at home talking than listening." Many politicians believe that, by virtue of popular election, they know what ordinary voters think, and they rate opinion polls well down the list of useful sources of information.[14]

Politicians tend to ignore evidence that does not point in the political direction they wish to go. For years, public opinion polls have shown that the nationalization of more industries is unpopular with voters, and revisionist Labour politicians have sought to have the party abandon this policy. Proponents of nationalization have denounced both the propriety and validity of evidence from opinion polls, and have lobbied successfully for extending nationalization. Public opinion polls have also shown that a clear majority of the electorate, and especially of Conservative voters, favor the reintroduction of capital punishment. Yet Conservative governments have refused to bring back the death penalty.

When the majority of English people speak out politically, they use actions, not words. Popular sayings about voting with your feet or voting with your pocketbook have real meaning in economic policy. A trade union can take strike action even after the government of the day, whether Conservative or Labour, declares that a strike is not in the national interest. Company directors can similarly act against government economic policy, withholding investment when the government wishes to stimulate it, and increasing investment when the government wishes to curb spending.

Citizens often voice demands for public services by actions taken without political intent. When people who formerly relied upon public transportation buy cars, the extra traffic they add to the roads constitutes a demand that something be done about the road network that they overload. When people have larger families, the increase in the number of children is a pressure to increase the number of teachers and schools.

The right to be heard is not the right to determine public policy. When individuals find that the government does not share their opinion, it is the government's view that becomes law. At the extreme, a citizen may communicate dissatisfaction by leaving the country; in fact, few people emigrate from England. More often, an individual seeks to exit from the effects of a particular policy. Parents dissatisfied with government education policy can send their children to a fee-paying school, if they can afford its fees. In many circumstances, a citizen cannot avoid the effects of public policy. For example, if a new road is built, it will affect all homeowners nearby. Individuals can communicate their opposition to a measure, but the government's view of what people get is authoritative.

PUBLIC MEDIA

The media, as their name implies, are means of communication. Among the media, television is the most popular means of following political news. It is preferred by 48 percent, while 20 percent prefer newspapers, 19 percent private conversations, and 5 percent radio.[15] But people do not rely exclusively upon one medium; they are exposed to politics by television, through the press, and in private conversation.

The major media are large, complex industries, and politics is not the sole interest of publishers, journalists, or the unions that organize media workers. Communicators care about journalistic practices, audience ratings, and money. Very few media organizations specialize in political reporting, and most stories are remote from the world of Westminster. Technical considerations, such as the need for visual materials to illustrate television news, also affect how the media operate. Most of the media are in the business of entertaining rather than informing a mass audience.

Broadcasting. Television and radio (collectively described as broadcasting) are highly centralized but competitive. The British Broadcasting Corporation provides two network television services and four radio services throughout the United Kingdom. Its regions provide additional programs, especially in non-English parts of the kingdom. Local radio stations, inaugurated in England in 1967, are a specialized news medium. The Independent Broadcasting Authority (IBA) licenses television companies to transmit and produce programs for a particular region; they exchange programs to provide a nationwide network. Independent Television News provides national and international news for the IBA stations. In 1982, Channel 4 started under IBA sponsorship as a network producing programs for specialist audiences. Commercial local radio stations also broadcast.

The broadcasting industry is subject to government licensing. The BBC's Board of Governors is appointed by the government, as are the members of the IBA. Each body operates under a government charter, subject to periodic review and renewal. Because the BBC depends for much of its revenue upon the license fee required of each household receiving programs (in 1984, £46 for color television), the government can exert influence by determining when this fee may rise. The annual profits of independent television companies, derived primarily from advertising, are affected by financial clauses in their license. Moreover, renewal of a license is not automatic. The government also influences broadcasting by decisions it makes about who gets broadcasting licenses and the conditions under which licenses will be renewed.

Because broadcasting authorities can never be sure which

party will be in office when their license is up for renewal, they have a strong incentive to report politics impartially, and statutes require companies to maintain a fair balance between differing points of view.[16] The bias toward caution in reporting party politics is balanced by the fact that novelty makes news. A study of the 1983 general election campaign found that BBC-1 divided its news coverage 34 percent for the Conservatives; 36 percent Labour; 26 percent, Alliance; and other candidates, 4 percent. Independent Television News (ITN) acted virtually the same.[17]

Parties and candidates are not permitted to purchase time to advertise themselves. The parties are allocated time for party political programs on radio and television roughly in accord with their electoral strength. In the 1980s the disparity between the Alliance's share of the popular vote and its low share of seats in Parliament has made the definition of "fair" shares contentious.

The general public trusts the impartiality of the broadcasting media.[18] In the 1983 election, 72 percent said they thought TV fair to parties and candidates, four times as many as those considering it unfair (Table VII.1). This confidence is not shared by all politicians. One set of complaints is nonpartisan. It alleges that the broadcasting authorities do not give enough time to programs that the viewers ought to watch, that is, programs about Parliament. Yet MPs themselves have been singularly unhelpful, repeatedly rejecting proposals to permit televising of Commons debates. Radio broadcasting of excerpts of debates began only in 1978. Politicians' complaints against television are motivated by the belief (or hope) that unpopularity

TABLE VII.1 *Perceived Fairness of Television Election Coverage*

In 1983 the channel treated:	BBC1 %	BBC2 %	ITV %	Channel 4 %	Overall %
All parties fairly	67	70	73	66	72
Tended to favour some parties	20	19	14	14	18
Don't know	13	11	13	20	10

Source: Barrie Gunter, Michael Svennevig, and Mallory Wober, *Television Coverage of the 1983 General Election* (London: BBC/IBA, 1984), tables 15, 16.

rests not with themselves but with those who communicate news about them.

Broadcasting staffs do not agree about the best way to treat political news. The BBC still reflects in part the ethos of Lord Reith, director-general during its formative years between the wars, who commented, ''It is occasionally indicated to us that we are apparently setting out to give the public what we think they need — and not what they want — but few know what they want and very few what they need.'' Lord Reith's high-minded ethic, it was alleged, resulted in few people ''at the top of the Corporation knowing, or indeed caring what the audience makes of the service it receives.''[19]

Competition from commercial television has made BBC staff more audience-conscious. But this awareness has only intensified differences within the BBC. In a study of BBC current affairs election staff, Jay Blumler found two contrasting outlooks: one group had a ''sacerdotal'' approach, seeing elections as intrinsically important events and the BBC as the quasi-priestly intermediary between politicians and people. ''Pragmatic'' producers, by contrast, wished to report the election only insofar as events were newsworthy; a crime story could be given more prominence than a Cabinet minister's repetition of a familiar campaign theme. As the campaign progressed, the communicators agreed on one thing: they saw themselves as public watchdogs guarding against politicians manipulating the media.[20]

The more the public is exposed to politics by television, the less interested it appears to be. Since 1970 surveys have asked voters whether they thought there was too much, not enough, or about the right amount of television coverage of an election campaign. Very few say that there is not enough coverage of politics. In 1970, 47 percent said there was too much coverage, and 30 percent about the right amount. In 1983 the proportion saying that TV gives too much attention to elections rose to 69 percent; the proportion satisfied with the amount of coverage fell to 21 percent.[21]

Studies of audience reaction to politics on television emphasize how little effect programs have on political outlooks. People principally judge programs by their *prior* party loyalty; they do not choose a party simply in response to a particular television program. Long-time Conservatives like Conservative broadcasts best, and Labour supporters like Labour best, regardless of style.

Viewers differ in the expectations that they bring to televised politics. A limited proportion use programs to help them decide how to vote; most wait to be informed about what politicians are thinking, gain reinforcement for their partisan loyalty, or enjoy the excitement of an election race. Programs can alter voters' impressions of individual political personalities, though not necessarily for the better. In 1964, Harold Wilson altered public perception of his personality, but the change emphasized "malevolent dynamism."[22] The less well known the personality or, for the Alliance, the less well known the party, the more important television is as a means of increasing popular awareness of a political cause.

The Press. Unlike the press in the United States, Canada, and many continental European countries, the English press is centralized. Morning newspapers printed in London circulate throughout England,[23] thanks to special night transport facilities. London-based papers account for two-thirds of daily newspaper circulation and nearly all Sunday circulation. Concentrated production is made necessary by the high costs of newspaper production and by competition for advertising. A popular newspaper needs at least 4 million readers to have a chance of breaking even financially. National papers with circulations smaller than that require a specialized readership to justify premium advertising rates.[24]

Today, no national daily paper is tied to a political party financially, though all express political preferences in their editorial columns. The view of the old-fashioned political proprietor, Lord Beaverbrook, publisher of the *Daily Express,* was, "I ran the paper purely for the purpose of making propaganda." But Beaverbrook also believed, "I do not think a paper is any good for propaganda unless you run it as a commercial success."[25] Today, proprietors run newspapers to make (or lose) money. Most readers see their newspaper as having a well-defined party orientation; this is offset by competition with television, which provides a bi- or tripartisan view of politics (Table VII.2).

The criteria for defining political news are broad. Although ministers complain that bad news is always news, claims of success will be printed if the speaker has high political status. As a Westminster lobby journalist once remarked, ''You may not believe what a person is saying, but if he is Prime Minister, he has a right to have his views known.'' Activities are deemed newsworthy if they are:

Immediate (the latest economic figures, not trends of a decade).

Novel within a familiar context (a Liberal party victory in a by-election).

Of interest to lots of people (an increase in pensions) or about a high-status individual (an increase in the Queen's grant from Parliament).

Factually ascertainable (a change in Cabinet ministers).

TABLE VII.2 *National Daily Newspaper Readership*

	Readership[a] % adults	Readers' view of paper's partisanship[a]			Own party preference[b]		
		Con %	All. %	Lab %	Con %	All. %	Lab %
Popular papers							
Sun	25	64	1	10	29	15	39
Mirror	21	5	1	80	19	16	51
Express	12	85	2	2	53	17	17
Mail	11	80	2	7	52	24	12
Daily Star	9	35	4	24	21	16	49
Serious papers							
Telegraph	8	86	2	1	62	19	7
Guardian	4	15	35	14	14	28	41
Times	3	66	0	0	50	24	12
Financial Times	1	60	0	0	51	19	17

[a]As reported in MORI, *British Public Opinion: General Election 1983*, p. 84; adding those who are don't knows about the partisanship of a paper would make the row totals sum to 100 percent.

[b]Unpublished figures supplied by NOP from survey of 4,357 respondents, 28 June–10 July 1984.

Close at hand (poor rubbish collection in London, not Newcastle-upon-Tyne).

Related to recognized areas of reporting (the wedding of a celebrity).

Occurring when little else is happening (a politician's speech when Parliament is not sitting).

News criteria also define the way in which events are reported. A demonstration may be reported in terms of its potential for disorder rather than in terms of the issue that the demonstrators are marching about.[26] Sometimes the opportunity to write a major story occurs fortuitously: a slum-property millionaire became newsworthy by being on the fringes of a scandal involving a minister, John Profumo. Because the slum landlord was dead, an unfavorable account of his property dealings could be printed without risk of libel. The exposé won a prize, and the publicity led to government legislation.

The Westminster lobby correspondent is the main figure in a paper's political reporting. The lobby correspondent usually writes the paper's lead political news story each day, because it is assumed that Parliament is the focal point of government. Since a lobby journalist is privileged in mixing daily with ministers and MPs, he can write with authority and inside knowledge. The professional role breeds detachment and skepticism about Parliament. One survey of lobby staff found that in party terms they divided into three almost equal groups: Labour, Conservative, and those who voted Liberal or abstained.[27]

If a lobby correspondent risks having a perspective affected by too close contact with politicians and events, the occupational hazard of a leader writer is detachment. Involvement in the daily routines of a newspaper office allows limited time to confront at first hand the problems about which editorials pronounce. The content of the day's leader page is likely to be decided by intraoffice discussion tempered by the paper's past position and readership. Byline columnists may gain an audience by cultivating a striking prose style or expressing an original point of view; to follow a party line is to be predictable, and risks dullness.

In an era when most publishers are not in their newspaper's

office every day because of having a multiplicity of business commitments elsewhere, the relationship between editor and owner is becoming more volatile. An editor is usually given a free rein for a substantial period. The proprietor may then object to a story and intervene in the paper's operation, for a multimillionaire owner will not be accustomed to having employees disagree with him. The editor will be affronted, regarding this as interference with editorial freedom. In the 1980s printing unions have from time to time also asserted an independent influence, compelling editors to print statements or free advertisements stating the views of union officials when they disagree strongly with the paper's editorial line.

For most of the daily press, the label newspaper is a misleading description of its contents. The five popular tabloid papers — the *Mirror, Sun, Express, Daily Star,* and *Mail* — carry little political news. Political stories consist primarily of headlines, photographs, and catch phrases, not detailed reports or analysis. These papers are sold for entertainment rather than information. The *Sun,* the biggest-selling paper in Britain, reached this position by featuring big photographs of bare-breasted models on page three. Only the readers of the four serious papers — the *Telegraph, Guardian, Times,* and *Financial Times* — receive sufficient domestic and international news each day to keep their readers reasonably informed about events.

The readership of the national press is determined partly by the education of readers, and partly by each paper's style. The popular press appeals to readers with a minimum of education; a majority of its readers are working class. By contrast, more than four-fifths of the serious papers' readers are middle class. Within each class papers compete for readers, and political positions are part of the image that each paper projects. Surveys show that however much an editor protests a paper's independence, most readers associate it with a party. Readers of popular papers differ in their party support: a majority of *Mirror* readers vote Labour, and a majority of *Express* and *Mail* readers favor the Conservatives. A paper's editorial line tends to match the distribution of views among its readers. The popular press today contains pro-Conservative (the *Express*) and pro-Labour (the *Mirror*) papers.

Media consumption is affected by an individual's political role. Politicians courting popular favor give most attention to television, because it reaches the largest audience. Those eager for the favor of the party faithful give particular attention to papers read by activists, whether party weeklies, local weeklies published in their constituency, or national dailies. Civil servants read serious and specialist papers. Among administrative-class officials, a survey found 88 percent read *The Times,* 72 percent the *Telegraph,* 36 percent the *Guardian,* and only one-quarter a popular paper. By contrast, among the clerical grade, the majority read a popular paper; only one-quarter read the *Telegraph,* and only 4 percent *The Times.* Whereas only a small percentage of the adult population read a serious weekly offering news and comments, 88 percent of administrative civil servants do so. *The Economist* is read by 68 percent, and *New Society,* specializing in social problems, by 33 percent.[28]

Studies of the influence of the press emphasize that class influences the choice of both party and paper. Within a class, individuals socialized into Conservative families are more likely to read pro-Conservative papers as adults, and those from Labour families, pro-Labour papers.[29] Class differences also affect the choice of TV programs.

The public media do not create public opinion; they tend to reinforce the predispositions of their audience. The creation of a multimedia system of political communication parallels the growth in the proportion of voters who no longer have a fixed party loyalty. Individual voters today are not exposed to news from a single partisan source. More and more readers are showing a readiness to switch between newspapers, and television provides virtually every newspaper reader with a view of public affairs different from, because less partisan than that contained in the press. With multiple sources of information, a voter is less likely to be certain that one party is always right.

COMMUNICATION IN WESTMINSTER

Politicians are involved in horizontal communication with their political peers within Westminster as well as vertical communication with those who elect them. Whereas vertical communication is usually public, horizontal communication is usually private.

Official Sources. Government departments differ enormously in the extent of their vertical communication with the peripheral public. The two chief Whitehall departments, the Treasury and the Foreign Office, have no organized channels of communication within England. Their listening posts are abroad in Washington, Brussels, Moscow, and elsewhere. Only through the marketplace can the public and Treasury officials speak to each other about economic policies. By contrast, the Department of Social Security has an elaborate domestic communications network, because its local offices deliver government benefits to millions. The problem of such a ministry is too much information; it is met by establishing fixed bureaucratic procedures. However, reliance on routine can cause a ministry to ignore warning signals about things going wrong.

To provide information about the changing demographic pressures on government services, the Central Statistical Office collects large quantities of information about social conditions in censuses and sample surveys. The information-gathering work of the Central Statistical Office is relevant to policy but does not determine policy. It provides facts about social conditions, but the facts *never* speak for themselves. Politicians evaluate and interpret their significance for government policy.

Whitehall departments commissioning surveys often stipulate questions that *cannot* be asked. Two academic researchers undertaking a study of the civil service on behalf of the Fulton Committee said in the second paragraph of their report, "Enquiry into such matters as political allegiance, religious affiliation, attitudes to career, and promotion opportunities was ruled out as too delicate and difficult."[30]

Publication by the government of forecasts of the state of the economy are often less valid than appears. Sophisticated mathematical models of the economy can be flawed by substantial errors inherent in efforts to forecast the future.[31] Whatever the immediate difficulties, official forecasts almost invariably stress favorable omens. No government wishes to publicize the possibility that it is steering the economy in the wrong direction. On occasion, the Treasury avoids risks by presenting forecasts so vague as to be meaningless in practice. In 1970 a Labour government divided over entry into the Common Market issued a white paper estimating the cost of entry at anything between £100 and £1,100 million. A Labour minister commented that this was like saying the score of a football match would be anything from 10-0 for one side to 10-0 for the other.[32]

Communication with intermittent public persons often takes place through an informal marketplace of ideas involving public officials, experts, and pressure group representatives. For example, defense policy involves the feedback of information between government ministers, senior military officers, defense correspondents of serious papers, members of the International Institute for Strategic Studies, a few MPs of each party specifically interested in defense, and spokesmen (sometimes former military officers) for firms producing armaments.[33] This elite network has few contacts with the mass of the population. Within its limits it is open to a variety of ideas throughout Europe and the United States.

If a government department wishes advice about a major issue of policy, it establishes an ad hoc Royal Commission or departmental committee; these committees deliberate upon such topics as metrication, the export of animals for slaughter, and the distribution of income. A Royal Commission is often formed when government is unable or unwilling to assume immediate responsibility for a policy decision. It can acquire information; identify and commend a course of action likely to be accepted by the majority of affected interests appearing before it; encourage public support for a policy that the government wishes to adopt; or stall decisions about a controversial matter. The government will prescribe terms of reference to ensure that the Commission does not publicize issues that the government wishes to leave unexamined.

An experienced committee man, Andrew Shonfield, has described how these bodies proceed:

> Just plunge into your subject: collect as many facts as you can;
> think about them hard as you go along; and at the end, use your

commonsense, and above all your feel for the practicable, to select a few good proposals out of the large number of suggestions which will surely come your way.[34]

Like a judge, a committee usually confines itself to listening to those who wish to testify before it. It may lack time, money, staff, or inclination to undertake any additional inquiry or research. For example, the Pilkington Committee on Broadcasting held 120 meetings over two years. It listened to dozens of pressure-group spokesmen, but it did not commission any sample survey of listeners' and viewers' attitudes. After it reported, a survey showed that public opinion was divided about a major Pilkington proposal. The pro-Pilkington group — those with education beyond the age of 18 — was about 4 percent of the population; the anti-Pilkington group was 96 percent.[35]

Mutual Interdependence. Although their professional interests are different, communicators and politicians need one another. Journalists need politicians as sources of news. Politicians need journalists to give publicity to their views and themselves. This communications loop can be complete only if it includes politicians and journalists; members of the general public may neither notice nor care about the publicity that results.

A lobbyman gets political news by learning how politicians think, spending fifty to sixty hours a week in and around the Palace of Westminster. Like back-bench MPs, a lobbyman has little time for Whitehall departments, or access there, for the most part depending upon ministers to provide information about government policy. Specialist correspondents in such fields as economics, defense, and education provide supplementary coverage of public affairs. The lobbyman, a paper's chief political correspondent, cannot act as a watchdog in Whitehall because he "stands guard in the wrong place."[36]

Lobby correspondents in the Palace of Westminster are involved in noncommunication as well as communication; spotlighting some topics necessarily leaves others in shadow. Communication within Whitehall and noncommunication with those outside its inner circle can be achieved by publishing stories in code. Everything important may be stated indirectly or by implication, so that only those who have private knowledge of public affairs can decode the document's significance. Most of the public cannot.

A report on *Control of Public Expenditure* by a committee under Lord Plowden, himself a former civil servant, illustrates how communication in code operates. The committee prepared both private memoranda and a formal report, so that the Treasury, the chief object of criticism, could decide which parts of the comment need be published.

Following publication of the coded report, W. J. M. Mackenzie, a former classical philologist and wartime civil servant, published a translation. The first paragraph of the official report reads:

> For these studies we co-opted the Permanent Secretaries of the departments with whose expenditure we are concerned or who had special experience of the general problems under review. In some cases we sought specialist advice from outside the civil service. We decided, however, not to take evidence from outside bodies: our review was primarily concerned with the inner working of the Treasury and the departments, and was necessarily confidential in character, and we decided that the group itself (except on certain specialist matters) provided a sufficient body of outside opinion to bring to bear on this task.

Mackenzie translated it thus:

> We proceeded on two principles: no dirty linen in public: outside critics are bores.[37]

The Importance of Noncommunication. Many conventions and laws of British government emphasize noncommunication. The philosophy is summarized in a government white paper entitled *Information and the Public Interest.*

> It does not follow, of course, that public consultation on tentative proposals is invariably the right course. It may result in slower decisions and slower action when prompt action is essential. Sometimes, too, conflicting views and conflicting interests are already well known. In such cases a prolonged period of consultation will merely impose delay without any compensating advantages. Each individual case has to be considered on its merits.[38]

The government declares that it favors prior publication of information about policy matters "whenever reasonably possible."[39] Whitehall remains the sole judge of what is reasonable and possible.

It is standard operating procedure for government departments to refuse the press information that it requests. When a *Times* reporter sought details of cases investigated by the Parliamentary Commissioner's (Ombudsman's) office, it was prevented by statute from even giving the name of the MP who had endorsed a complaint. Therefore, the press could not investigate consumer satisfaction with the Ombudsman's work. Similarly, when the National Council for Civil Liberties wrote to heads of each of forty-six police authorities in England and Wales requesting copies of their annual reports, only eighteen replied.[40]

Members of Parliament too are often frustrated in their inquiries into government policy. Question time in the House of Commons is of limited value in probing Whitehall's actions, because questions are not permitted on many topics, ranging from details of arms sales to purchases made by the National Health Service. Even when the Speaker allows a question on a delicate subject, the minister may refuse to answer. During the Suez crisis, Sir Anthony Eden refused Parliament an answer to a question asking whether or not the country was at war with Egypt![41] Because only a few minutes are allowed for an answer to each question, a minister can reply with words that evade the question. In the opinion of a former civil servant:

> The perfect reply to an embarrassing question in the House of Commons is one that is brief, appears to answer the question completely, if challenged can be proved to be accurate in every word, gives no opening for awkward supplementaries and discloses really nothing.[42]

Faced with such constraints, 91 percent of MPs believe that they are not adequately informed about the actions of government. Moreover, five-sixths of MPs think their lack of knowledge is caused in part by ministers wishing to limit what the Commons is told. One backbencher remarked:

The tendency of paternalism towards Government backbenchers is strong: "If you knew what I know you'd see I'm right." Meanwhile, father knows best.[43]

The constitutional justification for Whitehall's secretiveness is the doctrine of ministerial responsibility. Everything that a department does is said to be done in the name of its minister. The convention that the department reflects the mind of one individual has a corollary: no one else can speak for the department. Both junior ministers and senior civil servants are expected to make no public statement committing the department to a policy unless authorized by the minister. This convention is strengthened by Section 2 of the Official Secrets Act of 1911, which makes it a crime for any person to communicate any information received by virtue of being a minister or civil servant. This act even covers such matters as a circular from the minister to hospital authorities, asking them to convey Christmas greetings to all the staff on Christmas Eve.

The doctrine of ministerial responsibility is not valid empirically. Time is one obstacle to communication to and from the minister. There are not enough hours in the day for any minister to read everything about the work of a department or to draft or sign every statement issued in his name. A minister must communicate broad principles if ministry staff are to apply them in particular instances. When departmental scandals occur, the minister is formally responsible but can with truth plead that he did not know what was being done in his name. This plea can even be made on behalf of the Prime Minister. Lord Denning's inquiry into the 1963 Profumo scandal exculpated Prime Minister Harold Macmillan on the ground that the security services did not tell the Prime Minister what was going on.[44] The sequence of events leading up to the Falklands War in 1982 is another example of senior Whitehall ministers not being aware of (or not having time to think about) all that is important.

The doctrine of ministerial responsibility remains powerful politically because it appeals to the most important people in government: ministers and civil servants. Ministers do not wish to have news of differences within their department discussed in public prior to making a decision. They are also glad to take credit and blame for all that happens, trusting that a well-run department will more often than not make them look good by actions taken in their name. Civil servants regard confidentiality as the basis of trust in their dealings with ministers. Any alteration of arrangements would raise "major constitutional issues."[45]

When the Franks Committee was deliberating about liberalizing or amending the Official Secrets Act, very senior civil servants testified to the need to restrict public knowledge of departmental deliberations. Sir William Armstrong, the then head of the civil service, favored disseminating more information — but only if dissemination was controlled at a single point, in order to prevent the free flow of "good, bad or indifferent, inaccurate or accurate, embarrassing or unembarrassing" information. Sir Burke Trend, secretary of the Cabinet, opposed publication of news about the existence of Cabinet committees because it might breach collective responsibility.[46] Subsequently a leading academic lawyer, Professor Harry Street, commented that Whitehall's regulations prohibiting publication of information meant:

> Watergate could never have been exposed here. Our laws — the Official Secrets Act, contempt, libel and breach of confidence — would have prevented any journalist from investigating too closely.[47]

The complexities of contemporary government and changing standards of behavior among politicians have lowered the wall of secrecy a little. Occasionally, a government that has narrowed its policy options but not yet selected among them may publish a green paper to canvass political reaction to the choices before it. Doing so gives a minister the benefit of criticisms before officially committing the department. Individual civil servants now take part in public discussions of some pending legislation in an effort to increase public understanding of government measures. However, officials have been reminded that they "should not be drawn into expressing personal views on policy matters which could be represented as in conflict with those of their ministers, or as reflecting any political (that is, party political) bias."[48]

Cracks are appearing in the wall of official secrecy too, because of changing values among civil servants. Civil servants see ministers exploiting secrecy for their own ends, hiding evidence of their mistakes, and leaking information selectively, actions inconsistent with nonpartisan norms of good government. Such actions reduce civil service confidence in the absolute value of official secrecy. Even more important, when civil servants develop commitments to political opinions — whether about nuclear weapons, the payment of benefits to poor people, or vaguely defined standards of good government — then they have other claims to balance against absolute loyalty to their minister.

An increasing minority of civil servants is now prepared to put their idea of what is right and proper ahead of loyalty to a minister, and leak damaging information to the press. In 1984 a minor clerk, Sarah Tinsdall, went to jail for sending a photocopy of a nuclear weapons memorandum to the press. A senior civil servant, Clive Ponting, was indicted for leaking information to an MP contradicting a ministerial statement about actions during the Falklands War. Ponting argued that he had a duty to inform Parliament about government actions, even when this was against the wishes of the minister he was meant to serve. The interests of the state, he asserted, are broader than those of the government of the day. A jury acquitted Ponting.

The more widespread the unwillingness of civil servants to keep matters secret, the greater the difficulty in enforcing the Official Secrets Act, and the greater the pressure to change secrecy laws and to change assumptions about the privileges and duties of civil servants.

Politicians today are more interested in publicizing themselves than in protecting Whitehall. A determined politician can publish what he wishes without judicial punishment, for "the rules to be observed are voluntary obligations, known in advance and dependent for their observance upon no more than the decency and honour of those concerned." Richard Crossman established this point when three volumes of his political diary of six years as a Cabinet minister were published, in spite of objections from Whitehall about frequent references to civil servants who had worked with him, and the ex-minister's accounts of what was purportedly said in Cabinet.[49]

The leak is the politician's characteristic way of paying lip service to the doctrine of noncommunication, while ensuring that friendly journalists will print his version of current political controversies. The distinction between a leak, which is a breach of convention, and a briefing, which is accepted as a necessary means of giving background information to journalists, has been defined thus by James Callaghan: "Briefing is what I do; leaking is what you do." Technically, such disclosures are violations of the Official Secrets Act. But as the Director General of the Security Service has complained, "The chances of their being prosecuted . . . are minimal, if they exist at all, because the ministers can always say that they authorised themselves to disclose the information."[50]

WHAT PRICE COMMUNICATION?

The costs and benefits of secrecy and publicity differ from issue to issue. The greater the number required to cooperate if a policy is to work, the greater the need to seek information in advance, and to publicize the reasons behind the policy in the hope of mobilizing consent. The fewer the people involved in carrying out a policy, the less the need to communicate widely in advance of a decision. Every decision involves a trade-off between the speed gained by noncommunication and the risk of lacking widespread understanding and support.

Communication and noncommunication are complementary and concurrent. There is never enough time to talk to every group about every policy that the government is considering. In theory, representatives of all who need to know will be consulted, and those unaffected need not be consulted. Decisions about who should and should not be informed are usually made within Whitehall. Those in the know have a chance to act or react in their own interest. Those not consulted may sometimes consider that what they didn't know *has* hurt them.

The most economical form of communication is virtual representation; it requires understanding, not talk. When individuals know each other's mind, a wink and a nod may be sufficient, or one person may put himself in another's place and make the decision that the other would have taken. British government requires much virtual communication. Members of Parliament speak for their constituents by virtue of election, ministers speak for their departments, and departmental civil servants write letters speaking for ministers.

It is deceptively easy for people in Westminister to mistake the echo of their own voices for the views of a much larger public. In an essay on government in wartime, Sir Norman Chester remarked how the intensity of horizontal communication in Whitehall isolated it from the general public.

> What can come to be important, if one is not careful, is not how decisions affect people, but how they are thought to operate by people in the Whitehall circle. The leader or letter in *The Times* or *Economist* can become the reality by which one's actions are judged.[51]

The habits of wartime persist in peacetime. A study of the way public expenditure is controlled by the Treasury is aptly titled *The Private Government of Public Money.*[52]

Political communication is often urged as a good in itself, but even perfect communication cannot by itself resolve political problems, for by definition politics is about conflict. The communication of views on any issue of political significance will inevitably produce arguments and evidence supporting conflicting choices. The more representative the exchange of views the greater the likelihood that the result will be stalemate, or a three-, four-, or five-way division of opinion. In many political contexts, agreement is more important than anything else. Even in wartime, estimates of aircraft production were not reconciled by more information but by ''statistical bargaining'' leading to agreement upon a figure that all the Whitehall groups involved would accept.[53]

Busy policymakers want help, not information for its own sake. Sometimes Whitehall departments are prepared to spend months or years seeking information. At other times, they react to straws in the wind, or ignore facts that appear as palpable as handwriting on the wall. Politicians attend to information if the benefits of doing so are likely to be greater than the costs of ignoring it. A policymaker's attention is not a function of

the information's quality, but of immediate political requirements. In a political crisis, when the costs of inaction are great,
then any kind of information — statistical, literary, or half-
baked — will be seized upon for clues of what to do.[54]
The relative secrecy of Whitehall has been sustained by the
view that Whitehall knows what is best for the country. This
confidence has been undermined by the increasing difficulties
of British government. However, the habits of the past do not
disappear quickly, especially when they are integral to the status of both ministers and civil servants. The nation's governors
appear uncertain about whether it is in their interest to provide
more information about the problems facing government. The
less there is confidence that things are going well, the more
important it is for politicians to warn the electorate of troubles
in advance rather than have voters learn about them only when
the loud noise of failure shatters Whitehall's customary pose of
knowing silence.

NOTES

1. See Colin Seymour-Ure, *The Political Impact of Mass Media* (London:
Constable, 1974), chapters 1, 2. More generally, see Denis McQuail, *Mass
Communication Theory* (London: Sage Publications, 1983).

2. George Brown, *In My Way* (Harmondsworth: Penguin, 1972), p. 105.
See also Henry Brandon, *In the Red* (London: Deutsch, 1966), p. 43.

3. Samuel Brittan, *Steering the Economy* (London: Secker & Warburg,
1969), p. 29.

4. The title of a book by David Williams (London: Hutchinson, 1965);
see also K. G. Robertson, *Public Secrets* (London: Macmillan, 1982).

5. Quoted by Anthony Sampson, from a 1970 Official Secrets Act trial,
in *The New Anatomy of Britain* (London: Hodder & Stoughton, 1971), p. 369.
See also David Butler, "Cabinet Secrets," *The Listener,* 29 February 1968.

6. See the monthly *Gallup Political Index.*

7. See Anthony Downs, *An Economic Theory of Democracy* (New York: Har-
per & Row, 1957).

8. See "The Dons Who Want to Go to Market," *The Observer* (London),
24 October 1971, *Gallup Political Index,* No. 149 (December 1972), p. 205; and
British Attitudes Towards the Common Market, 1957–1971 (London: Gallup Poll,
1972).

9. On the referendum and the background to it, see David Butler and
Uwe Kitzinger, *The 1975 Referendum* (London: Macmillan, 1976); and Anthony King, *Britain Says Yes: The 1975 Referendum on the Common Market* (Washington, D. C.: American Enterprise Institute, 1977).

10. *Gallup Political Index,* No. 285 (May 1984), p. 19.

11. See Richard Rose, *The Problem of Party Government,* chapter 11, and the
discussion below in chapter 9.

12. See, e.g., Robert Worcester, "The Hidden Activists," p. 200; and Robert E. Dowse, "The MP and his Surgery," *Political Studies,* 11:3 (1963).

13. See Richard Rose, *Influencing Voters: A Study of Campaign Rationality* (London: Faber & Faber, 1967), and Robert M. Worcester and Martin Harrop, eds., *Political Communications* (London: Allen & Unwin, 1982).

14. See Dennis Kavanagh, *Constituency Electioneering* (London: Longmans, 1970), pp. 56ff.; and Robert Worcester, "Interview," *British Politics Group Newsletter,* No. 8 (spring 1977), p. 10.

15. David Butler and Donald Stokes, *Political Change in Britain,* 1st ed. (London: Macmillan, 1969), p. 220.

16. See chapters on broadcasting in successive volumes of the Nuffield election studies written by David Butler and others; the annual *BBC Handbook* (London: BBC); and a special issue of *Parliamentary Affairs,* 37:3 (1984) with varied studies of broadcasting.

17. See Martin Harrison, "Broadcasting," in Butler and Kavanagh, *The British General Election of 1983,* p. 148.

18. See Barrie Gunter, Michael Svennevig, and Mallory Wober, *Television Coverage of the 1983 General Election* (London: BBC/ITN, 1984), p. 19.

19. Tom Burns, "Public Service and Private World," in *The Sociology of Mass Media Communicators* (Keele: *Sociological Review* Monograph, no. 13, 1969), p. 71.

20. Jay G. Blumler, "Producers' Attitudes toward Television Coverage of an Election Campaign," in R. Rose, ed., *Studies in British Politics,* 3rd ed.

21. Gunter, Svennevig, and Wober, *Television Coverage.*

22. Jay G. Blumler and Denis McQuail, *Television in Politics* (London: Faber & Faber, 1968), p. 243.

23. What follows explicitly excludes the media in Scotland and Northern Ireland, which offer a different mixture of news than London-based papers. Cf. Richard Rose and Ian McAllister, *United Kingdom Facts,* chapter 7.

24. On the economics of the press, see Fred Hirsch and David Gordon, *Newspaper Money* (London: Hutchinson, 1975) and the Final Report of Lord McGregor's *Royal Commission on the Press* (London: HMSO, Cmnd. 6810, 1977).

25. Quoted in Colin Seymour-Ure, *The Press, Politics and the Public* (London: Methuen, 1968), p. 95.

26. See James Halloran, Philip Elliott, and Graham Murdock, *Demonstrations and Communication* (Harmondsworth: Penguin, 1970).

27. For details, see Jeremy Tunstall, *The Westminster Lobby Correspondents* (London: Routledge, 1970), pp. 20, 35, and 59ff.

28. A. H. Halsey and I. M. Crewe, "Social Survey of Civil Servants," *The Fulton Committee Report,* Vol. 3.1, pp. 32ff.

29. See Butler and Stokes, *Political Change in Britain,* 1st ed., pp. 232ff.

30. Halsey and Crewe, "Social Survey of Civil Servants," p. 1.

31. See Paul Mosley, *The Making of Economic Policy* (Brighton: Wheatsheaf Books, 1984), pp. 218ff.

32. George Thomson, "The Game's the Same," *Guardian,* 9 July 1971.

33. See L. W. Martin, "The Market for Strategic Ideas," *American Political Science Review,* 56:1 (1962).

34. "In the course of Investigation," *New Society,* 24 July 1969.

35. Cf. *Report of the Pilkington Committee on Broadcasting* (London: HMSO, Cmnd. 1753, 1962); and Harry Henry, *Public Opinion and the Pilkington Committee* (London: The Sunday Times, 1962).

36. Seymour-Ure, *The Press, Politics and the Public*, pp. 176ff., 311. Cf. Jeremy Tunstall, *Journalists at Work* (London: Constable, 1971).

37. Cf. W. J. M. Mackenzie, "The Plowden Report: a translation," in Richard Rose, ed., *Studies in British Politics;* and the original *Control of Public Expenditure* (London: HMSO, Cmnd. 1432, 1961).

38. *Information and the Public Interest* (London: HMSO, Cmnd. 4089, 1969), pp. 6–7.

39. *Ibid.*, p. 7.

40. See Tony Smythe, "Police Report," *New Society*, 9 November 1972, and George Clark, "Official Secrets of Britain's Ombudsman," *The Times* (London), 7 May 1970.

41. See House of Commons *Debates*, Vol. 558, cols. 1452–1454 (October 31) and cols. 1620ff. (1 November 1956). See also, "Speaker Helps MP to Update List of Questions Government Departments Refuse to Answer," *The Times* (London), 24 April 1978.

42. H. E. Dale, *The Higher Civil Service of Great Britain* (London: Oxford University Press, 1941), p. 105.

43. Or in the case of Margaret Thatcher, Mother knows best. Anthony Barker and Michael Rush, *The Member of Parliament and His Information*, pp. 150, 363ff.

44. *Lord Denning's Report* (London: HMSO, Cmnd. 2152, 1963).

45. *Information and the Public Interest*, p. 10. Cf. Michael Cockerell, Peter Hennessy, and David Walker, *Sources Close to the Prime Minister* (London: Macmillan, 1984).

46. See the report of Lord Franks's *Departmental Committee on Section 2 of the Official Secrets Act, 1911* (London: HMSO, Cmnd. 5104 1972). Cf. Hugo Young, "But who is responsible for burials?" *The Sunday Times* 12 April 1978.

47. Quoted in "Fear that Judges May Become 'Political,' " *The Times*, 29 September 1975.

48. *Information and the Public Interest*, p. 10.

49. See the symposium, "After Crossman," *The Sunday Times*, 30 March 1975 and Anthony Lewis, "The Crossman Diaries and the Legal Lessons of the Pentagon Papers," *The Sunday Times*, 3 August 1975. Ironically, colleagues and friends always regarded Crossman as a notoriously misleading reporter of events and discussions.

50. Quoted in Rudolf Klein's note in *New Society*, 5 October 1972. See also Hugo Young, "A Practised Leaker Meets his Match," *The Sunday Times*, 30 April 1978.

51. "The Central Machinery for Economic Policy," in D. N. Chester, ed., *Lessons of the British War Economy* (Cambridge: University Press, 1951), p. 30.

52. By Hugh Heclo and Aaron Wildavsky.

53. Ely Devons, *Planning in Practice* (Cambridge: University Press, 1950), pp. 155ff.

54. See Richard Rose, "The Market for Policy Indicators," in Andrew Shonfield and Stella Shaw, eds., *Social Indicators and Social Policy* (London: Heinemann, 1972), pp. 119–41.

CHAPTER VIII

Organizing Group Pressures

The unsectional Parliament should know what each section in the nation thought before it gave the national decision.

MILLIONS OF PEOPLE may be of the same mind politically, but without organization they will have no means of expressing their views and no one to represent their opinions. With organization, the same people will have spokesmen pressing government to act, and government can consult those who speak on their behalf. The trade unions, organized late in the nineteenth century, greatly increased the political influence of millions of formerly unorganized workers. Employers then organized to present a case on their own behalf to government.[1]

Both parties and pressure groups present demands to government; the chief distinction between them is that pressure groups do not contest elections. Because pressure groups do not seek the responsibilities of public office, their officials are free to advocate sectional interests without regard to the views of the mass electorate. By contrast a party, especially when in office, faces conflicting demands which it must try to reconcile in ways acceptable to the electorate. Pressure groups do not need to face government's problem of balancing competing claims against each other. Pressure groups are narrowly concerned with their own members' immediate and specific interests; they do not need to win votes.

A pressure group can have organizations rather than individuals as its constituent members. The Confederation of British Industries consists of business firms and associations, and the Trades Union Congress has trade unions as members. The nominal resources of an organization itself based upon large organizations are substantial, but the influence of such a confederation upon individuals is indirect and limited. It cannot speak for owners, employees, or consumers of member organizations. In the case of the Labour party, which has unions directly affiliated to it, Labour cannot count on the votes of upwards of one-half of members of the unions belonging to the party.

Parties and pressure groups are not independent as conventional terminology implies; they are interdependent. Both are parts of one political system, advancing political demands within a common policy process. Controversies about particular political issues often lead pressure group officials and party politicians to work together. Conservative politicians and businessmen can find common cause in debates about industrial legislation, as can trade union leaders and Labour politicians. Moreover, a federally or confederally organized group, such as the Confederation of British Industry or the Trades Union Congress, sometimes aggregates interests like a political party. Reciprocally, a party may present as a point of principle demands arising from the particular concerns of a group close to it.

Because the word group is a very general term, writings about pressure groups sometimes treat every political institution as a manifestation of pressure politics. At the extreme, writers can view "the government and various official agencies as a group actor in the same sense that we view the CBI and TUC as group actors in the policy process." But this view is a *reductio ad absurdum,* blurring all distinctions between those responsible for exercising the powers of government, and those groups that seek to influence government but not hold public office.[2]

To analyze pressure groups, this chapter first of all sets out essential structural characteristics by which organizations differ. Secondly, consideration is given to differences in political values between pressure groups, and between particular groups and government that affect the strategic location of groups within the political system. Thirdly, the chapter considers how the structure and process of government affect what pressure groups do. Since pressure groups are only a part of the policy process, they must adapt to changes in policy making, as shown by the large and sometimes abrupt shifts in the relationship of trade union and business groups with government.

DIFFERENCES IN GROUP RESOURCES

Because thousands of groups seek to influence government, only the most general of statements can identify resources common to organizations as diverse as the Association of County Councils, the Committee of London Clearing Banks, the Howard League for Penal Reform, the Distressed Gentlefolks' Aid Association, the Royal Society for the Prevention of Cruelty to Animals, the Transport & General Workers' Union, and the Automobile Association. A discussion of organizational features of pressure groups must show the extent to which the resources of groups differ from each other in terms of four characteristics.

Goals. In the abstract, groups can be distinguished according to whether their goal is the promotion of a standing interest or a particular cause. A cause group usually has an identifiable goal which it hopes to attain; attaining its goal, such as the abolition of capital punishment, can exhaust the rationale for its efforts. By contrast, a group concerned with a continuing interest, such as a trade union or a business association, has a permanent stake in politics and needs continuous representation. Trade unions, business groups, and such organizations as the Automobile Association expect to be active as long as society has workers, business firms, or motorists.[3] Causes can have relatively clear and finite targets, such as the enactment or repeal of a particular Act of Parliament. By contrast, an interest group can simultaneously be involved in discussions with half a dozen Whitehall departments about dozens of specific issues.

Cause groups can have an "all or nothing" approach to politics; they can demand the total adoption of their demands, whether it be the fluoridation of water supply, or the banning of a particular chemical preservative in foods. From their perspective, half a loaf may appear little better than none. By contrast, interest groups, whether their concern is with agricultural subsidies or public sector wages, try to get more for their members, or in hard times to avoid being given less. They do not expect to get everything; they are predisposed to compromise.

Such are the dynamics of organizations that the achievement of a goal will not necessarily make a pressure group dissolve. For example, groups organized to lobby for the adoption of race relations legislation can, if laws are adopted, turn their attention to the implementation and enforcement of that legislation. Many groups have both immediate and long-term goals, the former capable of achievement in the life of a Parliament, and the latter sufficiently ambitious to justify activity for generations.

Distinctions are sometimes emphasized between economic and ideological goals, and between groups defending sectional interests and altruistic promotional groups.[4] The difficulty with sustaining these distinctions is that what one group describes as a cause or ideological principle another may see as a vested interest. Business groups proclaiming that the profit motive is good for the British economy will be attacked as serving the interests of capitalists, and a trade union that campaigns against declaring workers redundant in a declining industry will be accused of trying to protect its own dues income at the cost of industrial change. Members drawing no money income from a group's activities can still gain a reward; campaigning for a cause can provide psychic income.

Capacity for Organization. Organization is necessary to convert people who may have a common attitude or attribute into a group that can articulate demands and be heard by government. Interests exist independently of organization, but those who share an interest have no means of pressing it upon government, nor do public officials have any way of negotiating as long as it is unorganized.

Producer interests are more readily organized than consumer interests because they are specific and immediate. Individuals and companies can often derive immediate material benefits by joining producer groups, whether trade unions or trade associations. Unions seek to enforce a closed shop so that all persons whose working conditions are bargained for by a union must belong. By contrast, consumer groups are difficult to organize because an individual does not need to belong to a consumer pressure group in order to enjoy the benefits it seeks; these will be available to everyone in the marketplace. The Consumers' Association organizes only 3 percent of the nation's consumers, whereas trade unions organize more than 40 percent of the nation's workers.

The more durable, the more frequent, the more numerous, and the more intense the contacts among individuals, the easier they are to organize. Miners have many of the characteristics that encourage cohesive organization. They usually work at mining all their lives, they always work in contact with fellow miners, and they frequently meet miners outside the pits, living clustered together in mining villages. The future of a mine becomes, in effect, the future of their community. By contrast, passengers on an air charter flight are almost incapable of organization, for they meet only once when waiting at an airport to board an aircraft.

The predisposition of an individual or organization to join a pressure group can readily lead to conflicts between organizational commitments, if an individual belongs to groups campaigning for opposing goals. For example, a teacher may belong to a union that campaigns for a higher wage in response to inflation, and belong to a consumer group that campaigns for a wage and price freeze to counteract inflation. A business firm may simultaneously belong to a group that protests about taxation, and to a trade association asking government to spend more money to help its particular industry. Multiple memberships can create cross-pressures; individuals can have their views cancelled out when they support groups that represent opposing positions.

Organizational Cohesion. The more committed members are to a pressure group's goals, the more confident a group's leaders can be that they speak with their members united behind them. This increases its leverage with government and also means that any agreement reached with government will be accepted loyally by its members. The less committed members are or the more they are cross-pressured, the more difficulty a group has, for policymakers will know that it cannot claim to speak with the full backing of its nominal supporters.

Whitehall prefers to deal with cohesive pressure groups, because it is administratively convenient to do so. An agreement between a government department and a cohesive pressure group is more likely to be carried out, or so it is believed in Whitehall. But decades of attempting to organize agreement about plans for the British economy demonstrate that leaders of business and unions cannot guarantee that a bargain they make will be carried out. Pressure-group leaders can articulate members' demands, but cannot force the members to accept a bargain if the members deem it against their interest. As one experienced British economist writes:

> Neither the trade unions nor management have systems of private government that can send plenipotentiaries to negotiate on their behalf and commit them to settlement, save on limited issues and particular occasions, when the negotiators can keep in touch with their constituents as the negotiations proceed.[5]

The 1984 coal strike demonstrated that group leaders also lack the ability to make all their members reject an agreement. During the strike the National Union of Mineworkers was split: miners in some areas worked, and in others they picketed.

The country's major pressure groups — trade unions and business firms — have difficulty maintaining group loyalty. Trade unions are perennially subject to conflicts of interest between members of different unions. From time to time unions dispute which one should have jurisdiction over workers in a given industry. In particular, they disagree about wage differentials between members of different unions, a problem exacerbated by the large number of craft unions dividing workers in one factory into many competing groups. For example, the railways have separate unions for locomotive drivers, clerks, and other workers, each with its own idea of the proper wage differential between them.

The Trades Union Congress (TUC), the coordinating federation of unions, is internally weak because of differences between its largest members. The TUC cannot make a contract with government about wages because its members are not committed to accept whatever agreement it might make. The comparative weakness of the TUC is illustrated by its ratio of headquarters staff to union membership, the lowest of any central labor organization in the Western world.[6]

Nominally capitalist institutions differ in many ways. Major functional and social differences distinguish the banks and financial institutions in the City of London from manufacturers who borrow from banks and retailers who seek to supply consumers with goods bought from the most economical sources, whether at home or abroad. The name of the Confederation of British Industry implies more unity than exists in fact. Corporate members of the CBI often prefer to rely upon trade associations or, in larger firms, upon direct contacts with government to advance their particular interests. Nationalized industries are owned by government, not capitalists, yet lobby Whitehall too.[7]

The trend toward creating fewer and bigger organizations to represent economic interests has been fostered by structural change in industry, and often by government policy. The rise in trade union membership in the postwar era has been paralleled by the reduction in the total number of unions; and business and trade associations have merged too. Yet merger usually does not eliminate the differences in interest that initially justified separate organizations. A review of the creation of pressure groups to represent interests within the City of London concludes that the net effect is that "the modern financial community is much more diverse and less easily manageable."[8]

Strategic Location. An organization occupies a strong strategic position if it commands resources indispensable in society, such as energy, money, or food. How much a group extracts from a strong strategic location depends on several considerations. The first is whether it is a monopoly supplier of a service. Communication is a necessity of modern society, but no group has a total monopoly. A postal strike can be circumvented by

greater reliance upon telephones and private messenger services, and newspaper strikes by using radio and television.
Dockers have a much stronger strategic position than cinema
owners, for England must import food through the docks to
live, but it does not need to import films to amuse itself.

A pressure group can extract the private benefit of its public
monopoly insofar as it is prepared to use its strategic location
for its own members. Groups representing occupations with a
service ethic, such as doctors, nurses, or teachers, have had
professional norms inhibiting them from refusing their services
to clients in need. However, in the face of economic difficulties
these groups now press their claims more actively, sometimes
working to rule, refusing all but emergency cases, or striking
in pursuit of their demands. At all times professional groups
enjoy the strategic advantage of monopolizing expertise in a
vital field of public policy. Generalist politicians and civil servants cannot claim that they know more about medical care
than doctors, and are inclined to let doctors have their way on
professional matters.[9]

Political perceptions greatly influence the extent to which a
group's location is strategically strong. In the early 1970s the
National Union of Mineworkers believed that the country was
so dependent upon coal that the government of the day would
have to force the publicly owned National Coal Board to meet
its wage demands, even when they were contrary to government policy. In 1984 the Thatcher government showed that the
consequences of a year-long coal strike could be accepted without bringing industry to a halt. While the technical expertise
of the Bank of England and its strategic role in managing the
pound in an open international economy is constant, the Bank's
actual influence upon government policy has varied with the
views of the government of the day.[10]

Resources of Little Importance: Money, Votes, and Publicity. Money
can ensure that an organization exists and that experts are
available to analyze and present the group's technical case.
Money can also be given to political parties. But money does
not buy favors from parties; it is given openly in recognition
of mutual interests. An MP may speak for a pressure group,

but party discipline sees to it that the MP votes with his party in the Commons. No pressure group in British politics can confidently claim that its members are so committed to it that they would switch their votes from one party to another at its direction. Even trade union leaders, who are Labour party members, must face the fact that only half their members actually vote Labour.

Pressure groups with a weak strategic position and few other organizational resources may turn to the media for publicity. Publicity gives the appearance of mass support by the multiplier effect of mass circulation. The simplest and cheapest publicity device is to issue a press release or write a letter to *The Times* signed by prominent persons, for names make news. But publicity can be a sign that the group in question is unable to advance its claims by quiet negotiations in Whitehall. In order to be influential, a group's publicity must reinforce predispositions already found within government, or call for action that the government of the day is not already committed against.

All groups press demands on Whitehall, but differences in resources affect their degree of success. When groups are lobbying against each other, then success for one side will be a setback for the other. For example, proabortion and antiabortion pressure groups cannot both succeed, for their demands are mutually exclusive. Because demands are varied, many groups can simultaneously achieve some satisfaction. But just because pressure group politics offers something to many groups, it does not mean that it offers the same satisfaction to each.

PRESSURE GROUPS AND POLITICAL VALUES

A political value of fundamental importance in Westminster is that all affected interests have the right to be consulted before the government announces a decision. When a government decision about the future of the British Museum was announced without consulting its trustees, the chairman, Lord Radcliffe, denounced failure to consult as "almost unbelievable administrative incompetence," being "not only a grave constitutional impropriety that all these agencies should be ignored and despised, but also a gross discourtesy.''[11] Pressure-group officials concede that their demands will not always be met by government, but they do expect that the government, whatever its party, will listen to what they have to say before making firm policy commitments.

Pressure groups do not press in a vacuum; they can influence government only within a context of political values and institutions. The value of collective action for political ends antedates democracy and the rise of liberal individualist values in the nineteenth century.[12] It is accepted in different ways by both Conservative and Labour politicians, and it is not rejected by the Alliance. But because the goals and values that pressure groups represent are political, they will inevitably generate controversy.

The extent of a pressure group's political support depends upon the congruence between its own demands and values and those of others in the policy process. The more consistent pressure-group goals are with general cultural norms, the easier it is for a group to equate its interest with the national interest. The greater the clash, the more difficulties a group will face in pursuing its aims. At least six relationships can occur:

1. *Harmony between pressure-group demands and general cultural norms.* Because pet animals command affection and support, the Royal Society for the Prevention of Cruelty to Animals is in a favored position. It does not need to devote much of its resources to gaining popular endorsement of its aims; they are already popular. Its resources are instead devoted to the different (and far from easy) tasks of negotiating details of administration, and seeking priority for its demands in competition with other groups making claims for laws and public money.

2. *A gradual increase in the acceptability of political values supporting pressure-group demands.* Groups lobbying for colonial independence saw their position change dramatically in the decades after the Second World War, as nationalists' claims for self-government in the colonies became accepted, first within the Labour party and then throughout the political system. Similarly, proponents of permissiveness increasingly found

government prepared to endorse their demands for changes in the laws governing divorce, homosexuality, theatrical censorship, drinking, and abortion.

3. *Bargaining with fluctuating support from cultural norms.* Although society always has some pro-union and some pro-employer sentiment, the balance fluctuates in response to events, sometimes favoring one or another party to industrial disputes, or refusing sympathy to both. Leaders of pressure groups with fluctuating popular support must be adaptable, pressing claims when support is high, and acting defensively when their opponents are dominant.

4. *Advocacy in the face of cultural indifference.* Indifference is a greater handicap than opposition. A pressure group facing opposition at least has its views discussed, whereas a group facing mass indifference will stimulate no reaction within or outside government. For example, for years the National Society of Non-Smokers suffered from public apathy. Although it claimed to represent 15 to 20 million nonsmokers in the country, the majority had no knowledge of this society. It took publication of evidence by medical experts that cigarettes can cause cancer to give political salience to antismoking policies.

5. *Advocacy in opposition to long-term cultural trends.* A pressure group that finds cultural norms changing to its disadvantage is forced to mount a holding operation. Groups such as the Lord's Day Observance Society once were strong enough to secure legislation regulating Sunday activities, and some of these laws remain on the statute books. With political support for religious values diminishing, the Society now must concentrate on forestalling repeal of Sunday observance laws.

6. *Conflict between cultural values and pressure-group goals.* Any group may advocate demands in conflict with prevailing norms, in the hope that cultural values will change and its goals will be realized. But groups advocating absolute values are handicapped because they cannot bargain with opponents; an all-or-nothing goal makes partial success appear a defeat. For example, pacifists cannot regard a reduction in arms expenditure as evidence of success, for they favor the abolition of all military force.

Political values concern parties as well as pressure groups, but affect them differently. Because pressure groups do *not* need to win majority approval of their views, they can promote policies that are unpopular. But parties must pay attention to the values of the electorate as a whole. That explains why a Conservative government may not adopt all the right-wing views with which such people as Mrs. Thatcher have sympathy (for example, reducing welfare services greatly) and why a Labour government may not adopt a variety of radical policies (for example, prison reform), for which Labour MPs express sympathy.

Mixing Group and Party Values. The interdependence of pressure group goals and political values results in the interpenetration of pressure groups and parties. The connection is formally recognized in the Labour party, which regards itself as one wing of the labor movement, complementing the trade unions and cooperative societies. The labor movement is thus two parts pressure group and one part political party. In the picturesque phrase of Ernest Bevin, a major leader of the labor movement, the party grew out of the bowels of the trade union movement.[13] Today, trade unions affiliate more than nine-tenths of the party's membership, elect 12 of the 29 members of the party's National Executive Committee, provide more than four-fifths of its income, and financially sponsor more than one-half of the party's MPs in Parliament.

The link between the Labour party and trade unions, while organic and strong, creates substantial difficulties. At times it can be a means for unions to achieve political goals; for example, the unions were able to veto a 1969 Labour government proposal to amend laws on trade union activity, and they secured the repeal by the 1975 Labour government of the 1971 Conservative government's Industrial Relations Act. But the two institutions have many different interests. For example, in the winter of 1978 trade unions sought to overturn Labour government guidelines to hold down wage increases; the resulting conflict between the two wings of the movement contributed to Labour's loss of the 1979 election.

Because the Labour party is closely identified with the unions, the Conservative party is inevitably linked with a variety of business interests. But the ties are less strong. The Conservative party existed before the Industrial Revolution and before businessmen gained the right to vote. For most of the nineteenth century, the party of businessmen was the Liberal party, committed to free trade and industry. The collapse of the Liberals led businessmen to become prominent in the Conservative party, especially in the interwar years. But the Conservatives have never had institutional links with business associations, as the Labour party has links with unions. Individual wealth, preferably in the hands of landed persons or those who aspire to noble status, has been the historic bulwark of the Conservative party.[14]

Mrs. Thatcher has identified the leadership of the Conservative party with the promotion of business values in the abstract. As she is fond of telling audiences, Mrs. Thatcher believes that the lessons learned as the daughter of a small-town grocer reflect values generally applicable in life. This stands in marked contrast to an alternative set of Conservative beliefs about social solidarity, promoted through semipaternalist care for all groups within society. Conservatives wishing to avoid identifying the party with business values signify their opposition by speaking about the social responsibilities of business, and making sympathetic comments about cooperation between government and trade unions.

The fortunes of every pressure group are much affected by whether or not its claims are considered partisan. A pressure group regarded as partisan will find its fortunes fluctuating according to which party is in power. In exceptional cases, a pressure group may enjoy bipartisan support, as the National Farmers' Union did for decades. But the NFU position was not permanent, for the country's membership in the European Community means that United Kingdom agricultural interests must now be promoted with the ten-nation Community.

In contemporary England, many pressure groups claim to be nonpolitical, that is to say, non-party-political, because they wish to be on good terms with the government of the day, whatever its party. One study of urban pressure groups found that more than four-fifths of their demands had little to do with party controversy.[15] However, the growth of the mixed economy has politicized many issues that pressure-group leaders would prefer to have resolved outside Whitehall.

Parties rather than pressure groups decide whether or not a group can secure nonpartisan status for its claims. By making a political issue of a group's activities, a party draws it into the arena of party conflict. The Labour party's tendency to make most of society's affairs the concern of government has led it to initiate partisan debate about everything from secondary education to fox-hunting. As the 1964–1970 Labour government's reform of education showed, education groups maintaining a nonpolitical status found themselves on the sidelines when major decisions were made about the future of secondary education.[16]

Many pressure groups today face a dilemma: Should they seek bipartisan status by cooperating with the government of the day, whatever its political color, in hopes that this will give them continuing influence in Whitehall on matters immediately affecting it? Such a goal may be pursued by sedulously cultivating politicians of all parties and refraining from public expressions of party preferences. Or should the group be outspoken in articulating its demands, even when this aligns it with the minority party in Parliament, in hopes of greater eventual success through a change of government?

GOVERNMENT AND PRESSURE GROUPS

The first rule of pressure group politics is to exert pressure where decisions are made. In England groups concentrate attention upon civil servants and ministers in Whitehall. As Lord Devlin's Report on Industrial Representation explained, "All executive policy and most legislation is conceived, drafted and all but enacted in Whitehall."[17]

Pressure groups give most attention to senior civil servants and departmental ministers because the largest number of decisions affecting pressure groups are made in a departmental context. For example, regulations about industrial injury claims in the glass industry are unlikely to be discussed in the Cabinet; they can most easily be settled by negotiations between the department and representatives of affected groups. To achieve success in negotiations, group representatives need only (*sic*) convince departmental officials that their position is reasonable, not contrary to Cabinet policy, and unlikely to cause conflict with other pressure groups.

A direct approach to ministers and civil servants is the normal channel of communication between established pressure groups and Whitehall departments. The channel may be institutionalized by appointing group spokesmen to departmental advisory committees. The spokesmen accept this in order to be able to put their case in Whitehall before decisions are made. Public officials prefer private approaches, because these expose them to a minimum of public criticism or unwelcome publicity. Such discussions allow each side to negotiate without public and sometimes acrimonious exchanges.

The Basis of Exchange. In communication between pressure groups and government, influence moves in two directions: government seeks to influence pressure groups, and groups press claims upon government. An exchange of influence occurs because each has things that the other wants, and each can offer things that the other needs.

Pressure groups seek four things from government. First they seek advance information about trends in Whitehall thinking, so that members can be informed of likely shifts in policies affecting them. Second, groups seek the good will of Whitehall officials with the discretionary power to decide whether or not a host of actions are allowable under established laws and regulations. The greater the government supervision of a field, the greater the importance a pressure group places upon frequent and friendly contacts in Whitehall. Third, pressure groups seek to influence government policy. The most dramatic example of influence stimulating new legislation is relatively infrequent. Usually a pressure group confines its attention to influencing the administration of existing laws in ways that will benefit its members. Fourth, pressure groups seek status. It may be given symbolically, by allowing an organization to add the prefix Royal to its title, or by a knighthood awarded to its general secretary. A group's status also rises by virtue of membership in official committees.

Government seeks four things from pressure groups. Information is the first of its needs. Groups accumulate from their members much information that does not otherwise come to the attention of Whitehall, and that is relevant in administering and reviewing policies. Secondly, Whitehall wants advice, so that it can know what pressure groups think ought to be done and how they would probably react to various proposals that a department is considering. Third, after a decision is made a department wants pressure groups to support what the government has decided. Finally, when a policy has been embodied in an Act of Parliament, government looks to pressure groups to cooperate in administering the law.

Because most of these wants are complementary, pressure groups and government find it easy to negotiate. Negotiations proceed without threats of coercion or bribery because each needs the other. The interdependence of pressure groups and government results in an exchange of influence in which policies can be the product of the dialectic, rather than the exclusive product of one group or the other.

Insiders and Outsiders. Continuous negotiation with Whitehall is the mark of an insider group.[18] While most pressure groups have contacts in Whitehall, access is not inevitable. Failure to achieve consultative status can arise from a number of causes: the weakness of the organization, the unacceptability of the group's demands to the government of the day; its membership; close identification with the opposition party; or the absence of a Whitehall department to act as the focal point of its particular concern. A group lacking consultative status will be an outsider in Whitehall.

Outsider pressure groups usually go public with their demands, using Parliament and the media to gain attention. The desire for publicity is often a second-best alternative to suffering political isolation in silence. In a House of Commons of 650 members, a pressure group can normally find at least a few MPs who are predisposed to support its cause. To some extent, back-bench MPs welcome the opportunity to join with a pressure group for the publicity they will gain as its advocate. In a highly diversified media structure, a pressure group can usually find a few periodicals willing to print its views, even if their circulation is very small. Media publicity encourages MPs to take more interest in a group's cause, and discussions in Parliament stimulate media attention, thus gaining the attention of ministers.

While some outsider groups are prepared to use conventional channels in hopes that their status will improve, groups seeking a radical change in government policy often protest in unconventional ways to publicize their cause. Protest movements engage in demonstrations, sit ins, and other forms of nonviolent but sometimes extralegal action. The Campaign for Nuclear Disarmament (CND) is the best-known British protest group. Protests have gained much publicity, but little influence. For more than a quarter century CND has been in the headlines, but its tactics have not been able to deter Conservative and Labour governments from continuing to rely upon nuclear weapons.

Conflicts Between Pressure Groups. Political organization carries the risk of stimulating countermobilization. The more strongly one group presses its claims, the greater the incentive for an opposing interest to organize pressure. Insofar as pressure groups deal with political issues, there will always be conflicting interests that can mobilize against them. For example, the political success of trade unions has led business groups to strengthen their lobbying activities.

Competition constrains the influence of any pressure group. Whitehall officials receive different and often conflicting demands. They are aware that a concession, say, to commercial broadcasting interests will be opposed by newspaper proprietors fearful of thus losing advertising revenue. Moreover, they are adept at playing competing pressure groups against one another, seeking an agreement that will be acceptable to the department's own interests as well as to groups lobbying it.

The influence a pressure group has on government policy depends chiefly on the scope and scale of the decision. The wider the scope of an issue, the greater the likelihood it will be controversial. The more complex the problem, the greater the likelihood that a number of Whitehall departments will be affected, thus requiring interdepartmental negotiations as well as negotiations between pressure groups and departments. Once a matter requires interdepartmental negotiations, the departments lobby on behalf of their own preferred policies. The greater the importance of a question, the greater the likelihood that the Cabinet will be consulted. Once a Cabinet decision has been made, the sponsor department, like the pressure groups associated with it, must accept the result as the collective decision of British government.

Pressure groups find that the centralized institutions of Whitehall are relatively difficult to influence. Pressure groups rarely expect to supplant government's authority. They do want to influence specific details and procedures of policies to which the government is committed. For example, group influence upon the drafting of Statutory Instruments that set out the details of a policy is far greater than their influence upon the Act of Parliament that lays down the framework of that policy.[19] A director-general of the Confederation of British Industry writes:

> Industry may or may not like the policy; and the CBI will say so on its behalf. But when the issue is decided, it may make a world of difference to industry how the policy is implemented and translated through administration into action.[20]

Government officials do not mechanically weigh the pressure that groups exert. The assessment of political pressures is uncertain. At a minimum, Whitehall influences policy by deciding how much weight each competing group can claim, and what it regards as appropriate terms for a settlement. Government's power to enact laws and allocate money can put public power in the scales on behalf of otherwise weak groups. In such cases as the nationalization of an industry, the party in office can use the lawful powers of government to take over private enterprise assets against the wishes of an industry. Equally, as the Thatcher government has demonstrated, it is possible to denationalize a public enterprise against the wishes of unions in an industry.

In the relationship between pressure groups and government, it is the government that is of primary importance.[21] The centralization of British government gives Whitehall the power to decide which groups can be classified as insiders, and which become outsiders. Party discipline gives the Cabinet of the day the capacity to impose its pattern of policy upon negotiations. A Labour government can start discussions with a business group with the chief agenda item how the group is to be nationalized, not whether nationalization is to occur. A Conservative government can lay down an agenda for discussion with trade unions in which the principal issue is how a new industrial relations act is to be written, not whether it is to be adopted. A pressure group can refuse to discuss policies that it rejects on principle, but doing so consigns it to outsider status. A group cannot by itself veto a policy it rejects in principle. If at odds with the party in power, it must await the outcome of an election that changes party control of government.

THE CHANGING POLITICAL CONTEXT

The object of negotiation is agreement. Public officials and pressure-group spokesmen know it is a matter of great convenience for a consensus to be achieved among all affected interests. Agreement is convenient for participants because it avoids having decisions made by remote politicians and officials who know less and care less about details that do those most involved. Agreement concentrates on a community of interest, disregarding the policy interests of those outside the circle.

In the past quarter-century British government has had to seek agreement among an increasingly wide range of economic interests. Changing economic forces have confronted the country with problems for which the government of the day has been deemed responsible: inflation, unemployment, and low rates of economic growth. The resolution of these problems is not solely within the command of Whitehall. It not only requires collective action within government, but also action involving government, business, and labor.

In pursuit of greater collective agreement within society, governments from the time of Harold Macmillan through James Callaghan have sought to create new institutions of consultation that could complement (or, their critics have charged, substitute for) Parliament and party. The names given the resulting tripartite institutions have varied. They are best referred to as tripartite bodies, because the three separate groups involved — government, business, and unions — have each maintained their separate identity. To refer to them as corporatist institutions suggests a degree of integration between the three bodies that has not been achieved.[22]

The Basis of Tripartism. Tripartite institutions have been based upon three assumptions. The first is a presumed consensus about immediate policies to deal with the economy, as well as a general consensus about goals concerning inflation, unemployment, and economic growth. Secondly, it has been assumed that the representatives in tripartite deliberations could secure the consent of those whom they represent. Thirdly, tripartite institutions have been seen as promising stable, long-term policies to deal with the country's deep-rooted economic difficulties.

While discussions between government, industry, and unions have been going on for generations, the particular contemporary impetus to tripartism came from the establishment of the National Economic Development Council (NEDC) in 1961. The intention was for the NEDC to set target rates for economic growth; to develop plans for overcoming economic difficulties and achieving target goals; and to coordinate actions by government, nationalized and private industries, and unions to implement these plans. In the 1970s a series of tripartite executive bodies were also established, such as the Manpower Service Commission and the Health and Safety Commission, each having immediate responsibility for delivering particular services.

The concern of tripartite economic bodies gradually shifted from optimistic plans for economic growth to measures to reduce inflationary increases in prices and wages, and then to the problem of rising unemployment. With the abandonment of economic growth targets promising more benefits for all participants, tripartite institutions have tended to fall apart, as recommendations for joint action against inflation and employment immediately threaten to impose more costs than benefits on members. The repeated establishment *and* abandonment of tripartite bodies demonstrates the dilemmas of choice facing a government seeking agreement with extraparliamentary pressure groups.

Difficulties of Tripartism. The first difficulty with the practice of tripartite policy making is that it requires consensus on means and ends. It is possible to identify actions that, temporarily at least, are consistent with the mutual interests of all three groups. For example, in 1975 a rate of inflation above 20 percent brought about the temporary acceptance of measures to limit wage and price increases. Extreme inflation forced groups to accept what they would not demand. But by 1978, in a winter of economic discontent, trade unions were no longer willing to forego wage claims, since the pay pause had not only reduced inflation but also reduced their members' real earnings.

Secondly, tripartite deliberations are fundamentally weak because the leaders of the participating groups cannot bind their members to accept what leaders agree with each other. The government of the day will not give trade unions and business groups the power to commit the Cabinet. Trade union leaders cannot bind their members, because union members are divided on many industrial issues, not least, wage differentials between different unions. The world of business is divided into a plethora of groups, lacking even a nominal peak organization like the Trades Union Congress. As Lord Watkinson, a former Conservative Cabinet minister and President of the Confederation of British Industry has pointed out, neither the CBI nor the TUC "has effective control over its membership to the extent that it can undertake to deliver a policy by ensuring that all its members will implement it."[23]

The third point follows: tripartite institutions to carry out major economic policies are inherently unstable. Their formation reflects a common desire to achieve collective action in pursuit of relatively general consensual goals such as increasing economic growth and reducing inflation and unemployment. But the attempt to identify agreed means to achieve consensual ends reveals disagreements between *and* within each of the three groups.

In reaction against the limitations of tripartite policy making, the Conservative government of Margaret Thatcher has adopted a strategy of arms-length dealings with both trade unions and business groups. The reliance of the Thatcher government upon monetary policy to reduce inflation and to promote economic growth has not required endless consultations with representatives of unions and businesses. Control of the money supply is within the hands of the government.

The conscious distancing of the Thatcher government from tripartite institutions not only reflects its aversion to trade union influence, but also a belief that business too ought not to expect Whitehall to resolve problems of industry. Victory at the 1983 election has given the Thatcher government a second term of office to test both its persistence in this policy and its ability to achieve its desired economic goals.

The limited resources of the economy constrain what government, firms, and union leaders can hope to achieve, whether acting through consensual tripartite institutions or independently pressing their distinctive demands. In 1977 a Labour Health and Social Security minister faced with demands to do more than the Treasury would finance, responded by calling representatives of pressure groups together for a meeting. The agenda listed each group's proposals and their cost. At the end of the paper was the total bill, approximately £13 billion, more than twice as much as the ministry was then spending on social services. Saying yes to each group would have required an increase of income tax of almost one-third.[24] Economic constraints have forced Labour governments to recognize that goodwill toward pressure group demands will not provide the money needed to finance all of them.

Pressure groups have the freedom to demand whatever they wish. But the government of the day does not have the resources to grant every demand, even if it wishes to do so. The Thatcher government's response is to emphasize that it would prefer government to spend less. It makes the refusal of demands a positive feature of its political credo.

Both government and pressure groups face the challenge of reconciling the benefits and costs of particular group demands with the total resources available to society. Pressure-group leaders have no difficulty in urging their specific claims, arguing that their relatively small cost is not the major cause of the government's difficulties. But that which is true in isolation is not true in the aggregate. Government has the specific responsibility of finding resources to meet the sum total of group demands. The government must do more than respond to particular group demands; it must also articulate policies that it regards as in the interest of the country as a whole.

NOTES

1. On the origins of groups, see Graham Wootton, *Pressure Groups in Britain, 1720–1970* (London: Allen Lane, 1975). For a classic study, see S. E. Finer, *Anonymous Empire,* rev. ed. (London: Pall Mall, 1966).

2. See J. J. Richardson and A. G. Jordan, *Governing under Pressure* (Oxford: Martin Robertson, 1979), p. 17; and comments by Ralf Dahrendorf, "The Politics of Economic Decline," *Political Studies,* 29:2 (1981), p. 290.

3. As the discussion emphasizes, the distinctions are not completely clear cut. See e.g., Allen Potter, *Organized Groups in British National Politics* (London: Faber & Faber, 1961), chapter 1; *The Guardian Directory of Pressure Groups* (London: Wilton House, 1976), pp. 1–20.

4. See David Marsh, ed., *Pressure Politics* (London: Junction Books, 1983), pp. 3ff.

5. E. H. Phelps-Brown, "The National Economic Development Organisation," *Public Administration,* 41 (Autumn 1963), p. 245.

6. Cf. Bruce W. Headey, "Trade Unions and National Wages Policies," *Journal of Politics,* 32 (1970), pp. 428f.; Gerald A. Dorfman, *British Trade Unionism against the Trade Union Congress* (Stanford: Hoover Institution Press, 1983); Ben Pimlott and C. Cooke, eds., *Trade Unions in British Politics* (London: Longman, 1982).

7. See Wyn Grant and David Marsh, *The Confederation of British Industry* (London: Hodder & Stoughton, 1977); Michael Moran, "Finance Capital and Pressure-Group Politics in Britain," *British Journal of Political Science,* 11:4 (1981), pp. 381–404; David Steele, "Government and Industry in Britain," *British Journal of Political Science,* 12:4 (1982), 449–504, and Leonard Tivey, "Nationalized Industries as Organized Interests," *Public Administration,* 60:1 (1982), pp. 42–55.

8. Moran, "Finance Capital and Pressure-Group Politics," p. 393.

9. See e.g., T. R. Marmor and D. Thomas, "Doctors, Politics and Pay Disputes: Pressure Group Politics Revisited," *British Journal of Political Science,* 2:4 (1972); and Maurice Kogan, *Educational Policy-Making: A Study of Interest Groups and Parliament* (London: Allen & Unwin, 1975).

10. Michael Moran, "Monetary Policy and the Machinery of Government," *Public Administration,* 59:1 (1981), pp. 47–62.

11. House of Lords, *Debates,* Vol. 287, cols. 1130ff (13 December 1967).

12. See W. H. Greenleaf, *The British Political Tradition,* Vols. 1–2 (London: Methuen, 1983); and Samuel H. Beer, *Modern British Politics: a Study of Parties and Pressure Groups,* 3rd ed. (London: Faber & Faber, 1982).

13. *Labour Party Conference Report, 1935* (London), p. 180. For implications,

see D. W. Rawson, "The Life-span of Labour Parties," *Political Studies,* 17:3 (1969). See also William D. Muller, *The Kept Men?* (Brighton: Harvester Press, 1977).

14. Cf. Nigel Harris *Competition and the Corporate State* (London: Methuen, 1972); and Wyn Grant, "Business Interests and The Conservative Party," *Government and Opposition,* 15 (1980), pp. 143–161.

15. Cf. J. Roland Pennock, "Agricultural Subsidies in Britain and America," *American Political Science Review,* 56:3 (1962); and Robert J. Lieber, "Interest Groups and Political Integration: British Entry into Europe," *ibid.,* 66:1 (1972).

16. See e.g., Paul E. Peterson, "The Politics of Comprehensive Education in Three British Cities," *Comparative Politics,* 3:3 (1971).

17. Quoted in Grant and Marsh, *The Confederation of British Industry,* p. 2.

18. See Wyn Grant, "The Role and Power of Pressure Groups," in R. Borthwick and J. Spence, eds., *British Politics in Perspective* (Leicester: University Press, 1984), pp. 132ff.

19. See David R. Miers and Alan C. Page, *Legislation,* p. 152.

20. Quoted in Samuel H. Beer, "Pressure Groups and Parties in Britain," *American Political Science Review,* 50:1 (1956), p. 8.

21. For evidence on this point, see the review article by Dilys M. Hill, "Pressure Groups and the Policy Process," *Parliamentary Affairs,* 32:3 (1979), pp. 343–346, and the books cited therein.

22. See Wyn Grant, "Corporatism and Pressure Groups," in Dennis Kavanagh and Richard Rose, eds., *New Trends in British Politics* (Beverly Hills: Sage Publications, 1977), pp. 167–190. For a comparative discussion, see e.g., Phillippe C. Schmitter and Gerhard Lehmbruch, eds., *Trends toward Corporatist Intermediation* (London: Sage Publications, 1979).

23. Lord Watkinson, *Blueprint for Survival* (London: Allen & Unwin, 1976), p. 88.

24. Calculated by the author from an unpublished Department of Health and Social Security briefing paper for a Seminar on Social Security Priorities, London, 5 July 1977.

CHAPTER IX

The Choice of Parties

Party organisation is the vital principle of representative government, but that organisation is permanently efficient because it is not composed of warm partisans. The body is eager, but the atoms are cool.

BRITISH GOVERNMENT IS PARTY GOVERNMENT[1] Parties organize the selection of candidates, enunciate policy intentions, and conduct elections. In a general election a voter does not vote for the policies that he or she wishes government to carry out; instead, votes must be cast for the candidate of the party deemed best at aggregating the outlooks of millions of citizens. Individuals cannot expect any party's program to match their own views perfectly. The choice offered by the parties forces voters to search for the party that best represents (or least misrepresents) their political outlook.

Voters do not determine who governs, but which party names the governors. The leader of the party with most seats in the House of Commons is invited to form a Cabinet. Once in office the Cabinet relies on party discipline to secure parliamentary support for its policies. If no party can secure a working majority, as happened in February 1974, another election is likely to occur shortly, for the contemporary conventions of British government assume that there is a partisan majority assuring the Cabinet the continued confidence of Parliament.

Political parties are complex organizations. Their members can be interested in many different things: ideological debates in obscure pamphlets, majorities in the House of Commons,

264

and/or fund-raising cake sales for the local party. Because parties are complex, the motives that lead people into party politics are usually multiple. Making policy is but one of many things that can bring satisfaction to a party member. Making a career is another. Intense personal contact between politicans can lead the party to dominate a person's social life too.

Collectively, parties form an interdependent system, for what happens to one party affects others. If the governing party loses popularity, then one or another opponent will gain support in response to cries to turn the rascals out. If one party announces that it favors a policy, such as increasing pensions, the pressure is on its opponents to adopt the same objective or risk losing votes of the elderly. When one party in a system favors trade unions (Labour), competitors can seek votes by favoring business (the Conservatives) or neither (the Alliance).

For generations, writers about British politics have praised the party system for fixing responsibility for government upon a single party, and assuring it effective legislative support. In the 1970s the party system came under criticism. Writers with strong left-wing or right-wing views criticized the established Conservative and Labour parties for not offering voters a wide enough political choice; each was said to pay too much attention to the middle ground in the competition for votes. Others complained that established parties offered the wrong choice, neglecting the views of individuals who do not accept orthodox trade union or business policies.[2]

Dissatisfaction with the choice between the Conservative and Labour parties has gone through two distinct phases. In the two 1974 general elections, the combined Conservative and Labour shares of the popular vote dropped to 75 percent. The Liberal vote rose to 19 percent, its highest since 1929. Altogether, the Liberals plus the Scottish and Welsh Nationalists and Ulster MPs won sufficient seats to deprive the Labour government of a working majority in the Commons. The 1979 election saw the vote for third-force parties decline to 19 percent of the total. More importantly, the decline in the Labour vote gave the Conservatives a majority in the House of Commons independent of the votes of third-force MPs.

The second phase has been marked by volatility. Whereas

the 1979–1983 Parliament commenced with a revival of Labour party fortunes, raising its Gallup Poll support to 49.5 percent in March 1980, internal disputes within the Labour party led some Labour MPs to break away in January 1981 to form a new Social Democratic party. The Social Democrats formed an Alliance with the Liberal party for electoral purposes; their combined support rose to 50.5 percent in the December 1981 Gallup Poll. Following the Falklands War, Conservative support rose to 46.5 percent by the July 1982 Gallup Poll.[3]

The June 1983, general election confirmed that if Britain can be said to have a two-party system, then it is temporarily a system with one whole party and two half-parties. The Conservatives won a landslide majority in the Commons (albeit with only 42.4 percent of the United Kingdom vote) and Labour and the Alliance each won one-quarter of the popular vote.

The British party system is temporarily destabilized by three parties competing for votes and seats in a Parliament built for two parties. To understand the choices that the party system now offers the British electorate, we must first consider the way in which elections translate individual votes into parliamentary strength or weakness. Second, we must see how the parties organize themselves to formulate policies and choose leaders to carry out policies. The third section compares the views of voters and parties to see how good is the fit between representatives and represented. Finally, an examination of coalition and competition between parties emphasizes differences within as well as between parties.

ELECTORAL CHOICE

A decision by one person — the Prime Minister — determines the date on which an election is held. Although an Act of Parliament states that an election must occur at least once every five years, the Prime Minister is free to request that the Queen dissolve Parliament and call a general election at any time the governing party chooses. But the difficulties of office are such that the government of the day trails behind the opposition in most monthly opinion polls. Hence, the governing party has limited opportunities to select a date when a combination of political and economic events will be in its favor.

In the twelve elections since 1945, the governing party has won seven and lost five.

Voting. The ballot offers a very simple choice. A voter is presented with a sheet of paper giving the name, address, occupation, and party label of each person who seeks to become the MP from the constituency. The ideas, arguments, and decisions of a multiplicity of politicians and party institutions are thus aggregated into a choice between standard-bearers for each party in the constituency. Nomination requires only the written endorsement of ten of the constituency's electors. To discourage frivolous contestants, each candidate is required to post a deposit of £500 with nomination papers. This deposit is forfeited if the candidate does not secure at least one-eighth of the vote in the constituency. In the 1983 election the Conservatives lost 5 deposits, the Alliance 11, Labour 119, and the Nationalists lost deposits in the majority of seats they contested.

Even when only two parties are on the ballot, there is always a third choice: not voting. The frequency of voluntary or involuntary abstention from voting is low in England compared with the United States, but high by European standards. Although nonpolitical reasons appear to explain most absentions, it is noteworthy that the proportion of eligible voters not voting in a general election rose from 16 percent in 1951 to 27 percent in 1983.

How a person votes reflects the cumulation of influences through the years, and not just the events of one election campaign. Five-sixths of British voters identify with a political party. When a general election is announced, those who have identified with a party are already predisposed to vote for it. However, Conservative and Labour difficulties have led to a decline in party identification. Whereas in 1964, 81 percent of the electorate identified with one of the two parties, in 1983 the proportion had fallen to 70 percent (Table IX.1). Moreover, those who very strongly identify with a party have declined from 44 to 26 percent of the electorate. The drop in Conservative party identification came in 1974; the Conservatives regained ground by 1983. Labour identifiers have declined by 30 percent from a peak in 1966. Identification with

TABLE IX.1 *The Decline of Party Identification in Britain, 1964–1983*

	1964 %	1966 %	1970 %	1974[a] %	1979 %	1983 %	Change 1983–1964 %
Party identification							
Conservative identifier	38	35	40	35	38	38	0
Labour identifier	43	46	42	40	38	32	−11
Both established parties	81	81	82	75	76	70	−11
Liberal-SDP-Nat.	12	10	8	15	14	16	+4
No party identification	7	9	10	10	10	14	+7
Strength of party identification (all electors)							
Very strong	44	44	42	26	22	26	−18
Fairly strong	38	38	37	40	46	38	0
Not very strong	11	9	11	24	23	22	+11
None	7	9	10	10	10	14	+7

[a]Combined responses to February and October surveys.

Source: Adapted by the author from British Election Surveys and BBC/Galllup surveys, as reported by Ivor Crewe, "The Electorate: Partisan Dealignment Ten Years On," *West European Politics*, 6:4 (1983), table 3.

third-force parties has not risen as much as that of major parties has fallen.

The weakening of psychological party identification has been complemented by a weakening of the influence of social class upon voting.[4] The proportion of the Conservative and Labour party share of the vote that could be explained by occupation, union membership, housing, and other socioeconomic characteristics has declined by nearly half since 1959. In consequence, the support for the Conservative and the Alliance parties is very much cross-class support. They attempt to appeal to middle-class and working-class supporters, and Labour is pressed to do the same if it wishes to regain the votes needed to win an election (cf. Table V.5).

Voters respond to parties today in accord with the general image of the party, and not by careful examination of the details of competing parties. Just as voter identification with parties is weakening, so too party images are now less clearly and favorably defined. Quarrels within the Labour party have even resulted in some Social Democrats claiming that they represent the heritage of the "old" Labour party. Under Margaret Thatcher the Conservatives have become more closely identified with a tough-minded economic approach to social problems, and given less emphasis to an older tradition of tender-minded Toryism. The failure of both Conservative and Labour governments to succeed as each wished in directing the economy has increased skepticism about the capacity of the opposition to do better next time in office when it did badly the last time.[5]

Individual party leaders contribute relatively little to long-term party images, for a leader is only in that post about half a dozen years on average. While the leader's personality remains the same, voters' opinions fluctuate more or less in keeping with their evaluation of the government's record and the performance of the opposition. As Prime Minister, Harold Macmillan saw his approval by Gallup Poll respondents fluctuate between 30 and 79 percent; Harold Wilson saw his swing between 27 and 66 percent; and Edward Heath from 31 to 45 percent. Margaret Thatcher led the Conservatives to victory in 1979 even though opinion polls consistently gave James Callaghan a higher personal rating. In her first term of office, approval of Mrs. Thatcher's performance as Prime Minister ranged from 52 percent to 25 percent.[6] The influence of a leader's personality upon the electorate is much less than in the United States, where party images are weaker.

The difficulties of the Labour and Conservative parties in and out of office have caused more and more Britons to become floating voters, shifting support between parties. In the 1951–1955 Parliament, support for the governing Conservative party was steady, ranging from 40 to 48 percent on the monthly Gallup Poll, and the party lost only one by-election. In the 1966–1970 Parliament, support for the Labour party fluctuated from 28 to 52 percent, and Labour lost fifteen by-elections. In the 1979–1983 Parliament, Gallup Poll support for the Conservative government fluctuated between 23 and 46 percent, and the Conservatives lost four by-elections.[7]

At any given general election up to half of the electorate behave differently than at the previous election. But the bulk of the movement is slight, a shift between voting and nonvoting or a move in or out of the ranks of Liberal or Alliance voters. Only a few percent switch across the divide between the Labour and Conservative parties.[8]

Because many movements of voters offset each other, the net fluctuation in the vote for the two major parties has been small by absolute or comparative standards. Since 1945 the difference between the highest and lowest Conservative share of the national vote has been 13.9 percent, and between 1945 and 1979 it was 11.9 percent for Labour (see Figure I.1). By comparison, in America the Republicans' share of the presidential vote since 1948 has varied by 22.2 percent between its peak and trough, and the Democrats' share by 23.6 percent.

The two major parties have been very evenly matched in their national electoral appeal (Figure IX.1). In the eleven elections between 1945 and 1979 Labour won an average of 44.9 percent of the vote, and the Conservatives, 43.5 percent. In the thirty-four-year period, Labour was in office for seventeen years, and the Conservatives for seventeen.

However, the 1983 election result marked a discontinuity from the past half-century. Labour's share of the vote fell to its

FIGURE IX.1 *Votes Cast in British General Elections, 1935–1983 (in percentages)*

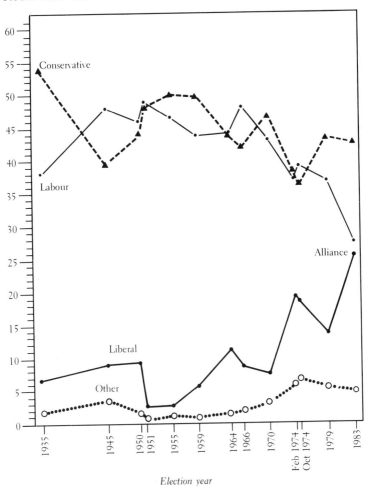

Election year

lowest total since it began contesting elections nationwide in 1922. The Liberal-SDP Alliance share was up nearly 12 percent from 1979, higher than the Liberals had won at any election since 1923. The Conservative share of the vote was *less* than the party secured in seven of the previous eleven general elections. Even though the Conservative vote went down by

1.5 percent, thanks to divisions between its opponents it won an additional fifty-eight seats in the House of Commons.

Winning Seats. To win election to Parliament, a candidate need not gain an absolute majority of the votes; the first-past-the-post electoral system gives victory to the candidate with a plurality (the largest number) of votes in a constituency. From 1945 through 1970 about three-quarters of MPs were elected with more than half the vote in their constituency. But the rise of third-force popular support resulted in only 36 percent of MPs being elected with an absolute majority in February 1974. In 1983, 48 percent of MPs were elected with half the vote in their constituency. The great majority of constituencies are electorally safe; fewer than one-tenth of seats in the Commons are likely to change hands in an election. But in the hundreds of seats in which the winner takes less than half the vote, victory depends upon divisions between opponents.

The distribution of seats in the House of Commons in 1983 bore little relation to a party's share of the popular vote (Table IX.2). The Conservatives won 121 more seats in the Commons than they would have won had seats been awarded strictly in proportion to votes. Labour's share of MPs was roughly proportional to its share of the vote, but the Alliance, with almost as many votes as Labour, won only 23 seats; it would have had 165 MPs with purely proportional representation.

It is normal for the electoral system to manufacture a majority in Parliament for a party with a minority of votes. No party has won at least half the popular vote since the 1935 gen-

TABLE IX.2 *The Relationship of Seats to Votes in Britain, 1983*

	Share of			Seats won		
	Votes %	Seats %	Difference	PR[a]	Actual	Difference
Conservatives	42.4	61.0	+18.6	276	397	+121
Labour	27.6	32.2	+4.6	179	209	+30
Alliance	25.4	3.5	−21.9	165	23	−142
Others	4.6	3.2	−1.4	30	21	−9

[a]Hypothetical result yielded by pure proportional representation.
Source: Calculated by the author.

eral election; the postwar high is the 49.7 percent share gained by the Conservatives in 1955. Yet in eleven of twelve elections since the war, one party has won an absolute majority of seats in the House of Commons. In the extreme case of October 1974, the Labour party won a parliamentary majority with only 39.2 percent of the popular vote.

A party can win seats if it concentrates its support in a limited number of constituencies. The Ulster parties do this, fighting only the seventeen seats of Northern Ireland; the Scottish Nationalists and Welsh Nationalists also win seats by concentrating their vote. The Liberals — and even more the Alliance in 1983 — win few seats in the Commons because their vote is spread relatively evenly among constituencies. In 1983 the Alliance finished second in 303 seats, and first in only 23. Labour did not so waste its support; it concentrated votes, winning a seat by either finishing first or finishing third.[9]

Debate about Electoral Systems. The British electoral system is a system of *disproportional* representation. It is not intended to allocate seats in Parliament in proportion to each party's share of the national vote. It is intended to vest control of government in one party by giving it an absolute majority of MPs without an absolute majority of votes. Proponents of the first-past-the-post plurality system argue that a difference in shares of seats and votes is a small price to pay in order to vest responsibility for government in the hands of a single party.[10]

Dissatisfaction with the performance of successive Conservative and Labour governments has given vigor to proponents of replacing the present electoral system by a proportional representation (PR) system.[11] One set of arguments is derived from the belief that as a matter of principle a party's representation in Parliament ought to match its share of the vote, as happens in Continental Europe, where proportional representation is normal. One consequence of proportional representation would be that no party would be likely to win a parliamentary majority.

The introduction of proportional representation would replace single-party government by coalition. Coalition is said to be a recipe for moderation and compromise, according to proponents of PR, preferable to the alleged extremism of adversary politics. It is a prescription for stagnation, according to critics. Arguments for PR advanced by the Liberals and Social Democrats reflects the Alliance interest. SDP politicians showed no interest in reforming the electoral system when they enjoyed its benefits as Labour MPs, nor did Liberals introduce PR when there was a Liberal government.

Participants in the debate about electoral reform often overlook two inconvenient sets of facts. The first is that MPs and parties victorious under the plurality system are unlikely to reject the system that has benefited them. To be certain of a parliamentary majority for PR, the Alliance would need to win a majority of seats under the present system that handicaps them. Secondly, proponents of the plurality system assume that the electorate is satisfied with choosing between only two parties. But since 1974 this has been arguable. In 1983 the collective share of the vote for "third force" parties — Liberals, SDP, Nationalists, etc. — was 30 percent, greater than popular support for Labour.

There is only one measure by which Britain can be said to have a two-party system: one of two parties, the Conservatives or Labour, has formed the government after every election since 1945. But from 1900 to 1945, coalition government occurred more often than government by a single-party majority.[12] From the perspective of a century, the period of two-party competition between 1945 and 1970 appears the exception rather than the rule.

By any measure of electoral competition, Britain has a multiparty (that is, more than two-party) system. This is shown in the following ways.

1. *Three candidates normally contest the majority of constituencies.* In 1983, 2,578 candidates contested 650 seats, an average of almost four candidates per constituency.

2. *Two parties do not monopolize the popular vote.* The closest that the Conservative and Labour parties came to a monopoly was in 1951, when their candidates collectively won 96.8 percent of the vote. But the two parties have not won more than 90 percent of the vote since 1959. In four elections since February 1974, the Conservative and Labour parties together have won

an average of 75 percent of the vote; in 1983 their combined share dropped to 70 percent.

3. *When voters change, they are more likely to switch to a third party, such as the Liberals or Alliance, than move between the Conservatives and Labour.* In 1983 the Conservatives as well as the Labour party had their share of the vote fall. The concept of swing, a measure of the average of the change in votes of the Labour and Conservative parties, is thus today a misleading abstraction. Theoretically, a 6 percent swing to the Conservatives from Labour was registered in 1983, but empirically the only net gainer in votes was the Alliance.[13]

4. *The pattern of party competition at constituency level involves three parties, not two.* In 1983 the Conservative and Labour parties were the two front-running parties in only 285 of 650 seats. By comparison, the Alliance was one of the two front-running parties in 336 seats.

5. *More than half a dozen parties consistently win seats in the House of Commons.* In 1983 three parties — the Conservatives, Labour, and Alliance — won seats in England; in Scotland, a fourth party, the Scottish Nationalists, was also successful; in Wales the fourth successful party was Plaid Cymru. In Northern Ireland another five parties won seats. In all, ten parties won representation at Westminster.

The party system today is best described as multiparty because the names and numbers of parties differ from election to election and among the nations of the United Kingdom. In Northern Ireland, British parties no longer contest seats. Ulster-only parties fight there. In Scotland, the Scottish Nationalists finished second in popular vote in October, 1974 and third in the other three elections of the 1970s. In Wales, Plaid Cymru finished third, ahead of the Liberals, in 1970. A distinctive feature of the 1983 election was that it was integrative: the Alliance attracted protest votes throughout Great Britain, pushing the Nationalists into fourth place in both Scotland and Wales.[14]

The Liberal party, which rotated in office with the Conservatives for most of the century up to the First World War, has the longest-standing claim to be the country's third party. But the Liberals split during the First World War, and Labour replaced it as the chief opposition party. The popular vote of the Liberals has fluctuated with the number of candidates the party has nominated, usually being about one-sixth of the vote in the constituencies contested.[15] Liberal membership in the House of Commons has ranged from six to fourteen seats since 1945.

The Social Democratic party, created in 1981, is organized independently of the Liberals in Parliament and in the country. But it has not yet demonstrated support independent of its alliance with the Liberals. It remains to be seen whether the SDP will succeed in becoming an established party on its own, or eventually merge with another party. An electoral alliance with the Liberals is a half-way house between complete autonomy and merger.[16]

The Conservative and Labour duopolistic control of government is not a reflection of class structure or of a popular preference for either/or choices. The preeminence of two parties first of all results from the small size of the non-English parts of the United Kingdom. Second, it reflects the Liberal and Alliance inability to break through the threshhold dividing gainers from losers in the first-past-the-post plurality system.

The present electoral system presents voters with much the same choice as a vote of confidence in the House of Commons: a choice between two parties, the Ins and the Outs. In 1983, a majority of voters indicated that their principal motive was negative: more voters said they felt a dislike of one or more of the principal parties rather than a positive liking for the party receiving their vote.[17] When support is principally negative and three parties compete for that support, then the choice of voters is widened, and the uncertainty of politicians enhanced too.

CONTROL OF THE ORGANIZATION

Party organizations are often referred to as machines, but the term is a misnomer. The parties do not have a machine to manufacture votes at election time, nor can party headquarters manufacture support for an unpopular party leader. Nor does party organization mechanically convert the preferences of voters into government policies. By the standards of American political parties, British parties are organizations, being formally established with a written constitution, permanent headquarters, routinized committee meetings, and bureaucrats whose careers depend on organizational loyalty rather than loyalty to an individual politician. But by comparison with a participative ideal, the Houghton Committee on Financial Aid to Political Parties in 1976 concluded: "British political parties frequently operate below the minimum level of efficiency and activity required."[18]

Because British government is party government, control of the party offers control of government. But neither the Conservative nor the Labour party can be controlled from any central position, for each is a complex of institutions. Each party can be divided into three major parts: the party in Parliament, the party at headquarters, and a network of constituency parties. Each party is differently composed and differently controlled. Much of the effort within a party is not directed toward the government of the country or against its electoral enemy. It is intended to keep together disparate parts. Fragmentation, not mechanical integration, is the chief feature of party organizations.

In Parliament. The party in Parliament enunciates and applies party policy routinely and in crises at Westminster. Events and issues arise so fast that pressures of time greatly limit consultation between the party inside and outside Parliament. Sometimes little prior consultation goes on among front benchers in Parliament or Cabinet, or between leaders and their own backbench MPs. Once party leaders in Parliament have made a commitment, this is an important political fact. Other sections of the party are expected to go along with the decision of party leaders, or else can be accused of fomenting disunity.

The organization of a party in Parliament varies with its electoral fortunes. The leader of the majority party becomes Prime Minister and forms a Cabinet that constitutes the frontbench leadership in Parliament. When out of office, the Parliamentary Labour party elects a Parliamentary Committee of twelve to act as its executive committee. The party leader allots shadow ministerial posts to the Committee members, as well as to some not elected to it. In the Conservative party in opposition, the leader selects people for shadow posts; the back benchers also elect a chairman for their own group.

Headquarters. Party headquarters are apart from the Palace of Westminster.[19] The size of the staff working for each party differs substantially. The Conservatives have more than twice the staff of Labour, and Labour five times that of the Liberal or Social Democratic party. At headquarters, the research staff is the largest group; it consists of university graduates. The research department is not so much concerned with long-term policy analysis as with briefing MPs and front-bench spokesmen, and assisting party policy committees. The briefing work overlaps with the efforts of the publicity department, which handles press releases, advertising, and television and the work of headquarters' agents liaising with constituencies.

The Conservative party has a dual structure; two organizations share facilities in Smith Square. One is the Conservative Central Office, which services the Conservative party in Parliament. The chairman of the Central Office is appointed by the leader of the party in Parliament. He is usually a front-bench MP, and when the party is in government, also in the Cabinet.

The second organization is the National Union of Conservative and Unionist Associations, which brings together constituency workers. At the Annual Conference of the National Union, constituency associations express their views about party policy. Votes at the Annual Conference are allotted in equal numbers to each constituency association. MPs have no voting rights; the gathering is technically not their conference. The parliamentary leadership exercises influence informally, by excluding resolutions that could embarrass the leadership and by speaking frequently in Conference debates. Because resolutions are usually phrased to avoid splits within the party and few delegates wish to vote against their parliamentary leadership, it is rare for a Conference debate to conclude with a formal ballot. Between 1950 and 1976, intraparty differences were pushed to a conference ballot on only eight occasions.

The Labour party is an amalgam of diverse organizations.

It incorporates independent centers of power, thus institution-alizing a potential for disagreement averted by the dualistic Conservative structure. The constitution of the Labour party states, "The work of the party shall be under the direction and control of the Party Conference."[20] The five-day Annual Conference debates policy resolutions which are pressed to a vote when they concern issues divisive within the party. Votes are distributed according to notional membership figures. More than nine-tenths of the Conference vote is in the hands of trade unions. The vote of each union is cast as a bloc, even though the union's membership may be divided on an issue. When a union's delegation to Annual Conference is almost evenly divided, then up to a million votes may depend upon a few delegates who hold the balance in deciding how a major union will cast its bloc vote. The half-dozen largest affiliated unions together have an absolute majority of the Conference vote. The bloc vote thus concentrates far more power in the hands of a few political caucuses than occurs in an American presidential nominating convention.

Between Annual Conferences, the National Executive Committee directs the Labour party's headquarters. Its membership is also dominated by trade union votes. The unions elect twelve of the Committee's twenty-nine members in their own name, and their votes dominate the selection of the five women's representatives and the party's treasurer. The constituency parties elect seven representatives, often back-bench MPs, and the Co-operative Societies and Young Socialists elect one member each. Seats are also reserved for the leader and deputy leader of the Parliamentary Labour party.

The headquarters staff work under the direction of the National Executive Committee and subcommittees. Rotating the party chairmanship annually by seniority limits its political importance. The leader of the Parliamentary Labour party is the chief spokesman for the party as a whole, but lacks the formal authority to issue directives to headquarters staff, or to countermand decisions of the National Executive Committee. One of the major reforms of the party constitution in 1981 gave the NEC a right to participate in drafting the election manifesto in consultation with the Parliamentary Labour party.

Constituency Organization. Local parties are organized according to parliamentary constituencies; usually their boundaries do not encompass a natural geographical community. The constituencies are larger than wards comprising urban neighborhoods, yet rarely the same size as a city or county. Where a party controls local government, there are immediate incentives to give priority to local politics. A high level of membership does not necessarily indicate great interest in parliamentary politics. It may indicate that the local party provides a good social club, can organize garden fetes and bazaars, or runs a well-organized lottery on football results. The interest of national headquarters in developing a mass-membership organization may not be matched by officials controlling a constituency through a small caucus. Only the Conservative party has a full-time election agent in a majority of constituencies. The Labour party maintains a full-time agent in less than one-sixth of the constituencies.

Constituency parties are important nationally, inasmuch as each separately selects a parliamentary candidate; collectively, the choices of constituency parties constitute the House of Commons. Party headquarters compile lists of hundreds of aspiring parliamentary candidates, vetoing applicants more for personal reasons (e.g., the individual has a criminal record or has very recently been a member of another political party) than on policy grounds. A constituency party then makes up a list of aspiring candidates to interview, some of whom are locally known and some from outside the constituency; a parliamentary candidate is not required to live in the constituency. The constituency candidate is selected after interviews with half a dozen to a dozen prospects. The final choice is made by a constituency committee, which may have anything from a dozen up to several hundred members. Decentralizing choice of the candidate to more than 600 associations in each party results in a great variety of candidates nationwide; it also prevents headquarters from dominating candidate selection.

Because the great majority of constituencies are safe seats for one party, nomination there is usually tantamount to election. Barring major changes in constituency boundaries arising from the population shifts or major political upheavals, most

MPs can regard their position in the Commons as secure from eviction by dissatisfied voters. A voter who does not like the nominee chosen by his local constituency party can vote against the party's candidate, abstain, or vote on party lines. Voters faced with a conflict between their allegiance to a party and their dislike of the local parliamentary candidate usually resolve it by casting their ballot along party lines.[21]

Conservative MPs assume that the association that initially nominated them will renominate them, as long as they avoid becoming involved in personal scandals, such as arrest for drunken driving or financial irregularities, and are not excessively casual in discharging their limited obligations in the constituency. Historically, it has been very rare for a Conservative MP not to be renominated by his constituency association, whatever the political views the MP expresses in the Commons.[22]

Within the Labour party, sitting Labour MPs used to be virtually certain of readoption, barring gross personal failings. But left-wing dissatisfaction with the policies of the 1974–1979 Labour government led to a demand for Labour MPs to be subject to mandatory reselection in every Parliament, and this is now the rule. Because of the limited membership of most constituency Labour parties, averaging less than 500, relatively small left-wing groups can sometimes dominate the reselection process. Eight Labour MPs failed to win readoption before the 1983 election; others defected to the Social Democrats before their constituency party voted whether to retain them as a candidate.[23] In 1985 constituency Labour parties once again started the process of deciding whether to renominate incumbent MPs.

Mandatory reselection gives constituency party committees a continuing influence over their MP's expression of views in Parliamentary Labour party meetings as well as on the floor of the Commons. This change has made some Labour MPs uneasy, because they believe that nonelected constituency party officers threaten their status as popularly elected representatives. As long as the MP, the dominant group in the constituency party, and voters are of one mind, then no problem need occur. But if differences of opinion arise, then a Labour MP must balance a claim to represent the electorate against the knowledge that continuing as an MP is dependent upon maintaining the confidence of the local party's general management committee, which has the power to approve or reject his bid for renomination.

Is Anyone in Charge? To ask who controls the party organization is to assume that some one individual or group must be in charge. The most obvious claimant is the party leader in Parliament. As the elected leader of the party and the party's recognized chief spokesperson in the media and in election campaigns, the party leader is inevitably important, defining by his or her actions where the party stands on controversial issues.

The processes for electing the leader in the Conservative and Labour parties reflect differences in the internal structure of the two parties. The Conservative leader is elected by a ballot of Conservative MPs, requiring an absolute majority to win. On the first ballot the candidate with the fewest votes is eliminated. A fresh compromise candidate may come forward subsequently; balloting continues until, by a process of elimination, one candidate wins. The system was first used to elect Edward Heath as leader in opposition in 1965; previously leaders had been chosen by a secret conclave of party elder statesmen. In 1975 Margaret Thatcher won the leadership in opposition by challenging the incumbent party leader and former Prime Minister, Edward Heath.

In the Labour party, the leader was elected solely by votes of Labour MPs until the party constitution was changed in 1981. The Labour party leader is now chosen by an electoral college in which the trade unions collectively have 30 percent of the vote, the constituency parties 30 percent, and the Parliamentary Labour party, 40 percent. In order to be elected leader, a candidate must win support from at least two of these three constituent elements.

The new Labour system was first used in a ballot for the deputy leadership of the party in 1981, when Anthony Benn and John Silkin challenged Denis Healey, the incumbent. On the second ballot, Healey retained the post by a margin of 0.9 percent of votes cast; Benn won a big majority in the constituency parties, and Healey a substantial lead among MPs and trade unions. The biggest union, the Transport and General Workers, switched support among the three candidates in maneuverings immediately before the final vote. The new system worked more smoothly in 1983, following the resignation of Michael Foot. Neil Kinnock was elected leader on the first ballot with a majority of votes in all three parts of the electoral college, and Roy Hattersley similarly won election as deputy leader.

In both parties the leader's position is strongest when also enjoying the authority of Prime Minister, an authority reinforced by control of government patronage. But only one party leader can enjoy the status of Prime Minister at any one time. The opposition leader's influence will depend upon whether he or she is expected to become Prime Minister after the next election.

The dynamics of electoral competition alter the leader's status during the lifetime of a Parliament. The leader of a newly elected government can claim popular justification for authority. Conversely, the leader of the opposition has just been repudiated, with disastrous effects on the ministerial ambitions of colleagues. Midway in the life of a Parliament, if the governing party becomes unpopular, the Prime Minister can appear to be the person who will lead it to defeat, if not replaced before the next election. At the same time, the leader of the opposition becomes the Prime Minister-apparent and his shadow patronage rises in value. As another general election approaches, the need to unite a party — whether in government or opposition — increases the influence of a leader as the person around whom others must rally. The party leader's influence is a variable, not a constant. It fluctuates according to the personality of the individual. Margaret Thatcher believes in leading a party from the front, whereas Clement Attlee believed in leadership from the rear. Attlee was prepared to follow the mood of the majority in the party, whereas Thatcher wishes to impose her views. The influence of a party leader varies within a term of office. For example, Harold Macmillan entered Downing Street without the full support of colleagues in 1957, but his victory in the 1959 general election made him dominant within the party until political setbacks and ill health brought Macmillan to a political nadir and resignation in 1963. Most party leaders resign after they have lost an election, and with it the confidence of their party.

The authority appropriate for the parliamentary leadership is disputed between and within the parties. A generation ago Robert T. McKenzie propounded the thesis that constitutional practice required that the leaders of all parties dominate their extraparliamentary party.[24] McKenzie asserted that elected politicians ought to be exclusively accountable to the electorate rather than to self-recruited party activists, and that this was a fortiori true of the Prime Minister and the leader of the opposition.

Within the Conservative party, the McKenzie doctrine was broadly acceptable, for the Conservative leader is independent of the extraparliamentary constituency association, and dominates the party's Central Office. The thesis was subject to one important qualification, noted by McKenzie. Differences of opinion about the leadership can be expressed among Conservative MPs, and this is the case, not least under Margaret Thatcher.

For most of the postwar era, the leader of the Labour party has been *primus inter pares* within the complex institutions of the Labour movement. But neither Clement Attlee nor Harold Wilson, Labour's two long-serving leaders, sought to impose their views on others. Each saw his role as conciliating disparate forces within the Labour movement, including the unions with the largest bloc votes. Hugh Gaitskell, leader from 1955 until his early death in 1963, sought to impose his own revisionist brand of policy upon the party. He failed in domestic policy, though successful in fighting off an attempt to commit the party to unilateral nuclear disarmament in 1960.

The multiplicity of policy-making organs within the Labour party compels continuing discussion and compromise, especially when the party is in opposition. At the height of one dispute, the party's general secretary summarized the practical political moral thus:

Within the party there are three centres of decision-making: the Annual Conference, the National Executive Committee and the Parliamentary Labour Party. . . . None of these elements can dominate the others. Policy cannot be laid down: it must be agreed.[25]

The adoption of constitutional changes in 1981 was evidence of the ability of the left to organize support for its views throughout the party. The reforms have changed the rules by which policies must be agreed. Constituency parties have become an important fourth center of decision making, because of their power to reselect (or deselect) MPs, their vote for the party leader and deputy leader, and their representation on the party's National Executive Committee and in Annual Conference. Left-wing groups within the extraparliamentary party have created a cohesive organization capable of sustaining a lengthy factional fight against the parliamentary leadership.

The Liberal party has been little concerned with problems of constitutional accountability, having been remote from office for generations. The Liberal party is like the Conservatives in being based upon individual members, not trade unions. It preceded Labour in electing its leader by extraparliamentary means. It differs from both parties in that its MPs are few. Neither Members of Parliament, extraparliamentary Liberals, nor political commentators view the Liberal party in terms of what it would do in government. The Liberals have been a loosely organized grass-roots campaign group, ready to seize tactical advantage to win seats in Parliament wherever and whenever practicable.[26]

By contrast, the Social Democratic party has been organized from the top by notables, former Labour Cabinet ministers. The circumstances of their departure from the Labour party meant that SDP leaders were suspicious of extraparliamentary influence. Yet the need to mobilize supporters quickly and to give them a sense of participating within the party meant that the SDP was pressured to give its well-educated activists a voice in party activities.[27] One innovation of the SDP is a computerized central membership list for collecting dues. Secondly, the SDP has not established constituency associations, concentrating its resources in 235 area councils, each covering several constituencies. Given its newness and small size, for the time being the party is particularly dependent upon its leader, Dr. David Owen, to gain visibility at Westminster.

Stratarchy is the term that best describes the distribution of

power in British political parties today.[28] Parties are not hierarchical organizations, led from the top like an army. Their
fragmentation makes it difficult for any group, whether a popular parliamentary leader or a dedicated group of Trotskyite
militants, to influence all parts of the party equally. One indication of the relative incoherence of the party is that neither
the Conservative nor Labour headquarters has an accurate
record of how many (or who) are party members.

In a stratarchy, each set of institutions tends to enjoy a degree of autonomy from others with which it is nominally linked.
Local councillors, whether Labour or Conservative, can defy
their party leadership at Westminster. Individual MPs can, with
the backing of their constituency association, defy parliamentary leaders. At party headquarters, many bureaucrats concentrate upon technical problems of maintaining voluntary
associations, as it were "keeping politics out of their work."
The Annual Conference provides an opportunity for anyone
and everyone to voice personal opinions from the rostrum —
but for only a few minutes a year. Labour's National Executive
Committe can be challenged by its parliamentary leadership to
moderate extreme positions. Reciprocally, a Labour leader
must respond to what the NEC has decreed; under party rules
he is powerless to veto their decisions.

The autonomy of different parts of parties is most clearly
demonstrated by party finance. Money is in principle an easy
commodity to transfer. Yet neither the Conservative nor the
Labour party has any institutional mechanism by which all
party funds can be centrally allocated. Each constituency party
and, in the case of Labour, affiliated union, has great discretion in raising and spending political funds. Although trade
unions raise substantial sums from levies on members' dues,
little more than half the funds go to Labour headquarters or
to constituency parties. The remainder is spent directly by the
unions or hoarded in cash reserves. In the Conservative party,
constituency associations raise more than twice as much money
as Central Office, and retain five-sixths of funds raised for local
activities. Central Office spends centrally most of the money
it raises.[29]

The fact that different parts of a party can often go their own way does not mean that they are all equal. Nationwide influences upon votes give every party member a stake in the success of the party at the center. The preeminence of Westminster in British government means that leaders of the parliamentary party will always be important vis à vis other parts of their party.

POLICY PREFERENCES

Whether parties do or should stand for different policies is a matter of controversy.[30] Elections give people the choice between different teams of leaders, but different leaders can still follow the same policies. Disagreements can have less to do with differences about goals than with different means to such agreed ends as peace and prosperity. Parties also stress differences in the personalities of their leaders. Competition to win votes tends to make all parties specially sensitive to views prominent in the electorate.

The eighteenth-century political philosopher Edmund Burke defined a party as a group of persons united by agreement on principles. This statement treats parties as political institutions concerned with articulating and resolving conflicts about government policies. But it is often argued that some issues, such as foreign policy, are too important for political dispute; every English person is said to have a common interest vis à vis other nations. It can also be argued that the chief differences between parties are not clear-cut ideological disagreements, but differences of degree: How much inflation or how much unemployment is tolerable? Or differences of timing: When should a social reform be adopted, or when should economic policies be altered?

Differences of Principle? At a very high level of abstraction, parties differ in their vision of an ideal society. No British party is explicitly ideological, deducing its election programme from a coherent theory of society. The Conservative party does not even offer a statement of goals in the constitution, as other parties do. Many of the goals enunciated in party constitutions are not specific to one party. The Liberals' endorsement of peace, prosperity, and liberty, and denunciation of poverty and ignorance could be echoed by almost any party anywhere.[31] The SDP constitution identifies a mixture of goals, some congenial to Labour, such as an open, classless, and egalitarian society, and others congenial to the Conservatives, such as promoting a strong economy and private enterprises.

Statements of principle must be abstract if they are to be of enduring significance, but generality reduces relevance to day-to-day politics. There is usually more than one way to interpret the applicability to contemporary events of ideas of eighteenth-century Conservatives or early twentieth-century Socialists. The gap between abstract goals and everyday reality is so great that goals may best be considered symbols to inspire partisans to battle. Harold Wilson caught the symbolic flavor of much debate about party principles when he said about efforts to abandon Labour's commitment to total nationalization:

> We were being asked to take Genesis out of the Bible. You don't have to be a fundamentalist in your religious approach to say that Genesis is part of the Bible.[32]

If contrasting political philosophies are to affect everyday politics, then the policy preferences of partisans should differ as do Conservative, Liberal, and Socialist philosophies. The first assumption in discussions of ideologies is that ideas about contemporary politics are coherent; that is, a person who holds egalitarian views about wages will also have egalitarian views about race relations, or that people who want to cut taxes will also want to cut spending on programs that benefit themselves.

No Ideological Coherence. In fact, when the views of a national sample of the electorate are examined statistically by factor analysis, the results show that the mass lacks any ideological framework for policy choices.[33] If attitudes were coherent, then the bulk of views on twenty-three issues examined by Donley Studlar and Susan Welch would constitute a single factor. In fact, five different factors are identified. The first concerns such class-related topics as the redistribution of wealth. This factor is completely independent of the second factor, the environment, and scarcely related to other factors concerning race relations, moral issues, and law and order.

While voters do have views on issues, their opinions tend to be specific to a given question rather than reflecting general ideological principles. If the latter were the case, then the five factors identified would explain nearly all the variation in opinions on particular issues. In fact, more than half of the variance (58 percent), is left unexplained.[34] Popular views about many issues are weakly or not at all related to more general values.[35]

Even if voters do not hold coherent views on a wide range of issues, their political outlooks could be characterized as partisan insofar as on any given issue Conservative, Labour, and Alliance voters differ from each other as their parties are meant to differ in the House of Commons. But a major Gallup survey of opinions on twenty varied issues (Table IX.3) demonstrates the following:

1. Most Conservative, Labour, and Alliance voters agree with each other on more than two-thirds of all major issues.

2. Alliance voters agree with the national majority on 19 of 20 issues, and Conservative and Labour voters on 17 of 20 issues.

3. The average difference between Conservative and Labour voters endorsing a policy is 16 percent.

4. Alliance voters on average differ 14 percent from Conservatives and 7 percent from Labour. Alliance voters take a middle position between Conservative and Labour voters on 14 of 20 issues.

Even though voters disagree about who should govern, most Conservative, Labour, and Alliance voters are like-minded on most issues. Moreover, the agreement is evidenced on many issues assumed to divide parties on ideological lines, such as spending more for the national health service, and letting council tenants buy their houses. Differences between partisans do exist — notably, on support for defending the Falkland islands, and on trade union legislation — but these differences are the exception. Differences of degree are so limited that on every issue there is a substantial overlap in Conservative, Labour, and Alliance views. Moreover, the similarities in outlooks between supporters of different parties have persisted through the years.[36]

TABLE IX.3 *The Similarity of Policy Preferences among Partisans*

	Total	Con.	All.	Labour	Con.-Lab. Difference
			(% endorsing policy)		
Plurality in all three parties agree					
Spend more on health	90	81	96	98	−17
Let council tenants buy their house	81	89	76	77	12
Have government guide wage, price rises	78	81	80	76	5
Spend more against pollution	78	78	82	78	0
Promote equal opportunities for women	77	73	80	80	−7
Spend to reduce unemployment	76	64	85	87	−23
Bring back death penalty	64	68	61	64	4
Redistribute wealth to poor	61	43	67	78	−35
Shift power to local govt., regions	51	44	53	56	−12
Reduce sex on TV and in magazines	50	53	52	48	5
Reestablish grammar schools	48	63	40	35	28
Allow abortion on National Health Service	46	44	45	51	−7
Send back coloured immigrants	29	29	25	30	−1
Give up nuclear weapons	22	8	35	27	−19
One or two parties disagree with national total					
Have stricter laws on unions	57	79	58	36*	43
Cut spending to reduce inflation	53	64	37*	48	16
Withdraw troops N. Ireland	50	37*	52	64	−27
Give more aid Africa, Asia	44	39*	54	42*	−3
Spend as needed to defend Falklands	39	58*	29	24	34
Leave Common Market	34	21	33	50*	−29

*Plurality of partisans disagrees with plurality of total electorate.

Source: Author's analysis of Gallup Poll survey for *Daily Telegraph*, 28 October 1983.

Notwithstanding efforts of Alliance leaders to claim that they are different, their voters do not endorse distinctive policies. On only one measure of relatively little national importance — aid to African and Asian countries — do a plurality of Alliance voters differ from both Conservative and Labour voters. Normally, Alliance supporters agree with either Conservative or Labour voters, or both.

Although party leaders depend on the mass electorate for votes, they depend on party activists to keep the party alive at the grass roots. Some political scientists have argued that active party workers hold extremist views; only people with both strong and extreme ideological commitments are expected to be willing to do the humdrum voluntary work of local party organization. The absence of jobs for the boys, as in a patronage party system, is assumed to increase the importance of extremist ideology in recruiting party activists.[37]

Studies of activists in constituency parties have found that only about one-third regard working for a cause as a principal satisfaction from political activity. Helping people and the social satisfaction of group meetings are at least as important. Less than one-third of the time of Labour party ward meetings appears to be devoted to discussing policy; more time is spent on organization and procedural matters. A large portion of resolutions put forward to Annual Conferences by constituency parties endorse views acceptable across party lines, for example, increasing pensions, or reducing accidents on the road.[38]

Even among Labour councillors, conference delegates, parliamentary candidates, and MPs there is a substantial amount of ideological incoherence. The crucial characteristic of these activists is that collectively they are divided in their opinions. Whiteley classifies 57 percent as center-left or left, and 43 percent as center-right or right. Even when activists are united, for example in wanting to nationalize land or abolish fee-paying education, Labour governments have refused to do what activists wish on grounds of electoral tactics (most voters would disapprove) or administrative infeasibility.[39]

During election campaigns, politicians do not compete with each other by comparing their own party's policies with the opposition party. In election addresses circulated by Conservative and Labour parliamentary candidates, only one of the top ten issues they mention — housing — appears on the lists of both parties.[40] Candidates stress the issues on which their party is popular, such as anti-inflation policies for the Conservatives, and welfare programs on the Labour side. Candidates do not advocate different solutions for the same problem; instead they describe the country's problems from differing perspectives, each choosing the issues on which his party's policies are most popular.

The emphasis on tactical differentiation rather than alternative strategies for governing is also clear in the speeches of the two party leaders. In 1970, the defending Prime Minister, Harold Wilson, devoted 75 percent of his major speeches and broadcasts to attacks on the Conservative opposition; Edward Heath, leader of the Conservative opposition, devoted 70 percent of his major speeches to attacks on the Labour government.[41] The choice that party leaders stress is often negative: reject my opponent.

When parties do make positive statements, as in their election manifestos, they can often be very general and anodyne. The titles of the manifestos since 1945 are virtually interchangeable between the Conservative and Labour parties: "Action not Words," "Time for Decision," "A Better Tomorrow," or "The New Hope for Britain" (Table IX.4). Nor did the Alliance break the mold in its 1983 manifesto, which was entitled "Working Together for Britain." Within the text of a lengthy manifesto, some pledges are controversial, but many are relatively uncontroversial proposals favoured by cross-party pressure groups.[42]

Members of Parliament are much more likely than voters to differ along party lines. Their greater involvement in politics gives them a stronger commitment to party policies than is found among the electorate as a whole. Their views have been analyzed by examining private responses to opinion surveys and parliamentary votes on conscience questions when party whips are not invoked. A majority of Labour and Conservative MPs disagree with each other on ten of fifteen domestic and foreign policy issues. Ironically, MPs in different parties disagree more consistently about issues of conscience, such as divorce law reform, abortion, or hanging, for which party whips are not invoked, than about issues for which there is a party line.[43] In neither the Conservative nor the Labour party is there a close match of views between voters and MPs.

TABLE IX.4 *Consensual Titles of Party Manifestos, 1945–1983*

	Conservatives	Labour
1945	Mr. Churchill's Declaration of Policy	Let us Face the Future
1950	This Is the Road	Let Us Win Through Together
1951	Britain Strong and Free	Labour Party Election Manifesto
1955	United for Peace & Progress	Forward with Labour
1959	The Next Five Years	Britain Belongs to You
1964	Prosperity with a Purpose	Let's Go with Labour for the New Britain
1966	Action Not Words	Time for Decision
1970	A Better Tomorrow	Now Britain's Strong — Let's Make It Great to Live In
1974 (F)	Firm Action for a Fair Britain	Let Us Work Together
1974 (O)	Putting Britain First	Britain Will Win with Labour
1979	The Conservative Manifesto 1979	The Labour Way Is the Better Way
1983	The Challenge of Our Times	The New Hope for Britain

Source: F. W. S. Craig, *British General Election Manifestos, 1900–1974* (London: Macmillan, 1975), and Richard Rose, *Do Parties Make a Difference?* 2nd ed. (London: Macmillan, 1984), p. 45.

The greater disagreement on issues between MPs than between voters results in party controversy in Parliament intensifying policy differences. While the gap between MPs and their voters can be found in both parties, it is greater in the Labour than in the Conservative party. Since the early 1950s Labour voters have been substantially less likely to endorse left-wing positions than Labour MPs. Harrop identifies a significant fraction of Labour's support as coming from "Labour-voting conservatives," that is, people who vote Labour because of working-class loyalties even though they agree with the Conservative party's position on many major policy issues.[44]

The extent to which the electorate and the parties differ is shown when a sample of voters is asked to place themselves along a left-right scale, and then to place the parties (Table IX.5). In the 1980s the electorate is divided into three groups unequal in size. The right and the center are each substantial;

TABLE IX.5 *Placement of Voters and Parties on a Left–Right Scale*

	Placement of Self	Placement of Parties			
	%	Con %	Lab %	Lib %	SDP %
Far Left	1	3	24	2	2
Substantially Left	3	1	26	2	4
Moderately left	9	1	16	7	8
Total left	(13)	(5)	(66)	(11)	(14)
Slightly left	9	2	8	14	17
Middle of the road	11	2	1	14	11
Slightly right	13	5	2	19	13
Total center	(33)	(9)	(11)	(47)	(41)
Moderately right	27	21	3	11	9
Substantially right	7	29	1	2	1
Far right	4	19	1	1	1
Total right	(38)	(69)	(5)	(14)	(11)
Don't know	16	17	18	29	33

Source: Calculated from Gallup Poll survey 22–27 June 1983. Q: In political matters people talk of the left and the right. How would you place the views of (yourself/the parties) on this scale?

the left is consistently much smaller.[45] Two-thirds of the electorate see the Conservatives on the right and Labour on the left. Labour's problem is not a failure to project its left-wing image, but that it has projected a left-wing image when the majority of the electorate is inclined to the center or the right.

During the 1983 general election campaign, 67 percent of the voters perceived important differences between the parties, the highest percentage recorded by the Gallup Poll since the 1955 election.[46] But the perception of differences between campaigning politicians does not imply big differences between most of their supporters. Nor does it imply popular support for confrontation politics, as the fall in votes for the Conservative and Labour parties since 1970 makes evident. As Bagehot observed a century ago, while parties are eager to go hot and heavy at each other in Parliament, the mass of their supporters remain cool.

CROSS-PRESSURES UPON PARTIES

Parties are subject to two different sets of pressures. On the one hand, they are concerned with winning votes, and on the other hand with satisfying the aspirations of those within the party organization. When these goals push in different directions, party leaders must decide whether to give greater weight to pressures within the organization or to trends in the electorate.[47]

Many of the problems of the Labour party were generated by electoral success that gave Labour fifteen years in office between 1964 and 1979. The result was a deterioration in relations between Labour's parliamentary leaders and the extraparliamentary party. The extraparliamentary party gained influence after Labour moved into opposition in 1979. Many internal divisions within the Conservative party have been papered over but not eliminated by Mrs. Thatcher's two successive election victories. The Liberal party is unique in being able to satisfy its members' ambitions without any major electoral success. It remains to be seen whether the ex-Labour ministers leading the Social Democrats will be able to gain electoral success or adapt their organization to the Liberals' low level of aspirations.

British parties are subject to more cross-pressures because they are fewer in number than in most European countries. Whereas proportional representation makes it easy for politicians to divide into five or ten relatively cohesive parties, the first-past-the-post electoral system encourages the maintenance of large coalitions under Conservative and Labour banners. In England large coalitions are more easily maintained in one party because of the absence of linguistic differences that multiply party divisions in Belgium, religious divisions that increase divisions in Italy, or working-class divisions creating parallel Socialist and Communist parties in France.

British parties are different coalitions than American parties for many reasons. The parliamentary system places a high premium upon party discipline. In England the voter chooses between parties. The primary system allows American voters to choose within as well as between parties. The ideological spectrum in America is different, extending further to the right and not so far to the left. The Thatcher government sustains far more welfare programs than the Reagan administration, and the center and left of the Labour party are well to the left of liberals within the Democratic party.

Parties, Factions, and Tendencies. British parties are large enough to divide into three distinctive groups: factions, tendencies, and nonaligned partisans.[48] *Factions* are self-consciously organized groups that persistently advance a program for government and a leader to govern. Factionalism gives stability to intraparty disputes and may even stimulate controversy, for old factional enemies can transfer their enmities to new issues. The left-wing Bevanite faction in the Labour party in the 1950s, often called a party within a party, is the outstanding postwar example of a faction. A *tendency* is a stable set of attitudes rather than a stable collection of politicians. The names and numbers of MPs adhering to right-wing or left-wing tendencies within a party can vary from issue to issue. *Nonaligned* MPs ignore intraparty differences in order to emphasize differences between parties. Factions and tendencies seek to convince nonaligned partisans that their own position is most in accord with the party's principles and interests.

The Conservatives have been preeminently a party of tendencies. An analysis of resolutions signed by back-bench Conservatives showed that "such disagreements as arise are struggles between ad hoc groups of members who may be left or right on specific questions; but as new controversies break out, the coherence of the former groups dissolves, and new alignments appear, uniting former enemies and separating old allies."[49] The leaders of the Bow Group, youthful Conservatives of potential front-bench stature, have carefully refrained from becoming a faction promoting specific causes and personalities. The members of the Monday Club have sought to change the party's policy in right-wing directions — but they have not become a fully fledged faction, lacking a leading figure in Parliament.

In Margaret Thatcher's period as leader, the Conservatives have divided into distinctive tendencies: the so-called wets who favor identifying the party with social reform and Keynesian economic policies; the drys, who favor free market and monetarist economic policies; and a substantial group of nonaligned Conservatives who try to avoid being caught up in this controversy. Mrs. Thatcher's own position is ambivalent. At the level of rhetoric, she is undoubtedly a dry. But her administration has not rolled back the state as the dries wished; instead, it has demonstrated the limited impact that a Conservative Cabinet can have upon contemporary big government. In party management, Mrs. Thatcher's key question about colleagues does not concern commitment to ideology but to herself: "Is he one of us?"

The Labour party has always had competing views put forward within its ranks, demonstrating the truth of the late Lord Samuel's dictum: "There is only one way to sit still, but there are many ways to go forward." Periodically the party has expelled members for being too far left, or suffered resignations from MPs who have moved to the right of the party. Under Clement Attlee's leadership from 1935 to 1955, Labour was a coalition led by a man who presented himself as a nonaligned partisan. Hugh Gaitskell tried but did not succeed in converting the party to the views of the Gaitskellite faction. Wilson reverted to the Attlee style of nonaligned leadership.

Since Labour left office in 1979 three groupings have crystallized: the hard left, the soft left, and a group of would-be ministerialists. The hard left comprises a number of energetic, well-organized bodies including the Campaign Group of Labour MPs, and the extraparliamentary Trotskyite *Militant* faction, which has more full-time paid staff in the field than does Labour party headquarters. The hard left stands for policies that have never been espoused by Labour in government. Suspicious of past Labour government actions, it campaigns for greater extraparliamentary influence upon MPs. Anthony Benn usually draws his support from the hard left. The soft left is to the left of previous Labour governments in foreign policy unilateral nuclear disarmament, and the direction of the economy.

The ministeralist tendency defends the 1974–1979 Labour government record. Ministerialists resist the left's push to abandon Labour government policies, while also rejecting former colleagues' claims that their cause can best be advanced by the Social Democratic party. All three groupings have long been active in the party under a variety of names, but there are big shifts in their relative strength. For the first time since the 1930s, the ministerialists are in a minority in the Labour party today.

The election of Neil Kinnock, who had never held office in a Labour government, as Labour leader, and Roy Hattersley, an experienced ex-minister, as deputy leader in October 1983, was an attempt to turn Labour from a party of faction fighters into a party uniting the soft left, where Kinnock has his roots, and the ministerialists, where Hattersley has his roots. It is supported by nonaligned Labour partisans too. The so-called "dream ticket" for the leadership had as its first priority the search for a program that would both unite the Labour party *and* appeal to the mass electorate.

Political groupings can exert pressures across party lines as well as within them. Entry to the European Community is a classic example. The decision was endorsed by Parliament in 1971 by a cross-party coalition consisting of 282 Conservative and 69 Labour MPs; 39 Conservatives and 189 Labour MPs voted against entry. The 1975 referendum on Community membership was called to avoid a split in the Labour party; it enabled Labour Cabinet ministers (and Conservative ex-ministers) to oppose each other in the referendum campaign, while continuing to accept party discipline in Parliament.

Today, the Alliance is most subject to cross-pressures. The Liberals are under tactical pressure to oppose the government of the day, whatever the party in power. Some Liberal voters are more inclined to the Conservatives, and others to Labour. The Social Democrats are under pressure to differentiate themselves from the Labour party, to which their leaders formerly belonged, while simultaneously wanting to project an image very different from the antisocialism of Mrs. Thatcher. To complicate matters further, both Liberals and Social Democrats put pressure on each other, as they compete with each other to get the most advantage from their electoral pact.

The extent to which partisan rhetoric reflects genuine differences about what government should do can be tested by examining divisions in Parliament. In the House of Commons, the governing party has the votes to put through as much partisan legislation as it wishes. Yet it is also subject to extraparty pressures from interest groups, to economic constraints, constraints within Whitehall, foreign pressures and, not least, electoral pressures. Insofar as these constraints are intrinsic to government, they will affect every governing party equally.[50]

Although the convention of party discipline requires MPs to vote together, it does not require that opposition MPs vote against all measures of the governing party. A vote takes place in the Commons only if an explicit request is made to divide the House. When the object of legislation is likely to be popular, such as providing greater welfare benefits, the opposition party will hesitate before going on record against a benefit. It will confine criticism to amendments challenging the operation of a bill but not its principles. Refusing to request a division in effect gives tacit consent to the government's legislation.

The division record of the House of Commons shows that, notwithstanding the rhetoric of party conflict, in office both Conservative and Labour governments usually put forward bills that will be acceptable to all sides of the House of Commons. In the 1970–1974 Parliament, 80 percent of all Conservative government legislation was *not* opposed on principle by the Labour opposition. In the 1974–1979 Parliament, 77 percent of all Labour's legislation was not opposed by the Conservatives. The bills that create major controversies in Parliament are newsworthy precisely because they are different from the average Act of Parliament.[51]

Cross-Pressured Voters. The organizational cross-pressures upon parties are also reflected in the political outlooks of individuals. Most people do not agree with every position advocated by the party for which they vote. One voter might favor permissive policies on moral issues, a position usually endorsed by the Labour party, but market-oriented economic doctrines usually advocated within the Conservative party. Another voter might favor government intervention in the economy, a Labour position, and Conservative views on moral issues. The Alliance may gain votes less by advocating new policies than by advocating a different mix than either of the two established parties, for example, support for market-oriented economic policies and for social welfare programs.

While more than five-sixths of the electorate identifies with a party, it is not an exclusive identity. A 1983 Gallup Poll found that 73 percent of all voters were prepared to vote for more than one party. When asked how they would mark a ballot allowing a voter to express a second as well as a first preference (a system used in Australia), 73 percent were ready to express a second choice. Conservative and Labour voters usually named the Alliance as their second choice: Alliance voters split their preferences more evenly between Labour and Conservatives.[52]

In times past, cross-pressures have led many major politicians to change parties. A list of party leaders who have switched from one party to another includes such Prime Ministers as Sir Robert Peel, William Gladstone, David Lloyd George, Ramsay MacDonald, Winston Churchill, and the youthful Harold Wilson, a Liberal as an undergraduate but Labour when he stood for Parliament less than a decade later. Dr. David Owen, formerly Labour foreign secretary and now Social Democratic leader, would like to see his name added to this list.

The everyday discourse of politics is misleading in concentrating attention upon differences between parties. By definition, politics is about the expression of different opinions about what government should do. But British political parties have quietly and repeatedly demonstrated that in social policy they are ready to assimilate ideas from their opponents. Many Conservatives are proud of their party's adaptiveness, arguing that it is good tactics to promote Tory men and Whig measures. Labour governments have shown it is also possible to have Labour men and Tory measures. The transfer of power from one party to another does not mean a great disruption in the actions of government. A newly elected government accepts as its inheritance virtually all the Acts of Parliament enacted by its predecessors, including many passed against its vocal opposition.

Everyday discourse is also misleading in fixing attention upon the present. The record of party competition in Britain since the introduction of the mass franchise in 1885 is a reminder that seemingly stable competition can be disrupted. The system of multi-party competition as of 1983 is the *fourth* system in a century, following a Conservative-Liberal era from 1885 to 1910; a three-party Conservative, Labour, Liberal system from 1918 to 1935; and a two-party Conservative-Labour system from 1945 until 1974.

The party system today is fluid, not stable. The four elections since February 1974 have shown so marked a departure from conventional two-party competition that a return to voting along the lines of the 1950s or 1960s would in effect be the creation of a fifth party system. Furthermore, the electorate shows no agreement about the direction in which the party system should evolve. When a 1983 survey asked voters—Which do you think is generally better for Britain: to have a government formed by one political party, or for two or more parties to get together to form a government?—the respondents divided almost evenly. Overall 47 percent said they preferred government by a single party and 49 percent government by a coalition of two or more parties; the median respondent was literally a don't know.[53]

NOTES

1. For a much fuller discussion, and evidence for themes developed here, see Richard Rose, *Do Parties Make a Difference?* 2nd ed.; and Richard Rose, *The Problem of Party Government* (London: Macmillan, 1974).

2. For arguments to this effect, see e.g., Samuel Brittan, *Left or Right: The Bogus Dilemma* (London: Secker & Warburg, 1968); and S. E. Finer, *The Changing British Party System, 1945–1979* (Washington, D.C.: American Enterprise Institute, 1980).

3. See Ian McAllister and Richard Rose, *The Nationwide Competition for Votes,* table II.3.

4. See Richard Rose, "From Simple Determinism to Interactive Models of Voting," *Comparative Political Studies,* 15:2 (1982), table 2.

5. James E. Alt, "Dealignment and the Dynamics of Partisanship in Brit-

ain,'' in R. Dalton, S. Flanagan, and P. Beck, eds., *Electoral Change in Advanced Industrial Societies* (Princeton, N.J.: Princeton University Press, 1984), pp. 298–329.

6. See Richard Rose, *The Presidency in Comparative Perspective* (Glasgow: U. of Strathclyde Studies in Public Policy No. 130, 1984), table IV.2.

7. See Richard Rose, ''British Government: The Job at the Top,'' in Rose and Suleiman, eds., *Presidents and Prime Ministers,* table I.2; and Ivor Crewe, ''Is Britain's Two Party System Really About to Crumble?'' *Electoral Studies,* 1:3 (1982), pp. 275–314.

8. Sarlvik and Crewe, *Decade of Dealignment,* p. 62.

9. McAllister and Rose, *The Nationwide Competition for Votes,* table IX.4.

10. For the impact that coalition would have upon many features of British government, see David Butler, *Governing Without a Majority* (London: Collins, 1983). For arguments for the present electoral system, see Philip Norton, *The Constitution in Flux,* chapter 12, and sources cited therein.

11. See Vernon Bogdanor, *The People and the Party System* (Cambridge: Cambridge University Press, 1981).

12. See David Butler, ed., *Coalitions in British Politics* (London: Macmillan, 1978); cf. R. O. Bassett, *The Essentials of Parliamentary Democracy* (London: Macmillan, 1935).

13. Cf. Butler and Kavanagh, *The British General Election of 1983,* pp. 336ff., with McAllister and Rose, *The Nationwide Competition for Votes,* pp. 196ff.

14. See McAllister and Rose, *The Nationwide Competition for Votes,* especially chapter 9.

15. Butler and Sloman, *British Political Facts, 1900–1979,* (5th ed.), pp. 206–210.

16. Cf. Geoffrey Pridham, ''Not So Much a Programme — More a Way of Life: European Perspectives on the British SDP/Liberal Alliance,'' *Parliamentary Affairs,* 36:2 (1983), pp. 183–201.

17. *Gallup Political Index,* No. 274 (June 1983), p. 5.

18. *Committee on Financial Aid to Political Parties* (London: HMSO, Cmnd. 6601, 1976), p. 54.

19. For a full description of party organizations, see Rose, *The Problem of Party Government,* chapters 6–10.

20. See Lewis Minkin, *The Labour Party Conference* 2nd ed. (Manchester: University Press, 1980).

21. See Roger Jowell and Colin Airey, *British Social Attitudes: the 1984 Report* (Aldershot: Gower, 1984), p. 17.

22. Cf. Alison Young, *The Reselection of MPs* (London: Heinemann, 1983).

23. See Byron Criddle, ''Candidates,'' in Butler and Kavanagh, *The British General Election of 1983,* pp. 219ff.

24. R. T. McKenzie, *British Political Parties,* 2nd ed. (London: Heinemann, 1963).

25. Morgan Phillips, *Constitution of the Labour Party* (London: Labour Party, 1960), p. 4.

26. For an early organizational study, see Jorgen S. Rasmussen, *The Liberal Party:* (London: Constable, 1965). For a collection of analyses, see Vernon Bogdanor, ed., *Liberal Party Politics* (Oxford: Clarendon Press, 1983).

27. See Herbert Doering, ''Who are the Social Democrats?'' *New Society,* 8 September 1983.

28. Cf. S. J. Eldersveld, *Political Parties: a Behavioral Analysis* (Chicago: Rand McNally 1964). For a similar idea, distinguishing high and low politics, see

Jim Bulpitt, *Territory and Power in the United Kingdom* (Manchester: University Press, 1983).

29. See Michael Pinto-Duschinsky, *British Political Finance 1830–1980* (Washington, D.C.: American Enterprise Institute, 1981).

30. McKenzie, *British Political Parties* p. iv, rules out party ideologies and programs from consideration in his preface.

31. See J. D. Lees and Richard Kimber, eds., *Political Parties in Modern Britain* (London: Routledge, 1972) pp. 14ff.

32. In a radio interview reprinted in *The Listener* (London) 29 October 1964.

33. Donley T. Studlar and Susan Welch, "Mass Attitudes on Political Issues in Britain," *Comparative Political Studies,* 14:3 (1981), pp. 327–355.

34. Moreover, Studlar and Welch (*ibid.*) found that after controlling for demographic influences, the five attitude factors explained only 12 percent of the Labour vote and 13 percent of the Conservative vote in October 1974.

35. If only those questions loading at least .50 on a factor analysis are considered part of a more general ideological syndrome, then 15 of 23 issues are not associated with any factor. See also Paul Whiteley, *The Labour Party in Crisis* (London: Methuen, 1983) pp. 25ff.

36. See Rose, *The Problem of Party Government,* chapter 11; and Rose, *Do Parties Make a Difference?* chapter 3.

37. See Susan Welch and Donley T. Studlar, "The Policy Opinions of British Political Activists," *Political Studies,* 31:4 (1983), pp. 606–615.

38. See Rose, *The Problem of Party Government,* table VIII.4; Barry Hindness, *The Decline of Working Class Politics* (London: Paladin, 1971), pp. 70f; Rose, "The Policy Ideas of English Party Activists," *American Political Science Review,* 56:2 (1962), pp. 360–371.

39. Whiteley, *The Labour Party in Crisis,* tables 2.6, 2.8.

40. See David Robertson, Appendix IV, in David Butler and Michael Pinto-Duschinsky, *The British General Election of 1970* (London: Macmillan, 1971).

41. See Rose, *The Problem of Party Government,* table XI.2.

42. Rose, *Do Parties Make a Difference?* 2nd ed., chapter 4.

43. See Allan Kornberg and Robert C. Frasure, "Policy Differences in British Parliamentary Parties," *American Political Science Review,* 65:3 (1971); and, on free votes, P. G. Richards, *Parliament and Conscience* (London: Allen & Unwin, 1970), p. 180.

44. See Ivor Crewe and Bo Sarlvik, "Popular Attitudes and Electoral Strategy," in Z. Layton-Henry, ed., *Conservative Party Politics* (London: Macmillan 1980), pp. 244–275; I. Crewe, "The Labour Party and the Electorate," in D. Kavanagh, ed., *The Politics of the Labour Party* (London: Allen & Unwin, 1982), pp. 9–49; and Martin Harrop, "Labour-Voting Conservatives; Policy Differences between the Labour Party and Labour Voter," in R. M. Worcester and M. Harrop, eds., *Political Communications* (London: Allen & Unwin, 1982), 152–163.

45. For data from 1980 to 1983, see *Gallup Political Index* No. 278 (October 1983), pp. 17ff.

46. See Rose, *Do Parties Make a Difference?* 2nd ed., table 3.5, Epilogue table 1.

47. Richard Rose, and Thomas T. Mackie, *Do Parties Persist or Disappear? The Big Tradeoff Facing Organizations* (Glasgow: U. of Strathclyde Studies in Public Policy No. 134, 1984).

48. See Richard Rose, "Parties, Factions and Tendencies in Britain," *Political Studies,* 12:1 (1964), pp. 33–46.

49. S. E. Finer, Hugh Berrington, and D. J. Bartholomew, *Backbench Opinion in the House of Commons 1955–59* (Oxford: Pergamon Press, 1961), p. 106. See also Robert C. Frasure, "Backbench Opinion Revisited," *Political Studies,* 20:3 (1972).

50. Rose, *Do Parties Make a Difference?* 2nd ed., chapter 8.

51. *Ibid.,* table 5.1

52. *Ibid.,* Epilogue table 2.

53. Jowell and Airey, *British Social Attitudes: The 1984 Report,* p. 16.

CHAPTER X

The Policy Process

If we think what a vast information, what a nice discretion, what a consistent will ought to mark the rulers of that empire, we shall be surprised when we see them. We see a changing body of miscellaneous persons, sometimes few, sometimes many, never the same for an hour.

THE CREATION OF GOVERNMENT IN ENGLAND was initially a process of concentrating power at the center: the Crown was concerned with those activities that had to be centrally determined, such as the declaration of war, control of the state Church, and providing a final court of appeal in disputes about laws. Policy making was isolated as well as centralized; its impact did not extend far beyond the Royal court.[1]

The evolution of government is a story of the development of institutions not only enforcing its authority nationwide, but also delivering a host of programs from one end of the land to the other. The creation of a multiplicity of institutions to deliver the programs of the mixed-economy welfare state has made central government exchange independence for interdependence. To be effective, Whitehall ministries must give direction to organizations that are not accountable to Parliament and, in the case of local government, are accountable to a different electorate. Equally important, the impact of government often depends upon social trends and economic events that government can influence but not control.

To understand how policies are made, we must look inside the black box of government. Instead of treating government as a unitary decisionmaker we must face up to realities. The Crown's formal unity is not matched by a unified policy process. Government is best conceived as a plural noun; it is not a singular organization. It embraces a myriad of organizations in central London as well as local authorities, nationalized industries, and the health service, and distinctive institutions for Scotland, Wales, and Northern Ireland.

Making policy is a lengthy and complex political process. Analytically, we can start by conceiving a routine steady-state when no decisions are required of politicians, and government's only task is to supervise and administer policies determined by past choices. Routine administration is challenged by political controversy's demanding a departure from this routine. For example, from the passage of the 1944 Education Act guaranteeing free secondary education until the mid-1950s, the system of universal selective secondary education was routinely praised by all parties. In its 1955 election manifesto, the Labour party began to urge a policy of comprehensive schools instead, and in 1965 a Labour government made this government policy as well. By the mid-1970s comprehensive education had become the new routine.

Government policies are statements of intent, not accomplishment. A policy indicates what politicians would like to do about a condition in society. A policy usually aggregates a multiplicity of demands from parties and pressure groups (including Whitehall departments) into a more or less agreed-upon statement of intent. Stating a policy intention is meaningless if it is not followed by actions intended to direct government institutions to realize policy objectives. A policy intention is a hypothesis about what might happen; it is not an accomplished fact.

To translate a statement of good intentions into a specific program requires "running the Whitehall obstacle race."[2] A minister with a program to promote must first of all secure agreement within his department that the proposal is administratively practicable. Next, the minister must gain consent from other Whitehall departments affected by it. If money is to be spent, the Treasury must also grant its approval. Once over these hurdles, the minister will ask the Cabinet for formal approval and to find room in a crowded parliamentary timetable to enact a law if legislation is required. The effort necessary to secure an Act of Parliament can be so great that ministers often regard it as an end in itself.

Passing an Act of Parliament is not proof that intentions will be realized; the record of any Parliament includes monuments to intentions that were never fully realized. Policymakers face a variety of social and economic constraints. Government is powerful, but not all-powerful. This is most evident in laws against crime; they are not so much intended to prevent crimes occurring as to punish those who violate Parliament's rules. The central concern of government today, the management of the economy, is not easily controlled by legislation. Laws cannot make the economy grow faster or repeal the market forces inhibiting economic growth or inducing inflation or unemployment.

To see how policies are made, we first examine the influence that party politicians can have upon government policies. It is then necessary to look at the limits of central control of policy making, starting with constraints upon the Prime Minister. In a complementary manner, we consider the limits of decentralization within England, and then elsewhere in the United Kingdom. Finally, we ask whether any one individual or institution is invariably the maker of policies, or whether influence is contingent upon the type of policy at hand.

THE LIMITS OF PARTISAN INFLUENCE

The policy process is about ends as well as means. The ceaseless activity of governing is not an end in itself; it is also about the means to achieve larger public purposes through the adoption of particular programs. But programs are not mechanical in their operation: there are disputes about program goals, and uncertainty about effectiveness.

The policy process works easily when an issue involves applying a known, predictable technology to uncontroversial choices. A known technology makes the results of a choice predictable, and the absence of differences makes it easier to reach a political accord. For example, decisions of the Property Services Agency about building government offices are minor, for the technology of the construction industry is predictable, and government office-building is rarely in dispute between parties. The presence of a known technology, such as nuclear physics, does not simplify choices if the issue is controversial, such as the development of atomic energy.[3] When an issue involves an uncertain technology and conflicting political interests as well, policymakers face great difficulties.

When uncertainty and controversy arise, it is not possible to resolve disputes by invoking a simple dictum: give the people what they want. Deciding what is wanted by the electorate is no simple task; nor is there any reason why government should be expected to be able to satisfy all the people all of the time.

Parties can be the source of values directing policies, and justifying government actions when challenged. The very name of the Conservative party implies that it will make choices intended to keep society as it is. But such a belief does not permit a do-nothing approach to government, for society is continually in flux. Hence, a Conservative government is always actively enunciating policy intentions. The Labour party's intention, stated in the party constitution, of promoting the welfare of workers by hand and brain, is too general to provide unambiguous criteria for choice. A Labour Cabinet must decide how to interpret Socialist principles.

Parliamentary conventions make British government party government. But to be *ex officio* in charge of the policy process is not necessarily to be the *de facto* policymaker. "Parties live in a house of power," Max Weber wrote in one of his most gnomic sentences; he did not say whether the party in office resided as master, prisoner, or spectator.[4] To answer this question one must consider what a party has to do if it is to give positive direction to government, as well as being formally responsible for what government does. The basic requirements are as follows.

1. *Parties must formulate policy intentions for enactment once in office.* The Conservative and Labour parties have well-established procedures for formulating policy intentions in opposition, and stating them in a detailed election manifesto. Social Democratic leaders, with substantial previous experience of govern-

ment, have been concerned that the Alliance too show its seriousness by preparing detailed policy intentions.

2. *A party's policy intentions must be matched by specification of the programmatic means to achieve desired ends.* A statement of intent without reference to means, such as a pledge to seek peace and prosperity, is not a basis for action, but a vague and perhaps vain statement of hope. The conventions of Westminster make it difficult for an opposition to prepare detailed programs. Because there is no chance of any of its parliamentary proposals becoming law, an opposition party may simply adopt a negative policy: throw the rascals out. This is convenient, for it absolves the leader of the opposition from committing himself on issues about which the party may disagree. It also avoids premature commitment in advance of practical advice that Whitehall civil servants offer after a party moves from opposition to office.

In effect, opposition parties have neither the staff nor the political incentives to draw up programs in sufficient detail for prompt presentation to Parliament before an election. This task is usually delayed until after a party wins an election. The result is that once in office MPs can be surprised by the difficulties of governing. This view was given classic expression by Emanuel Shinwell, minister responsible for nationalizing the coal mines in the 1945 Labour government:

> We are about to take over the mining industry. This is not as easy as it looks. I have been talking of nationalization for forty years, but the complications of the transfer of property had never occurred to me.[5]

3. *Partisans must occupy important positions in government, and partisans must be sufficiently numerous to dominate government's major organizations.* Within hours after an election result is known, the leader of the winning party takes office as Prime Minister, and begins appointing a Cabinet of up to two dozen colleagues. The constitutional fiction of one minister being personally responsible for the whole of a department inhibits the appointment of many partisans to form a directing core in each ministry, or their dispersal throughout complex ministries, as

happens in Washington. With a few junior ministers and a policy or partisan advisor, a minister will still feel isolated, and tend to depend upon civil servant advisors.

4. *Partisans in office must have the skills needed to control large bureaucratic organizations.* The skill that a Cabinet minister is most likely to have is that of managing Parliament. The ability to deal with fellow MPs in the Commons is not, however, the same as the ability to deal with the inheritance of programs of a ministry. The conventions of a parliamentary career make it difficult for an aspiring minister to acquire experience of directing a large organization outside government before becoming a minister. There is also a limited likelihood that a new minister will have firsthand knowledge of the substantive social and economic conditions that the ministry is meant to deal with.

5. *Partisans in office must give high priority to carrying out party policies.* A politician in office must face up to many pressures that party supporters are not acutely aware of, because they are not in office. These constraints include the established program commitments of the department; pressures from groups that are not partisan supporters but are necessarily involved in Whitehall (for example, trade unions with a Conservative government, and business with a Labour government); pressures from abroad, especially trends in the international economy; and, not least, problems arising from the fact that the governing party itself may be more divided about issues than was apparent in opposition.

A systematic analysis of the difference that British parties can make in office, covering the period from 1957 to 1983, found that while one party might initiate measures that the other would not have, there were many areas of agreement. Similarities do not mean that opposing parties espouse the same intentions: "Necessity more than ideological consensus is the explanation for similarities in behaviour."[6]

6. *Civil servants must cooperate in carrying out party policies.* According to Sir Kenneth Wheare, a civil servant "is not a one-party man; he is a government-party man. He offers his best services to the party in power, to the government of any party."[7] But civil servants are also concerned with ensuring that their ministers are aware of what Sir William Armstrong,

former head of the civil service, has referred to as "ongoing reality,"[8] that is, circumstances that constrain the choices of any minister. It is these constraints that ministers need reminding of, since policy intentions voiced in opposition are unlikely to give them much weight.

If a minister does have clear and distinctive policy intentions and understands how to relate them to the continuing programs of government, party policy *can* give direction to government, or at least, particular party preferences can direct particular government programs. If not, there is likely to be much continuity from a Labour to a Conservative government, or vice versa. As a former Conservative Chancellor of the Exchequer said about the economic policy of the successor Labour government, they inherited "our problems and our remedies."[9]

The limits of partisan influences can be illustrated by considering the likely consequences of the different economic policies offered by the Conservative, Labour, and Alliance parties in the 1983 general election. While all three parties wanted to do something about unemployment, inflation, and low rates of economic growth, each argued that it would act differently from its competitors. Differences in the means of policy imply differences in economic results.

The development of sophisticated statistical models of the economy makes it possible to simulate the likely impact of different parties' economic measures.[10] Even though the government of the day can adopt only one policy (or one policy at a time), each party's economic proposals can be applied to a computerized model of the British economy in order to estimate what the net effect of each would likely be. The bottom line in comparing simulations is the numerical difference between policies said to make all the difference by their advocates. While models can only give an estimate of outcomes, the results are more coherent and more precise than the self-interested forecasts made by campaigning politicians.

Unfortunately for the country, simulations indicate that none of the policies advanced by different parties would make a big difference to the state of the British economy (Table X.1). The four models forecast an average level of 3.2 million unemploy-

TABLE X.1 *The Economic Consequences of Different Parties: A Simulation for 1983-1987*

| | Unemployment | | | Inflation | | | Growth GDP | | |
| | Con | All | Lab | Con | All | Lab | Con | All | Lab |
	mn	mn	mn	%	% *(average annual rate)*	%	%	%	%
London Business School	3.2	2.9	2.8	5.4	6.2	8.7	2.3	2.8	3.2
ITEM	3.0	2.8	2.4	7.3	7.8	9.7	2.2	2.8	4.5
National Institute of Econ. & Soc. Research	3.2	3.1	2.8	7.2	6.5	8.5	1.8	4.3	2.5
Henley Centre	3.3	2.9	2.9	5.1	7.2	11.3	1.7	2.4	2.8
Average	3.2	2.9	2.7	6.2	6.9	9.5	2.0	2.6	3.7

Source: Compiled from "Cold Comfort Forecasts," *Observer Business Review*, 5 June 1983; and Andreas Whittam Smith, "Tory Economics Gain the Edge by Promising Less," *Daily Telegraph*, 21 May 1983.

ment under the Conservatives, 2.9 million unemployment with Alliance, and 2.7 million unemployment if Labour prescriptions were followed. Consistent with economic theories, inflation would be highest by following Labour's prescriptions, averaging an estimated 9.5 percent, and lowest with the Conservatives, at 6.2 percent. Labour's higher inflation rate would be the cost of a higher growth rate, just as Conservative prescriptions intended to keep inflation down would result in higher unemployment and a lower growth rate.

Economic models demonstrate that there is a marginal difference in the likely impact of different parties upon government. But the size of the margin is far less than voters or politicians would like it to be. For years politicians have unsuccessfully sought an economic growth rate double that actually achieved in the past decade, and to maintain unemployment and inflation at a level one-half or two-thirds less than the record of the governing party of the day.

THE CENTER AND ITS LIMITS

The formal theory of British government is unitary. The powers of government are vested in the Crown in Parliament, which is effectively in the hands of the leaders of the majority party in Parliament. Those seeking political influence invariably head toward Whitehall, in search of the center of central government. More than one institution there can claim to be central at the center.

The Prime Minister. Within Westminster the Prime Minister is the person most often named as the leading policymaker in government. This reflects the Prime Minister's unique eminence in Parliament and in Cabinet, as well as the spotlight that the media shine on whoever holds that office. Yet publicity should not be confused with power.

Because of the Prime Minister's prominence, some writers go so far as to argue that England now has Prime Ministerial government. While often invoked, the phrase is rarely defined. R. H. S. Crossman, a former Labour minister, has argued that "primary decisions" are made by the Prime Minister and "secondary decisions" are made by departmental ministers in consultation with the Cabinet; any decision made solely by a minister becomes by definition "not at all important."[11]

A professor turned back-bench Labour MP, John P. Mackintosh, asserted, "The country is governed by the Prime Minister, who leads, co-ordinates and maintains a series of ministers."[12] But Mackintosh immediately retracted the full force of this statement by saying that some decisions are made by the Prime Minister alone, others in consultation with senior ministers, and still others by the Cabinet, Cabinet committees, ministers, or senior civil servants. Even proponents of a theory of power centralized in Downing Street hedge their generalizations with statements about the limits of what the Prime Minister can do.

The weaknesses in the theory of Prime Ministerial government are substantial. The first is vagueness. The distinction between important and unimportant decisions is never clearly defined. Yet without a clear definition of what is an important decision, the tautological implication is that important decisions are those made by the Prime Minister, and unimportant decisions are those made by others. Although individual decisions in crises of the greatest importance are usually reserved for the Prime Minister, the decisions in which she does not involve herself can be *collectively* more important than the dramatic but occasional crisis.

Second, writers such as Mackintosh pay less attention to the decision-making activities of the Prime Minister than to his or her survival in office.[13] To argue that the Prime Minister's significance arises from remaining in office is to apply a criterion that treats the incumbent like a constitutional monarch, who is far more secure than a Prime Minister. At times, the price a Prime Minister pays to retain office is giving way to Cabinet and extra-Cabinet pressures. The choice is summed up in Peter Jenkins's description of Harold Wilson's position in 1969, when the Prime Minister abandoned a proposal for a major industrial relations bill.

> The power of the Prime Minister was thus sufficient for him to remain in office, but insufficient for him to remain in office *and* have his way.[14]

Third, Prime Ministers are overloaded; their responsibilities far exceed their ability to deal with all problems at first hand. Mackintosh portrays the Prime Minister as "at the apex, supported by and giving point to a widening series of rings of senior ministers, the Cabinet, its committees, non-Cabinet ministers and departments."[15] But this view from the top can be remote. Only a small portion of activities occurring lower down the pyramid filter to the top. The Mackintosh metaphor can be interpreted to show that bureaus within departments are the base of government, with senior civil servants and ministers almost as remote as the Prime Minister.

Because of the opportunity to intervene in so many issues, the Prime Minister pays a very high opportunity cost for any action. Time is finite, and it is exhaustable. To participate in foreign policy negotiations is to forego the opportunity to discuss other issues with other ministers. One person cannot keep abreast of the complexities of foreign affairs, defense, internal security, economic policy, industrial relations, the environment, housing, education, health, social security, and public order — especially when there are other tasks besides. For every Cabinet minister whom the Prime Minister sees often to discuss policy issues, many more will be seen infrequently or not at all.

In their memoirs, retired Prime Ministers emphasize the time spent on foreign affairs because they are expected to speak for the country internationally. The Prime Minister receives Foreign Office papers as a matter of course, but not papers from domestic departments. As long ago as 1900 Sir Henry Campbell-Bannerman commented, "It is absolutely impossible for any man who conducts the foreign affairs of the country at the same time to supervise and take charge of the general action of the government."[16] By appointing a relatively weak Foreign Secretary, a Prime Minister can easily give directives to the Foreign Office. However, when Britain no longer has as much international influence as it did in Queen Victoria's time, the Prime Minister's involvement abroad in matters that Britain's government can scarcely influence is a sign of weakness, not power.

A fourth limitation on the Prime Minister's influence in

Whitehall is the lack of a large personal staff. Since 1964 successive Prime Ministers have had one or more personal policy advisers in Downing Street in addition to a handful of civil service advisers; together the two groups number about a dozen. The head of the Cabinet Office is also in a crucial position to assist the Prime Minister. In numbers and political status, the staff of a Prime Minister is slight compared with the staff of an American president. Downing Street staff lack both the constitutional status and the political weight to give direction to departments with their own ministerial heads.

Although the Prime Minister is invariably the most important person in government, one person cannot dominate the whole of government. The direction of more than 7 million public employees and the expenditure of more than £100 billion is more than any one person could supervise, let alone determine. In the words of one civil servant, transferred from a department directly concerned with programs to 10 Downing Street: "It's like skating over an enormous globe of thin ice. You have to keep moving fast all the time."[17] Describing the Prime Minister as at the apex of government aptly symbolizes the small space that the post occupies among a range of public institutions.

The Prime Minister keeps in touch with the activities of government through the papers and information that flow through the Cabinet and its committees and from the House of Commons. "Touch" is the word. The great bulk of the information is tangential to the imperative concerns of the Prime Minister with party management, parliamentary performance, media performance, and winning elections. At any given time a Prime Minister is restricted to selective intervention in a few issues important to the government as a whole.

The Cabinet. The Cabinet is constitutionally the chief institution for the central determination of government policy. It is large enough to include persons with day-to-day executive responsibilities for major areas of public policy, such as education, agriculture, and the social services, yet small enough so that every member can sit around a table and participate in its deliberations. In theory, the most important persons in government can deliberate in the Cabinet on the general wisdom of particular measures, and consider priorities among policies. Once a Cabinet decision is minuted, ministers are collectively responsible.

Every Cabinet minister has great incentives to deemphasize his collective Cabinet role and bury himself in his department. Within the department, he is the chief personage; the limits on his ability to influence other departments are also a defense against interference by colleagues. A study of Cabinet ministers revealed that half made no mention of their Cabinet role; only one in ten saw himself as in any way a *Cabinet* minister. Bruce Headey comments, ''Insofar as the Cabinet is important to ministers, it is seen as an interdepartmental battleground rather than as a forum for collective deliberation on policy.''[18] Government policy can come to mean no more than the sum of matters that individual ministers will approve or defend departmentally.

Cabinet ministers head departments that compete with each other for scarce resources, such as money, skilled manpower, and parliamentary time for legislation. This competition divides ministers from each other. Barbara Castle entered the 1964 Labour Cabinet believing ''in my innocence'' that it would make major policy decisions in collective deliberation. But ''I was soon disabused of that . . . I wasn't in a political caucus at all. I was faced by departmental enemies.''[19] Departmental disagreements are at bottom institutional; differences between ministers in personality or political tendency reinforce this competition. Disagreements arise from overlapping areas of responsibility; for example, the Department of Education and Science, the Home Office, and the Department of Health and Social Security each has some responsibility for children. Differences are further enhanced because often the delivery of programs for which ministries are nominally responsible rests in the hands of extra-Whitehall bodies, such as local councils and health boards.

The chief formal mechanisms for resolving interdepartmental differences are Cabinet committees of ministers and parallel committees of their civil servants. Before 1914 there was only one Cabinet committee, Defense. Today dozens of committees meet on subjects ranging from nuclear defense to agricultural policy. Ministers may also privately meet each other or the Prime Minister, seeking wider support for departmental policies and the informal resolution of disputes.[20]

If affected ministers can agree among themselves about an issue before it goes to Cabinet, the matter will be presented for information only. An uninvolved minister can contribute little that has not already been discussed before an issue reaches Cabinet. If every minister sought to speak about each item on the agenda, there would only be time in a meeting to discuss two or three topics. Individual Cabinet ministers engage in tacit logrolling, remaining silent on matters outside their responsibility in expectation that other ministers will be quiet when they themselves put forward proposals.

Strict control of the Cabinet's agenda is necessary because time for discussion is scarce. Meetings of the Cabinet occupy about six hours a week. By convention, the agenda regularly includes discussion of foreign affairs and of parliamentary business, as well as matters of major political controversy, however transitory their significance. Before a matter can be placed on the Cabinet's agenda, the Cabinet Office must be satisfied that it is sufficiently important to merit discussion there, and that the necessary preparatory work for discussion has been undertaken in committee.

The Cabinet can veto or delay a minister's policy if it decides a proposal is politically undesirable. When a crisis requires prompt action, it cannot veto a policy unless an alternative can be found. Often time is too short for nonexpert ministers to challenge a departmental minister involved in crisis negotiations. There may not even be time for the Cabinet to be told about a decision until it is a *fait accompli*.

In Cabinet deliberations, ''The one thing that is hardly ever discussed is general policy,'' that is, underlying priorities and objectives. ''Nothing, indeed is more calculated to make a Cabinet minister unpopular with his colleagues, to cause him to be regarded by them as Public Enemy No. 1, than a tiresome insistence on discussing general issues.''[21] The Cabinet is not an institution for coordinating policies; it enforces collective responsibility but not collective decision making. In the words of Colin Seymour-Ure:

> The Cabinet seems to have disintegrated in the literal sense of that word. Every member of the Cabinet is important, but his importance depends on functions that are performed almost entirely *outside* the Cabinet.[22]

Trying to give more political coordination to government policy, Prime Minister Edward Heath in 1970 created super-departments in which one minister, such as the Secretary of State for Environment, was responsible for policies previously divided among three ministries: transportation, public works, and housing and local government. It was argued that a superdepartment would be better able to coordinate major policy decisions, because within a large department one minister could see the interdependence of policies about housing, roads, and local government planning decisions. Moreover, within a superdepartment a minister has to rank policies by their importance; only one issue can come first at a time.[23]

But changing the names of government departments and adding another ministerial layer to an already high pyramid has not centralized the making of policy. There is only a limited amount of time in which one minister can deal with the multitude of problems arising beneath him. Resolution of disputes within a superdepartment also makes it more difficult for the Cabinet to see and correct the mistakes that individual ministers inevitably make.

The Cabinet's position in British government is part fact and part fiction. It is a fact that the Cabinet meets regularly, and membership in it is an important political asset to a politician. But it is a fiction, insofar as the Cabinet does not take most of the decisions promulgated in its name. Most of the effective work of Cabinet ministers occurs in intradepartmental and interdepartmental settings. The important constitutional fiction symbolized by the Cabinet is that the political decisions of ministers are related, because they involve the collective fate of the party in control of government.

The limits on central direction to government in 1970 also

led Edward Heath to establish a Central Policy Review Staff (CPRS) within the Cabinet Office. The unit was intended to provide a comprehensive review of government strategy, evaluating alternative policy options and considering how policies of different departments related to more general objectives of the governing party. With a staff of fifteen, less than one person for each government department, the CPRS could not be compared with the Executive Office of the President in Washington. Its creation was evidence of weakness in Downing Street. When asked to name the CPRS's major achievement, its first head, Lord Rothschild, said:

> I don't know that the government is better run as a result of our work. I think the highest compliment I ever got paid was from a Cabinet minister who said: "You make us think from time to time." I thought that was a great achievement, considering how much ministers have to do. They don't have much time to think.[24]

After being neglected by Heath's successors, the CPRS was abolished in 1983.

The Treasury. Because it reviews the programs of all other government departments annually in order to recommend how much (or how little) money they should have to spend, the Treasury has a unique coordinating responsibility among Cabinet departments. The Treasury's formal authority is also enhanced because it attracts civil servants of very high caliber — many of the leading positions in Whitehall are held by persons who have made their careers in the Treasury — and the Chancellor of the Exchequer is always a leading member of Cabinet.

The Treasury's control of public spending starts before a new measure is put to the Cabinet. The Treasury must be consulted about costs, and the measure must have Treasury approval before being considered in Parliament. The annual budget cycle provides another opportunity for departmental programs to come under review, especially if they involve a large increase in expenditure. The Treasury's responsibilities for overall management of the economy lead it at irregular intervals to require departmental spending cuts when deflation is the norm, and increased spending when the economy is deemed in need of inflation.

Treasury control no longer deals primarily with "saving candle ends," in Mr. Gladstone's picturesque phrase equating economics with parsimony. Instead, it deals with pervasive concerns of government insofar as they affect or are affected by economic considerations. When major national or international problems appear, such as domestic inflation or foreign pressure on the pound, the Treasury may be able to dictate reductions in the programs of spending departments. But the Treasury is subject to strong political pressures as well. In the months leading up to a general election, the Treasury is expected to allow public spending to increase in order to provide more social benefits or, as a tax-conscious opposition might argue, "to bribe the public with its own money."

Within the Treasury sanctum, disagreements are frequently articulated. Treasury economists are no more likely to agree than are academic economists. In the past Treasury officials could unite in dismissing proposals deemed to be invalidated by economic theories. In the 1980s Treasury economists have lost much self-confidence. In the words of Sir Douglas Wass, a former head: "Both the Keynesian and the monetarist explanations, which are anyway not mutually exclusive, have been found to be inadequate."[25] In such circumstances, a party that is very clear about its economic priorities — and Mrs. Thatcher's team entered office in 1979 with a commitment to specific objectives — is in a strong position vis à vis uncertain advisors.

The Treasury's policy objectives are multiple, and its organizational priorities pose dilemmas for choice. All areas of economic policy are or ought to be related. But the number of tasks are more than one minister can handle. Three activities of utmost importance are related, yet at times can be in conflict. First, the Treasury is manager of the domestic economy, seeking desirable levels of economic growth, inflation, and employment. Second, it is responsible for maintaining a favorable balance of payments in trade between the sterling area and other parts of the world. A third Treasury function, budgeting annual expenditure, is no longer viewed as an end in it-

322 *The Policy Process*

self. Because of the influence of public sector spending upon the economy, budgeting has now become a means to the end of managing the economy as a whole.

Given conflicts among economic objectives and negative side effects of many policies, since the Second World War governments have intermittently sought to undertake economic planning. The history of Whitehall's efforts shows a slow but gradual increase in the Treasury's economic sophistication, introducing a new form of planning, then abolishing it, leaving behind a residue of improvements. Administrative machinery cannot by itself resolve political conflicts or guarantee economic success. The performance of the British economy in the past three decades demonstrates the limits of central influence.[26]

Important as the Treasury is in the control of Whitehall departments, it is misleading to assume that it is thereby able to control the economy as a whole. To do this would require perfect knowledge of future events, abroad and at home, as well as dictatorial powers within the country, and great influence upon other lands. To speak of controlling the economy as if it were a machine is to be deceived by a verbal sleight-of-hand. Even at the best of times, the Chancellor of the Exchequer cannot do this. In the words of former Chancellor of the Exchequer Denis Healey, "Running the economy is more like gardening than operating a computer."[27]

DECENTRALIZATION AND ITS LIMITS

Formally, the Crown in Parliament represents authority at the center; in practice government is nationwide. Responsibility for delivery of most services of the mixed-economy welfare state is not in the hands of civil servants working for Whitehall ministries; it is decentralized. Decentralization is both spatial (to local elected councils) and functional (to nationalized industries and expert executive agencies). The power that Westminster retains to abolish these agencies is, as a minister once privately remarked, "Like the atom bomb, so awesome that it is difficult to use." The financial powers of the Treasury affect non-Whitehall organizations, but the determination of how (as distinct from how much) money is spent is outside the Treasury's hands. Whereas central government raises 90 percent of total tax revenue, ministries directly spend only a limited portion, transferring money to local authorities, the health service, and nationalized industries, and ministries employ only one-seventh of all public employees.[28]

High and Low Politics. The operational theory of the Constitution, according to Jim Bulpitt, distinguishes between two sets of policies, matters of "high politics" concerning the center, and "low politics," said to be of little central concern.[29] High politics are matters of traditional status affecting the Crown, relations with foreign countries, command of the armed services and intelligence systems, the courts, and matters of little practical importance today such as relations between Church and State, and concerns of landowners and aristocrats. By contrast, low politics are the result of the rise of the welfare state, such matters as rubbish collection, health services, education, pensions, unemployment benefits, and personal social services. Whitehall is predisposed to keep responsibility for high politics in its own hands, and place the administration of low politics in other organizations. The result is what Bulpitt calls a "dual polity," in which each of the two parts has been responsible for different sets of policies.

In European countries organized on the Napoleonic model, each ministry can establish an elaborate system of field offices to deliver its services, with centrally employed prefects installed in each locality to monitor affairs of state there. In England, the practice has been to strengthen organizations outside Whitehall ministries. Whereas the Napoleonic system results in complex problems of direction within very large hierarchical organizations, the British system results in problems of interorganizational relations. Interorganizational politics occur within an *intra*governmental framework, for the Crown in Parliament remains unique in its power to abolish other organizations if relations become too difficult.

Whereas matters of high politics are determined by status, low politics requires large sums of money. Since the concerns of the welfare state have no traditional status, its evolution has increasingly concentrated the resources of government in low politics. At least four-fifths of public expenditure today is concerned with such untraditional matters as health, education, pensions, and unemployment benefits.

Westminster uses its authority to give direction to government, but not to deliver goods and services. Acts of Parliament set limits and conditions upon the actions of public-sector organizations, the Treasury allocates and monitors financial expenditure, and Cabinet ministers have ill-defined supervisory or "oversight" responsibility for programs. Although Whitehall pays the piper, it does not have its hands on the pipes.

The delivery of health, education, housing, social services, and the outputs of nationalized industries are in the hands of organizations separate from Whitehall. These organizations are seen in Whitehall as agents that ought to respond to central directives. But agents in local government are responsible to those who elect them; in the health services, to professional standards and clients; and in public enterprises, to customers.[30] The result is uncertainty and conflict between Whitehall departments and organizations that are more than mere agents of the center.

Many motives lead ministers to decide that they do not wish direct responsibility for public programs. Ministers may wish to insulate activities from charges of political interference (for example, the National Theatre); to provide flexibility in commercial operations (the Gas Board); to give an aura of impartiality to quasi-judicial activities (the Monopolies Commission); to respect the extragovernmental origins of an agency (the British Standards Institution); to allow qualified professionals to regulate their affairs (the Royal College of Physicians and Surgeons); to remove controversial matters from Whitehall (the Family Planning Association); or to concentrate efforts for a special purpose (a fund for disaster relief).

Of all the rationales for a public organization's form, the particular historical circumstance in which Whitehall became concerned with it is inevitably important. In consequence, there are few general rules to identify the organizations that collectively constitute British government.[31] *The Civil Service Year Book* divides central government into five types of organizations: the Royal Households and Offices; Parliamentary Offices; Ministers and Departments; three territorial ministries for Northern Ireland, Scotland, and Wales, each described as consisting of Departments and other Organizations; and a fifth category of Libraries, Museums and Galleries, Research Councils, and Other Organizations.[32] Complex as this classification is, it nonetheless omits the whole of local government, nationalized industries, and the health services, because they are independent of the civil service and Whitehall.

Most public-sector organizations outside Whitehall ministries can be grouped under three headings, depending upon whether or not their directors are elected, and whether an organization gives or sells its services: local authorities (directly elected, and providing major services such as education without charge); nationalized industries (nonelected, and selling their outputs); and the expert directed national health services (neither directly elected nor charging recipients for services). In addition, there are a host of nonelected fringe organizations, making few claims on public funds, for their duties are advisory or small-scale.

Local Government. In constitutional theory English local government reflects a top-down conception of authority. All local councils operate under Acts of Parliament that prescribe their boundaries and powers. Parliament can reorganize local government, transforming powers and boundaries radically; this was last done in the Local Government Act of 1972, and to a limited but politically symbolic extent in the second Thatcher administration.

Policymakers at the center see their authority justified by virtue of being accountable to a Parliament elected by a *national* constituency; local councils are pejoratively seen as reflecting local interests. Equally important, central government sees itself as a necessary and positive instrument for achieving territorial justice, ensuring that where a person lives makes little difference to the range and standard of public services that he or she receives.[33] This leads the Treasury to redistribute money from richer areas to poorer areas through a complex block grant system. Central concern with efficiency and equity causes Westminster to downgrade elected local councillors. In the words of one leading academic expert and Labour activist, Professor J. A. G. Griffith, "Councillors are not necessary political animals. We could manage without them."[34]

The framework for local government activities is laid down in Westminster and Whitehall. Under the *ultra vires* rule, local councils can do only what they are legally authorized to do by an Act of Parliament. By contrast, the American Constitution leaves states the power to do anything that is not explicitly forbidden. When local authorities wish to spend money, they are normally subject to Treasury guidelines affecting both current and capital expenditure. The Treasury gives more money to local authorities than the local authorities raise in local rates (property taxes). Central government lays down standards for the cost of building local council houses, and subsidies are related to cost standards.

Central government departments exercise a variety of supervisory powers as well. Inspectors examine schools and police services. Auditors examine both small and large expenditures to make sure they are sanctioned by statute. The salaries and terms of appointment of many local authority employees are also affected by central government decisions. The land-use planning decisions of local authorities may be challenged by an appeal to central government. In extreme cases, a minister can override decisions made by elected local councils, or even suspend councillors and assume administrative powers directly.

Local government in England is of three different types: the *shire counties,* with 59 percent of the population; *metropolitan county councils* in major cities, 25 percent; and the *Greater London Council* (GLC), 16 percent. Each of these local authorities has a lower tier of elected government: district councils in the counties and metropolitan areas, and borough councils in Greater London. County councils have responsibility for education, strategic land use planning, roads and transport, and personal social services. In metropolitan areas the district councils have responsibility for education and personal social service elsewhere assigned to the upper-tier county councils. Housing, with more than one-quarter of the population living in municipally owned council houses, is primarily a district council or borough responsibility. In the Greater London Council area most local authority responsibilities are in the hands of boroughs, and exceptional arrangements are made for education and police.[35] So few are the GLC powers that the Conservative government was able, to secure its abolition by statute in 1985, following conflicts with the Labour-controlled GLC.

Each local council divides into departments. The departments differ from Whitehall ministries in that they are accountable to a committee of the council rather than to a single minister. While the committee chairman will often be of substantial importance, the chairman is part-time rather than full-time. Moreover, a committee chairman does not have the authority to direct a department: only a committee vote, upheld by the council, can do this.

The crucial political relationships within local authorities are between the councillors who chair the most important committees of the council and the professionals who are the chief officers directing the services that these committees provide. Within each committee the chief local officer, a full-time council official appointed for expertise, merit, and seniority, is in charge of operations, exercising great influence by having technical knowledge and commitment to professional values. In major local authorities, chief officers can be of the same caliber as Whitehall civil servants, and be paid as much too.

National professional associations of educationists, town planners, architects, social workers, traffic engineers, and so forth are an important vertical link in the making of policy. These associations can simultaneously promote policies in relevant Whitehall departments and in local authorities. Chief officers look to their professional associations for leadership in developing new programs, and also as a defense against unwanted directives from Whitehall. In turn, Whitehall looks to professional associations to promote change in local authorities in accord with what Whitehall regards as desirable.

Insofar as professional officers become strong, each gives priority to the policy of greatest importance in his or her profession. It is difficult to coordinate decisions among architects, traffic engineers, and social workers, for each responds to different professional standards and directives from different

Whitehall ministries. Notwithstanding its nominal responsibility for a precisely defined and limited geographical area, local government is divided internally by different program responsibilities, as is Whitehall.

Within local authorities, elected councillors are meant to give direction to government. Their effectiveness is limited because the office is unpaid, limiting the kind of people who can afford to participate. The presence of disciplined parties in most local authorities usually produces a few more or less full-time politicians at the top of local authorities. Low turnout for local elections — often half that at a parliamentary election — indicates limited popular interest in local politics.[36]

The reorganization of local government in the early 1970s produced three major changes in the links between elected councillors and electors. First, it meant that local government is no longer local. The average English shire county now has a population of nearly 1 million; the locality with which an elector identifies is usually a small neighborhood, ward, or district within a large local government area. Second, the great majority of local government elections are now contested on party lines. Third, the power of the local party is enhanced, because a small number of local party members effectively decide who is nominated, and in one-party areas, who is in charge of the local council.

The coincidence of local government reorganization in 1974 and the onset of major fiscal difficulties at all levels of government has placed substantial strain upon central-local government relations.[37] Following the 1976 International Monetary Fund loan, the Labour government of the day sought to impose cash limits upon local government spending as well as that of Whitehall ministries. While the principle was opposed by many Labour councils, party loyalties argued for cooperation between councils wanting to spend more money and constraints imposed by a Labour government. Controversy was contained within the Labour party.

Since the return of a Conservative government in 1979, controversies have escalated by the opposition of some locally elected Labour councils to a nationally elected Conservative government. As part of its plans for containing public expenditure, the Conservative government first sought cooperation in expenditure reductions from local councils. When some Labour councils refused cooperation, it mandated expenditure limits by a series of increasingly restrictive laws involving penalties, such as the reduction of central government grants, and prohibitions upon councils deemed by Whitehall to be overspending. In reaction, some Labour councils have urged defiance of central directives, and canvassed methods of protest or evasion by all means available, ranging from expensive advertising campaigns in national newspapers to actions that courts can be challenged as illegal.

The interdependence of central and local government, arising from central government's legal and financial powers and local government's responsibility for service delivery, has meant that the autonomy of each from the other, assumed by the dual polity model, no longer exists. Whitehall has hoped to replace it with a cooperative relationship, in which agreement upon professional standards and technical criteria of efficiency would promote harmony, and acceptance of Westminster's overriding authority would resolve disputes. The financial and party political pressures of the 1980s, however, have emphasized a third alternative, conflict between central and local government, albeit a conflict in which the two sides have unequal resources.[38]

Nationalized Industries. Because the Labour party, unlike Socialist parties in Sweden or Germany, emphasizes public ownership, a wide variety of British industries have been nationalized. Publicly owned organizations are responsible for electricity, coal, gas, railways, air, shipbuilding, steel, the post office and a variety of other services. Each nationalized industry is a hybrid: it is in the market selling its products, yet because it is publicly owned there is a presumption that it has nonmarket purposes as well. In the words of a government white paper:

> The nationalized industries cannot be regarded only as very large commercial concerns which may be judged mainly on their commercial results; all have, although in varying degrees, wider obligations than commercial concerns in the private sector.[39]

Nationalized industries are distinctive public institutions in that their directors are not elected but appointed by ministers. They are meant to be nonpolitical (in the sense of nonparty), yet to have a public purpose. In legal form they are usually public corporations empowered to borrow money from the private sector as well as from the Treasury; to derive revenue by selling their goods and services; exempt from many forms of parliamentary scrutiny applicable to Whitehall ministries; and to recruit employees on terms appropriate to industry rather than the civil service.

Nationalized industries are important in the British economy, because they employ more than 2 million workers, about 8 percent of the total labor force, and account for an even larger proportion of the gross national product and national investment. However, nationalized industries are not conventional trading enterprises, for they are not solely dependent upon the market for revenue. They can borrow money from the Treasury, and industries such as British Railways and the National Coal Board have for years run substantial deficits met from tax revenue.

Differences between industries in public ownership mean that generalizations about their economic performance drawn from a priori assumptions about the presumed virtues or vices of the market or socialism are usually *not* correct for all industries.[40] The industries differ greatly in whether they are capital-intensive (for example, gas) or labor-intensive (for example, the post office); this affects their ability to increase efficiency and output. Nationalized industries also differ greatly in that some supply products for which there is an increasing demand (electricity), whereas others are in a contracting market (the railways). Industry-specific characteristics are important determinants of the financial accounts of nationalized firms.

Politically, all nationalized industries have a common problem, an unclear division of responsibilities. On the one hand, each industry is immediately responsible to its own board and full-time executive directors. On the other hand, the board can be called to account by the minister who oversees and appoints it. A minister normally has vaguely specified statutory authority to give directions of a general character to the board about matters that the minister deems affect the public interest. The Treasury's role in funding industry deficits and authorizing capital investment and loans further increases dependence. The powers of a minister may be used for a variety of ad hoc purposes, such as preventing price rises and preventing the layoff of workers in the period leading up to a general election, or encouraging these after an election in order to reduce public sector deficits.

Since 1979 the Conservative government of Margaret Thatcher has sought to resolve the dilemma of conflicting objectives by reversing the process that created the problem, and privatizing public enterprises by selling them. Conservatives justify privatization on the ground that market accountability is better than the present ill-defined hybrid system. Labour opposes it on the ground that it reduces public influence in the economy.[41] To date, the government has succeeded in selling interests in British Aerospace, in telecommunications, and some interests in North Sea oil. But it faces a dilemma: the nationalized industries that are easiest to sell are those with the greatest actual or potential profit. Industries causing the most problems, such as the British Steel Corporation and the National Coal Board, are unattractive to potential buyers because they are losing hundreds of millions of pounds annually.

National Health Service. While the goals of the health service are consensual, the organization and operation of the health service is complex. The National Health Service Act 1946 established the principle of comprehensive treatment of health problems through a range of hospital services, treatment by qualified general practitioners, specialists, and dental and opthalmologist staff, plus provision of pharmaceutical supplies, artificial limbs and appliances, ambulances and community health services. Its scale is very big: every year one-third of all families have a least one member receiving medical treatment, and more than one-quarter receive hospital treatment. Public expenditure on the health service accounts for about one-tenth of total public expenditure.

From the top, the organization of the health service resembles a mountain range rather than a pyramid.[42] One Cabinet minister, the Secretary of State for Health and Social Security, is formally responsible for paying out pensions and supplementary income benefits as well as nominally having oversight of the health service. The connection between the minister and service delivery is very weak. Responsibility is vested in the National Health Service, which employs more than 1 million people, ranging from surgeons and psychiatrists to hospital orderlies and kitchen staff.

The structure of the National Health Service has been subject to reorganization from time to time, in search of a formula that maximizes coordination between its parts and related local government responsibilities such as social services, yet leaves each with sufficient autonomy to concentrate on its particular tasks. The service is now organized into fourteen regional health authorities responsible for planning activities within England, and 192 district health authorities. In turn each district health authority is meant to devolve responsibilities to particular operational units, such as hospital or clinic.[43]

From the bottom up, the doctor's office remains the initial point of reference for the individual. The doctor is chosen by the patient, and the doctor remains, as the German term puts it, a free professional. Instead of being paid for each treatment, doctors are primarily paid by the number of persons registered with them. This gives a doctor an economic interest in maintaining patients in good health, for income is not increased by patients visiting more frequently. The doctor is also important as a gate-keeper, recommending whether a patient requires specialist treatment, admission to a hospital, or a variety of specialist services.

Whilst medical treatment is of basic importance, an individual is far less capable of assessing health treatment than assessing the supply of food, another basic human need. Restaurant cooking can be compared with home cooking, but treatment by a doctor or a hospital is not comparable to home medication. This is true whether medical care is provided through the public sector, as in Britain, or by the private sector, as in the United States.

Because health care is usually provided free of charge to individuals, there is no limit on potential demand, except the limits resulting from central allocation of money for hospitals and medical treatment. The British Treasury has succeeded in keeping costs of the health service low by European standards, and even more by comparison with the United States. Its decisions determine the number of hospital beds available, and affect the length of lines in a doctor's office. Access free of charge does not mean instant access.

Within the health service expert medical practitioners and administrators are the most important decisionmakers. Doctors use their command of specialist knowledge to prescribe priorities. Knowing which facilities are in short supply can affect decisions at the margin about patients entering hospital or receiving special treatment. When facilities are in good supply, hospital treatment is more readily prescribed than when there is a long line. The very complexity of the organization of the health service limits pressures to spend more money, by discouraging doctors from making lots of demands on behalf of their patients. The Treasury can keep overall health costs within public expenditure constraints, because medical experts have little autonomy in revenue raising. Within Treasury expenditure constraints, doctors have great scope to determine priorities for expenditure.[44]

Fringe Organizations. Given that the character of each public organization is influenced by a distinctive history and that Westminster is free to authorize any organizational form, there are a host of organizations such as the Red Deer Commission, the Gaming Board for Britain, the College of Arms, and the Women's Royal Voluntary Service, which cannot readily be fitted into standard categories.

Organizations that are not headed by elected officials or classified as public corporations are sometimes attacked because they are not accountable to Parliament. Academics have anatomized the many different varieties of *quangos* (that is, quasi-nongovernmental organizations). So large and heterogeneous have been the types of organizations thus identified that the coiner of the word quangos, Anthony Barker, has concluded: "As a means of describing anything, however, the word is useless."[45]

Most fringe bodies are advisory rather than executive; their membership typically addresses comments to a minister or an executive agency. One study found that Whitehall departments named more than 23,000 people to unpaid advisory appointments, about 6,000 to part-time appointments for which a fee is paid, and 1,600 to more or less full-time salaried posts.[46] The total cost of fees and salaries to the Exchequer, a few million pounds, is trivial in the hundred-billion budget of government, albeit large by comparison with the resources of many voluntary bodies.

The significance of so-called quangos is not reflected by the material resources that they claim, which are few. It arises from the fact that appointment to a government advisory body, whether unpaid or paid, gives those who sit there privileged access to government. It also enhances government's capacity to mobilize support from those appointed, and such organizations as they represent.

A Paradox. Central authority and decentralized responsibility for service delivery are meant to be complementary but may also be contradictory. In the view of John P. Mackintosh:

> Central government can plan, control, guide, review, audit and so on but never actually execute. Foreign students find it scarcely credible that in Britain a Ministry of Housing has never built a single house and a Ministry of Education has never run a single school.[47]

The center's power to set minimum standards and maximum costs is balanced by the decentralized bodies' powers of execution. Although local government officials complain about the restrictiveness of central government, ministers complain about their own lack of influence. Lord Hailsham, a minister with experience in many departments, has contrasted being a defense minister in command of the armed forces and being a minister in a department whose program is administered by local authorities.

> In the Admiralty you are a person having authority. You say to one person "come" and he cometh, and another "go" and he goeth. It is not so in the Ministry of Education. You suggest

rather than direct. You say to one man "come" and he cometh not, and another "go" and he stays where he is.[48]

Decentralization exists because the central government cannot administer all its services in all parts of the United Kingdom without overloading the center. The desire to push administration out from Whitehall has become a prominent feature of administrative reorganization. Yet central government does not wish to reduce its power to constrain the organizations that it has created.

UNION WITHOUT UNIFORMITY — THE UNITED KINGDOM DIMENSION[49]

The United Kingdom is a Union created by royal inheritance and conquest; its unity is expressed in the centralist doctrine of the Crown in Parliament. But the institutions that exercise that authority are in no sense uniform throughout the territorial jurisdiction of that Crown. The result is a maze of institutions, whether plotted functionally on an organization chart or territorially on a map.

The Mace. The Mace—the medieval symbol of the authority of the crown in Parliament—is effectively in the hands of the Cabinet. The Cabinet expresses both the unity and diversity of government. It brings together some ministers whose responsibilities are denominated in functional terms, for example, Defense, Education, Housing, Health & Social Security; and some ministers with territorial responsibilities in Scotland, Wales, and Northern Ireland. England is unique in being the one nation of the United Kingdom without a territorial minister in Cabinet.

Membership in Cabinet constrains territorial ministers to abide by collective choices. As a general rule, the more important the issue, the narrower the tolerance for territorial variations in policy within the United Kingdom. No Cabinet minister would wish to defend different levels of unemployment benefit or different school-leaving ages or different income tax rates in different parts of the United Kingdom. Yet all of these vary between states in the American federal system.

Three types of policies can be differentiated on territorial grounds. Most Acts of Parliament stipulate *uniform* policies, laying down procedures that are meant to apply equally throughout the United Kingdom, whether administration is nominally in the hands of a functional or a territorial department. Secondly, territorial ministers can make variations in clauses in an Act in accord with local circumstances, or separately writing Acts for Scotland and Northern Ireland and placing administration in territorial ministries. When this occurs one can speak of *concurrent* policies. While administrative responsibility is in different hands, there is consistency of principle. For example, education acts make distinctive arrangements for each nation in the United Kingdom but the principles — reading, writing, and arithmetic — are taught much the same. Thirdly, and rarely, legislation can be *exceptional* — for example, about public order in Northern Ireland, the Welsh language in Wales, or conditions exclusive to the Scottish Highlands.

Territorial Ministries. In every political sense the territorial ministers are much more part of Whitehall than part of Scotland, Wales, or Northern Ireland. The Secretary of State may in name be said to look after affairs in Scotland, but the authority exercised is that of a *British,* not a Scottish, Parliament. There is lots of government in Scotland, Wales, and Northern Ireland, but there is no such thing as a Scottish government or a Welsh government, and today no such thing as a Northern Ireland government. Decisions affecting the parts of the United Kingdom are the prerogative of British government at Westminster.

The organization of British government is confusing, because there is no uniform principle for assigning territorial and functional responsibilities to ministries. Within Whitehall, some ministries are responsible for the United Kingdom as a whole, such as the traditional defining ministries of the Foreign Office, the Ministry of Defense, and the Treasury. There are some ministries whose responsibilities are principally for Great Britain, such as the Department of Energy. There are also some ministries whose responsibilities are mostly confined to one part of the United Kingdom, such as the Department of Education, (England) or the Scottish Office (exclusively Scotland).

Differences in territorial responsibilities exist within ministries as well as between them. For example, the Department of Education and Science is responsible for the administration of research councils for the whole of the United Kingdom, whereas its responsibility for primary and secondary education is for England only. Reciprocally, the Scottish Office has responsibility for primary and secondary education in Scotland, but responsibility for university education in Scotland is in the hands of the Department of Education and Science.

Because programs are of primary concern, each territorial ministry is divided internally by function. For example, the Scottish Office is divided into education, health, and agriculture departments that have little in common with each other and much in common with counterparts in London with concurrent responsibilities.

When the distribution of public resources is examined, three considerations must be taken into account. The first is that public expenditure in every part of the United Kingdom is substantially in proportion to population, because many programs provide benefits for individuals and families. Secondly, allowance must be made for differences in the composition and distribution of population within each part: an area with more children will need more money spent on education, and an area with greatly dispersed population will need more money spent on roads. Rather than credit a territorial minister for all the money spent under the department's auspices, the appropriate question to ask is: How much difference does a territorial ministry make, after allowance for differences in population characteristics?

Systematic analysis of spending in different parts of the United Kingdom in the late 1970s, when allegations of regional deprivation were often voiced, shows that variations in public expenditure for major programs are limited in degree (Table X.2). More than five-sixths of the variation in Northern Ireland could be accounted for by the very great social needs of that area, and more than two-thirds of additional expenditure in Scotland. Wales was unique in losing expenditure that its

TABLE X.2 *Territorial Public Expenditure Adjusted for Need and Political Muscle*

	English Norm	Needs Allowance	Political Muscle Allowance	Total per Capita
Northern Ireland	100	+31	+5	136
Scotland	100	+16	+7	123
Wales	100	+9	-8	101

Source: Derived from *Treasury Needs Assessment Study,* pp. 5, 25; figures for 1976–1977.

needs merited because of the lack of political clout of the Secretary of State for Wales.

Overall, the application of policies in the United Kingdom — always excepting the unique challenge to public order in Northern Ireland — reflects two major principles. The first is the political premise that economic and social programs should be governed by functional criteria, whether administration is in the hands of one ministry or four. The second is that some allowance should be made for different needs in different parts of the United Kingdom, and that some revenue raised in better-off areas should be allocated to less-well-off areas.

The visibility of territorial ministries and of different geographical regions of the United Kingdom should not be confused with political autonomy. Geographical distance is not important politically. Although 400 miles from Westminster, St. Andrews House, Edinburgh, is more immediately subject to Westminster's authority, since its head is a Cabinet minister, than is the Greater London Council, an assembly of locally elected politicians meeting across Westminster Bridge from Whitehall. A Prime Minister can dismiss a Scottish Secretary but cannot dismiss an elected local government leader.

THE CONTINGENCY OF INFLUENCE

Every generalization about the policy process is contingent upon circumstances; it will fit some policies but not others. Decisions about war and peace may be confined to a few people at the top of government, whereas decisions affecting land-use planning will be dispersed nationwide among local councils. As Bagehot's epigraph to this chapter emphasizes, a country's rul-

ers need not be fixed and few. Collectively, a heterogeneous
stream of different people can influence different policies,
rather than government actions being the product of a single,
centralized decisionmaker.

To test the extent to which the policy process involves the
same few people or many different persons, C. J. Hewitt analyzed twenty different case studies of domestic and foreign policy covering many different fields of government concern.[50]
The results emphasize the contingency of influence: each of six
models was appropriate for at least one policy field.

A *ruling clique* model is most appropriate to describe the making of foreign policy in Britain. Major decisions about diplomacy and defense are consistently made by a small group of
people around the Prime Minister, the Foreign Office, the
Ministry of Defense and, when financial considerations are significant, the Treasury. To describe those involved as a group
is not to say that they always agree, but to emphasize relative
isolation from influences outside their narrow circle. One constraint upon the foreign affairs ruling clique is the dependence
of British foreign policy upon limited manpower and public
money. Another constraint is the military power of other nations.

Balance-of-power pluralism occurs when a few groups consistently compete in the same policy arena with each winning some
of the time; it characterizes the making of domestic economic
policy. Typically, business and financial interests are arrayed
on one side and unions on the other, with the government's
senior economic officials acting as something more than disinterested brokers. The weight of each group in the balance
varies with changing economic and political circumstances. For
example, in the course of three decades the British steel industry was nationalized, denationalized, renationalized, and
then drastically reduced in size.

Social policies display *segmented pluralism;* a stable number of
groups are involved with an issue, but these differ from issue
to issue. The cluster of groups involved with education are few
and stable, as in the balance-of-power model, but they are not
the same as those involved with health. Teachers and doctors
have different professional associations, assuring each a con-

tinuing role within their own segment of public policy. Policies cutting across segmented interests are particularly difficult to negotiate.

Amorphous pluralism describes policy arenas in which those with interests to defend or articulate are constantly changing. Controversies arising in land-use planning always involve specific plots of land. Whereas planners expect consistency of principles from case to case, most participants care only about land that may literally be their own back yard. The personalities and groups in planning controversies are thus ad hoc and transitory, depending on the particular site in dispute.

Policy making is *populist* when the mass of the electorate is directly involved in determining the outcome. When government policy depends on consumer response, the decisions of masses become crucial. The decision many Englishmen have made to buy cars and rely less on railways and buses has incidentally had a great influence on government transportation policy. In race relations, popular opinion, as reflected in MPs' perceptions as well as in popular expression, has increasingly been used to justify laws intended to restrict the entry to England of nonwhite Commonwealth citizens.

A *veto* model describes the frustration of government policy by extragovernmental groups. Occasionally, policy proposals are vetoed by public opposition from strategic pressure groups. More often, the veto power of a group prevents an issue from being put on the political agenda. For years the Trades Union Congress successfully prevented governments from proposing legislation affecting them, and banks and insurance companies are well mobilized to resist any threat of nationalization, a fact that discourages the Labour party from casually adopting such a policy.

Collectively, the case studies examined by Hewitt confirm the contingency of influence. A total of 339 extragovernmental organizations were involved in the 20 case studies. More than five-sixths were involved in only one major issue, and only 6 percent with three or more issues. Hewitt found that when opinion poll data indicated a clear popular preference, it almost invariably favored the actual outcome.[51]

The case studies emphasize that for any given issue, policy

making is oligopolistic; that is, only a relatively small number of groups are involved. In no sense does this mean that those involved constitute a cosy few; for example the balance of power in the economy involves heated disputes between leaders of peak business and trade union groups. In an oligopolistic process, deliberations involve organizations that depend upon each other to cooperate in order for outcomes to be generally desirable. But those involved are unequal as well as few, and there is usually one leader within the negotiations, or two groups contesting dominance. The groups most consistently involved in the policy process—business firms and trade unions—enjoy both victories *and* defeats.

The Pervasiveness of Public Affairs. The contingent and limited involvement of many groups gives special advantage to those most consistently involved in the policy process, public officials. Ministers and civil servants must be involved in matters that require government action. They are not only participants but also the persons who define what government is to do. Ministers do not dominate in all areas of policy, but they can take initiatives to which others must react. Governors are not only experienced players but also the referees who, at the end of the day, arbitrate between group demands.

The making of policy by nominally sovereign governments is constrained at all times by government itself being a cluster of organizations, not a monolith. Studies of policy making within government emphasize that it is *inter*organizational. Different Whitehall departments have separate identities and distinctive ideas about what should be the policy of the Crown in Parliament. Questions of public policy are as likely to pit different Whitehall departments (or Whitehall and extra-Whitehall institutions) against each other as they are to involve major differences between political parties. But because of the centralization of authority in the Cabinet, the conflict is *intra*governmental.

The nature of intragovernmental conflict is illustrated by disputes in land-use planning. A nationalized industry may claim that the industrial use of a plot of land is in the public interest, but a local authority may wish to keep the land free of industry because it feels green spaces are even more important for the common good. Central government cannot eliminate disagreement; it hears arguments and often after a lengthy delay determines which of the competing public organizations has the most persuasive notion of the public interest.

Whitehall's influence is itself subject to influence by many groups outside government. Bargaining between governmental and nongovernmental organizations is not bargaining between equals. Insofar as the issues at stake are amenable to legislation, the government of the day can claim to have the ultimate weapon of an Act of Parliament. But insofar as the problem at hand is not determinable by legislation — for example, a discussion about improving productivity in industry — government depends upon the cooperation of others.

Because Britain is part of an open international economy, many matters central to economic importance are subject to decisions made in other countries, or to such transnational influences as the international movement of money that directly affects the foreign exchange value of the pound. Britain's membership in the European Community reinforces the country's openness to the international economy, but it is not the cause. The British economy has been open for nearly a century and one-half.

The great concern of policymakers today is whether the conventional institutions of the policy process are adequate to the demands placed upon them. From an administrative perspective, this is a question of political management. But the problem is more than that. In policy terms it is substantive: Does British government have the resources to meet a reasonable number of demands placed upon it? Or even, as has been suggested in a study of the national health service: Is administrative overload, delaying and dissipating responses to demands, the best way to deal with requests that cannot be satisfied because of the country's economic state?[52]

The difficulties of managing the British economy today emphasize that there is no guarantee of an effective way to make policy for every problem at hand. Moreover, policies intended to encourage economic growth, rising wages, full employment, and low inflation may contradict each other. As the scope of government policies expands, the prospect increases of government incorporating within itself all the contradictions found within English society.

NOTES

1. See Richard Rose, *From Government at the Centre to Nationwide Government* (Glasgow: U. of Strathclyde Studies in Public Policy No. 132, 1984).

2. Hugh Dalton, *Call Back Yesterday* (London: Muller, 1953), p. 237.

3. See Richard Rose, "Disciplined Research and Undisciplined Problems," *International Social Science Journal*, 38:1 (1976), pp. 105ff.

4. The following paragraphs summarize Richard Rose, *The Problem of Party Government*, especially chapters 15, 16.

5. Quoted in Alan Watkins, "Labour in Power," in Gerald Kaufman, ed., *The Left* (London: Anthony Blond, 1966), p. 173. For a detailed account of what it feels like to be a Cabinet minister unprepared for government, see the three-volume *Diaries* of R. H. S. Crossman (London: Hamish Hamilton, 1975–1977).

6. Richard Rose, *Do Parties Make a Difference?* 2nd ed., p. 146.

7. Sir Kenneth Wheare, *Government by Committee* (Oxford: Clarendon Press, 1955), p. 27.

8. Sir William Armstrong, "The Role and Character of the Civil Service," (text of a talk to the British Academy, London, 24 June 1970), p. 21.

9. Reginald Maudling, quoted in David Butler and Michael Pinto-Duschinsky, *The British General Election of 1970* (London: Macmillan, 1971), p. 62.

10. Rose, *Do Parties Make a Difference?* 2nd ed., pp. 182ff.

11. See R. H. S. Crossman, "Introduction" to an edition of Bagehot's *The English Constitution* (London: Fontana, 1963), pp. 51ff.

12. John P. Mackintosh, *The British Cabinet* (London: Stevens & Sons, 1968) 2nd ed., p. 529.

13. The same confusion is evident in R. T. McKenzie's discussion of the "power" of party leadership in *British Political Parties*.

14. Quoted in Peter Jenkins, *The Battle of Downing Street*, p. 163.

15. Mackintosh, *The British Cabinet*, 2nd ed., p. 531.

16. Quoted in H. J. Hanham, ed., *The Nineteenth Century Constitution* (Cambridge: Cambridge University Press, 1969), p. 69.

17. Quoted in Richard Rose, "British Government: The Job at the Top," p. 43.

18. Bruce Headey, *British Cabinet Ministers*, chapter 1.

19. "Mandarin Power," *The Sunday Times* (London), 10 June 1973.

20. See T. T. Mackie and B. W. Hogwood, *Cabinet Committees in Executive Decision Making*.

21. L. S. Amery, *Thoughts on the Constitution*, p. 87.

22. Colin Seymour-Ure, "The 'Disintegration' of the Cabinet," *Parliamentary Affairs*, 24:3 (1971), pp. 196–207.

23. See Sir Richard Clarke, *New Trends in Government* (London: HMSO, 1971), and Christopher Pollitt, *Manipulating the Machine* (London: Allen & Unwin, 1984).

24. "Thinking about the Think Tank," *The Listener* (London), 28 December 1972.

25. Quoted by Hugo Young, "Wreckers or Obedient Servants," *The Times,* 25 February 1983. cf. Paul Mosley, *The Making of Economic Policy* (Brighton: Wheatsheaf Press, 1984); Joel Barnett, *Inside the Treasury* (London: Andre Deutsch, 1982); and Hugo Young and Anne Sloman, *But Chancellor* (London: BBC, 1984), pp. 34ff.

26. See Richard Rose, *Do Parties Make a Difference?* 2nd ed., chapter 7 for a detailed exposition of the evidence summarized here.

27. Quoted from Paul Mosley, *The Making of Economic Policy,* p. 44, where this remark is set in its full empirical and theoretical context. More generally, see Richard Rose and Edward Page, "Can Government Control Itself?" the first chapter of their edited book, *Fiscal Stress in Cities* (Cambridge: University Press, 1982), pp. 1–12.

28. Richard Rose, *From Government at the Centre to Nationwide Government* (Glasgow: U. of Strathclyde Studies in Public Policy No. 132, 1984).

29. See Bulpitt, *Territory and Power in the United Kingdom;* and comments thereupon in Richard Rose, *Understanding the United Kingdom,* pp. 157ff.

30. For a typology, see Richard Rose, "Accountability to Electorates and the Market," *Politique et Management Public* (Paris), No. 9 (1985).

31. For a critical discussion and demonstration of this, see Christopher Hood and Andrew Dunsire, *Bureaumetrics* (Farnborough: Gower, 1981).

32. *Civil Service Year Book* (London: HMSO, 1983).

33. For a discussion of territorial justice, see David Heald, *Public Expenditure* (Oxford: Martin Robertson, 1983), chapter 10.

34. J. A. G. Griffith, *Central Departments and Local Authorities* (London: Allen & Unwin, 1966), p. 542.

35. For overviews of local government, see e.g., Alan Alexander, *The Politics of Local Government in the United Kingdom* (London: Longman, 1982) and Tony Byrne, *Local Government in Britain,* 2nd ed., (Harmondsworth: Penguin, 1983), and sources cited therein. On policy dimensions, see Ken Young, ed., *National Interests and Local Government* (London: Heinemann, 1983).

36. See John Gyford and Mari James, *National Parties and Local Politics* (London: Allen & Unwin, 1983).

37. For an analysis of causes and implications, see Richard Rose and Edward Page, eds., *Fiscal Stress in Cities.* For a committed discussion, see George Jones and John Stewart, *The Case for Local Government* (London: Allen & Unwin, 1983).

38. For case studies of detachment, cooperation, and antagonism, see Gyford and James, *National Parties and Local Politics,* chapter 7. Note that the example of antagonism involved conflict between a local Labour council and a Labour government nationally.

39. *Financial and Economic Obligations of the Nationalized Industries* (London: HMSO, Cmnd. 1337, 1961).

40. See e.g., Robert Millward and D. M. Parker, "Public and Private Enterprise: Comparative Behaviour and Relative Efficiency," in R. Millward et al., *Public Sector Economics* (London: Longman, 1983), pp. 199–274.

41. For a careful discussion of the issues, see Heald, *Public Expenditure,* chapter 13.

42. For an overview, see Rudolf Klein, *The Politics of the National Health Service* (London: Longman, 1983).

43. On the complicated division of health responsibilities between England, Scotland, Wales, and Northern Ireland, see D. J. Hunter, "Organising

for Health: the National Health Service in the United Kingdom," *Journal of Public Policy,* 2:3 (1982), pp. 263–300.

44. See Rudolf Klein, "Costs and Benefits of Complexity: the British National Health Service," in Richard Rose, ed. *Challenge to Governance* (Beverly Hills: Sage Publications, 1980), pp. 107–126.

45. Anthony Barker, editor *Quangos in Britain* (London: Macmillan, 1982), p. 1.

46. See e.g., *A Directory of Paid Public Appointments Made By Ministers 1978* (London: HMSO, 1978), and P. Holland and M. Fallen, *The Quango Explosion,* (London Conservative Political Centre, 1978).

47. "The Report of the Review Body on Local Government in Northern Ireland, 1970," *Public Administration,* 49 (Spring 1971), p. 20.

48. Quoted in Maurice Kogan, *The Politics of Education* (Harmondsworth: Penguin, 1971), p. 31.

49. For a full discussion of points raised in this section, see Richard Rose, *Understanding the United Kingdom: The Territorial Dimension in Government,* chapters 4–7.

50. See C. J. Hewitt, "Elites and the Distribution of Power in British Society," in P. Stanworth and A. Giddens, eds., *Elites and Power in British Society* (Cambridge: Cambridge University Press, 1974); and his "Policy-making in Postwar Britain," *British Journal of Political Science,* 4:2 (1974).

51. Hewitt, "Elites and the Distribution of Power," p. 57.

52. See Klein, "Costs and Benefits of Complexity."

CHAPTER XI

Converting Policy Intentions into Outputs

What grows upon the world is a certain matter-of-factness. The test of each century, more than of the century before, is the test of results.

THE RESULT OF IMPLEMENTING A POLICY is not necessarily what governors intend. Measures adopted to secure peace and prosperity may be followed by war or depression. In a world in which causation is complex, many things in society change independently of (or in spite of) government's actions.

If a policy is to be anything more than a minister's statement of pious intentions, Whitehall must create a program that can plausibly be expected to advance the government's stated intention. A program prescribes in bureaucratically meaningful language the means — money, laws, and personnel — to achieve policy intentions.[1] Often more than one program is related to a policy intention; many Whitehall departments, for example, have programs intended to promote economic growth. A program may also have more than one purpose: programs to reduce unemployment are also meant to protect the governing party from losing votes. Creation of a program is no guarantee that a policy will be a success. But without a program, a government has not identified any means for achieving a stated intention.

The first test of a program is in Westminster: will a measure secure endorsement by the Cabinet and Parliament? But the greater test of a program is at the stage of implementation: How can it be implemented? Will the program work as intended?

In logic, the design of a program should follow decisions about the ends of policy, for means reflect ends. But in politics, the choice of ends often depends on the acceptability of means. Ministers and senior civil servants spend much time discussing the acceptability of measures with groups inside and outside government. A "good" program may even be defined as one that is easily implemented and acceptable to all interested parties.

Examining program outputs shifts attention from government as a reactive institution responding to popular demands to government as an active force influencing conditions in society. Models of the positive state are especially consonant with collectivistic values, whether of paternalistic Toryism, Socialism, or technocracy. Ironically, Mrs. Thatcher's desire to roll back government commits her to take positive action in efforts to make changes in both government and society.

Although the policy intentions of governors may be unclear or even contradictory, government's activities are everywhere palpably evident. The multiplicity of organizations that collectively constitute British government employ millions of people to spend tens of billions of pounds under the authority of thousands of laws and regulations. To the ordinary citizen, the most important feature of public programs is their impact on society. Even if governors enunciate vague intentions and social scientists have difficulty in measuring precisely the impact of government outputs, the actions of government, for better and worse, greatly affect society.

To understand the complex process by which the government converts policy intentions into program outputs, we must first review the resources of government. The second task is to see how policies are implemented, and made to run more or less routinely. Once this is done, it is then possible to consider the potential impact of government programs upon society, bearing in mind the importance of economic and social conditions independent of determination by Act of Parliament. The concluding section assesses popular reaction to government's outputs.

MOBILIZING RESOURCES FOR PUBLIC PROGRAMS

To understand the dynamics of contemporary government we must think about what government does (produce a variety of program outputs) as well as what government is (a set of formal institutions in Westminster and elsewhere).[2] Government organizations mobilize resources of law, money, and personnel, and combine these resources into program outputs concerned with health, pensions, defense, trade and industry, education, and so forth (Figure XI.1).

The resources that government mobilizes are very different in character; laws are verbal statements drafted in Whitehall and approved by Parliament, and meant to authorize programs.[3] Tax revenues are extracted from individuals, corporations, and other taxpayers; the money thus extracted is used to finance program outputs. Public employees, whether in roles

FIGURE XI.1 *The Conversion of Government Resources into Program Outputs*

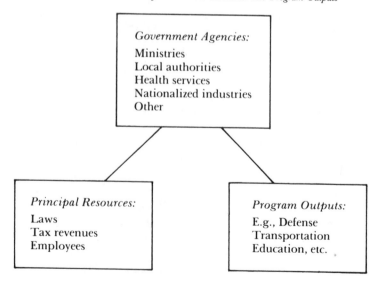

Government Agencies:
Ministries
Local authorities
Health services
Nationalized industries
Other

Principal Resources:
Laws
Tax revenues
Employees

Program Outputs:
E.g., Defense
Transportation
Education, etc.

unique to government (policeman) or common to many organizations (secretary or clerk) provide services to citizens, but they are first of all servants of government. The intentions of politicians and parties can have an impact only if public organizations adopt programs to implement these intentions. If this does not occur, then politicians' statements will remain rhetorical statements of intent, and little else.

Law. The unique resource of government is legislation. The power to make rules that ought to be binding upon all members of society distinguishes government from other organizations that employ large numbers of people and disburse large sums of money. Private organizations can use economic power to influence other organizations, but they cannot invoke political authority to legitimate their intentions and to compel popular compliance. Long-standing legitimacy makes law a particularly valuable resource for British government. People voluntarily follow most government directives not because they are necessarily rewarding financially but "because it is a law."

The most familiar rules are those contained in Acts of Parliament. Continuity of government from medieval times results in a vast accumulation of legislation through the centuries. The *Chronological Table of the Statutes,* giving the title of each Act of Parliament, runs to more than 1,300 pages. The earliest statute still in force dates from 1267. One in ten laws date from before Queen Victoria's accession to the throne in 1837, and more than one-third date from her death in 1901. Every program of government is derived from a succession of laws enacted at different times before, without a logical and comprehensive analysis of their cumulative and multiple effects.

Drafting a law is a test of how carefully policymakers have thought about their intentions.[4] Legislation requires politicians to state to draftsmen of parliamentary bills precisely what they intend to do about a problem. A law is not like a speech, a form of words that can be as vague as a politician desires. Nor do the consequences of a law disappear at the end of an evening, as often happens with a speech. Even civil servants may find it difficult to transfer their attention from drafting speeches and white papers for ministers to drafting legislative instruments to realize proclaimed intentions. One civil servant experienced in drafting legislation comments:

> Very often you don't see the pitfalls and traps until you write your instructions to parliamentary counsel. Having to be so specific, you suddenly realise you have been talking nonsense for months.[5]

The difficulties of legislation are compounded in Britain because party politicians are usually excluded from the legislative process before entering office. As ordinary Members of Parliament they can only criticize the laws that others propose. Whitehall avoids detailed consultation with MPs when drafting legislation; legislative plans are treated as official secrets. Nor do MPs individually have the political position to compel officials to discuss draft bills, as American congressmen have.

Once a measure is introduced, it is subject to a series of procedural reviews that are not only time-consuming but also of dubious relevance for improving a policy. Amendment procedures intended to clarify a bill in Parliament may be used by the opposition to reiterate differences about principles. Even though opponents realize that what they dislike will become law, they often concentrate their speeches upon criticizing the bill in principle, rather than seeking to remove particular drafting defects in the legislation.[6]

Each year Parliament enacts an average of fifty-eight bills proposed by the government and an additional thirteen measures not directly reflecting government policy.[7] Because the government can be nearly certain of success for almost any bill it cares to introduce, its efficiency, as measured by the ratio of bills proposed to laws enacted, is very high. Since 1951 Conservative and Labour governments have been similar in the amount of legislation that each has sponsored annually.

Every newly elected government inherits responsibility for thousands of Acts of Parliament prepared by its predecessors. This limits its room for maneuver. First of all, any new proposal must be carefully scrutinized for its effect on preexisting legislation, as well as in relation to immediate government objectives. Secondly, adapting new legislation to old, or old to new is laborious and often time-consuming. Thirdly, from time to time it is necessary to consolidate a large mass of preexisting legislation into a single new Act to avoid obsolescence, or because this is the only way in which to accommodate old enactments to new circumstances.

The growth of government programs in postwar Britain depends upon legislative authorization, but it does not necessarily require the enactment of new laws. For example, a new social security act is not needed for more money to be spent on pensions. If more people live to pensionable age, expenditure automatically increases because of already existing statutory entitlements. Some seemingly new acts simply consolidate and update a variety of acts passed by previous Parliaments.

Between 1945 and 1980, a period of great growth in government, the number of Acts of Parliament actually decreased by 38 percent. Successive governments repealed almost twice as many acts as they approved (Table XI.1). In most cases, a large number of measures enacted at different times were consolidated into a single omnibus act. Hence, the number of pages in the statute book increased by 64 percent. This not only reflected an input of new measures, but also a very substantial updating of old measures.

The government enjoys great powers to make binding rules

TABLE XI.1 *The Gross and Net Increase in Acts of Parliament, 1945–1980*

	N
Acts on statute book, 1945	5,583
New Acts approved, 1945–1980	+ 2,399
Acts repealed, 1945–1980[a]	− 4,570
Acts on statute book, 1980	3,412
Percentage change, 1945–1980	− 39%

Source: Denis Van Mechelen, *Has There Been a Growth of Legislation in Britain since 1945?* (Glasgow: U. of Strathclyde Studies in Public Policy No. 123, 1984), Table 10.

outside the exhausting business of parliamentary legislation. In such fields as foreign affairs and defense, the government can justify actions by invoking the unlimited prerogative powers of the Crown derived ultimately from medieval concepts of royal sovereignty. In domestic policy, a British government can enact legislation retrospectively giving ex post facto authority to what it has done.

Acts of Parliament can delegate authority to make detailed regulations. In some fields executive decrees can be issued as Orders in Council, with the full force of law. Statutory Instruments, typically rules of relatively minor importance, provide another means of executive rule making. The Statutory Instruments Committee of the Commons scrutinizes these measures; it can call to the attention of the Commons measures that it believes exceed powers authorized by Act of Parliament. If this is done, the instrument becomes binding. The number cited as objectionable is usually less than ten a year, hardly 1 percent of the annual total.

Every program at some time involves the discretionary use of statutory powers; discretion is particularly great in managing the economy and foreign affairs. Many acts of discretion are limited in scope, but the result can be of intense significance to a few people, for example, planning permission to add a room to a house. Many decisions involving discretionary use of statutory powers are made by special-purpose administrative tribunals. Industrial tribunals, local valuation courts, national insurance bodies, rent tribunals, supplementary benefit appeal tribunals, and other bodies together hear more than 250,000 cases a year.[8]

Money. The second major resource of government is money, and taxation is the principal source of government revenue. Tax revenue is first of all defined by laws that set the rate of tax to be levied (for example, 30 percent as the standard rate of income tax, and 15 percent Value Added Tax on purchases) and define the economic base to which the rate applies (for example, stipulating the allowances that reduce gross income to net taxable income). The actual revenue yielded by a particular tax reflects the overall state of the economy, the buoyancy of tax bases in an inflationary era, and the efficiency of tax administration, which in Britain is high.

The total tax revenue of British government is large, and continuously growing. In money terms, total tax revenue increased more than 2,200 percent from 1948 to 1981. After allowing for the effects of inflation, total tax revenue still increased more than one and one-half times in the period. When tax revenue is viewed in terms of tax effort — that is, the proportion of the gross domestic product claimed as taxes — then the increase, 3.4 percent, is very small, rising from 35.5 percent in 1948 to 38.9 percent in 1981. The purchasing power of tax revenue rose far more than that, since the national product has itself grown greatly in the postwar era.[9]

Taxes exist in the plural: no one tax can provide British government with most of the revenue it needs, and hundreds of taxes produce very small yields (Table XI.2). Taxation is highly centralized; nine-tenths of tax revenue is raised by the Treasury as against one-tenth levied in local authority rates subject

TABLE XI.2 *The Principal Sources of Tax Revenue, 1948–1981*

Type of tax (1981 revenue)	As % National Tax System		As % Gross Domestic Product	
	1948	*1981*	*1948*	*1981*
Income tax (£27.7)	31.8	28.6	11.3	11.1
National insurance (£18.2bn)	8.0	18.8	2.9	7.3
Purchase & Sales/ VAT[a] (£13.7bn)	7.2	14.1	2.6	3.3
Local authority rates (£10.3bn)	7.6	10.7	2.7	4.2
Oil & Petroleum[b] (£8.4bn)	1.3	8.7	0.5	3.4
Other taxes (£17.6bn)	44.1	18.8	15.5	9.6
Total	(£4.1bn)	(£96.9bn)	35.5%	38.9%

[a]Value Added Tax (VAT) introduced in 1975 in place of purchase taxes.

[b]Revenue from hydrocarbon oil tax plus revenue from tax on North Sea oil extractors of petroleum.

Source: Richard Rose and Terence Karran, *Increasing Taxes, Stable Taxes, or Both? The Dynamics of United Kingdom Tax Revenue since 1948* (Glasgow: U. of Strathclyde Studies in Public Policy No. 116, 1983).

to Treasury influence. The British taxpayer has only one major taxing authority to worry about, by contrast with Americans, who can pay income tax to three different levels of the federal system, and be subject to several additional taxing jurisdictions.

A few taxes account for the great bulk of tax revenue. The most important sources alter slowly, for certainty of revenue collection is one of the most important concerns of government. The five most important taxes, collectively accounting for 81.2 percent of revenue, are (last share in parantheses):

1. *Income tax* (28.6 percent). Income tax, initially introduced as an emergency measure to help finance the wars against Napoleon, is today the single biggest source of government revenue. When income tax was orginally introduced, it applied to only a small wealthy stratum of the population, and claimed a very small portion of their income. In 1900 the standard rate levied on those liable to income tax was 3.3 percent; in 1984, it was 30 percent. Income tax is progressive; it assumes that those earning more money should pay higher taxes. As the income of middle-class and manual workers has risen with economic growth, nearly all wage-earners are now liable to income tax, and weekly deductions from wages and salaries ensure that it is collected. Income tax claims more than £1200 a year from the average employed person.

2. *National insurance* (18.8 percent). The income-maintenance programs of the welfare state are normally based on a *quasi*-insurance principle. Intended beneficiaries of pensions and unemployment benefit make a weekly contribution from wages, and so too does their employer. On weekly wages of up to £250, the standard contribution in 1984 for an employee is 6.5 percent, and for the employer, 10.45 percent. The earmarking of the revenue to pay for social security benefits is unusual; it vests the right to a benefit in individuals and makes it very difficult for any government to pass an Act of Parliament to reduce, let alone repeal, benefits. National insurance is quasi-insurance for two reasons: the payments are compulsory rather than voluntary, and are insufficient to meet claims fully, due to increases in benefit levels and inflation devaluing past con-

tributions. Benefits are partially funded from general tax revenue, which now accounts for approximately 43 percent of current expenditure on pensions and unemployment benefit.

3. *Value Added Tax* (14.1 percent). Prior to British entry to the European Community, the tax on goods purchased took the form of purchase taxes with rates varying between so-called luxury goods and essentials. To increase harmony between tax systems within the European Community, the government introduced a Value Added Tax in 1974. Initially the standard rate was 10 percent; the rate was raised to 15 percent in 1979. The tax is levied upon goods at each stage of the production process. The effect is to leave more earnings in the hands of taxpayers, but to increase the price of goods and services bought with these earnings.

4. *Local authority rates* (10.7 percent). The taxation of property in England dates back to the sixteenth century. The particular rate levied on houses, and commercial and industrial property is determined separately by each local council and is its sole taxing power. The rapid increase in rate bills in the 1970s, principally because of inflation, provoked political controversy. The continued rise in local authority rates in the 1980s, in part to compensate for the reduction of central government financial grants to local authorities, has increased the controversiality of rates. Yet neither Conservative nor Labour governments has abolished rates. If this were done it would be necessary to place responsibility for funding local government (and perhaps, for administering its services) entirely in the hands of the Treasury, or local authorities would have to be given the power to levy a local income tax, sales, or poll tax, in compensation for the loss of revenue from the rates.

5. *Oil* (8.7 percent). When cars were few in Britain, the government raised revenue from taxes on simpler ''luxuries'' instead of taxing oil heavily. In 1948 14.3 percent of tax revenue came from tobacco, and 10.2 percent from beer, wine, and spirits taxes. The increase in the number of cars and in the use of oil for central heating has caused a gradual shift to oil taxes. The oil price shock of 1973, fortuitously coinciding with the start of oil production in Britain's North Sea oil fields, led to

the collection of oil taxes from producers as well as consumers. Oil now provides substantially more revenue than taxes on tobacco, beer, wines, and spirits combined.

When the costs of public programs exceed the revenue that government can raise from taxation — because of either an unexpected downturn in the economy or political resistance to increasing taxes — then government turns to borrowing. The amount of borrowing varies with government policy and economic conditions. Borrowing to finance a deficit of public revenue as against expenditure has been rising gradually. In 1961 government borrowing was equivalent to 8.7 percent of tax revenue; in 1971, 6.8 percent. It then rose as high as 27.3 percent in 1975. Unlike President Reagan's administration, Mrs. Thatcher's government has made the reduction of public borrowing a major political goal in the belief that this will reduce inflation. In consequence, by 1983 borrowing added 10.0 percent to tax revenue.

A few activities of government are distinctive because they generate revenue. This is most obviously the case with such nationalized industries as electricity and gas, in which revenue can exceed expenditure. Government derives revenue by selling offshore oil rights which it owns because of laws of the sea, as well as by taxing oil producers and consumers. Rent from council housing is another major nontax source of revenue; it is particularly important for local authorities. As landlords to a large number of voters, local authorities wish to keep rents low yet simultaneously need rent revenue to balance their housing accounts.

In effect, taxation is both a resource and a burden of government. It is a resource, because it provides the billions of pounds needed to meet the costs of contemporary big government. It is a burden insofar as there are political costs in being identified with taxing. As long as the economy was relatively buoyant, the costs of government could be met painlessly from the fiscal dividend of economic growth. But since the world recession of the 1970s, this option has not been available to successive British governments.

The generalization that taxes are rising is true in the literal sense, for the money values paid in taxes continuously go up because of inflation. When revenue from taxes is calculated as a proportion of the national product, then a very different picture emerges. Some taxes increase their share of the national product (for example, national insurance); some taxes have a relatively constant share of the national product (for example, income tax); and some taxes claim a declining share of the national product (beer and tobacco). The increase in total government revenue reflects the net effect of taxes changing in more than one direction.

Public Employees. Labor is the third major resource of contemporary government. Whereas classic concerns of the nightwatchman state required the employment of few people, the contemporary mixed-economy welfare state requires millions of people to produce and deliver its goods and services. Very few measures of government can be implemented simply by the enactment of laws or the payment of money. Typically, the largest portion of the money that government spends to implement a program is spent on the wages and salaries of public employees.

Government does not hire people to surround itself with loyal retainers as a medieval monarch might. Public employees are hired to perform program functions.[10] Some functions are much the same for many programs; secretaries, computer technicians, bookkeepers, and general administrators can help produce many different kinds of goods and services. But many more are specific to a particular program, such as the skills of teachers, nurses, or soldiers. Public employees can be grouped under three major headings (Table XI.3).

1. *Social programs* are the principal cause of public employment today: health and education together account for more than one-tenth of all jobs in Britain, and in all social programs account for 45 percent of all public jobs. The growth of public employment in postwar Britain has been the result of a major expansion of two central programs of the contemporary welfare state, education, and health. Education has added nearly a million to the public payroll due to the baby boom, an increasing number of years of education per pupil, lower pupil:teacher ratios, and addition of ancillary services. Health has increased

TABLE XI.3 *The Program Functions of Public Employees in Britain, 1951–1981*

	1951	1981 (000)	Change
Social programs			
Health	492	1,316	824
Education	618	1,616	998
Personnel social services	116	370	254
Social security, employment	86	156	70
Total	1,312	3,458	2,146
Economic programs			
Transportation	1,017	526	−491
Post office & telecommunications	340	444	104
Gas, electricity, & water	371	343	−28
Coal mining	775	294	−481
Steel	292	121	171
Other nationalized enterprises	3	455	452
Other economic programs	191	218	27
Total	2,989	2,401	−588
Defining concerns			
Defense (uniformed & civilian)	1,228	561	−667
Police, fire, tax, and general admin.	755	1,212	457
Total	1,983	1,773	−210
Total public employment:			
Number	6,284	7,632	1,348
As % workforce	26.6	31.4	4.8%

Source: Richard Parry, "Britain: Stable Aggregates, Changing Composition," Table 2.3; in Richard Rose et al., *Public Employment in Western Nations* (Cambridge: Cambridge University Press, 1985).

by 824,000, due to the aging of the population, the provision of health services without charge, and the consequent expansion of demand.

2. The nationalized industries that constitute the major *economic programs* of government have tended to contract in the postwar era. Transportation (railways, buses, airlines) today employ scarcely half their number in 1951, due to the spread of the private ownership of cars. Coal mining has contracted

nearly two-thirds, due to a shift of consumer preference to oil, electricity, and other forms of energy. Steel has declined by more than one-half, as steel production has become more capital intensive, and international competition has depressed world demand for British-made steel. In total, economic programs have contracted by nearly one-fifth. Whereas in 1951 they were the principal public employer, in the 1980s public enterprises account for 31 percent of public employment.

3. Defense, the chief *defining concern* of government, was the largest single cause of public employment at the height of cold war mobilization in 1951. With changes in world affairs and Britain's role in the world, numbers in defense have fallen by more than half. The principal cause of expansion has been the need for more general administrators. Public employees classified as dealing with the basic defining concerns of British government today account for 23 percent of total public employment. However, that proportion would be substantially reduced if general administrators servicing economic and social programs could be assigned to those categories.

In aggregate, public employment has changed relatively little in thirty years, increasing its proportion of the total labor force by 4.8 percent. If employment in the private sector had not contracted by nearly half a million because of mechanization in agriculture, then public employment would have grown by only 3.0 percent. If unemployment had not increased tenfold, then public employment would have increased its share by less than 2 percent in the period. The relative stability of total public employment in postwar Britain is atypical. It reflects the fact that Britain was *already* a big government in 1951. Expansion during the Second World War was confirmed and extended by major measures of the 1945–1951 Labour government.

The relative stability of public employment in aggregate is not, however, matched by employment in specific programs. A striking feature of Table XI.3 is that most major programs have seen very substantial changes in *opposite* directions. The total has been relatively stable only because some programs, such as health and education, have increased greatly, while others, such as defense, public transport, and coal mining have contracted greatly. Thus, the dynamics of public employment cannot be explained by general theory; they must be explained by program-related factors. One important consideration is whether or not programs provide benefits free of charge to their recipients. Programs providing social benefits without charge to citizens have increased their employment more than two and one-half times since 1951. By contrast, nationalized industries selling their goods and services have had employment fall.

Changes in composition have accentuated the nationwide dispersion of public employment. A basic feature of social programs is that they must be delivered where recipients live. Since three-quarters of the population of Britain does *not* live in London or the Southeast of England, most social program employees must work at a distance from the capital. Nationalized enterprises such as the post office and public transport similarly distribute employment in proportion to population. Those nationalized industries that do concentrate employment, such as coal mining or steel, do so at a substantial distance from London, which is a political and financial center of Britain but not its industrial center. Within England public employment as a proportion of the labor force is highest in the industrial North; it is below average in the Southeast.

Analysis separates what government unites. The resources catalogued above — laws, money and personnel — are brought together in a manifold of public programs. Laws authorize government to act, and create agencies to carry out programs. In turn, these organizations take money from the pool of government revenue. Programs usually combine all these factors. For example, children are legally compelled to attend school, and citizens must pay taxes supporting education whether or not they have children. Hundreds of local education authorities employ hundreds of thousands of teachers in tens of thousands of schools to provide this major program of government.

PROGRAM INERTIA AND IMPLEMENTATION

At any given point in time, most programs of government run easily, because they are driven by inertia forces ensuring that what government did yesterday will continue to be done today and tomorrow.[11] The bulk of government's activities do not involve the consideration of new policies or the implementation of fresh choices. Most of government's resources are devoted to the routine administration of long-established programs. Far more public employees are engaged in carrying on programs implemented a long time ago than in carrying out measures for the first time.

Inertia is a force in motion. Whereas the activities of individual politicians are transitory, government is continuing. A newly elected government is not so much the custodian of an inert constitution as it is a group temporarily on board public organizations continuing in motion. Already enacted laws, public employees in place, and revenue routinely flowing in maintain government outputs. Big government was established before any of today's Cabinet ministers stood for Parliament, and before the median voter was born.

In theory a newly elected British government could repeal most of the program commitments of government, assuming that its own back benchers in Parliament would be willing to endorse proposals to end compulsory education, the national health service, old-age pensions and so forth. But even if a government of the day had the votes in Parliament to do this, it would produce chaos in society. So numerous and large are the programs of government today that they can be altered only gradually and incrementally. As the Thatcher government has shown, elected Conservative politicians have not attempted the immediate and wholesale repeal of major government programs, any more than Labour ministers have sought the wholesale transformation of the economy and society.

A newly elected government need not regard the persistence of public programs as a justification for doing nothing. Its ministers will want to make a mark by introducing new measures that will subsequently be carried forward as routine by their successors, and selectively altering programs inherited from their predecessors.

In an era of big government it is often more appropriate for politicians to think in terms of modifying established programs than adopting completely new programs. By definition, ministers are immediately responsible for many established programs. Any initiative they may take is likely to have an impact upon established programs.

Adapting existing programs makes implementation much easier, for organizations are already in place. But a minister must also redirect the program from the course it follows by inertia. The more complex and well institutionalized a program, (for example, pensions or education) the greater the force needed to alter the direction in which inertia is carrying it.

Of all the forms of policy succession, the replacement of an established program by a completely new program is usually the least likely.[12] What a minister presents as a new measure may simply be the result of further elaborating or developing actions already undertaken within an existing program; extending or reducing the scope of a program; or consolidating, dividing, or otherwise reorganizing the agencies responsible for delivering a program. The less the substantive change, the greater the probability that a proposed change can be implemented.

In theory, politicians could start from a statement of political objectives and then develop a plan designed to achieve stated ends. While every program involves a measure of planning for the future, planning is *not* to be confused with control of future events. Government cannot control how citizens will respond to its proposals, or even how other organizations within government respond. Insofar as the outcome is uncertain, there will be a tendency to substitute a prospect of what is desired to happen for a realistic estimate of what will probably result.

Logically, the implementation of a more or less new government program should start from the identification of its objectives. But identifying the aims of a government measure is not easy. There are enormous variations in the clarity with which the intentions of major laws are stated. The National Health Service Act of 1946 is exceptional in clearly stating objectives: to secure improvement in physical and mental health by the prevention, diagnosis, and treatment of illness — and specifying program means to these ends. The preamble of the landmark 1944 Education Act, making secondary schooling free to everyone, is more typical; it simply enunciates a vague intention "to promote the education of the people of England and Wales."

An Act of Parliament is not required to state any objectives. For example, the Act to end capital punishment contains no statement of its intent, whether it be to encourage the rehabilitation of murderers, to reduce the cost of judicial errors, or to shed governmental responsibility for taking human life. Many programs enumerate a great many objectives for good political reasons. Each Whitehall department has distinctive departmental goals, and pressure-group clients reinforcing them. The greater the number of objectives, the more interests that can be satisfied. Rather than identify precise program targets, the Prime Minister often enunciates broad, even vague themes comprehensible and appealing to the ordinary voter.

Because British government has so many objectives, its actions can easily appear confusing or contradictory. The Coal Industry Nationalisation Act of 1946 states as objectives: to get coal from the mines, to secure efficient development of the industry, and to sell coal "at such prices as may seem to the directors best calculated to further the public interest in all respects." Collectively, these objectives can be contradictory. If maximizing the output of coal were the sole objective, then the Coal Board could concentrate upon increasing supplies of this major energy resource, whatever the cost. If efficiency were the sole objective, then the amount of coal extracted would depend on the marginal cost of production, greatly reducing the present size of the industry. If the miners' interest is reckoned as part of the public interest, the Coal Board might provide good working conditions, secure jobs, and high wages to the miners regardless of cost. Determining which among many objectives is the *dominant* objective of the moment is a political choice.[13]

Busy public officials do not have time to be bothered by confusion about objectives. Confusion, after all, can be a sign of intense political interest and activity. The denizens of Whitehall and Westminster are not logicians, or engineers designing mechanical systems. They are English empiricists, content to pursue a policy of muddling through, ready to implement programs even if unsure about the purpose of their actions.

To avoid the many frustrations that arise in trying to implement a program, Whitehall ministries usually engage in a lengthy process of consultation. Consultation occurs first of all among the myriad organizations of government. If the organizations meant to act as agents of the ministry are skeptical about their ability to carry out a measure or actively hostile, its chances of effective implementation are much reduced. Consultation with pressure groups representing potential beneficiaries are also important.

The process of bargaining within government and with affected pressure groups can greatly facilitate implementation. If the objectives stated are attractive to pressure groups and the means stated are regarded as feasible by administrators, then there is good reason to expect that a new program can easily be introduced. But to make administrative and political acceptability the criteria for adopting a new program means that a minister is not starting from what he would like, but engaging in a consensus-seeking process of bargaining to seal a deal. Sealing the deal becomes the object, rather than anything more substantive.[14]

The easiest programs to design and implement are those applying a proven technology to the physical environment.[15] The British government can successfully carry out a program of building bridges across rivers or motorways, because civil engineering is a well-understood technology, and the costs are calculable within limits. Moreover, the physical environment in England offers few difficulties to bridge builders or highway engineers. Yet even seemingly simple tasks face political obstacles. Construction costs escalate with inflation, making it more and more difficult to calculate the economics of large building projects. Even more important, citizens can be organized into environmentalist groups protesting against public engineering proposals in the name of a previously mute environment.

Programs that involve giving away money are usually easy to implement. All that is required is a statutory definition of the persons entitled to receive benefits, and Treasury appropriation of the funds to pay out. The most expensive British government program — pensions for the elderly — is administratively very simple. An elderly person can claim a pension by referring to his or her age and work record, which is already on file within the ministry. Post office branches are authorized to pay cash over the counter to pensioners when they produce their claim book. Cash benefits become difficult to implement as discretion enters in, for example, questions such as: How much earning power has been lost by a partially disabled worker? or, How much supplementary benefit does a problem family really need to be paid?

The difficulties of implementing government economic policy illustrate how nongovernmental as well as governmental actions determine policy outcomes. At any moment the state of the economy can be influenced by government policies affecting public spending, the size of the public deficit, and specific policies encouraging investment and employment. But the state of the economy also reflects conditions that the British government does not control, such as wage demands voiced by trade unions, and investment decisions of businessmen. The British economy is also affected by changes in the international economic environment.

Many major programs of the welfare state are easy to implement up to a point, namely, the production of program outputs. From a Whitehall point of view, a new education policy is implemented when buildings are built and teachers are at work on a new task, say, providing compensatory education classes for children from disadvantaged homes. But providing such a service is not an end in itself, as the term output implies. It is an input intended to improve the education of disadvantaged children. Because their learning is influenced as well by family, community, and other influences beyond the control of government, it is simplest for public officials to concentrate on producing outputs rather than worry about the impact that their efforts have.

THE OUTPUTS AND IMPACT OF GOVERNMENT

Within government, money is the single most important measure of program outputs. The responsibilities of ministries conventionally determine the program headings by which public expenditures are classified. The annual round of budget negotiations between the Treasury and the spending ministries is the process by which government outputs are collectively reviewed.

The principal objects of public expenditure are what are

popularly thought of as "good" goods and services, namely, pensions and other social security payments, education, the health service, and personal social services. Together, these four programs account for more than half of total public expenditure (Table XI.4). In every European country, government spends a substantial portion of its tax revenue on these services. Social programs are popular because they provide benefits to many families. Because so many people benefit, these programs also cost a large amount of money, and their claim on public expenditure has been growing slowly but steadily through the years.

Second in spending are programs that concern the core defining activities of government. The amount of money spent on each program is in no sense proportionate to its importance. In international affairs, diplomacy is as important as military force, yet the armed services cost six times what is spent on diplomacy and foreign aid. Maintaining law and order, a *sine qua non* of social life, claims only 4 percent of total public expenditure. An increase in government borrowing and interest rates since the 1973 oil crisis results in debt interest payments today being one of the five biggest programs of government. The cost of repaying past borrowing is about equal to public spending on health or education.

The government's impact on the economy is only in part registered by public spending on housing, which also generates revenue from rents. Similarly, the importance for the economy of the trading activities of nationalized industries is understated by public expenditure, since their costs are mostly met by trading revenues. Moreover, a host of macroeconomic policies affect both the size of the national product and its composition.

The sum total of public expenditure has risen more than twenty times through the years, principally because of inflation. It has also been increasing because of economic growth. Since the economy has been growing, public expenditure as a proportion of the national product has increased by 8.3 percent.

Because programs vary in their mix of resources, public expenditure cannot by itself be regarded as the sole measure of the political importance of programs. International affairs claim

TABLE XI.4 *The Principal Programs of Public Expenditure, 1953–1983*

	1953	1963	1973	1983	Change
		(as % total public expenditure)			
Social Welfare					
Social security payments	14	19	18	25	11
Education	9	13	14	12	3
Health service	8	10	10	12	4
Personnel social services	0.5	0.8	2	2	1.5
Total	32	43	44	51	19
Defining concerns					
Defense	27	18	12	12	−15
Debt interest	13	12	9	11	−2
Intl. relations	1	2	2	2	1
Police, prisons, law	2	3	3	4	2
Finance and tax collection	2	1	1	1	−1
Total	45	36	27	30	−15
Economic programs					
Housing and environment	13	10	13	9	−4
Roads, transport[a]	3	5	6	4.	1
Employment	0.3	0.3	0.7	2	1.7
Industry, trade[a]	−0.5	0.7	6	1	1.5
Agriculture, food	5	4	2	2	−3
Total	21	20	28	18	−3
Miscellaneous	2	1	1	1	−1
Totals (current £bn)	£6.3	£10.7	£30.1	£136.2	£129.9
(as % GDP)	36.9	34.7	40.6	45.2	+8.3

[a]For 1953 and 1963 investment by public corporations excluded.

Source: Central Statistical Office, *National Income and Expenditure, 1963–1973*, and *United Kingdom National Accounts 1984* (London: HMSO), tables 1, 47, 48; 1,51; 1.26, 2.5 respectively. Minor adjustments required to establish continuity. Percentage subtotals may differ slightly because of the effects of rounding off. Not trading capital consumption (£2.1bn in 1983) omitted, as not attributed to a specific program.

little money or personnel, but questions of war and peace are undoubtedly very important. Moreover, programs claiming similar sums of money are not equal in other respects. For instance, most citizens give education and health a higher priority than debt interest payments, yet the three programs are equal in the burden they place on the Treasury.

While every program of government will be important to some within government and to some outside government as well, a few programs claim the great bulk of government's principal resources (cf. Tables XI.3, 4).

> *Money-intensive programs.* Social security and debt interest payments are very different in objectives, but alike in one respect: administration is simple and routine. The principal action required for each program is check-writing.
>
> *Both money-intensive and labor-intensive.* Health, education, defense, and housing and environmental services are similar in one respect: much money goes to pay the public employees who produce the goods and services that constitute the output of these programs.
>
> *Labor-intensive more than money-intensive.* Nationalized industries are unique among public organizations in that the bulk of their revenue comes from activities as trading enterprises. Their significance for government's role in the economy is out of all proportion to the limited sums expended through the budget.
>
> *Law-intensive.* The maintenance of order cannot be purchased. Order results from the coincidence of two things: the requirements of the statute book, and popular norms concerning rightful conduct. When the two are congruent, then laws do not need to be enforced by public officials: they are obeyed voluntarily. This is usually the case in England.

Any attempt to reduce all public programs to a single measuring rod, such as the measuring rod of money, is misleading, for every government program requires an element of legal authorization, personnel, and organization as well as (or instead of) money. To ignore nonmonetary elements in public programs is to dismiss as unimportant the maintenance of law and order, and the conduct of foreign relations. To ignore the role of public employees is to forget the fundamental distinction between programs that put money in peoples' hands to spend as they like, and services that pay public employees to do what they think best to help people.

Any attempt to equate the outputs of public policies with their social impact will reveal as much about the narrow perspective of policymakers as about the conditions of social and economic change. From a politician's or a civil servant's point of view, programs may be considered the ultimate objective of months or years of political effort. But program outputs are only inputs to society.

Government is not the only major institution influencing English society. The influences affecting society can be categorized under three broad headings: (1) government programs, (2) other organizational activities outside the direct control of government, and (3) many other factors that neither governors nor social scientists can identify or understand.[16] Conditions in the social world are more complicated and far harder to control than actions within the world of government.

The impact of government varies with the subject matter. Government's power is greatest when it can claim a lawful monopoly (printing money) or powers of compulsion (fixing the age for starting school attendance). Usually government can be confident that its program outputs will have some impact on social conditions, but not a monopoly of influence. For example, government can influence transportation by the building of roads, and through pricing policies of nationalized railways and buses. But it does not force people to travel by rail or bus if they wish to go by automobile. Nor can it force people to travel at all. In some fields government avoids stating a policy objective, such as population policy. As one Cabinet minister explained, ''It would mean a policeman in every bedroom.''[17]

Any major program will have multiple impacts, some intended and some unintended. A scheme for slum clearance will not only remove rundown buildings, but also may uproot communities whose residents have lived as neighbors for years. Many consequences of a policy are not so much unintended as they are ignored. Politicians prefer to stress benefits, such as new houses, rather than costs, such as social dislocation. Fearing that government's influence would often be harmful,[18] an extremely disillusioned senior civil servant remarked during the 1974 crisis, "Thank God, the government's influence is so little."

The difficulties of anticipating, measuring, and evaluating the impact of a public policy concern the Treasury even more immediately than social scientists. In a negative sense, the Treasury is aware that spending more money on a program does not guarantee increasing its impact proportionately. An extra £100 million spent on health services might reflect the success of doctors, nurses, and hospital workers in pressing claims for higher wages rather than improving the nation's health by as much as the health services budget rose.

When making judgments about competing public priorities, the Treasury often falls back on evaluating policies by the inputs of government resources: "numbers of staff employed, goods and services purchased, and so on . . . because of the difficulty of measuring the social output of the services."[19]

Except in pathological or perverse situations, a very substantial increase in public expenditure can normally be expected to make some positive impact in society. But that is not the problem facing governors: their everyday concern is with determining whether a little more *or* a little less input of resources would have *any* discernible impact. Budget increases or budget cuts, which are invariably expressed in terms of marginal changes of expenditure, cannot be equated with a proportional increase or decrease in benefits to society.

The total production of welfare in society is the sum total of activities of government, the market, and the family.[20] The industrial revolution saw a great shift from production of welfare within the predominantly rural household to the availability of welfare services in the market. The twentieth century has seen the gradual evolution of public programs to promote welfare.

Today, 89 percent of families receive from the welfare state at least one benefit of major importance (Table XI.5); education, hospital treatment, or a pension would cost weeks or months of wages if purchased in the market. The average

TABLE XI.5 *Households Receiving a State Welfare Benefit, 1984*

	Receive %	Do not receive %
Dependent on public transport	38	62
Pension	36	64
Regular treatment, doctor	35	65
Education	34	66
Housing	30	70
Hospital care, past year	29	71
Unemployment benefit	23	77
Personal social services	5	95
Total	89	11

Source: Calculated by the author from a Gallup Poll survey for the *Daily Telegraph*, 2–3 April 1984. Food omitted from the survey, as state provision is negligible.

household receives 2.3 welfare benefits, for example, having a council house and using subsidized public transport, or drawing a pension and receiving national health service treatment. Independence of all major state benefits is a temporary phase in the life-cycle. A young single person with good health and a car, and living in a privately rented flat is likely to marry, start a family, and rely upon public education, health services, and then a pension in old age.

Welfare Programs. The growth of welfare provision by government has increased the amount of welfare produced in society. More pensions and education are provided by government today than half a century ago. But the gross increase in public provision need not be the same as a net increase in welfare provision. For example, the growth of programs giving midday meals to school children does not mean that no child had a midday meal before the program was introduced. To some extent, public provision "fiscalizes" the provision of welfare, transferring responsibility from the household or market to the public purse. The day after the national health service was introduced in 1948, there were not more doctors or hospitals in Britain. The change realized immediately was that the public purse, rather than private funds, became responsible for health care.

The importance of public provision differs greatly between major dimensions of welfare. Through public employment, pensions, unemployment benefits, and other social security payments, the British Treasury maintains the incomes for more than one-third of people in society today. The market provides a money income for almost one-third of the population, who neither are in paid work nor receive a public benefit, such as children and nonemployed spouses, receive an income from transfer payments within the household. Government, the market, and the family are each important in the distribution of money incomes in Britain today.

Education is today the only major welfare need provided almost exclusively by government. Private fee-paying education is limited, and parental instruction is slight. Even here, however, what a child learns is not only a function of what a teacher is paid to teach, but also of effort that the individual pupil puts into the process of learning.

By contrast, nearly all personal social services, such as care for the elderly and the young, are provided within the household. Household care is very important for health too. Four-fifths of those certified as ill enough to be away from work are not sent to a hospital. Instead, they stay at home, being looked after by other members of the family or themselves, rather than by national health service employees.

The most basic of human necessities — food — is not given free. Instead, it is sold in the marketplace. Nor does the British government try to control food consumption by issuing food stamps, as in America. People are given money which they can spend for foods of their own choice, or in other ways if they prefer. The conversion of food into meals is principally the concern of the household. The great majority of meals are produced outside the market rather than being bought in restaurants or cafes, or provided free in public canteens and institutions.

Because welfare can be produced by a variety of sources, the average British family has a degree of choice. The growth in the national product has not only given government more money to spend on public programs, but also given citizens more money to spend in the market. Transportation — a necessity in modern life — is an example of declining popular dependence upon public provision. Demand for public bus and railway service has fallen, as an increasing proportion of households have been able to buy a car.

The net effect of postwar economic growth is that the great majority of families today receive more welfare than at any time previously. A survey by Social and Community Planning Research found that 67 percent believe that poverty today is not a question of people lacking food and clothing, but rather of not being able to keep up with the living standards of most people.[21] A 1984 Gallup Poll found that only 4 percent of the population said they lacked proper meals, 6 percent suitable clothes, and 8 percent something special for birthdays and Christmas. The chief things that people lacked — a car to get about in (14 percent) and suitable heating (13 percent) — would have been considered luxuries unavailable to the mass of people a generation ago.[22]

The Economy. Today, the economy is at least as mixed as the provision of welfare. While ministers and MPs speak casually about the government managing the economy, the phrase implies a power that politicians in England lack. The economy is neither owned nor controlled by the state, as is an economy in Eastern Europe. It is a mixed economy, with a substantial private sector having trade unions, industrialists, and financiers able to make many decisions as they think best. Sometimes they act in ways that the government of the day says is against the national interest, such as striking for higher wages when the government is seeking to maintain a voluntary incomes policy, or refusing to invest when the government is trying to encourage investment.

The government's influence over the economy has increased substantially by comparison with before the Second World War, but the influence of world economic conditions on the British economy has been increasingly great. In the competitive world economy Britain has usually done less well than other nations.

The most visible indicator is the falling value of the pound, compared with other major currencies such as the dollar and the Deutsche Mark.

One explanation for the failure of British government to give more effective direction to the economy is that politicians have been too ready to take into account the views of business and trade union groups meant to carry out plans. Consent has been placed ahead of effectiveness in mobilizing resources. A wish for due process has triumphed over a sense of purposeful growth. Another explanation is that British people have not wished to make the effort to increase wealth, as Germans and Japanese had to do after their military defeat in 1945. This unwillingness to abandon customary business and trade union practices or to forego consumption for the sake of investment is encouraged by material living standards higher than in the past. A third explanation is that a small offshore island such as Britain lacks the resources to maintain its world economic hegemony of a century ago, now that international trade is open to competition with other large countries often better endowed with resources. A fourth explanation is that economists have yet to find the appropriate policies that would be both applicable and effective in securing economic growth. It is possible that all four of these explanations are true.

Every Prime Minister since Harold Macmillan entered office in 1957 has sought to achieve economic growth and low rates of unemployment and inflation. The electorate has also put the economy at the top of its list of priorities for government action. The rotation of Conservative and Labour governments in office has given leaders of both parties the opportunity to try, again and again, to improve Britain's generally lackluster economic record.

A systematic examination of the performance of the economy under four changes of party control, six different Prime Ministers and ten different Chancellors of the Exchequer shows that their good intentions are not enough. While every government has intended to improve the government's record, in fact this has not happened. Britain's economic growth has consistently remained among the lowest in Europe. Even worse, the economy has deteriorated in the past quarter-century: unemployment and inflation rates have each increased, government borrowing has risen, and interest rates have risen too (Table XI.6). The achievements of the late 1950s or the 1960s, regarded at that time as inadequate, in retrospect appear successful compared to the state of the economy under Conservative and Labour governments since.

Judged by historical standards, the economy has succeeded in the postwar era, whether the government is given the credit for this, or is said to be the cause of it failing to do better. From 1951 through 1981 the national wealth available for public and private consumption more than doubled. The economy's growth rate rose in the 1960s, and then fell in the 1970s in line with experience elsewhere in the Western world. In this period Britain maintained a higher annual rate of growth than at any earlier time in the twentieth century. Because growth rates apply to an increasing economic base, the absolute value of the fiscal dividend of each year's growth is high. But by international standards, the economy has not grown as quickly

TABLE XI.6 *The Continuing Deterioration of the British Economy, 1957–1982*

Economic Indicator	Con govt '57–64	Lab govt '64–70	Con govt '70–74	Lab govt '74–79	Con govt '79–82
	(annual average percent for period of office)				
1. Lending rate	4.9	6.7	7.5	10.5	14.4
2. Public sector borrowing requirement as percent of GDP	2.3	1.2	3.6	7.2	5.8
3. Public expenditure as percent of GDP	33.3	37.1	38.1	42.6	42.3
4. Annual growth in gross domestic product	2.7	2.2	3.9	1.4	1.4
5. Annual change in take-home pay	2.0	0.4	3.4	−0.04	−0.5
6. Unemployment	2.0	2.2	3.2	4.9	9.3
7. Inflation	2.5	4.4	12.1	16.1	11.7

Source: Richard Rose, *Do Parties Make a Difference?* 2nd ed. (London: Macmillan, 1984) p. xxx.

as that of major European competitors or as the country's political leaders have wished.

International Affairs. The distinction between government output and policy outcome is most evident in foreign policy, for no nation can impose its own will unilaterally. The first decades of the postwar era saw government making a retreat from its great power commitments in Asia, Africa and the Middle East, and Europe. Today Britain's membership in the North Atlantic Treaty Organization reflects its dependence upon American military power, and membership in the European Community reflects a grudging awareness of the need to pool influence with European neighbors in a world of superpowers.

For forty years since the end of the Second World War English people have not been a major participant in an international war. England has enjoyed its longest period of continuous peace since the end of the Crimean War in 1856 until the commencement of the Boer War in South Africa in 1899. Avoidance of war is more the result of a global balance of power than of British diplomacy. For better or worse, the United Kingdom's most significant military engagement since 1945 has been an internal war in Northern Ireland.

As government goes "deeper in" to society, undertaking a wider range of policies, it reduces its claim to unilateral sovereignty. Instead of achieving its intentions by fiat, government becomes one of many influences upon social conditions. The nation's welfare, economic resources, and international security are influenced not only by government's policies but by other factors as well. The difficulties that government faces in implementing programs are not unique to England. Only the government of a totalitarian society would claim to determine everything that happens therein. The record of history demonstrates that even totalitarian aspirations are doomed to frustration.

Insofar as the purpose of government is thought to be mobilizing national resources to achieve political goals, then limitations upon government's power are frustrating. But if maintaining consent is considered to be the chief purpose of government, then the frustrations of government appear in a different light. Government is not an organization acting in response to orders from the top, like a military command hierarchy. A representative government is meant to do what citizens want and what they will accept. The unitary power of government is more apparent than real. Within a network of institutions involved in policy implementation, Cabinet ministers must bargain to secure political cooperation by consent.

POPULAR REACTION

English people evaluate the impact of government in the light of established values and beliefs. People have ideas, grounded in experience, about what government ought (and ought not) to do, and what it can realistically be expected to achieve. Government has flourished through the centuries in both good and bad economic conditions. Yet so widespread is the belief in economic determinism among political commentators that many forecast in the 1970s that the failure of government to sustain increases in both public spending and private affluence could lead to a popular reaction threatening the authority of the regime. This has not happened.[23]

If English people put material standards of living first, then they would emigrate to more prosperous countries such as America, Canada, or Australia, or to other member-nations of the European Community. But large-scale emigration does not take place. Political dissatisfactions are not so intense as to create refugees from the political economy. In their everyday lives, people adapt to the things that government does and fails to do.

Frustration with the shortcomings of government presupposes a prior expectation of success. In fact, most English people do not expect government to succeed most of the time, let alone all the time. Each year since 1957 the Gallup Poll has asked a national sample about their expectations for the economy in the year ahead. For a generation most English people have normally expected the coming year to be worse than the one before, with rising taxes, more unemployment, higher prices, and economic difficulties (Table XI.7). Paradoxically, this means that a government responsible for a deteriorating economy would actually be meeting popular expectations! Any

TABLE XI.7 *Popular Expectations of Economic Conditions in the Year Ahead, 1957–1985*

| | Number of years in which largest group expects: | | |
	Increase	No change	Fall
Taxes	28	0	0
Prices	22	3	3
Unemployment	22	1	5
Economic difficulties[a]	20	1	4

[a]Question asked for twenty-five years.

Source: *Gallup Political Index No. 293* (London: Gallup Poll January, 1985), p. 28.

indication of success — or simply less deterioration than expected — could be counted as doing better than expected.

A generation of media criticisms of the British economy has generated a negative set of popular expectations about what will happen to the economy, whatever the government of the day. Negative expectations are partially justified. Prices have risen annually, albeit by very different amounts, sometimes more and sometimes less than the price increase of the previous year. Taxes normally rise, if only as a consequence of inflation. But by historic standards unemployment has been very low for most of the past quarter-century; from year to year the unemployment rate has often fallen rather than risen, reflecting cyclical trends in the economy. The economy has actually grown in most of the years covered by the Gallup surveys.

Insofar as people have learned from the shortcomings of past governments, the ability of government sometimes to do better (or less worse) than expected is the basis of a politics of reprieve.[24] When the economy grows a little, then people who have felt threatened because they were expecting worse may enjoy a sense of reprieve. Ordinary voters, like politicians, are adaptable, and can learn from government's past shortcomings not to expect much in the future.

Consistently, the great majority of English people report that they are getting by with what they have. When the Gallup Poll asks people whether they are able to save a little of what they earn, just managing to make ends meet, or having to draw on savings or run into debt, five-sixths normally report that they are managing to make ends meet or even saving; less than a sixth report having to draw on savings or temporarily running into debt. Most people do not see their own circumstances as immediately determined by changes in the national economy. In nearly every year more than half of the Gallup Poll respondents think that the year ahead will be better or much the same.[25]

When voters are asked directly to give an overall assessment of how democracy works in Britain today, the responses are moderate. In 1983 only 12 percent reported that they were very satisfied, and the same proportion was very dissatisfied. The largest group, 49 percent, said they were fairly satisfied, and the second largest, 20 percent, said that they were not very satisfied. In the face of continuing economic difficulties, the proportion reporting themselves satisfied has increased from 44 percent in 1973 to 61 percent in 1983.[26]

Consistently, studies of public opinion find that the great majority of English people are generally satisfied with the life they lead. In 1973, shortly before a decade of economic difficulties began, 85 percent reported themselves satisfied with their lives; a decade later, after much economic difficulty and shocks to the party system, the proportion reporting themselves satisfied with their life remained very high, 83 percent (Table XI.8). Moreover, those saying that they are very satisfied with

TABLE XI.8 *Level of Life Satisfaction in Britain, 1973–1983*

	1973 %	1975 %	1977 %	1979 %	1981 %	1983 %
Very satisfied	33	29	30	27	32	29
Fairly satisfied	52	53	57	59	52	54
Not very satisfied	11	12	10	11	10	11
Not at all satisfied	3	5	3	3	5	4
Don't know	1	1	—	—	1	1

Source: *Euro-Barometre* No. 20 (Brussels: European Commission) Table 5, and Appendix 23A.

life consistently outnumber by a wide margin those who are very dissatisfied.

The contrast between unfavorable economic expectations, qualified assessments of the system of government, and very positive satisfaction with life overall emphasizes how the most important concerns of the great majority of people are insulated from the major political controversies of society. Time and again, when surveys ask people to evaluate their lives, the same pattern recurs: people are most satisfied with their family, friends, home, and job, and least satisfied with major institutions of society for which government is responsible. Individuals generalize their view of life primarily from face-to-face experiences, and not from actions of distant political institutions communicated vicariously through the media.

NOTES

1. See Richard Rose, "The Programme Approach to the Growth of Government," *British Journal of Political Science,* 15:1 (1985).

2. For a full development of this model, see Richard Rose, *Understanding Big Government: the Programme Approach* (London & Beverly Hills: Sage Publications 1984).

3. For a related but more abstract analysis of resources, see Christopher C. Hood, *The Tools of Government* (London: Macmillan, 1983).

4. See the Report of the Committee chaired by Sir David Renton, *The Preparation of Legislation* (London: HMSO, Cmnd. 6053, 1975).

5. Quoted in John Clare, "Who Makes the Decisions that Change our Environment?" *The Times* (London), 9 May 1972.

6. Gavin Drewry, "Reform of the Legislative Process," *Parliamentary Affairs,* 25:4 (1972).

7. Material in this and following paragraphs are drawn from Denis Van Mechelen, *Has There Been a Growth of Legislation in Britain since 1945?* (Glasgow: U. of Strathclyde Studies in Public Policy No. 123, 1984).

8. *Social Trends,* vol. 14 (1983), table 11.21.

9. Data in this and subsequent paragraphs come from Richard Rose and Terence Karran, *Increasing Taxes, Stable Taxes, or Both?* (Glasgow: U. of Strathclyde Studies in Public Policy No. 116, 1983).

10. Data on Britain are drawn from Richard Parry, "Britain: Stable Aggregates, Changing Composition," in Richard Rose et. al., *Public Employment in Western Nations* (Cambridge: Cambridge University Press, 1985).

11. See Richard Rose and Terence Karran, *Inertia or Incrementalism? A Long-Term View of the Growth of Government* (Glasgow: U. of Strathclyde Studies in Public Policy No. 126, 1984).

12. Cf. Brian Hogwood and B. Guy Peters, *Policy Dynamics* (Brighton: Wheatsheaf, 1983).

13. For preambles to major laws, including those cited here, see G. Le May, *British Government, 1914–1953.*

14. See Richard Rose, *What is Governing? Purpose and Policy in Washington* (Englewood Cliffs, N.J.: Prentice-Hall, 1978), pp. 142–146.

15. On the conditions affecting program implementation, compare Jeffrey Pressman and Aaron Wildavsky, *Implementation* (Berkeley: University of California Press, 1973; 2nd ed., 1979), and Elinor R. Bowen, "The Pressman-Wildavsky Paradox," *Journal of Public Policy*, 2:1 (1982), pp. 1–22.

16. Social scientists identify many influences upon social conditions that are in the second rather than the first category. Statistically, the third category represents the error term.

17. Reginald Maudling, quoted in David Wood, "Birth of a Population Policy," *The Times*, 8 March 1971.

18. See "Sir William Armstrong talking with Desmond Wilcox," *The Listener*, 29 March 1974.

19. See Her Majesty's Treasury, *Public Expenditure White Papers: Handbook on Methodology* (London: HMSO, 1972), p. 23.

20. For full explanation and documentation of the data cited here and in following paragraphs see Richard Rose, "The State's Contribution to the Welfare Mix in Britain," in Richard Rose and Rei Shiratori, *The Welfare State East and West* (New York: Oxford University Press, forthcoming).

21. Roger Jowell and Colin Airey, *British Social Attitudes: the 1984 Report* (Aldershot: Gower, 1984), p. 94.

22. See *Gallup Political Index*, No. 285 (January 1984), p. 17; No. 281 (May 1984), p. 34 and, more generally, James E. Alt, *The Politics of Economic Decline*.

23. For a review of this literature, see A. H. Birch, "Overload, Ungovernability and Delegitimization: the Theories and the British Case", *British Journal of Political Science*, 14:2 (1984), pp. 125–160.

24. See Richard Rose, "Misperceiving Public Expenditure — 'Feelings about 'Cuts,' '" in Charles H. Levine and Irene Rubin, eds., *Fiscal Stress and Public Policy* (Beverly Hills & London: Sage Publications, 1980), p. 228.

25. See e.g., *Gallup Political Index No. 288* (London, August 1984), p. 12.

26. *Euro-Barometre* No. 20 (Brussels: European Commission, December 1983), p. 32.

CHAPTER XII

A Changing England?

It is needful to keep the ancient show while we secretly interpolate the new reality.

ANY SPECULATION ABOUT A CHANGING ENGLAND is conditioned by what is expected to alter when politics changes. Focusing upon the Constitution might lead one to argue that no fundamental change has occurred in England since the Glorious Revolution of 1688. By contrast, focusing on parties might suggest that every election that changes the party in government inaugurates a new politics. Changes in one sphere of politics do not necessarily produce changes in another. England could turn from a monarchy into a republic with little alteration in public policies. Equally, the persistence of an institution in name does not mean that nothing of consequence has altered; Parliament today is very different from what it was a century or two ago.

Political changes can be grouped into three categories: nominal, ordinal, and continuous. The biggest changes are nominal, a change in kind. For example, the introduction of a small proportion of New Commonwealth immigrants into English society represents a new way of thinking about British citizens in terms of color. Some nominal changes occur at precise times: election of a new government or enactment of an Act of Parliament. Often, changes that cumulatively result in discontinuity—for example, when Labour replaced the Liberals as the alternative governing party — take years to accomplish.

Many changes of great political importance are best measured ordinally. British government had been financing some
health services prior to the passage of the National Health Service Act in 1946. But the comprehensive service established
then was different in scale from its predecessor. The increase
in unemployment between 1974 and 1984 can similarly be described as a major ordinal change, a shift from low to high
unemployment.

The everyday issues of politics often lead to small increments
of change along a continuum of choice. Typically, welfare policies involve changing the money value of a benefit by a few
percent. Changes in the rate of economic growth are measured
in tenths of 1 percent. Small changes along a continuum provide the best opportunity for compromise. In a debate about
whether interest rates should be increased by 1 percent or 2
percent, an increase of 1.5 percent is readily available as a compromise.

Some political changes have special significance because they
are irreversible. Once a government has declared war, in a literal sense it can never go back to what was before. Politics in
England at the end of the First World War was different from
politics at its outbreak; the same was true after the Second
World War. Because of strong cultural values, many policies
are in effect irreversible. It would be legally possible to take
away the vote from women or from persons lacking a specified
income. But no party hoping for political success would conceivably advocate such a change.

Other political changes are cyclical, like the exchange of government and opposition roles between the Conservative and
Labour parties. While such movements have no pendulum-like
regularity, there have been many ups and downs in the fortunes
of the two parties since 1945. In economics, government moves
back and forth between policies giving priority to economic
growth and those keeping price increases down. The inflation-
deflation cycle is known as a stop-go policy.

A disturbing feature of the political and economic difficulties
facing Britain in the mid-1970s was that they could not be fitted
into any of the foregoing descriptive categories. The abrupt
and erratic fluctuations in the rate of inflation, the contraction

and then expansion of the economy, the volatility of the electorate, and divisions within and between parties produced a
pattern that could be described as chronic instability.[1] A major
aim of the Conservative government elected in 1979 was to
reintroduce predictability and consistency — on terms laid
down by Mrs. Thatcher.

Forecasting the content, direction, and pattern of future
changes in society is inevitably risky. The biggest changes —
nominal shifts in the political system — are the most uncertain.
An attempt in 1964 by a reputable industrial planner to forecast the state of Britain in 1984 illustrates the difficulties. The
long-term forecast expected unemployment to be at about 2
percent rather than above 10 percent as is now the case, and
inflation to be 1 to 2 percent annually, rather than two to ten
times as much.[2] A textbook on British government published
in 1980 opened with the statement that abrupt changes in the
United Kingdom Constitution were being forced by pressures
from the European Community, violence, nationalism, the referendum, opposition to the Official Secrets Act, and minority
government in Parliament.[3] Five years later, little change had
been induced.

British government must give thought to the future when
preparing each year's statement about public expenditure. But
the task of planning even a year ahead is very difficult, because
crucial influences on events cannot be known with the degree
of certainty required to "fine-tune" the management of the
economy, or to control public expenditure. Estimates of growth
rates in the economy, inflation rates, and revenue totals must
be adjusted during the course of a fiscal year. The difference
between anticipated and actual rates of change is such that the
actual budget deficit, a particularly important target in both
Keynesian and monetarist forms of economic management, is
often significantly different from what the government expected.[4]

In looking ahead, it is easier to see countervailing pressures
for and against change than it is to see the direction of change.
To avoid overestimating the speed with which an established
society such as England can change, constraints should be considered first. Next we consider pressures promoting change.

Even if government cannot determine change by political planning, it must cope with its consequences. The assumption that there will always be an England mkes no assumption about the character of the England to be.

CONSTRAINTS UPON CHANGE

Few political changes take place as quickly as a Prime Minister can take office; this can occur hours after the result of a general election is conceded. Yet the event alters few things in the control of government. It takes several days for a Cabinet to be formed, months for ministers to become familiar with their new departments, and substantially longer for ministers to make an imprint upon public programs. Moreover, once new people enter office, the constraints of office may change ministers more than they can alter government.

The resources that past governments have effectively allocated become constraints upon a new Cabinet. Once resources are mobilized to produce programs, the programs continue with the force of inertia. A newly elected government that wants to act differently from its predecessors is greatly inhibited by this force.

Every newly elected government is sworn to uphold the laws of the land — and most laws it must uphold have been enacted by its predecessors. After its first year in office, the Thatcher government elected in 1979 found that 98 percent of the laws for which it was responsible had been enacted by its predecessors, as against 2 percent that it had itself put forward (Table XII.1). In the life of a Parliament, a government can introduce no more than one-tenth of the laws on the statute book.

Organizations institutionalize responsibilities for carrying out Acts of Parliament. A newly elected government could in theory reorganize Whitehall ministries in any way it wished — but the programs for which the old ministries were responsible would remain responsibilities of the new institutions. The most visible changes in government — the many alterations in the names of Whitehall departments — are not matched by alterations in public programs. A "reorganization" of government is typically a reshuffling of program responsibilities, requiring a change in the department's letterhead but little or no move-

TABLE XII.1 *The Limits upon Change in Laws*

	Number of Acts	As % all Acts in force, 1980	Cumulative %
Before 1760	132	4	4
1760–1836	215	6	10
1837–1901	866	25	35
1902–1918	192	6	41
1919–1945[a]	479	14	55
1945–1951	200	6	61
1951–1964	438	13	74
1964–1970	284	8	82
1970–1974	195	6	88
1974–1979	328	10	98
1979–1980	81	2	100

[a]For the period up to 1945, calendar years. From the return of the Labour government in 1945, sessions of Parliament.

Source: Calculated from data reported in Denis Van Mechelen, *Has There Been a Growth of Legislation in Britain since 1945?* (Glasgow: U. of Strathclyde Studies in Public Policy No. 123, 1984).

ment of personnel between buildings.[5] The Queen's government carries on with a great momentum of its own.

Public employees too exert great pressures for continuity. Reform ought to be easiest within Whitehall, especially among the senior civil servants responsible for advising and carrying out policies. However, their response to the 1968 Fulton Committee's proposals for reform is an excellent example of obstacles to change. By the time that consultations had taken place between the proponents of reform and the civil servants responsible for administering the new program, the proponents had exhausted their political strength. Civil servants were left to reform themselves to the extent that they deemed change necessary and proper. Insofar as changes have occurred in the higher civil service since then, they often reflect unintended consequences of unexpected pressures as much as conscious intentions.[6]

Government at Westminster is not well placed to reform the bulk of public employment, for more than nine-tenths of public employees do not work in Whitehall ministries. They are in local government, the health services, nationalized industries, and other bodies that recruit personnel, independently set pay and conditions of work, control promotion, and decide staff numbers. Mrs. Thatcher's efforts to cut the size of government by reducing the number in the home civil service by 10 percent from 1979 to 1983 has been an exercise in hunting rabbits rather than bigger game. A 2 percent cut in public employees omitted from the Thatcher directive would reduce public employment more than a 10 percent cut in civil servants employed by Whitehall.[7]

Members of Parliament are in no position to criticize Whitehall for resistance to change, for Parliament, which institutionalizes procedures developed over seven centuries, is itself slow to accept change. Abolishing the House of Lords has been debated ever since its powers to obstruct legislation were greatly curbed in 1911. Liberal, Conservative, and Labour governments have pondered the subject — but none has yet abolished hereditary membership. Changes in House of Commons practices have been numerous, but Sir T. Erskine May's guide, *The Law, Privileges, Proceedings and Usage of Parliament,* first published in 1844, remains, in suitably amended form, the standard work on the Commons.

The views of the electorate are a major influence upon change. Few politicians would wittingly fly in the face of public opinion — as they see the public. Since the perception of mass opinion by MPs is likely to be colored by partisan inclinations, there is ample scope for politicians to influence or, through misperception, to ignore public opinion. Once politicians have acted in what they think is the best interest of the country, ordinary citizens then have the opportunity to react to what government has done.

The decade from 1964 to 1974 was a period in which both Labour and Conservative governments actively sought to promote change in society. Politicans were confident that they not only knew what was wrong with Britain but also could put things right. Moreover, there was a big generational change in Parliament. Socially conservative values rooted in Victorian England were rejected by a new generation of MPs socialized into favoring a more permissive era.

When people were asked in 1974, at the end of a decade of

reform, whether they felt government actions had gone too far, not far enough or were about right, the responses indicated that the government was ahead of the mass electorate in favoring change (Table XII.2). On four of the nine issues, an absolute majority felt that the government had gone too far; low respect for authority, public displays of nudity and sex, treatment of lawbreakers, and tolerance of demonstrations. For five issues, a plurality said that the government had introduced just about the right amount of change. There was no issue for which the majority felt the government should have gone further.

Initial reactions to policy changes may be altered by experience. Hence, answers to the same questions in 1983 are even more revealing of popular acceptance (if not active desire for) change. After a further nine years of exposure to the effects of change, there remained three subjects about which an absolute majority still felt things had gone too far — low respect for authority, public nudity and sex, and penalities for criminals — and another, modern methods of education, where a plurality were against change. On five subjects — demonstrations, abortion, welfare benefits, equal opportunities for nonwhite Britons, and equal opportunities for women — a plurality or majority believed the amount of change was about right. There was no change that most people felt had not gone far enough.

Constraints here and now.   Government must start from what is already there. Policymakers struggling with the problems of remodernizing the world's first industrial nation sometimes wish for the advantages of developing new industries without the incubus of declining ones. For the foreseeable future, these thoughts must be classified as wishful thinking. There is no escaping the immediate fact: England is a large, old industrial society and its immediate prospects for change are highly constrained by this inheritance.

In time, almost anything can be changed. The island of Britain may even be joined to the Continent of Europe by a bridge or tunnel. The longer it takes to achieve political action, the greater the delay in realizing benefits. To politicians involved with immediate events this is an argument against action, for it means that they must accept all the political costs of introducing change while themselves being unlikely to reap many

Table XII.2 *Popular Responses to Policy Changes, 1974–1983*

	Gone too far %	About right %	Not gone far enough %
Showing less respect for authority			
1974	78	9	8
1978	71	13	11
Nudity and sex in films and magazines			
1974	61	29	5
1983	62	30	4
Going easier on people who break the law			
1974	57	8	32
1978	58	10	27
The right to have protest marches and demonstrations			
1974[a]	(51)	(37)	(8)
1983	33	59	3
Abortion on the National Health Service			
1974	38	38	13
1983	26	46	11
Modern methods of teaching children			
1974	34	35	12
1978	43	31	12
Welfare benefits available today			
1974	32	40	21
1983	19	49	28
Attempts to give equal opportunities to blacks and Asians in Britain			
1974	25	41	27
1983	18	49	26
Attempts to give equal opportunities to women			
1974	18	44	33
1983	9	56	31

[a]In 1974, the question asked about police standing firm in handling demonstrations; answers reversed to establish approximate comparability.

Source: October 1974: British Election Survey, ESRC Survey Archive, Colchester; 1978: *Gallup Political Index* No. 220 (November 1978), p. 11; *British Election Study* 1983 (Social & Community Planning Research, Oxford University and Pergamon Press). For all questions, don't knows omitted.

benefits. To those working for future generations, it may be an argument for beginning work today, so that posterity may enjoy the benefits.

The time required for government policy to have an impact varies from policy area to policy area.

Immediately Changeable. Many features of the economy for which government is responsible can (or must) be altered quickly. This requirement is notably true of the interest rates that influence the exchange value of the pound, for in an open international economy money can move in or out of Britain on an around-the-clock basis.

Changeable in a Few Months. The public esteem of political leaders and parties can rise or fall significantly in a few months. These fluctuations, reflecting very crude political judgments, occur at a much faster rate than substantive changes in parties or in the basic personalities of politicians. The 1970 British general election provided an especially vivid demonstration. In January, the Labour party badly trailed the Conservatives in all opinion polls, only to be ahead in all the polls in May, and on the losing side when the election result was declared in mid-June.

Changeable in up to Five Years. An Act of Parliament normally takes several years to process, from the time a minister decides that a bill should be prepared to formal enactment. Consultations must be undertaken with affected pressure groups, with the administrators responsible for the bill, and with lawyers drafting the language of the statute. The Cabinet must give the measure priority in the queue for legislation, and Parliament will require months to discuss it. Once the bill is enacted, administrators require time to implement the new measure, and the public to feel its impact. If a newly elected governing party does not commence preparing legislation within a year of election, it is unlikely to have time to see its measures through before once again risking its future with the electorate.

Changeable in a Decade. Many major activities of government require substantial time to plan and implement. A particularly long lead time is required by major capital investment programs for school buildings, hospitals, or roads. For example, to help meet the rising demand for university education, seven completely new universities were founded in England between 1961 and 1965. Because each literally commenced on a green field site, growth came slowly. By 1976, the seven new universities had a total enrollment of only 22,000, scarcely half that of the long-established University of London, and by 1983 they had 29,000, a quarter less than London. The bulk of additional students were accommodated by expanding established universities.

Changeable in a Generation or More. Health is always a major concern of citizens. But life expectancy cannot show the full effect of the National Health Service until well after the year 2000, at which time the whole population will consist of persons who have had its benefits all their lives.

Past choices limit present policies. A newly elected government will find itself committed to many decisions that it is too late to stop or reverse, except at a very high political or monetary cost. For example, the roads and highways policy of any newly elected government must start from the fact that in the lifetime of a Parliament, more than 95 percent of traffic will be traveling on roads planned or built under previous governments.

Present choices constrain future actions. Like its predecessors, a newly elected government can make some major decisions that its successors will find difficult to reverse. It can assume that most of the legislation that it places on the statute books will not be repealed by its successor. The resistance of inertia makes it difficult to put new programs into effect. But once a new program is established, momentum carries many programs along for decades after the original sponsors have left office.

PRESSURES FOR CHANGE

Even if the government intended to pursue a policy of no change, this would not result in unchanging consequences, because of alterations in the society that programs are intended to influence. The more socially conservative a government is, the more it must *actively* pursue policies designed to limit or prevent the effects of social change.

Demographic change. Ironically, the most inevitable of all changes in society, demographic change, is strong in its influence upon public programs but little amenable to influence by legislation. An increase of 10 percent in the population means that the economy must expand by 10 percent in order to keep constant the gross national product per capita. Problems increase if population growth occurs disproportionately among children and the elderly, who are respectively especially heavy consumers of education and of health and pensions. In the past forty years, both the number and the proportion of people of pensionable age has doubled in Britain.

Population change creates pressures to provide more of the same public services (expanding universities in the 1960s) or different services (geriatric programs in the 1980s). Doing nothing in response to population change also has consequences. If demand rises more quickly than supply, then the benefits of public programs will be harder to obtain, whether these are conceived as a place in higher education or a bed in a nursing home for the elderly.

Today very great uncertainties surround future trends in the population. In 1970 the Central Statistical Office estimated that the population of the United Kingdom would increase by 2.8 million people by 1981, with all that implied in increased demand for public services. In fact, in 1981 the population had grown by only one-quarter the forecast rate. Whereas in 1970 official forecasts anticipated a 6 million population increase by 1991, twelve years later official forecasts scaled down by more than three-quarters anticipated population growth to 1991. Whereas the 1971 official forecast anticipated the population to rise by 10 million by the year 2001, as of 1983 the forecast increase was only 1 million.[8]

Changes in population put pressures on government social programs and on the economy. The decline in the number of babies born in the 1970s means that primary schools that expanded to meet the earlier baby boom are becoming short of pupils in the 1980s. The impact upon higher education is less clear, for in the 1980s universities are still under pressure to expand in response to high birth rates nearly two decades before. Forecasting what the demand for higher education will be in the 1990s is more difficult than forecasting the number of 18 to 21 year olds, for attendance at university reflects variable influences upon this age group, including youthful and potential aspirations, labor market pressures, and government policy itself.

The population of working age is growing in the 1980s, for it consists of persons already born by the beginning of the 1970s. Because birthrates in the 1960s were generally higher than between the wars, the numbers entering the labor market are currently greater than those retiring. Furthermore, the proportion of women seeking work rather than remaining at home as housewives is also increasing. Hence, there are great demographic pressures to produce more jobs in response to demands from youths and women. But the increase in demand occurs at a time when the economy is actually decreasing the total number in employment. In consequence, unemployment rises because the growth of those of working age has exceeded growth in the economy.

Even if the population remains constant, members of society will inexorably change, for millions of elderly persons die each decade, and millions of youths mature into adults. The passing of the elderly removes the last of those who have a first-hand recollection of England's role as a world power prior to the First World War, and diminishes the proportion who recall the years of depression between the wars. The entry of youthful cohorts to adulthood increases the proportion who have no personal experience of the Second World War, or of times when affluence was not the expectation of most people in society. In the 1945 general election, the median voter was born about 1900 and had been socialized into awareness of all these things. In the election of 1983, the median voter was born during the Second World War. By the next general election the median voter will be a child of the Second World War who started work in time to become part of the generation that saw the founding of the Beatles.

The processes of political socialization by family, older friends, and established institutions of society are important in maintaining continuity in society. The population changes slowly, with about 2 percent of the electorate dying each year. From one election to another, about 85 percent of the electorate is the same.

Young adults, like the elderly, are one among many minorities. Young people cannot dominate politics by their numbers. Unlike the elderly, young people do not have sufficient experience to have many very firm political views. Because young voters are new voters, they are less likely to be fixed in their political behavior, and are readier to swing from party to party, or to alter political attitudes.

Insofar as generational differences are more important than party loyalties, young people should differ more from old people than Conservative voters do from Labour voters. This hypothesis is particularly appropriate in the 1980s, as party loyalties have been in decline and differences between the young and elderly appear to be increasing. However, the hypothesis is rejected by the evidence.

Comparing the views of young people born in the 1950s and 1960s with those of older persons born before or during the First World War shows only a small difference between the two age groups, averaging 11 percent for twenty different issues (Table XII.3). For at least half the issues, the difference between young and old is so small that it is likely to reflect sampling fluctuations. The greatest difference — a 48 percent gap between young and old in attitudes toward showing sex on TV and in magazines — is remote from party politics. On only one other issue — the repatriation of colored immigrants — is there a difference between the generations of as much as 20 percent. A plurality of young and old people have much the same policy preference about the great majority of issues.

Even though most Conservative and Labour partisans normally agree on most issues (cf. Table IX.3), the differences that remain are usually greater than the differences between young and old. On average, the two groups of party supporters differ by 16 percent in their policy views. The differences between partisans are greater than the differences between the generations on thirteen of twenty issues. Moreover, the differences

TABLE XII.3 *Comparing the Effect of Age and Party on Policy Preferences*

				Difference	
Party more important than age (13)	*Total*	*Young*	*Old*	*Age*	*Party*
		(% endorsing policy)			
Stricter laws on unions	57	53	66	13	43
Redistribute wealth to poor	61	66	55	11	35
Spend as needed to defend Falklands	39	45	36	9	34
Take Britain out of Common Market	34	30	35	5	29
Reestablish grammar schools	48	40	57	17	28
Withdraw troops N. Ireland	50	47	51	4	27
Spend to reduce unemployment	76	78	75	3	23
Give up nuclear weapons	22	24	19	5	19
Spend more on health	90	93	83	10	17
Cut public spending to reduce inflation	53	55	46	9	16
Shift power to local govt., regions	51	49	49	0	12
Let council tenants buy their house	81	80	84	4	12
Promote equal opportunities for women	77	79	77	2	7
Age more important than party (7)					
Reduce sex on TV and in magazines	50	29	77	48	5
Send back colored immigrants	29	20	43	23	1
Give more aid to Africa, Asia	44	51	32	19	3
Bring back death penalty	64	57	71	14	4
Allow abortion on National Health Service	46	49	38	11	7
Have government guide wage, price rises	78	75	81	6	5
Spend more against pollution	78	75	79	4	0
Average differences, 20 issues				11	16

Source: Author's analysis of Gallup Poll survey for *Daily Telegraph,* 28 October 1983. See Table IX. 3 for full details of party differences. Young, age 18–34; old, age 65 plus.

between partisans tend to be greatest on matters of major dispute in Parliament, such as the distribution of wealth and the regulation of trade unions. By contrast, generational differences tend to relate to issues that are often considered conscience matters, unlinked to party, such as the death penalty or abortion.

Overall, party differences are much more likely to divide the British electorate than are differences in age. The effect of age is further diminished because the median voter is neither young nor old but middle age, mediating the small political differences between young and old.

Economic change. Changes in the economy can occur far more quickly than changes arising from the passing of generations. Yet the difficulties of the British economy have a lengthy history; the problems of the political economy today have been compounding for a generation.

The spending commitments of British government require economic growth in order to finance continuing growth in public expenditure. In 1951 the cost of public policy accounted for less than one-third of the national product. In the 1950s the economy grew more rapidly than the costs of public policy. But in the period from 1961 up to the 1973 oil shock, the costs of public policy grew at a faster rate (4.2 percent) than the national product (2.8 percent). By 1972, half the annual growth in the economy was claimed by the Treasury to finance the growth in public expenditure. Since 1973, public expenditure has continued to grow at virtually the same rate as in the 1960s. But the already slow rate of growth in the economy has been halved to 1.3 percent a year. In such circumstances, the government can finance the expansion of public expenditure only by raising taxes that cut workers' take-home pay, or by increased borrowing that threaten to reduce the purchasing power of earnings by stimulating inflation.[9]

The pressures for change are neither new nor unpredictable. For decades, even generations, writers have been warning that the British economy was vulnerable to changes in world trade, and politicians have been trying to reduce this vulnerability. But their efforts have yet to show success. In a 1971 budget speech, the then Conservative Chancellor of the Exchequer, Anthony Barber, said:

> For many years, under one government and another, the economic performance of our country has been poor. If we are realistic, we should recognise that unless there is a change in the trend — a change not only compared with the last five or six years, but with the trend over the last two decades or more — the prospect is that by 1980 our standard of living in this country will have fallen considerably behind that of most of the countries of Western Europe.[10]

The forecast was accurate. When the statement was made in 1971 it was still possible to see England competing with France and Germany as major and prosperous economies. By 1980 England had been relegated to the second division of European economies, with a per capita national product closer to that of Italy or Ireland than to that of the most prosperous Northern European countries.

The consequences of government growing faster than the economy as a whole have been felt by both Labour and Conservative governments. In 1976 economic difficulties led a Labour government to seek a loan from the International Monetary Fund, and impose severe cash limits on public spending. In 1979, a Conservative government under Margaret Thatcher was elected with the promise to do even more to reduce public spending, and to make the economy grow. Inertia pressures have proven stronger, causing the continued deterioration of the economy (See Table XI.6).

Policymakers in Britain are today cross-pressured. A decade of economic recession has emphasized that government programs cannot be financed indefinitely by relying on economic growth to produce what Heclo has characterized as ''policy without pain.''[11] Concurrently, the economic recession has made government's role in providing incomes to the unemployed of far greater significance, and its impact is heightened by the very weakness of the private sector. Faced with the prospect of insecurity, popular opinion has tended to support maintenance of present levels of high taxes and big benefits (cf. Table

IV.5). It is easier for policymakers to feel the pressures to act than to be confident that they will succeed in realizing their intentions.

COPING WITH CHANGE

The biggest challenge immediately facing politicians is not whether British government can cope with its problems, but *how* can it do so. As Prime Minister James Callaghan once remarked to an advisor: "I do not need to be told how difficult things are. I want to know the way through." History demonstrates that British government has succeeded, time and again, in surmounting great difficulties. After the event, coping with change looks easy and obvious. But politics is about actions taken in moments of uncertainty and conflict.

Wartime offers extreme examples of government's need to cope quickly and successfully with unexpected and great challenges. Both the First and Second World Wars imposed many burdens upon an unprepared Whitehall. Both also involved mobilizing civilians. Intervention in wartime has had important carryovers to the years of peace that followed. War-time brought new institutions to Whitehall as well as expanding greatly the services of the welfare state.

But the wartime success of British government is not a good guide to the coping strategies of peacetime governors. Wars were not won by relying upon Whitehall's standard peacetime procedures, but by introducing institutions and personnel that were not (or could not be) accepted in peacetime. In the Second World War, three of the most important members of the Cabinet — Ernest Bevin, Lord Beaverbrook, and Sir John Anderson — were respectively a trade union leader, a press lord, and a senior civil servant. None would have found himself in the Cabinet but for the war. The same is true of the Prime Minister, Winston Churchill.

No peacetime political event can create a crisis with the intensity, scope, and duration of war. Many so-called crises in domestic politics are extremely trying while they last, but very short-lived in their consequences. Few people today refer to the Profumo scandal of 1963 or the Bank Rate Tribunal of 1957, even though each at the time received great political attention.

When important issues do arise unexpectedly, government must act in circumstances that do not allow much time for thought about long-term consequences. For example, the British government's decision to put troops in the field in Northern Ireland in August 1969 was made under the immediate pressure of riots; no plan was made for getting the troops out.

The standard operating procedures of Whitehall are meant to avoid the possibility of major difficulties erupting, concentrating on difficulties already at hand. The Fulton Report on the Civil Service describes how Whitehall routinely copes with problems:

> The operation of existing policies and the detailed preparation of legislation, with the associated negotiations and discussions, frequently crowd out demands that appear less immediate. Civil servants, particularly members of the Administrative Class, have to spend a great deal of their time preparing explanatory briefs, answers to parliamentary questions, and ministers' cases. Generally, this work involves the assembly of information to explain to others (civil servants, outside bodies and so on) the policies of the department, how they are operating and how they apply in particular cases. Almost invariably, there are urgent deadlines to be met in this kind of work. In this press of daily business, long-term policy planning and research tend to take second place.[12]

When there is time to plan what to do, there may not be any political pressure to act. There is always one good political argument for maintaining the status quo: the fact that it is there. The introduction of decimal coinage illustrates how slow and cautious government can be before acting upon a proposed policy. The abandonment of the old £.s.d. (pounds-shillings-pence) system of coinage was first debated in Parliament in 1817. At that time, the Napoleonic Wars had created a shortage of metal coins in England. But the wars with France also made suspect the introduction of an alien decimal form of coinage. Two decades later, Charles Babbage, Cambridge professor and pioneer of ideas basic to modern computing, offered a detailed scheme for converting the currency into decimal coinage. In 1855 a government report recognized the advantages of decimal coinage. The government did not respond positively until

106 years later, when it established a committee to review the subject once again. In 1971, 154 years after the topic was first raised in Parliament, England adopted a system of decimal currency along the lines recommended by early nineteenth-century reformers.

The best descriptive and normative justification for standard governmental practices is given by the doctrine of muddling through, or, as it is known in its most elaborate form, the theory of serial disjointed incrementalism.[13] Politicians are expected to make decisions one at a time, reacting empirically to problems immediately before them. They are not expected to worry about the further consequences of what they do, because these consequences cannot be completely known; they will become tomorrow's problems. If the consequences of today's decisions are bad, they should be reversed tomorrow, for this is better than consistency in pursuing unsuccessful or unpopular measures. In this model of coping with change, a policy is not so much a statement of intent; it is the after-the-fact description of decisions made over a significant length of time.

Muddling through is an ambiguous phrase; everything depends on whether one emphasizes the muddle or the winning through. Those who are caught in the muddle are likely to be less satisfied than those who see the problem in a broader analytic framework. Cumulatively, muddling through can by trial-and-error process lead policymakers to hit upon an acceptable and durable policy. A decade of trying first one policy then another can also result in muddling around in circles.

The arguments for incremental adjustment of programs appeal to politicians who worry first about surviving until the next general election. Short-term incrementalist tactics are appropriate to conditions of great complexity and high uncertainty, for they give policymakers great flexibility. But the impact depends upon the implicit assumption that conditions will improve in the long run, or at least remain acceptable as the cumulative consequence of many ad hoc choices.

The arguments against incremental ad hoc policy making are also formidable, particularly if it is *not* assumed that a benign "hidden hand" will always guarantee favorable results in the long run. Compounding small difficulties can add up to big difficulties. If the shortcomings of one government are rein-forced rather than offset by the next — and this often appears to be the case in the direction of the British economy — then the long-term effects will be big, and bad. Incremental choices deal with current problems, but they do nothing to avoid future difficulties inherent in past choices.

To sustain government, politicians do not need to act. Doing nothing can also have formidable consequences. A half-century ago Andre Siegfried canvassed a variety of strategies available to British government for coping with the 1931 crisis. He con-cluded pessimistically that "what is much more likely is that England will not choose at all."[14]

A QUESTION OF VALUES

The most important of all political changes — alterations in the values and beliefs of the political culture — are the most difficult to anticipate. Yet once the meaning of politics alters, then much else changes in consequence. Values cannot be ex-trapolated by a line on a graph, nor can they be predicted with the actuarial certainty of forecasting the primary school pop-ulation from knowledge of the number of infants under age 5.

The economic difficulties of the mid-1970s stimulated a rash of forecasts of political disorders by writers on both the left and right. The common assumption was that popular consent to political authority rested upon government providing a high (or rising) level of material benefits to its citizens. An econo-mist and former advisor to the Labour government could then write:

> The performance of the economy since 1964 had been worse than most observers would have thought possible; and the situation in 1976 was so bad that it was reasonable to wonder whether the sacrifices, needed to get the economy back into internal and ex-ternal balance could really be exacted by a government which had to rule by consent.[15]

Such generalizations were ahistorical, ignoring the relatively pacific nature of England in the interwar years, when depres-sion persisted. Moreover, the country's standard of living in the 1970s was higher than ever before — and rising. The re-

ductionist mentality that defines economic problems as the
worst problems that could face a government is remarkably
blinkered. Any English person need only watch television reports from Northern Ireland to see what *real* challenges to political authority within the United Kingdom are.[16]

Within England the political values that people rank highest
are meant to remain constant rather than change: the liberty
of the individual, freedom of speech, and the right of the electorate to dismiss the government of the day. Real or imagined
actions deemed threatening to these basic political values are
attacked by the left if proposed by the right, or by the right if
proposed by the left. The hyperbole of political controversy
leads MPs in opposition to accuse the government of the day
of seeking to subvert the Constitution. But these allegations are
normally forgotten by both sides once fiercely resisted political changes are assimilated into government.

Within a competitive party system, value changes often reflect one party catching up with the ideas of another, once the
ideas have been tested and found generally desirable. In the
1930s, for example, the Labour party opposed rearmament of
the country, and the Conservatives opposed many welfare measures proposed by Labour. During and after the Second World
War, the majority of the Labour party came to accept military
force as a necessary part of foreign policy, and Conservatives
accepted that they would conserve major welfare state programs. In the dynamics of party competition, yesterday's disputed issues are often buried in today's consensus, to be
succeeded by new issues that may excite passionate disagreement, then subsequently are incorporated in an interparty consensus.

Attempts to forecast the direction of future political change
are inevitably affected by the different value assumptions of
forecasters. A tradition-minded English person might emphasize conserving achievements from the past, not least maintaining the fully legitimate authority of government. Socialists
think less about forms of government and more about achievements, especially the redistribution of wealth, status, and political power. Economists assert that all talk of change is
meaningless, unless there are the material resources to attain

that to which politicians aspire. Humanitarians argue that the next major development in English society should assist the handicapped and deprived rather than productive groups in society, and environmentalists foresee the need to reduce rather than increase material change. Libertarians argue for removal of government constraints on behavior.

Amid the troubles between the wars, R. H. Tawney, a leading Socialist theorist, remarked that the idea of reflecting upon alternative futures is "uncongenial" to the bustling people who describe themselves as practical, because they face problems as they occur.

> The practical thing for a traveller who is uncertain of his path is not to proceed with the utmost rapidity in the wrong direction: it is to consider how to find the right one. And the practical thing for a nation which has stumbled upon one of the turning points of history is to consider whether what it has done hitherto is wise, and if it is not wise to alter it.[17]

A prominent conservative philosopher, Michael Oakeshott, viewed the failure of grand designs to bring about a new order in Europe, and wrote, in an equally apposite but opposite way:

> In political activity, then, men sail a boundless and bottomless sea; there is neither harbour for shelter nor floor for anchorage, neither starting-place nor appointed destination. The enterprise is to keep afloat on an even keel: the sea is both friend and enemy; and the seamanship consists in using the resources of a traditional manner of behaviour in order to make a friend of every inimical occasion.[18]

In contemporary England, political leaders are ambivalent about change. A desire to conserve past achievements is often commingled with a desire to remove present grievances and promote future improvements. A study of young political leaders found that characteristically these politicians use "the language of the future when talking of modernization, but they seek to join it with the values of the past: balance, stability and unity."[19] A majority of would-be innovators explicitly state that the things they like most about England — moderation, tolerance, a capacity for compromise, and continuity — are also the cause of what they most dislike: resistance to change.

404 A Changing England?

NOTES

1. See Richard Rose and Edward Page, "Chronic Instability in Fiscal Systems," in Rose and Page, eds., *Fiscal Stress in Cities* (Cambridge: Cambridge University Press, 1982), pp. 198–245.

2. Cf. Ronald Brech, then head of Unilver's Economics and Statistics Department, *Britain 1984* (London: Darton, Longman, Todd, 1964); and Michael Prowse's retrospective review, "The Future that Britain Never Had," *Financial Times,* 17 August 1984.

3. Cf. Max Beloff and Gillian Peele, *The Government of the United Kingdom: Political Authority in a Changing Society* (London: Weidenfeld & Nicholson, 1980), Chapter 1.

4. See Paul Mosley, *The Making of Economic Policy,* especially pp. 218–225.

5. See Christopher Pollitt, *Manipulating the Machine: Changing the Pattern of Ministerial Departments, 1960–83* (London: Allen & Unwin, 1984).

6. See the bitter testimony to the slowness of change by proponents of change Peter Kellner and Lord Crowther-Hunt, *The Civil Servants.* Cf. Richard Rose, "The Political Status of Higher Civil Servants in Britain," in E. Sulerman, ed., *Bureaucrats and Policy Making* (New York: Holmes & Meier, 1984).

7. Cf. Richard Parry, "Britain: Stable Aggregates, Changing Composition," in R. Rose *Public Employment in Western Nations* (Cambridge: Cambridge University Press, 1985).

8. For basic statistics, see *Social Trends,* vol. 9 (1979), table 1.2 and vol. 4 (1983), table 1.2. For a discussion of implications, see John F. Ermisch, *The Political Economy of Demographic Change* (London: Heinemann Educational Books 1983).

9. See Richard Rose and Terence Karran, *Inertia or Incrementalism? A Long-Term View of the Growth of Government,* table 6.

10. Hansard, House of Commons *Debates,* vol. 814, cols. 1358–1359 (30 March 1971).

11. Hugh Heclo, "Toward a New Welfare State?" in Peter Flora and Arnold Heidenheimer, eds., *The Development of Welfare States in Europe and America* (New Brunswick, N.J.: Transaction, 1981). The whole of Heclo's essay is very relevant here.

12. The Fulton Committee, *Report,* vol. 1, p. 57.

13. David Braybrooke and C. E. Lindblom, *A Strategy of Decision* (New York: Free Press, 1963).

14. André Siegfried, *England's Crisis,* p. 311. For a fuller development of the critique of incrementalism, see Rose and Karran, *Inertia or Incrementalism?*

15. Michael Stewart, *The Jekyll and Hyde Years* (London: Dent, 1977) p. 234, quoted approvingly in the doom-laden last chapter of Keith Middlemas, *Politics in Industrial Society* (London: Weidenfeld & Nicolson, 1979), p. 447.

16. These challenges have political, not economic roots. See Richard Rose, *Governing without Consensus,* especially chapters 14–15.

17. R. H. Tawney, *The Acquisitive Society* (London: Bell, 1921), p. 2.

18. *Political Education* (Cambridge: Bowes & Bowes, 1951), p. 22.

19. Erwin Hargrove, *Professional Roles in Society and Government: The English Case* (Beverly Hills: Sage Papers in Comparative Politics, 01–035, 1972), p. 14.

Index